Psychopathology in Persons With Mental Retardation

Clinical Guidelines for Assessment and Treatment

D1298628

Christine M. Nezu
Arthur M. Nezu
Mary Jane Gill-Weiss

Research Press Company
2612 North Mattis Avenue
Champaign, Illinois 61821

Advisory Editor: Frederick H. Kanfer

Cover design by Doug Burnett
Composition by Wadley Graphix Corporation
Printed by McNaughton & Gunn

ISBN 0-87822-329-0
Library of Congress Catalog No. 90-64044

To our fathers: In loving memory
Frank J. Maguth and Tetsuo Nezu

—C. M. N. & A. M. N.

And to William J. Coneys

—M. J. G. W.

Contents

Figures and Tables   ix

Foreword   xi

Preface   xv

Acknowledgments   xix

SECTION I

Chapter 1   **Mental Illness and Mental Retardation   3**

Introduction   3

Mental Illness and Mental Retardation:
Why the Gap?   5

Mental Illness in Persons With Mental Retardation:
Prevalence and Epidemiological Issues   7

Psychopathology in People With Mental Retardation:
Pathogenic Mechanisms   23

Chapter 2   **A Problem-Solving Model of Decision Making
and Case Formulation for Clinical Interventions
With Dually Diagnosed Individuals   29**

Introduction   29

Toward a Problem-Solving Conceptualization
of Clinical Interventions   32

The Problem-Solving Process   35

Summary   43

SECTION II

Chapter 3   **A Problem-Solving Approach to Clinical Interventions With Dually Diagnosed Persons: Focus on Assessment   47**

Introduction   47
Screening   48
Problem Analysis and Selection of Focal Target Problems   53
Summary   69

Chapter 4   **Assessment of the Individual   71**

Introduction   71
The Need for a Multimatrix Assessment Model   72
Issues Concerning Differential Diagnosis   73
Components of Client Assessment   81
Specific Categories of Disorders   90
Initial Clinical Diagnostic Formulation   95
Summary   95

Chapter 5   **Assessment of the Caregiving System   97**

Introduction   97
Evaluation of the Caregiving System   99
Assessment of Caregiver Competency   108
Combining a Functional Systems Assessment With Evaluation of Need for Caregiver Training   116
Summary   116

Chapter 6   **Assessment of the Environment   119**

Introduction   119
Aspects of Environmental Assessment   124
The Role of Frustration   134
Assessing the Environment for Success in Fostering Community Integration   135

Assessing Qualitative Aspects of the Environment   140

Assessing Resource Management   140

Summary   140

SECTION III

Chapter 7   **A Problem-Solving Approach to Clinical Interventions With Dually Diagnosed Persons: Focus on Treatment   145**

Introduction   145

Designing Treatment   145

Implementing and Evaluating Treatment   156

Summary   160

Chapter 8   **Treatment Guidelines: Focus on the Individual Client   161**

Introduction   161

Behavioral Approaches   162

Nonbehavioral Approaches   183

Summary   189

Chapter 9   **Treatment Guidelines: Focus on the Caregiving System   191**

Introduction   191

Stress Associated With Caregiving   192

Models of Coping   194

Caregiver Training   196

Caregiver Systems Interventions   204

The Reciprocity of Adaptation: Integrating Systems Perspectives, Caregiver Training, and Stress/Coping in the Treatment Plan   209

The Role of Social Support   209

Summary   213

**Chapter 10   Treatment Guidelines: Focus on the
Environment   215**

Introduction   215
The Physical Environment   215
The Social Environment   216
Aid to Programmatic Interventions   217
Qualitative Aspects of the Environment   217
A Model Residence for Dually Diagnosed
Individuals   218
Therapeutic Groups   220
Key Components of Residential Treatment   226
Addressing the Goal of Increased
Visibility and Integration   227
The Importance of Proactive Intervention   233
Summary   234

**Appendix   The Behavioral Role-Play Activities Test
(BRAT)   235**

Administering the BRAT   237
Introduction and Role-Play Descriptions   241
Role-Play Scripts   245
Scoring Forms   253

References   267
Author Index   299
Subject Index   307
About the Authors   321

Figures and Tables

FIGURES

3.1   Three-Dimensional, Tripartite Model for Assessment,
        Treatment, and Therapy Evaluation   59

3.2   Sample Clinical Pathogenesis Map (CPM) for Client
        Displaying Aggressive Behavior   65

7.1   Evaluation Form for Treatment Alternatives   153

7.2   Sample Goal Attainment Map (GAM)   155

8.1   Target Behavior Frequency Across Treatment
        Phases for John   187

TABLES

1.1   Prevalence of Psychiatric Disorders and Behavioral
        Problems Among Individuals With Mental
        Retardation   8

1.2   Prevalence of Anxiety Disorders Among Individuals With
        Mental Retardation: Representative Studies   19

3.1   Alternative Strategies to Enhance Client Motivation   54

3.2   Decision-Making Criteria for Selection of
        Key Focal Problem Areas   66

4.1   Measures of Intellectual and Adaptive Functioning   76

4.2   Components of Assessment   82

6.1   Environmental Assessment Measures   138

7.1   Potential Strategies, Tactics, and Methods for Addressing
        Problems of Aggression   149

7.2   Decision-Making Criteria for Evaluation of Alternative Treatment Ideas   150

7.3   Troubleshooting Questions to Ask If Treatment Appears to Be Ineffective   159

9.1   Useful Coping Skills for Caregiver Stress Management   197

9.2   Outline for Caregiver Behavioral Training   199

Foreword

From the title of this book, one might suspect that it is written primarily for clinicians. Don't be misled by the title—this work is much more than a "clinical" contribution. First, it addresses a most problematic population—one typically either underserved or inappropriately served by the profession. The profession has been begging for a book that takes such a comprehensive, balanced look at a total model of treatment for "dually diagnosed" individuals, or people with some degree of both mental disability and illness. But even more important, the book offers a blueprint for comprehensive program development that has a utility for all of the professional disciplines involved. Much of the material can also be adapted for the parents and paraprofessionals who are so often the primary caregivers.

As the authors argue, an interdisciplinary approach is necessary for the development of state-of-the-art programs and services for people with mental disabilities. No one individual or profession can be the critical element in successfully analyzing needs and implementing an effective treatment plan. Yet, too often, when confronted by a client or patient presenting multiple problems and challenging behaviors, one discipline tends to dominate the treatment process and, thus, comes to be regarded as the sine qua non. Because the intervention typically occurs when a client is in crisis, and the steps taken are viewed as preventing an emergency, the psychologist or psychiatrist emerges as the "expert," and others learn to extend due deference.

There is really nothing wrong with the perception of the psychologist or psychiatrist as expert. It is nice to have experts available to make sense out of a dangerous or perplexing series of behaviors. What *is* critical is that the clinicians in this role have the proper perspective on what is being done to bring reason and order back into the life of the client. In most such cases clinicians are not doing anything esoteric or unique. Rather, they are figuring out where the interactions of the individual, the caregiving system, and the environment went awry. Doing so is not wizardry; it is just one part of the treatment process. It is a highly visible and crucial part of the process, but it is only a beginning.

Inherent in the authors' discussion of the need for interdisciplinary cooperation, and present throughout the book, is the concept of *professional judgment*. This judgment is a vital component of the clinical balance the authors insist on. Professional judgment demands planning for a client using the best strategies and technology available. And certainly one of the keys to making the most effective judgments is addressing considerations from the variety of disciplines relevant to the treatment program.

Professional judgment as a concept is not only sound clinically, it is a necessary safeguard in serving this type of population. Underlying most treatment decisions today is an often unspoken but very real concern about what will happen if something goes wrong with the treatment. Clinicians and caregivers must be able to defend their decisions and actions—professional judgment is legally as well as ethically defensible.

Particularly relevant to the authors' considerations of professional judgment is their discussion on pharmacology. They do not rule out the appropriateness of prescribing drugs in certain instances, but rather urge clinicians following this approach to exercise their professional judgment with great care and with due regard to other types of support. Again, this discussion points to the clinical balance so typical of this book.

The authors' expertise in the various components of the treatment process, as well as their "hands-on" experience, is evident throughout the book. In presenting their material, they recognize that every reader has a practical mode, and they have made every attempt to address that reality. The assessment model, for example, demands a dynamic approach to diagnosis and treatment options, but the presentation is so clear and logical that readers will feel immediately comfortable with the material and confident that they can use it.

The major contribution of this work, however, may well be the section on the development and presentation of Nezu, Petronko, and Nezu's (1990) pioneering effort—the Behavioral Role-Play Activities Test, or BRAT. In this era of accountability, we seek newer and better ways to ensure that professionals in the field know what it is they are doing when prescribing strategies for dealing with aberrant behavior. The BRAT goes beyond paper-and-pencil verification of the efficacy of staff training and introduces structured simulation, wherein people can be rated on their actual performance of teaching strategies. The test, thus, becomes not only a means for measuring performance, but also a means for remediation. As such, it is a powerful tool for those charged with ensuring proper staff development.

The decision-making model presented here bears some striking similarities to approaches adopted by other fields, perhaps the most obvious of which is management. The authors' methods of generating treatment strategies are very much like the development of a business plan or the formulation of a series of goals and objectives for an organizational strategic plan. In this regard, the book has great utility for those who run organizations and want to ensure proper procedures and guidelines for service delivery. In fact, it would be a bonus if public officials would use material like this to evolve systems that would prevent so many dually diagnosed individuals from "falling between the cracks."

Some final points should be mentioned because they have a substantial impact on the importance of this work. First, the book is very strong in relating systemic research to the authors' experience. In addition, the authors do not advocate the *same* treatment for the *same* problem every time—this will pose a much-needed challenge to those who will use this work to improve their service delivery. And finally, there is a strong commitment to considering weighty ethical and moral issues before reaching a decision about a treatment program. The book's inclusion of these points adds strength to this solid piece of scholarship.

The professionals who will benefit the most from applying the principles presented in this book are those who are clinically strong and confident, are able to relinquish power and control when necessary, and are comfortable letting others share in the credit for successes. The clinical reward comes from knowing that the proper application of the strategies herein will allow caregivers and other professionals to encourage appropriate changes in the life of the client.

Readers will undoubtedly feel better about their ability to manage difficult situations and symptoms after reading this book. Although some of this material may seem familiar, it will also be obvious that it has never before been structured or presented in such an effective fashion. The synthesis of current ideas and technology is one of the great strengths of the book. And this synthesis speaks, again, to the credibility of the authors—they have had the experiences, they have worked out the strategies for treatment, and now they are sharing this highly effective problem-solving model with the profession.

ROBERT G. GRIFFITH, ED.D.
PRESIDENT, THE WOODS SCHOOLS
PAST PRESIDENT, AMERICAN ASSOCIATION
ON MENTAL RETARDATION

Preface

People with mental retardation constitute a population that is most in need, but least in receipt, of quality mental health services. People with dual diagnosis of mental retardation and coexisting psychiatric or behavioral disorders have historically experienced particular difficulty in receiving mental health services. Several authors have described dually diagnosed individuals as falling between the cracks in mental health and mental retardation service delivery systems (Evangelista, 1988; Matson & Barrett, 1982a).

Despite a continuing data base that reflects a high incidence of mental illness among persons with mental retardation (Eaton & Menolascino, 1982; Reiss, Levitan, & McNally, 1982; Stark, Menolascino, Albarelli, & Gray, 1988), we have repeatedly observed this unfortunate phenomenon in many clinical settings, particularly with regard to outpatient facilities. It is not uncommon to see dually diagnosed individuals shuffled from one facility to another, receiving indiscriminate dosages of neuroleptics in the absence of a clear diagnosis or adequate integration of multiple treatment components. For example, a client may receive psychopharmacologic therapy, crisis intervention, family therapy, and behavior modification, all at different facilities that do little to communicate or coordinate efforts. A multitude of problems—such as variable competency of community caregivers, turnover of direct care staff, lack of empathic involvement of mental health professionals, and bureaucratic complications—seem to exacerbate the difficulty of providing effective mental health services to dually diagnosed clients.

However, a refreshing and optimistic movement has recently begun, thanks to scientist-practitioners in psychology, psychiatry, special education, and social services who are attempting to change public policy by developing more scientifically rigorous and ethically responsible mental health treatment protocols for individuals with dual diagnoses. The urgent need for such efforts has been voiced for over a decade—since the special advisory panel to the President's Committee on Mental Health concluded that clients with mental retardation and mental illness had, been sorely neglected by health care delivery systems (Gettings, 1988). Moreover, the clients themselves continue to make their needs visible through maladaptive behavioral characteristics that cannot be ignored.

Because this movement is only of recent origin, the current literature provides few guidelines for evaluating and treating clients with dual diagnoses, particularly in outpatient settings. The existing literature tends to focus on psychological or behavioral problems of institutionalized patients, primarily from a behavioral perspective. In the aftermath of the deinstitutionalization movement, there is an urgent need for effective approaches to outpatient treatment. Toward this end, drawing on our own research and clinical work with such outpatient populations, we attempt to provide these needed guidelines. Because of the paucity of experimental literature regarding the issue, we advocate adopting a creative but empirical approach to clinical interventions with dually diagnosed clients. Thus, a major underpinning of this book is a clinical decision-making framework that urges mental health professionals to respect the complexities involved in providing clinical interventions to persons with multiple disabilities and advocates flexibility in applying strategies from the treatment literature.

In Section I we provide an historical perspective on the relationship between mental health and mental retardation. Summarizing much of the literature concerning prevalence and epidemiology, we conclude that persons with mental retardation do experience the full spectrum of psychiatric disorders. Further, persons with mental retardation appear more at risk than others for developing such disorders. Because many studies concerning these topics are methodologically problematic and limited in number or focus, we attempt to illustrate the complexities of working with dually diagnosed clients and argue for use of a systematic clinical decision-making process in assessment and treatment. We present a model for decision making with specific regard to outpatient populations and offer guidelines for application of the problem-solving model to three major areas of concern: the individual client, the caregiving system, and the physical and social environments.

The chapters in Section II provide more specific guidelines concerning assessment considerations for each of these areas. Believing that a well-defined problem is half solved, we stress comprehensive assessment as the essential first step toward efficacious treatment. We further highlight an integrative approach to assessment of the individual client and dispel the notion that behavioral and more traditional medical assessment cannot coexist. Indeed, we view different aspects of assessment as complementary rather than conflictual. We also propose several ways of assessing a client's caregiving system. Regarding assessment of caregiver behavior management skills, we emphasize hands-on competency beyond mere knowledge of behavioral principles. Moreover, we offer an empirically derived measure of caregiver competency regarding the use of behavior management principles (the Behavioral Role-Play Activities Test, or BRAT). In the chapter dealing with assessment of the environment, we discuss how the client and the caregiving system can be significantly helped or hindered by the prevailing physical and social milieu. Many case examples are included to demonstrate important means of assessing this milieu.

Section III describes intervention issues and strategies regarding each of the three areas of concern. Inherent in this section is the understanding that the onset and maintenance of psychiatric disturbances in individuals with developmental disabilities is influenced by a multitude of biological and psychosocial factors. Clinical application of the decision-making model can result in treatment strategies based on a combination of factors that are salient and individualized for each client.

Although a clinical decision-making approach appears valid and consistent with a multicomponent approach to the treatment of clients with dual diagnosis, it should, like any untested theory, be subjected to empirical scrutiny. In this light, we hope that presentation of our model will prompt mental health professionals to both use and critique it so that we may all work toward improving mental health services for developmentally disabled persons.

We believe that efforts to develop a strong body of literature on the treatment of mental health problems of persons with mental retardation have reached a critical turning point. The need for services to this population has never been greater; awareness of the problem is well documented. Yet most clinicians are obliged to make clinical decisions without the security of a comprehensive treatment literature base. With or without more well-designed treatment outcome studies, this population will continue to be treated. What kinds of services people with dual disabilities ultimately receive—which way the balance will tip—will depend upon all of us.

We have attempted to provide a clinical decision-making model for mental health professionals who are seeking ways to make current treatment decisions. Clinicians will continue to grapple with many medical, psychological, ethical, and legal problems regarding patients with dual diagnosis. We hope that this book will help to provide one avenue through which to seek resolution to these problems.

Acknowledgments

Our sincere appreciation goes to the people who helped bring this book to fruition. First, we would like to thank the significant people in our daily lives who continue to provide us with the love, support, and motivation to keep going. They include Linda, Ali, and Frank Nezu (C. M. N. & A. M. N.) and Joan Coneys and Daniel Weiss (M. J. G. W.).

We also thank two colleagues, Michael Petronko and Sandra Harris, who, having served as role models, mentors, and friends, continue to assist us in our problem-solving efforts regarding treatment of persons with mental retardation.

Thanks also to Joan Jones, whose secretarial skills and clerical assistance at Hahnemann University made completion of this book possible.

Our sincere gratitude is especially extended to Ann Wendel, Karen Steiner, and everyone at Research Press for their patience, tolerance, and helpful comments.

Finally, we would like to extend our appreciation to all the persons with dual diagnoses, and their caregivers, whom we have come to know through our clinical work. They have touched us through their challenges in a way no others could. We have learned much from knowing them.

Section I

Chapter 1

Mental Illness and Mental Retardation

INTRODUCTION

Early History

Historically, the relationship between the concepts of mental illness and mental retardation has undergone dramatic changes. Early thinkers tended to view both forms of "abnormality" as similar. For example, ancient Greeks and Romans treated mentally "dull" and mentally ill persons alike—unfortunately, in a persecutory manner. Because any form of mental deviance was often attributed to possession by evil spirits or demons, treatment often included flogging, starvation, and even death.

A more "scientific" conceptualization of mental pathology was that of Hippocrates, who offered a somatogenic, rather than religious, hypothesis to explain mental disorders. Mental illness and dullness were attributed to natural causes, namely, to a disruption of the delicate balance of the four basic bodily humors or fluids (blood, black bile, yellow bile, and phlegm). Melancholia or depression, for example, was caused by a preponderance of black bile; mentally dull or sluggish individuals came to be that way through an excess of phlegm.

Although the next few centuries saw major fluctuations in the manner in which deviant persons were treated, ranging from compassion to ridicule and scorn, little distinction was made between mental retardation and mental illness. By the 18th and 19th centuries, however, advances in medical science led professionals to draw a conceptual line between them. Intellectual deficit was viewed as the primary characteristic of mental retardation, whereas emotional impairment represented the outstanding feature of psychiatric disorders (Ollendick & Ollendick, 1982). One unfortunate outcome of this distinction was a generally limited interest in mental retardation on the part of the scientific community until Itard, in 1801, published his extensive treatment devoted to an "education of the mind" with Victor, the "Wild Boy of Aveyron." Although professional attention to mental retardation grew considerably as a function of Itard's work, the perception of mental retardation and mental illness as distinct disorders persisted until very recently, despite intervening conclusions by professionals such as R. M. Phelps (1897) that both forms of mental disorder should be viewed along a continuum rather than as distinct entities.

Recent History

Although surveys conducted early in this century began to document more empirically the existence of bona fide emotional and psychological disorders in people with mental retardation (e.g., Penrose, 1944; Potter, 1922; Tredgold, 1908), the fields of mental illness and mental retardation continued to diverge considerably. With the emergence of the Binet test to assess intellectual functioning psychometrically, traditional psychiatric evaluations of people with mental retardation were often replaced by IQ evaluations (Fletcher, 1988).

Menolascino and McCann (1983) have characterized the early 20th century as the "tragic interlude" when the gap between mental illness and mental retardation widened. For example, Humphreys (1935, as cited by Herskovitz & Plesset, 1941), in reviewing the proceedings of the American Association on Mental Deficiency between 1876 and 1935, noted the significant lack of presentations regarding emotional development and psychiatric disorders of this population. Further, in a paper presented at a joint meeting of the American Psychiatric Association and the American Association on Mental Deficiency in 1944, Pollock argued that "ordinarily, we regard the mentally ill and the mentally defective as separate and distinct groups . . . comparatively little thought is given to the mental hygiene needs of mental defectives" (pp. 361, 363). Over three decades later, little appears to have changed, as observed in Gualtieri's (1979) remonstrance to the field of psychiatry: "Psychiatry needs to reconsider its stance towards retarded people, because a terrible barrier has grown up between the fields of mental health and mental retardation" (p. 26). A psychiatrist himself, Gualtieri further notes that, in 1977, of the 612 articles published in the four American psychiatric journals, only 20 were concerned with mental retardation. Matson (1985) reminds us further that clinical psychologists may be similarly guilty of a lack of interest in the emotional problems of individuals with mental retardation.

Although the 1950s saw a growing concern for the overall treatment of people with mental retardation (e.g., in 1952 the National Association for Retarded Children, now called the Association for Retarded Citizens, was formed by concerned parents), it is only during the past two decades that the scientific community has acknowledged the coexistence of psychopathology and mental retardation. Indeed, it was only in the early 1980s that a group of concerned professionals formed the National Association for the Dually Diagnosed, a multidisciplinary association specifically concerned with the mental health needs of persons with mental retardation. As will be evident throughout this chapter, however, this increase in professional interest has not produced a plethora of empirical information about the incidence, prevalence, evaluation, diagnosis, and treatment of various psychopathological disorders in the population concerned.

Our primary purpose in this chapter is to offer a brief overview of mental health issues of people with mental retardation. First, however, we will discuss several factors that have impeded (and continue to impede) progress toward a better understanding of those issues.

MENTAL ILLNESS AND MENTAL RETARDATION: WHY THE GAP?

Unfortunately, the distinction between mental illness and mental retardation led to the belief commonly held among professionals that mentally retarded persons somehow enjoyed immunity to mental illness as a specific function of the retardation. For example, with regard to affective disorders, mentally retarded individuals were viewed as too psychologically immature to develop a depressive illness (Gardner, 1967). Moreover, as Fletcher (1988) notes, "The mildly retarded have been characterized as worry-free and thus mentally healthy. The severely retarded have been considered to express no feelings and therefore do not experience emotional stress" (p. 255).

A second factor perpetuating the gap is the perception that any emotional problem observed in a mentally retarded person is actually a feature of the retardation itself. Moreover, the existence of intellectual deficits takes precedence over the presence of any psychiatric symptoms. In other words, mental retardation diagnostically overshadows any accompanying emotional disturbance. In a series of investigations, Reiss and his colleagues provided substantial support for this observation. In the first study (Reiss, Levitan, & Szyszko, 1982), three groups of psychologists received a case description of an individual with a phobic reaction precipitated by a stressful experience. Each group received a slightly different version: One case suggested that the individual was mentally retarded, the second suggested the individual was alcoholic, and the third described the individual as having average intellectual ability. Results indicated that the psychologists rated the phobic reaction as less likely to represent a neurosis or an emotional disturbance if the subject was also mentally retarded as compared to intellectually average. A second study described in the same article extended these findings of diagnostic overshadow-ing to case descriptions involving schizophrenia and personality disorder.

Reiss and Szyszko (1983) continued this line of research and found that professionals who actually worked with mentally retarded persons were not immune to diagnostic overshadowing. Levitan and Reiss (1983) further found this phenomenon among a group of advanced students in psychology and social work.

In a related phenomenon, the label of "mental retardation" has also been associated with negative biases on the part of professionals. For example, Alford and Locke (1984) found that doctoral level psychologists rated the psychopathology described in a brief therapy transcript as less severe when the client was labeled mentally retarded. Further, when this label was applied, the client's level of intellectual functioning tended to assume more importance in the assessment process. Moreover, these results were consistent across theoretical orientations. Collectively, such studies provide convincing evidence that professionals, regardless of therapeutic orientation and experience with persons who have mental retardation, continue to see such persons as unlikely to experience mental illness.

Perhaps a major reason for the persistence of such diagnostic errors is the significant lack of training across mental health disciplines. Few graduate and professional training programs in mental health (psychology, psychiatry, social work) provide substantial training in mental retardation in general; even fewer offer training in the evalua-tion and treatment of emotional disorders of persons with mental retarda-tion. For example, Phelps and Hammer (1989), using survey data, found that 75% of clinical psychology and 67% of counseling psychology graduate programs do not address the personal and social adjustment of persons with mental retardation in their training curricula. Lack of specialized training in the mental health needs of mentally retarded indi-viduals can allow the effects of diagnostic overshadowing and bias to go unchallenged, thus perpetuating the gap between the fields of mental illness and mental retardation.

Unfortunately, federal and state regulatory bodies have tended to reinforce the distinction made by the professional community. Adminis-tratively, mental hygiene services in most states generally are divided into an office or department of mental health and a separate office or department of mental retardation. Each delivery system often develops policies and procedures independently of the other related system. The gate-way to either system, but not to both, is the diagnosis: An individual found to have mental retardation would be referred to the mental retardation office—referral to the mental health system would then be unlikely. This system of dual but separate institutional tracks reinforces professionals' perceptions about the orthogonality of the two diagnostic constructs.

Much worse, because of this policy of separateness, the mental health needs of persons with mental retardation are grossly underserved (President's Commission on Mental Health, 1978; President's Committee on Mental Retardation, 1985). Given the recent trends toward deinstitutionalization and mainstreaming of persons with mental retardation, this deficiency is especially serious. Community-based programs serving the mental health needs of nonretarded individuals are relatively easy to locate; similar facilities for those with mental retardation are extremely rare.

MENTAL ILLNESS IN PERSONS WITH MENTAL RETARDATION: PREVALENCE AND EPIDEMIOLOGICAL ISSUES

Despite the weak interest displayed until recently by the professional community regarding mental illness in persons with mental retardation, the association between maladaptive behavior and mental retardation has been noted in the literature for several decades. Table 1.1, which lists investigations addressing this relationship, provides ample evidence that persons with mental retardation experience psychiatric disorders. These studies consistently document the relationship for both institutional (e.g., Balthazar & English, 1969) and community settings (e.g., Benson, 1985), as well as across various cultures. For instance, the list includes investigations conducted in Canada (e.g., Dewan, 1948), Denmark (e.g., Dupont, 1981; Haracopos & Kelstrup, 1978), England (e.g., Birch, Richardson, Baird, Horobin, & Illsley, 1970; Rutter, Tizard, Yule, Graham, & Whitmore, 1976), Japan (e.g., Ando & Yoshimura, 1978), Sweden (e.g., Gostason, 1985), and the United States (e.g., Borthwick-Duffy & Eyman, 1990; Jacobson, 1982, 1990).

Further scrutiny of these studies, however, reveals vastly different rates of prevalence (10% to 100%) of mental illness among people with mental retardation. Why? One problem involves the use of differing definitions of mental retardation across studies. As we will discuss in greater detail in chapter 4, the most widely accepted definition of mental retardation (and the one we adopt here) includes elements of subaverage cognitive abilities as well as behavioral deficiencies in adaptive functioning. This definition, originally put forth by the American Association on Mental Deficiency (now known as the American Association on Mental Retardation), states that "mental retardation refers to significantly subaverage general intellectual functioning existing concurrently with deficits in adaptive behavior and manifested during the developmental period" (Grossman, 1983, p. 1). Some studies rely solely on psychometric evaluation (i.e., IQ scores) to identify individuals with mental retardation, whereas others include measures of adaptive functioning.

Table 1.1 Prevalence of Psychiatric Disorders and Behavioral Problems Among Individuals With Mental Retardation

Authors of study	Study sample	Method of assessment	Overall results
Ando and Yoshimura (1978)	128 mentally retarded children aged 6–14	Teacher ratings of maladaptive behavior	Prevalence of maladaptive behavior significantly related to IQ level (actual incidence not reported)
Balthazar and English (1969)	288 severely and profoundly retarded institutionalized persons	Behavioral inventory (Balthazar Scales of Adaptive Behavior)	16% of sample found to suffer from moderate to severe emotional and behavioral disturbance
Benson (1985)	130 mentally retarded adults and children referred to out-patient mental health clinic (extension of report by Reiss, 1982)	Clinical interview and examination of case records	Approximately 85% of sample accounted for by three broad diagnostic categories: schizoid-unresponsive/psychotic disorder; conduct disorder; and anxious-depressed withdrawal disorder
Birch, Richardson, Baird, Horobin, and Illsley (1970)	Total population of 8–10-year-old mentally retarded children in British city	Clinical interviews with child; parent and teacher questionnaires	Approximately 52% of sample considered psychiatrically abnormal

Study	Method	Findings
Borthwick-Duffy and Eyman (1990)	78,603 clients receiving services from state developmental disabilities office	Client Development Evaluation Report (multitrait-multimethod evaluation of all state clients)	Approximately 10% of state clients assigned diagnoses of both mental retardation and psychiatric disorder
Chess and Hassibi (1970)	52 mildly retarded children aged 5–11 living at home	Observations of child at home and school; parent and teacher interviews	Approximately 60% of sample showing significant psychiatric impairment
Connecticut MR Planning Project, 1966 (cited in Jakab, 1982)	827 residents of mental retardation training school	Psychiatric evaluation	42.7% of children identified as emotionally disturbed
	670 mentally retarded residents under age 20	Psychiatric evaluation	47.2% of sample found to be dually diagnosed
Corbett (1979)	402 mentally retarded adults	Psychiatric interviews	Approximately 46% of sample found to be psychiatrically impaired
Craft (1959)	314 adult inpatients certified as "mentally defective"	Clinical interview and review of case records	Approximately 33% of sample found to evidence abnormal personality disturbances
Day (1985)	357 mentally disabled adults over age 40	Review of case records	Approximately 30% of sample showing significant psychiatric disorders
Dewan (1948)	Approximately 2,000 Canadian army recruits (of original cohort of 30,247) identified as mentally retarded	Psychiatric examination	Approximately 47% of sample found to be emotionally unstable

Table 1.1 (cont'd)

Authors of study	Study sample	Method of assessment	Overall results
Donoghue and Abbas (1971)	293 moderately and pro-foundly retarded children	Identification by nurse and physician	Approximately 51% of sample judged to have disturbed behavior
Dupont (1981)	22,000 mentally retarded persons	National data registration information (Denmark)	Of 6,000 persons with moderate to severe retardation, 11.4% found to have neuroses and 11.3% psychoses
Eaton and Menolascino (1982)	798 mentally retarded persons across wide age range participating in community-based program	Clinical interview	Of original 798 receiving general services, 168 referred for psychiatric assessment; of those, 114 found to be dually diagnosed (14.3% of overall population)
Gillberg, Persson, Grufman, and Themner (1986)	146 mentally retarded children aged 13–17	Clinical interview	Approximately 64% of severely mentally retarded and 57% of mildly mentally retarded children found to evidence psychiatric conditions
Gostason (1985)	132 mentally retarded adults	Clinical interview plus infor-mation from relative or staff member	71% of severely retarded and 33% of mildly retarded adults given one or more psychiatric diagnoses

Study	Sample	Method	Findings
Groden, Domingue, Pueschel, and Deignan (1982)	1,114 mentally retarded children and adolescents from a community clinic	Examination of case records	Approximately 25% found to evidence serious behavioral and emotional problems
Haracopos and Kelstrup (1978)	Combined sample of 392 mentally retarded institutionalized children (random sample plus sample previously considered psychotic)	Clinical interviews and direct observations	Approximately 37% given specific psychiatric diagnoses
Heaton-Ward (1977)	1,251 mentally retarded, institutionalized patients	Examination of case records	Approximately 5% showing serious psychiatric impairment
Hill and Bruininks (1984)	2,271 mentally retarded individuals residing in community or public facilities	Assessment of behavior problems via interviews with direct care staff	47% of community facility residents and 60% of public facility residents found to display significant behavioral problems
Iverson and Fox (1989)	165 randomly selected mentally retarded adults	Behavioral inventory (Psychopathology Instrument for Mentally Retarded Adults—PIMRA)	35.9% of sample evidencing at least one psychiatric disorder
Jacobson (1982)	State data base of 30,578 mentally retarded persons	Survey-based protocols completed by clinical staff	11.6% of sample classified as having psychiatric disabilities
Jacobson (1990)	Extended state data base as originally contained in Jacobson (1982)	Same as Jacobson (1982)	20% of sample classified as having psychiatric disorders

Table 1.1 (cont'd)

Authors of study	Study sample	Method of assessment	Overall results
Jakab (1982)	595 referrals to mental retardation facility	Psychiatric evaluation	194 mentally retarded children also diagnosed as having psychiatric disorders
James (1986)	50 moderately and severely mentally retarded inpatients aged 60 and above	Behavioral questionnaire completed by nursing staff	56% of sample displaying significant behavioral problems requiring psychotropic medication
Koller, Richardson, Katz, and McLaren (1983)	Follow-up of 221 mentally retarded young adults previously identified in epidemiological study	Structured interviews using behavior disorders classifications	Approximately 60% of sample at childhood evidencing behavior disturbances; 20% rate at young adulthood
Larson and LaPointe (1986)	77 students attending school for educable retarded adolescents	Achenbach Childhood Behavior Checklist	20% or more of sample scoring abnormally high (above 98th percentile) on 6 of 8 female and 7 of 9 male subscales of deviant behavior
Linaker and Nitter (1990)	168 institutionalized mentally retarded patients (aged 16–65)	PIMRA	146 satisfying criteria for DSM-III Axis I diagnosis; 153 satisfying criteria for one or more disorders on Axis I or II

Study	Sample	Method	Findings
Lund (1985)	302 mentally retarded adults sampled by epidemiological criteria	Clinical interview of individual and relevant caretaker (parent or institutional staff member)	27.1% of sample diagnosed with psychiatric disorders
McQueen, Spence, Garner, Pereira, and Winsor (1987)	221 mentally retarded children aged 7–10	Review of case files	9% of sample found to have psychiatric disorders
Menolascino (1969)	1,025 children referred for evaluation of mental retardation	DSM-I diagnosis made by multidisciplinary team	Approximately 25% of sample judged to be emotionally disturbed
Menolascino (1970)	95 Down syndrome patients aged 1–24	Psychiatric examination and review of behavioral history	Approximately 35% of sample identified as behaviorally/emotionally disturbed
Penrose (1966)	Institutionalized mentally retarded inpatients	Review of case files	Approximately 16% of sample found to be psychotic or neurotic
Philips and Williams (1975)	100 mentally retarded children referred to a psychiatric clinic	Clinical interview with child and parent; physical, neurological, and psychological testing	87% of sample given psychiatric diagnoses
Pollock (1944)	444 mentally disabled inpatients newly admitted to state hospitals	Unspecified	Approximately 70% evidencing significant psychiatric disturbances
Reid, Ballinger, Heather, and Melvin (1984)	100 severely and profoundly mentally retarded adults in a hospital	Nursing staff observations and psychiatric interviews	50% of original sample judged to have psychiatric disorders; 51% of remaining cohort judged to have such disorders at follow-up 6 years later

Table 1.1 (cont'd)

Authors of study	Study sample	Method of assessment	Overall results
Reiss (1982)	66 mentally retarded out-patients aged 6–60	Clinical interview, psychological testing, and review of case records	100% of sample found to evidence significant psychopathology, where four diagnostic groupings (schizo-phrenic symptomatology, antisocial behavior, depres-sion, personality disorders) accounted for over 77% of the sample
Reiss (1985)	5,637 mentally retarded chil-dren in a public school system	Review of case files	10.2% of sample identified as having mental health disorders
Reiss (1990)	205 adults and adolescents participating in community-based day programs for mentally retarded persons	Two-stage procedure: (a) initial identification of psychiatric problems via Reiss Screen for Maladaptive Behavior and (b) confirmation via clinical evaluation	Dual diagnosis (MR/MI) prevalence rate found to be approximately 39%
Rutter, Tizard, Yule, Graham, and Whitmore (1976)	Isle of Wight cohort of 10–12-year-old children initially identified as intellectually retarded (initial cohort = 2,199)	Comprehensive evaluation including clinical interviews of child and parents, behavioral questionnaires completed by teachers	Approximately 30% to 42% of sample showing psychiatric disorders of sufficient severity "to have caused a social handicap"

Weaver (1946)	8,000 military inductees classified as intellectually retarded	Psychiatric examination	44% of males and 38% of females exhibiting significant psychiatric disturbance
Webster (1963)	159 mentally retarded children aged 3–6	Neurological, psychiatric, and psychological evaluations; parent interviews, review of previous medical records	Of entire sample, 35% considered mildly emotionally disturbed, 48% moderately disturbed, and 17% severely disturbed
Wright (1982)	1,507 mentally retarded institutionalized patients	Survey including verbal and nonverbal criteria	7.3% of sample evidencing serious psychiatric conditions

A related problematic issue leading to differing rates of prevalence across studies involves the grouping of all individuals with mental retardation into one overall cohort in a given study. Often investigators fail in their research designs to address the vast differences between, for example, persons with mild and severe retardation. Just as nonretarded people are heterogeneous along a wide variety of dimensions (e.g., age, sex, socioeconomic background, cultural diversity, severity of disability, presence of additional disabilities), so are persons with mental retardation. Thus, when level of retardation is taken into account, studies indicate that prevalence of maladaptive behavior varies as a function of IQ and age (e.g., Ando & Yoshimura, 1978).

Just as differences in the diagnostic criteria for mental retardation affect the outcomes of epidemiological investigations, so do differences in the manner in which psychiatric disorders are defined. Diagnostic criteria, as well as methods of assessing such criteria, have differed across studies. Historically, psychiatric diagnostic categories—as defined, for example, by the various versions of the *Diagnostic and Statistical Manual of Mental Disorders* (American Psychiatric Association, 1952, 1968, 1980, 1987)—tend to change with the availability of new research data and new developments in mental health philosophy. Thus, studies conducted earlier in the century are difficult to compare with more recent ones.

However, even studies conducted contemporaneously have often used different methods to assess the presence of psychopathology, ranging from a review of case files (e.g., Reiss, 1985) to a comprehensive series of interview and testing sessions (e.g., Philips & Williams, 1975). Several investigations have focused on classifying persons with mental retardation according to formal psychiatric diagnostic categories (e.g., Reiss, 1990), whereas others tend to address the issue of prevalence according to the presence of serious behavioral and/or emotional disturbance (e.g., Groden, Domingue, Pueschel, & Deignau, 1982). Inconsistency in criteria for the diagnosis of mental illness has made comparisons across studies extremely tenuous.

A final issue that accounts for variation in psychopathology prevalence rates among people with mental retardation involves differences in situational factors concerning the studies' subjects. These factors include (a) the subjects' residence (community versus institution), (b) the method used in selecting subjects for inclusion (referral to mental health center versus random selection from census data), and (c) the sources of information used to evaluate psychiatric symptoms. With regard to residence, studies have shown that behavior problems are much more prevalent in institutions than in community-based samples (e.g., Eyman & Call, 1977). Second, a higher incidence rate would probably emerge among subjects referred to a mental health center than among individuals identified randomly through a census list.

Finally, differences in prevalence rates can be a function of data source. This fact is best exemplified by the famous Isle of Wight studies conducted by Rutter and his colleagues (Rutter et al., 1976), a major epidemiological undertaking considered one of the best sources of information about the relation between mental illness and retardation among children. The Rutter studies avoided many of the methodological problems just discussed. Psychiatric disorders were identified in a two-stage process. The first stage involved screening questionnaires regarding a cohort of children aged 9, 10, and 11. The questionnaires, focusing on ratings of psychiatric symptoms, were completed by the parents and teachers of the subjects. Direct clinical interviews and collection of other measures constituted the second stage. All evaluation methods were assessed for their psychometric soundness. This comprehensive assessment methodology incorporated data from several sources, including the clients themselves, parents, and teachers. Pertinent to the issue of the effects of data source on varying rates of prevalence, 30% of children with mental retardation were found to have psychiatric disorders when parental ratings were used; however, the rate increased to 42% when based on teacher ratings.

Despite the problems leading to wide variation in reported prevalence rates, existing studies collectively lead to the inescapable conclusion that persons with mental retardation do in fact suffer from mental illness. Experts currently agree that the actual rate of incidence of mental illness among persons with mental retardation ranges from 20% to 35% (e.g., Stark, 1989). In fact, many investigations show that people with mental retardation experience higher rates of psychopathology than do people without retardation. Indeed, according to the third and revised edition of the *Diagnostic and Statistical Manual of Mental Disorders* (DSM-III-R; American Psychiatric Association, 1987), other mental disorders are at least three to four times more prevalent among people with mental retardation than among the general population. For example, in the Isle of Wight study (Rutter et al., 1976), the rate of psychiatric disorders among the children with mental retardation ranged between 30% and 40%, in contrast to a rate of approximately 7% among the total population of children matched for age.

Further, Koller, Richardson, Katz, and McLaren (1983) found that the overall rate of behavioral disturbance among young adults with mental retardation was about 2.5 times greater than in a matched control group. Dewan (1948) noted that about 47% of army recruits identified as mentally retarded were considered emotionally unstable, whereas the rate for the nonretarded cohort was about 20%. On the basis of another large-scale epidemiological investigation of mental retardation in a Swedish population, Gostason (1985) found that 71% of a severely retarded group and 33% of a mildly retarded group received at least one psychiatric diagnosis via a comprehensive assessment procedure. This again is in contrast to a rate of 23% for a matched control group of nonretarded individuals.

A related question that emerges is whether people with mental retardation experience the same types of psychopathology as persons without retardation. Philips and Williams (1975) attempted to answer that question in a study of 100 children with mental retardation who were referred to a psychiatric clinic. Of the 100 children, initial diagnostic evaluations indicated, 38 were found to be psychotic and 49 showed symptoms of characterological, neurotic, behavioral, and/or situational disorders. Thirteen children showed no evidence of psychiatric disorder. When the nonpsychotic retarded children were compared to a control group of 79 emotionally disturbed, nonretarded children, symptoms in general were not found to differ. This comparison supported earlier clinical observations by Philips (1967) regarding 227 children with retardation and their families. He noted the misconception, common among professionals at that time, that "emotional disorder in the retarded is different in kind from the normal child" (p. 30). Clinical observations by Reid (1980) of 60 mentally retarded children also support the notion that mentally retarded and nonmentally retarded persons experience similar types of psychological disorders.

To clarify some of these issues, the following section will describe specific psychiatric disorders experienced by persons with mental retardation.

Anxiety Disorders

A review of studies addressing anxiety (and anxiety-related disorders) and mental retardation suggests two general conclusions about prevalence. First, although investigations have produced widely varying rates of incidence (probably for the reasons previously noted), persons with mental retardation are in fact susceptible to anxiety disorders, as Table 1.2 shows.

Moreover, several studies strongly suggest that anxiety levels are higher among mentally retarded persons than among their nonretarded counterparts (Cochran & Cleland, 1963; Malpass, Mark, & Palermo, 1960). For example, Feldhausen and Klausmeier (1962) focused on differences in scores on the Children's Manifest Anxiety Scale (CMAS) among groups of low IQ (Wechsler Intelligence Scale for Children scores between 51 and 81), average IQ (scores of 90 to 110), and high IQ (scores of 120 to 146) grade school children matched for age. Results of this investigation indicated significantly higher CMAS scores for the low-IQ children than for the average and high-IQ groups (no differences were noted between the latter two groups).

Table 1.2 Prevalence of Anxiety Disorders Among Individuals With Mental Retardation: Representative Studies

Authors	Overall results
Benson (1985)	25% of sample characterized by "anxious-depressed withdrawal disorder"
Craft (1960)	10.8% of sample diagnosed with "anxiety states"
Eaton and Menolascino (1982)	1 out of 114 cases diagnosed as "psychoneurotic anxiety disorders"
Gillberg, Persson, Grufman, and Themner (1986)	4.5% of severely mentally retarded individuals exhibiting anxiety disorders; 10% of mildly mentally retarded individuals characterized by anxiety disorders
Lund (1985)	2% of sample diagnosed with anxiety disorders
Neuer (1947)	13% of sample classified as "neurotic" (i.e., exhibiting extensive symptoms of restlessness, anxiety, and compulsions)
Penrose (1938)	10.3% of sample characterized as "psychoneurotic" (i.e., exhibiting symptoms of "nervous energy" and anxiety)
Philips and Williams (1975)	5% of sample diagnosed with anxiety disorders; over 23% of sample reporting problems that included anxiety symptoms
Pollock (1944)	16% of sample characterized by severe anxiety
Reid (1980)	22% of sample exhibiting "neurotic disorders" (i.e., symptoms of worry, depression, and school phobias)
Richardson, Katz, Koller, McLaren, and Rubinstein (1979)	17% of sample characterized by neurotic disorders (i.e., symptoms of anxiety and depression)

A study by Knights (1963) indicated that both institutionalized and noninstitutionalized mentally retarded children reported more test anxiety than did nonretarded matched controls. No differences among the children with mental retardation were found as a function of institutionalization, although this variable did account for significant differences in test anxiety among the nonretarded children.

With specific regard to fears, Guarnaccia and Weiss (1974) conducted a factor analysis of responses to the Louisville Fear Survey for Children provided by parents of 102 mentally retarded children and young adults (age range from 6 to 21). Four types of fears emerged from their analysis: separation (e.g., getting lost), natural events (e.g., thunder), injury (e.g., being wounded or injured), and animals (e.g., snakes). On the basis of these results, the authors concluded that mentally retarded persons show the same dimensions or types of fear behavior as do nonretarded individuals. Moreover, in a study by Duff et al. (1981), 20 mentally retarded adults were found to be more fearful in general and to display more intense fear than did their chronological age-matched control counterparts.

Affective Disorders

In 1983, Sovner and Hurley published an article entitled "Do the Mentally Retarded Suffer From Affective Illness?" Reviewing the 25 published reports then available regarding the occurrence of affective disorders (i.e., depression, mania, bipolar disorder), they concluded that individuals with mental retardation manifested the full range of affective illnesses. A review published the previous year by Matson and Barrett (1982) led to a similar conclusion. Investigations conducted since the publication of those reviews serve to reinforce this conclusion (e.g., Benson, 1985; Gillberg, Persson, Grufman, & Themner, 1986; Iverson & Fox, 1989; James, 1986; Koller et al., 1983; Lund, 1985). In fact, according to Laman and Reiss (1987), depressed mood is among the most common psychiatric symptom experienced by adults with mental retardation.

Two recent studies further indicate that depression is more prevalent among mentally retarded children than among their nonretarded counterparts. Matson, Barrett, and Helsel (1988) compared the Child Depression Inventory and Child Behavior Profile scores of 31 mentally retarded, emotionally disturbed, hospitalized children with those of 31 children matched for age and sex from a regular school setting. Results indicated that depression was more prevalent in the group with mental retardation and that overall psychopathology was highly correlated with depression. Further, the investigators found evidence that the types of depression experienced by mentally retarded children and nonretarded children were similar.

Reynolds and Miller (1985) examined differences in depression levels between a sample of 26 educable mentally retarded (EMR) adolescents and a group of 26 nonretarded adolescents who were matched on age, sex, and race. Their results indicated that the EMR adolescents manifested depressive symptomatology significantly greater than that of their nonretarded peers. Moreover, the adolescents with mental retardation were found to score higher on a measure of learned helplessness.

Psychoses and Schizophrenia

Although reported rates of prevalence vary, a multitude of studies document the existence of psychotic and schizophrenic disorders among individuals with mental retardation. Neuer (1947) reported that among 300 consecutive admissions to a state school for mentally retarded children, 11% were found to be psychotic. Angus (1948), focusing on a similar population, found that 28% of a sample of 150 new admissions were schizophrenic. Among Eaton and Menolascino's (1982) community-based sample of 114 mentally retarded persons, 24 were diagnosed as schizophrenic. The category of schizophrenia was found to account for over 24% of the 66 mentally retarded outpatients in Reiss's (1982) sample.

Researchers have also addressed the question of whether schizophrenia is related to degree of retardation. For example, among a sample of 64 children with severe mental retardation living in an urban area of Sweden, 50% were diagnosed as psychotic, as compared to 14% among a group of children with mild mental retardation residing in the same area (Gillberg, Persson, Grufman, & Themner, 1986). A contrasting finding was reported by Gostason (1985), who also focused on a Swedish population but found no difference in the occurrence of schizophrenic disorders as a function of differing levels of retardation.

Confounding this issue is the controversy about the validity of a diagnosis of schizophrenia in a person with severe mental retardation. On the one hand, clinicians have argued that it is impossible to obtain the kind of information needed for such a diagnosis with a person whose IQ is less than 50 (e.g., Hayman, 1939; Herskovitz & Plesset, 1941). However, others (e.g., Eaton & Menolascino, 1982) have argued that careful observation of symptoms such as altered affective responding, bizarre rituals, and the use of interpersonal distancing strategies can support a diagnosis of schizophrenia for even severely retarded individuals. Further compounding the diagnostic dilemma is the difference between adult onset schizophrenia and childhood schizophrenia and autism. Most cases of severe retardation diagnosed as psychosis occur in very young children, who in consequence are often considered autistic. Indeed, the incidence of infantile autism among individuals with mental retardation is significantly greater than within the general population (Wing, 1978).

The lack of solid medical and psychiatric documentation often makes it difficult to ascertain the validity of information that would be used in diagnosis. Further, this difficulty often coexists with the problems previously noted. Despite the methodological and clinical problems leading to differential estimates of schizophrenia among differing samples of mentally retarded persons, we can conclude that mentally retarded persons do experience schizophrenic and psychotic disorders.

Personality Disorders

Perhaps the diagnostic category that has received the least attention in the context of mental retardation is that of personality disorders. This is due in part to the inherent difficulty of defining and evaluating person-ality disorders among the general population as well as to the unique obstacles in identifying abnormal problems of personality among persons with severe mental retardation (Gostason, 1985). However, attempts to study the prevalence of personality disorders among individuals with mental retardation have yielded findings generally consistent with those concerning other psychiatric disorders: (a) that they do exist in this popu-lation and (b) that they occur at a high rate. For example, Eaton and Menolascino (1982) reported the presence of various personality dis-orders (e.g., antisocial, passive-aggressive, schizoid) in 27.1% of their community-based sample. Of the first 70 referrals to an outpatient clinic at a major New York medical center for dually diagnosed adolescents and adults with mental retardation, 11 were characterized by personality disorders (Nezu, Miescher, & Solgan, 1989). Reiss (1982) reported that 10 of 66 mentally retarded outpatients were classified as having person-ality disorders. However, his diagnostic criteria excluded schizoid person-ality disorder (which was included in the schizophrenia subgrouping) and psychopathy. If those criteria had been included, the number of patients placed in the personality disorder category would probably have increased. For example, the subgroup of psychopathy was included in an "antisocial behavior" category, which accounted for an additional 16 of the 66 cases.

In a sample of 357 long-stay mentally retarded hospital residents aged 40 and over, Day (1985) found that more than 50% were classified as presenting behavioral and personality disorders. In a second sample of 215 new admissions (over a 7-year period) to a psychiatric unit for men-tally disabled individuals, he further found over 35% evidencing person-ality disorders. Sixteen of 100 mentally retarded children in Philips and Williams's (1975) sample were diagnosed with personality disorders.

Particularly telling is a recent study by Reid and Ballinger (1987), who randomly selected from a pool of 260 hospital residents 100 mildly and moderately retarded adult inpatients. Assessment of personality disorders was conducted according to the procedures of the Standardized

Assessment of Personality (Mann, Jenkins, Cutting, & Cowen, 1981) procedure, which entails completion of an inventory based on a structured interview with a significant caretaker (in this case, the nurse in charge of the hospital ward). The procedure used personality disorder classifications included in the International Classification of Diseases. Results of the investigation indicated that 56% of the sample showed features of abnormal personality. Moreover, in 22% of the cases, the abnormality was markedly sufficient to support the diagnosis of a bona fide personality disorder.

In sum, a brief review of the literature focusing on specific psychiatric diagnostic categories (anxiety disorders, affective disorders, psychotic and schizophrenic disorders, personality disorders) provides further evidence that persons with mental retardation certainly experience a wide variety of psychiatric and psychological disorders, and that in many cases, those disorders are significantly more prevalent than in the general population.

An important question that emerges from these conclusions is, What factors account for this increased vulnerability to psychopathology? Unfortunately, the answer is complex and difficult because of the paucity of research specifically addressing this issue. However, in the next section, we will briefly discuss several variables that may play a role in the increased prevalence of psychopathology among people with mental retardation.

PSYCHOPATHOLOGY IN PEOPLE WITH MENTAL RETARDATION: PATHOGENIC MECHANISMS

Assuming that the reader accepts our previous conclusions about the strong association between psychopathology and mental retardation (despite our often repeated caveats regarding the methodological limitations characterizing most of the relevant research), the logical question emerges: What are the specific mechanisms or factors underlying the increased vulnerability to mental illness in persons with mental retardation? Although we can acknowledge that those individuals experience the full spectrum of psychiatric disorders, providing a comprehensive and detailed answer would be tantamount to explaining why *anyone* is vulnerable to psychopathology, a task far beyond the scope of this book. However, on one level, this perspective suggests strongly that (a) psychopathology in mentally retarded persons is probably multiply determined and (b) individuals with mental retardation may become psychiatrically impaired through the same pathogenic mechanisms that operate for persons without mental retardation. Nevertheless, particular etiological variables may be more characteristic or salient for individuals with mental retardation.

A specific example of this latter point involves the causal relationship between certain psychological constructs and depression. With regard to nonretarded individuals, various psychological theories point to the etiological role of poor social skills in clinical depression (e.g., Lewinsohn, Hoberman, Teri, & Hautzinger, 1985; Nezu, Nezu, & Perri, 1989). Recent studies suggest a similar relationship of poor social skills and depression among mentally retarded individuals (Benson, Reiss, Smith, & Laman, 1985; Helsel & Matson, 1988; Laman & Reiss, 1987). In addition, Reiss and Benson (1985), studying a group of adults with mental retardation, reported a significant association between depression and low levels of social support, a variable also highly related to depressive symptomatology among subjects without retardation (Billings & Moos, 1982).

In addition to lack of social skills and social support, a third construct that has guided research in depression concerning the general population is learned helplessness (Seligman, 1975). Reynolds and Miller (1985) explored this construct with regard to adolescents with mental retardation. A group of educable mentally retarded adolescents were found to manifest levels of depressive symptoms and learned helplessness higher than that of a comparison group of nonretarded adolescents matched for age, sex, and race.

Collectively, such findings suggest that mentally retarded persons become depressed for the same reasons nonretarded individuals do, at least with regard to the etiologic roles of inadequate social skills, low social support, and feelings of learned helplessness. The next question then is, Are mentally retarded persons more likely to show ineffective social skills and learned helplessness than nonretarded individuals? By definition, persons with mental retardation are below average in adaptive functioning and exhibit poor coping ability, ineffective problem solving, and inadequate social skills (Nezu, Nezu, & Arean, 1991). Further, research findings strongly suggest that mentally retarded persons are more likely to feel helpless than nonretarded individuals. For example, Floor and Rosen (1975) compared scores on a helplessness test among two groups of adults with mental retardation (one institutionalized and the other community residents) and a control group of adults matched for chronological age. The test consisted of several behavioral items designed to assess coping ability in simple problem-solving situations in which intellectual capacity did not play a dominant role. Results indicated that both groups of individuals with mental retardation exhibited significantly more signs of helplessness than did the controls.

Weisz (1979) provides evidence to support the notion that helplessness tends to be learned over time by the child with mental retardation, who is continuously exposed to failure experiences and helplessness-inducing feedback. For instance, youngsters with mental retardation are more likely to evidence deterioration in intellectual performance following failure feedback than are their nonretarded counterparts (Weisz, 1981a). Moreover, adults in their lives may actually foster and reinforce these beliefs and failure expectations. In a series of studies, Weisz (1981b) found evidence that college student subjects rated insufficient ability as a more important cause of failure for a retarded than for a nonretarded child and insufficient effort as the more important cause of failure for the nonretarded youngster. Further, they rated the retarded child as less likely to succeed in the future, a result suggesting that retardation itself sufficed to reduce one's likelihood of being urged to persist after a failure experience. Using a similar methodology, Nezu, Shenouda, and Taylor (1984) found that adults would be less likely to use various behavioral change strategies to help adolescents with mental retardation overcome self-control problems because they perceived the youngsters as incapable of responding in a positive manner.

Even though research has demonstrated that persons with retardation can overcome this low expectancy of success through structured reinforcement training (e.g., Ollendick, Balla, & Zigler, 1971), an unresponsive social environment can serve not only to condone helplessness but actually to foster its development. In such an environment, the person with mental retardation can remain particularly vulnerable to inadequate adaptive behavior, poor social skills, and feelings of helplessness. In turn, these problems can increase this person's susceptibility to psychopathology.

Although research is lacking to provide definitive conclusions, this model that emphasizes the increased relevance of certain psychopathology-related variables for mentally retarded individuals probably accounts for such individuals' increased vulnerability to psychiatric difficulties per se. The example regarding learned helplessness and depression is but one illustration of this concept. Several additional factors can be shown to be (a) etiologically involved in the pathogenesis of various forms of psychiatric disorders and (b) particularly prevalent among people with mental retardation as compared to the general population. These factors include lowered socioeconomic level (Baumeister, 1988); increased presence of physical disabilities (Larson & LaPointe, 1986), especially epilepsy (Corbett & Harris, 1974); heightened family stress (Richardson, Koller, & Katz, 1985) and maternal stress (Quine, 1986); increased probability of central nervous system damage (Baumeister & MacLean, 1979); increased presence of reading and language dysfunctions (Rutter et al., 1976); decreased opportunities to learn adaptive coping styles (Nezu et al., 1991); increased likelihood of chromosomal abnormalities, metabolic diseases, and infections (Abramowicz & Richardson, 1975); increased likelihood of institutionalization (Eyman & Call, 1977); significant problems related to emotional and personality development (Levitas & Gilson, 1989; Webster, 1963); and decreased inhibition in responding to stressful events (Myers, 1986). As mentioned earlier, it is likely that psychopathology in individuals with mental retardation is multiply caused—that any combination of these factors increases the likelihood of a person's experiencing significant psychiatric symptomatology.

SUMMARY

Not until the latter half of this century have researchers attempted to investigate systematically the relationship between mental illness and mental retardation. For a variety of reasons, the mental health needs of persons with mental retardation have traditionally been ignored. These reasons include the notion that individuals with mental retardation are immune to mental illness, the influence of diagnostic overshadowing, the presence of professional biases related to the label "mental retardation," the significant lack of systematic training for mental health professionals regarding mental retardation, and the demarcation between mental health and mental retardation in governmental service provision.

Despite these obstacles, a significant amount of research has led to the inescapable conclusions that (a) persons with mental retardation do in fact experience the full spectrum of psychiatric disorders, (b) these disorders are similar to those experienced by nonretarded individuals, and (c) psychiatric disorders are more prevalent among mentally retarded persons than in the general population. The increased relevance of various psychopathology-related factors (e.g., learned helplessness) can explain why mentally retarded persons are more at risk for psychological dysfunctions.

Unfortunately, although a plethora of studies collectively support the validity of these conclusions, the literature as a whole is characterized by methodological limitations. With specific regard to the variability among investigations yielding prevalence rates of psychiatric disorders, several problems were identified: (a) use of differential definitions of the construct of mental retardation, (b) failure to discriminate among levels of retardation, (c) diagnostic problems regarding the assessment of psychiatric disorders, and (d) various situational factors (i.e., residence of subject, subject selection procedures, source of data).

Given these methodological limitations, in addition to the paucity of research addressing the pathogenesis of various psychiatric disorders in persons with mental retardation, it is not surprising that literature focusing on the effective treatment of such disorders among these persons is also sorely lacking. Elsewhere (Nezu & Nezu, 1989a) we have vehemently argued that there is no "cookbook" in which mental health professionals concerned with the general population can locate "the" treatment approach to use in a particular case, given the vast array of differences (e.g., previous history, age, sex, severity of symptoms, life-style, social support, race) among people suffering from the same disorder. How, then, to answer—with regard to persons with mental retardation who experience psychological disorders—the question that psychotherapy out-come researchers have been asking for the past several decades: "What treatment, by whom, is most effective for this individual with that specific problem, under which set of circumstances?" (Paul, 1969, p. 111). Admittedly, this is a tremendously complex and difficult question to address. The remainder of this book attempts to answer the question within the context of the clinical decision-making model we have articulated in detail elsewhere (Nezu & Nezu, 1989b).

The next chapter will delineate a model of clinical decision making for the provision of mental health services for dually diagnosed persons, particularly in outpatient settings. The model is based on a prescriptive model of problem solving (D'Zurilla, 1986; Nezu & Nezu, 1991) that can aid the mental health professional in identifying optimal treatment for a client who has mental retardation and a concomitant psychiatric disorder. A major theme of this book is the need for an idiographic perspective on assessment and treatment. A second theme involves a tripartite approach to assessment and treatment, considering the client, the caregiving system (e.g., parents, siblings, direct-care residential staff), and the client's physical and social environment. Sections II and III of the book, dealing with assessment and treatment, respectively, will reflect this tripartite approach.

Chapter 2

A Problem-Solving Model of Decision Making and Case Formulation for Clinical Interventions With Dually Diagnosed Individuals

INTRODUCTION

Recently, we articulated a problem-solving model for clinical decision making as one way to help guide mental health professionals in the difficult process of making clinical judgments in general (Nezu & Nezu, 1989b). Such judgments can include differential diagnosis, clinical assessment, problem behavior identification, goal setting, selection of therapeutic interventions, and treatment evaluation. The desirability of such a systematic approach to clinical interventions is based on three premises: (a) the absence of a "treatment cookbook," (b) the complexity of most clinical cases, and (c) the negative influence of a variety of judgmental errors on clinical decision making.

Lack of a Treatment Cookbook

As mentioned in the previous chapter, there is no "treatment cookbook" for the general population that would permit mental health professionals to consult a comprehensive index and locate the ideal clinical intervention for a given client. Even among individuals suffering from the same psychological dysfunction or displaying similar maladaptive behaviors, heterogeneity is the rule rather than the exception. Differences among individuals exist along a wide range of parameters, including demographic variables (e.g., age, sex, ethnic background, socioeconomic status); disorder-related dimensions (e.g., presence of additional disorders, severity of symptoms, previous psychiatric history, age at onset, symptom duration); psychosocial variables (e.g., coping ability, social support, personality factors); and biological factors (e.g., presence of medical complications, specific biological vulnerabilities). Each of these elements can impact on the efficacy of a treatment plan: Thus, a specific therapeutic strategy to alleviate Jack's depression may not be the optimal treatment for Jill, who also is depressed. In addition, variations in adaptive behavior and intellectual functioning greatly increase the heterogeneity of dually diagnosed individuals, heightening the need for an individualized or idiographic approach.

Complexity of Cases

To say that the treatment of persons with mental retardation who suffer from concomitant psychological disorders is complex is a gross understatement. In particular, we would like to highlight the multidimensional nature of the distal and proximal causes of both mental retardation and psychiatric dysfunction. In other words, the pathogenesis of a mentally retarded person's emotional difficulties is likely to be pluralistic. In problem-solving terms, the obstacles to goal attainment are multiple and varied. Therefore, any attempt to explain psychopathology that focuses on a single phenomenon is likely to fall short of clinical reality. Similarly, any clinical intervention that uses only a single technique is likely to fall short of success.

Errors in Clinical Judgment

Psychological research has consistently demonstrated several ubiquitous factors that interfere with reliable and valid decision making by people in general (Kahneman & Tversky, 1973) as well as by health and mental health professionals in clinical settings (Arkes, 1981; Nezu & Nezu, 1989a). Often, errors in clinical reasoning are due to the limited capabilities of humans to process large amounts of information simultaneously. This concept has been termed *bounded rationality* (Newell & Simon, 1972). In other words, to cope more efficiently with large amounts of information, people tend to resort to various strategies to overcome their inherent cognitive limitations. Thus, clinicians may focus only on information that is considered important, to process this information in serial rather than parallel fashion, and to represent the clinical situation in very laconic terms. Although many of these strategies are generally necessary in the solving of complex problems (Nisbett & Ross, 1980), they can often lead to errors in judgment (Nezu & Nezu, 1989a).

Tversky and Kahneman (1974) have identified three such strategies or *judgmental heuristics:* availability, representativeness, and anchoring. The availability heuristic is invoked when one attempts to estimate the frequency of a class or the probability of an event by the facility or ease with which examples of that class or event can be recalled.

The representativeness heuristic is often used when one attempts to answer such questions as, What is the probability that A is associated with B? What is the probability that A is a member of group B? What is the likelihood that event A caused event B or that B caused A on the basis of perceived resemblance of A to B? Use of such heuristics, when coupled with a lack of experience regarding dually diagnosed persons, can often lead to the conclusion that such persons do not experience psychological difficulties. For instance, for a clinician attempting to predict whether a person with mental retardation can suffer from depression, such cognitive strategies can lead to a biased answer because there might be little perceived resemblance between a person with mental retardation and one with depression.

The third heuristic, that of anchoring, is associated with a shortcut method of estimation or prediction in which final decisions are based more on initial impressions than on subsequent information. Meehl (1960), for example, noted that a clinician's identification of clients' personality traits stabilized between the second and the fourth therapy sessions but changed little after several months of contact. This would suggest that information gleaned during those later sessions was often ignored.

In addition to the three judgmental heuristics, other phenomena lead to biased clinical judgments. For example, *overconfidence* in one's abilities has been found to produce systematic error in clinical reasoning, whereas confidence has been found unrelated to clinical accuracy (Oskamp, 1965). The *hindsight bias* can often reinforce overconfidence in clinical judgments. This bias is seen when a person claims after the fact that he or she would have predicted a given outcome if asked in advance of its occurrence.

In situations that necessitate gathering of information to help make judgments (as in clinical assessments and the process of differential diagnosis), the appropriate strategy itself often inadvertently contributes to erroneous conclusions. For example, *confirmatory search strategies* have been shown to be common attempts to verify inferences and make predictions (Wason, 1969). These strategies are designed to obtain data that support one's original hypotheses rather than facts that may help to adjust one's initial impressions. Research has shown that people tend to disregard evidence that actually contradicts their current judgments or opinions (Koriat, Lichtenstein, & Fischhoff, 1980).

Given the relative paucity of empirical information regarding psychological treatments for individuals with mental retardation (and considering especially that the need to target psychological and emotional problems within this population has been acknowledged only recently), our three premises—lack of a treatment cookbook, complexity of cases, and systematic errors in clinical reasoning—appear even more salient regarding clinical interventions for mentally retarded persons with concomitant psychiatric disorders. To address the difficulty, we will describe briefly a model of clinical decision making that provides a heuristic framework within which to conceptualize assessment and treatment of the dually diagnosed population. (See Nezu & Nezu, 1989a, for a detailed version of this model across various clinical populations.)

TOWARD A PROBLEM-SOLVING CONCEPTUALIZATION OF CLINICAL INTERVENTIONS

To delineate a decision-making model that can aid clinicians in formulating interventions for persons with mental retardation and mental illness, we will adopt a problem-solving framework. Our paradigm incorporates the principles of problem solving that are the basis of social problem-solving training as described by D'Zurilla and Goldfried (1971) and D'Zurilla and Nezu (1982). Although the original model was a prescriptive approach with the goal of enhancing people's problem-solving ability with regard to stressful life circumstances (cf. Nezu & D'Zurilla, 1989; Nezu, Nezu, & Perri, 1989), the present model represents the mental health professional as the problem solver (Nezu, Petronko, & Nezu, 1982; Nezu & Nezu, 1989a).

In other words, at the outset of treatment planning with any prospective client, the clinician is faced with a problem. Nezu and Nezu (1989a) define this problem as

> a clinical situation in which a therapist is presented with a set of complaints by an individual for which help is sought to reduce or minimize such complaints. This situation is considered to be a problem since the current state of affairs (i.e., presence of complaints) represents a *discrepancy* from the individual's *desired* state (i.e., goals). A variety of impediments (i.e., obstacles or conflicts) exist that prevent or make it difficult for the client to reach his or her goals at the present time without a therapist's aid. Such impediments may include variables relevant to both the client (e.g., behavioral, cognitive, and/or affective excesses or deficits) and/or his or her environment (e.g., lack of physical and/or

social resources; presence of aversive stimuli) . . . treatment, then, represents the clinician's attempt to identify and implement a *solution* to this problem situation. (p. 36)

An effective solution within this framework is represented by clinical interventions that reduce or minimize the initial complaints. The treatment plan might include components aimed at (a) changing the nature of the impediments or obstacles (e.g., increasing social skills), (b) reducing the negative impact that they exert on the client (e.g., reducing anxiety symptoms), or (c) both. The important point is that, because of individual differences, the same clinical intervention may not be effective with different people experiencing the same clinical problem.

In addition to representing clinical intervention globally as a problem-solving process, we further suggest that a variety of important subproblems require active decision making on the part of the therapist working with mentally retarded individuals who have emotional difficulties. These subproblems include differential diagnosis, client problem identification, selection of problems to be targeted for change, treatment implementation, and treatment evaluation. To a great degree, the success or effectiveness of the clinician's decision making during each of these clinical tasks influences the success of subsequent activities. In other words, there is a synergistic relationship among the outcomes of all these clinical processes. For example, if the therapist inaccurately identifies the factors underlying the persistence of a given problem, it is likely that subsequent treatment plans will be ineffective. Therefore, in order for clinical interventions to be successful, each of the subproblems also must be effectively solved.

This synergy is illustrated by the case of Brad, a 22-year-old mildly retarded male referred to an outpatient clinic by his group home staff for problems of aggressive behavior. The overall question that his therapist must answer is, How can I help Brad to behave less aggressively? In problem-solving terminology, impediments or obstacles (factors causally or functionally related to the presenting problem) that make it difficult or impossible for a client like Brad to solve the problem on his own can be quite varied—for example, lack of social skills, unresponsive environment, inconsistent environmental contingencies for aggressive behavior, poor social relationships, poor expressive speech, medical difficulties, presence of severe stressors, inadequate social problem-solving skills, or any combination of these factors. Given this variety of causal elements, the therapist must address the initial subproblem of accurately identifying the specific impediments that affect Brad. The clinician is then ready to develop a treatment plan that might address any or all of these target areas. After a comprehensive assessment, Brad's therapist might determine that an intervention plan should entail social skills training to help him interact more effectively with people during anger-arousing situations. In addition, Brad might learn to use his feelings of anger as a signal that a problem exists and then attempt to resolve the problem without an aggressive response.

The case of another client, Judy, illustrates the need for a treatment plan based on an accurate assessment of causal factors. Judy is a 19-year-old with moderate retardation who, like Brad, engages in aggressive behavior. A comprehensive assessment might reveal that her immediate family's continuous reinforcement of her temper tantrums is the major impediment to goal attainment. Hence, Judy's treatment plan would be quite different from that designed for Brad; her parents might receive training in various behavioral strategies such as contingency management to decrease aggressive behavior and increase adaptive responding.

For a third client, Bob, a 28-year-old mildly retarded male, evaluation of causal factors underlying aggressive behavior might reveal a combination of relevant variables, such as poor social skills, heightened arousal threshold, lowered self-esteem, and inadvertent peer reinforcement for aggression. An appropriate treatment plan for Bob should therefore include intervention strategies targeting each of these important areas.

After developing an overall treatment plan based on the unique features of the case, the therapist then needs to carry out the various clinical intervention strategies and monitor their effects. Continuous scrutiny of the client's progress is necessary to determine whether the implemented treatment plan is, in fact, an effective solution. If progress results in overall goal attainment, then treatment can be terminated, and the clinician's problem is solved. If the goals are not reached, the therapist should recycle through the problem-solving tasks to determine what changes, if any, are required.

Of course, clinical treatment of dually diagnosed individuals is rarely that straightforward. As noted earlier in this chapter, simple cases do not exist. One common complication involves the identification of problems that emerge only after treatment has begun. In Judy's case, for example, the therapist might implement parent training, only to discover that the family is experiencing major difficulties of their own, independent of Judy's aggressive behavior. Such problems might only be revealed as family members are engaged in actual training and their interactions observed. The therapist might then decide to shift the focus of treatment toward family therapy as a means of resolving family problems as well as preparing family members to help implement Judy's contingency management program.

A second type of complication involves changes in a client's goals that arise as a function of progress. Such changes occurred in Brad's case: As his interpersonal skills improved (with a concomitant decrease in aggressive responses to frustrating situations and rise in self-esteem), Brad voiced a strong desire to engage in more social activities with women. Given Brad's newly articulated desire to date, his treatment plan was reformulated to involve training in dating skills, as well as sex education.

Because clinical reality suggests that such complexities are the norm rather than the exception, our model of clinical decision making emphasizes the need for flexibility in treatment planning. Moreover, the therapist should always be cognizant of the reciprocal influence among treatment goals, effects, choices, and decisions (Nezu & Nezu, 1989a).

To summarize, we conceptualize treatment for dually diagnosed individuals within a problem-solving framework, where the discrepancy between a client's initial state and his or her ultimate goal state is the problem for the mental health professional to solve. In addition, given our bias toward a social learning perspective regarding clinical interventions, we identify several specific subproblems that the mental health professional must address in order to resolve this discrepancy. These subproblems include problem identification, target behavior/problem selection, treatment selection and design, treatment implementation, and treatment evaluation.

In our model of clinical decision making, mental health professionals view themselves as active problem solvers in addressing the components of case formulation, treatment planning, and treatment implementation and evaluation. We advocate use of problem-solving principles to optimize the effectiveness of these clinical endeavors. Chapter 3 will focus on the problem-solving approach to the broad area of assessment, whereas chapter 7 will address treatment planning and implementation. The remainder of this chapter will describe the five components of our problem-solving model.

THE PROBLEM-SOLVING PROCESS

The problem-solving process is best viewed as consisting of a series of specific skills rather than a single unitary ability. The components of the process include (a) problem orientation, (b) problem definition and formulation, (c) generation of alternatives, (d) decision making, and (e) solution implementation and verification. Each component makes an important and distinct contribution to effective problem resolution (Nezu, Nezu, & Perri, 1989). Brief descriptions of the five components follow. (See D'Zurilla & Nezu, 1982; Nezu, Nezu, & Perri, 1989, for a more complete description of the problem-solving process as well as research supportive of its effectiveness in training programs.)

Our model is prescriptive and does not represent the way expert problem solvers or clinicians address problems in real life. Nor does the sequential depiction of the five components of the process imply that problem solving always proceeds in an orderly, unidirectional manner. Rather, effective problem solving is likely to involve continuous and reciprocal movement among the five components as an adequate solution is reached.

Problem Orientation

Problem orientation, the first component in the problem-solving process, is a general response set that an individual uses in understanding and reacting to problem situations. Orienting responses include a general sensitivity to problems, as well as a host of relatively stable beliefs, assumptions, appraisals, values, and expectations concerning problems and one's own problem-solving ability. Depending on the nature of these cognitive variables, this orientation may either facilitate or disrupt later problem-solving activities. For example, a clinician who believes that persons with mental retardation cannot experience emotional difficulties would probably tend to avoid active attempts at problem resolution (providing psychologically based interventions) for dually diagnosed individuals.

Several orienting beliefs are particularly relevant to clinical interventions for persons with both mental retardation and mental illness. These include the assumptions that (a) persons with mental retardation do experience bona fide psychiatric disorders and psychological problems, (b) psychosocial intervention is a viable approach for the treatment of such disorders, and (c) least restrictive approaches to treatment are preferable from both clinical and ethical perspectives (Turnbull, 1981).

On a more global level, problem orientation reflects the influence of the therapist's worldview on both assessment and treatment planning. A worldview is a cohesive philosophical framework within which a person attempts to understand how the world works (Pepper, 1942). For the mental health professional, the worldview centers around the manner in which people function. In other words, one's worldview provides a perspective that helps one understand, predict, and explain human behavior and psychopathology. It incorporates several assumptions about cause-effect relationships pertaining to thoughts, emotions, behaviors, the environment, and their interrelations.

For our clinical decision-making model, we advocate adopting a worldview that emphasizes a multiple causality perspective within a bio-psychosocial framework. In this framework, a particular set of symptoms can be expressed via a plurality of potential paths, and a variety of biological (genetic, neurochemical, physical), psychological (affective, cognitive, overt behavioral), and social (social and physical environmental) variables may act or interact as causal factors (Nezu & Nezu, 1989a). This framework is consistent with recent calls for multivariate analytic perspectives for understanding psychopathology or deviant behavior in general (cf. Craighead, 1980; Hersen, 1981; Nezu, Nezu, & Perri, 1989). In addition, the framework is an example of planned critical multiplism (Cook, 1985; Shadish, 1986), a conceptual methodological approach that attempts to minimize the biases inherent in any univariate search for knowledge. *Multiple* in this context can refer to both independent and dependent variables, methods to measure these variables, and general constructs (e.g., multiple methods to assess a variable, multiple variables being assessed, multiple statistical procedures used to analyze data, multiple hypotheses tested simultaneously).

In practical terms, planned multiplism means considering various options that have inherent, competing biases. Attention to the broad array of variables that may be causally related to the client's presenting problems can yield important clinical information while also highlighting possible judgment biases when disconfirmations of the therapist's original hypotheses occur. Within our model, these variables, or *focal problem areas,* embedded within the biopsychosocial conceptualization are seen as impediments to achievement of the clinician's goal (reducing or eliminating the client's presenting problems).

In emphasizing multiple causality, we are not advocating a haphazard and time-consuming search for all possible causal factors. Rather, we underscore the notion of *planned* multiplism and urge the therapist to consult the experimental literature, a rich source of information that can provide guidelines to delimit the search. However, given the scarcity of information specifically regarding psychopathology of persons with mental retardation, the search for causal variables is difficult (and the need to adopt a problem-solving perspective especially great). When assessing a nonretarded person with clinical depression, the mental health professional can turn to a broad array of literature for potential clues to the pathogenesis and treatment of this disorder. On the other hand, for the depressed person who is also mentally retarded, scant information is available. Whether the literature on depression (or any psychological disorder) among nonretarded persons is directly applicable to a population of retarded individuals remains an empirical question. Therefore, therapists providing clinical interventions to dually diagnosed clients face an additional task—that of determining the relevance for their clients of much of the literature on psychopathology and its treatment in the general population. Until more data are available, we suggest using this literature as a source of potentially relevant guidelines. Applying this information to a population of mentally retarded individuals requires the active application of the problem-solving model.

Until recently, many therapists were reluctant to look to the general literature on self-control and self-regulatory treatment strategies regarding its applicability for a population of mentally retarded individuals (Whitman, 1990). This reluctance may be an extension of the myth that people with mental retardation, owing to psychological immaturity, could not experience emotional difficulties: Because mentally retarded persons, by definition, evidence limited cognitive abilities, then self-control treatment options, which rely heavily on cognitive constructs, would not be relevant for this population. Such bias has led to heavy reliance on neuroleptic drugs, aversive contingency management protocols, or placement in more restrictive environments. Despite accumulating evidence of the efficacy of a variety of cognitive-behavioral approaches for a variety of clinical disorders with nonretarded persons, such treatment strategies have only very recently been adopted for dually diagnosed persons (Nezu et al., 1991). In a framework of planned multiplism, inclusion of the broader literature, with all its potential treatment options, is imperative.

Related to the multiple causality perspective is the view that clinical intervention is a set of strategies rather than a set of tactics. A *strategy* is an overall approach that includes statements identifying subgoals and/or focal problem areas—for example, anxiety reduction, anger management, coping skills training, contingency management, and relationship enhancement. *Tactics,* on the other hand, are specific means for implementing such strategies—for attaining the subgoals. For example, tactics for implementing an anxiety reduction strategy would include muscle relaxation training, biofeedback, flooding, exposure, cognitive restructuring, and diaphragmatic breathing.

Practically speaking, if various strategies are considered initially, a wide range of tactics can then be identified. However, if clinical interventions are viewed as merely a set of techniques, it is more likely that a particular tactic will be misapplied. For example, automatically implementing a token economy system in a group home without considering a wide range of factors (e.g., individual differences in reinforcer saliency, staff readiness to implement a complex procedure, availability of back-up reinforcers) can lead to treatment failure.

Problem Definition and Formulation

Whereas problem orientation is a general set or approach to problems, the other four components of the problem-solving process are best viewed as specific skills or tasks. The purposes of problem definition and formulation are (a) to identify the aspects of the situation that make it a problem for the individual and (b) to identify a realistic set of goals or objectives. The importance of this task for effectively guiding subsequent problem-solving activities cannot be overemphasized: Clear definition of the problem can help in the generation of possible solutions, improve decision making, and contribute to the accuracy of solution verification (Nezu & D'Zurilla, 1981a, 1981b).

Within the clinical decision-making model, the therapist must accurately define and formulate each of the subproblems constituting the treatment process: problem identification, target problem selection, treatment design, and treatment evaluation. Whereas the goals may already be implicit in the nature of the particular task (to identify accurately the most important client problems), each of these subproblems must be idiographically defined: The therapist needs to identify the most important problems for *this* particular client, with *this* particular set of presenting complaints, given *this* particular set of circumstances and conditions.

To improve the accuracy of problem definition, the therapist needs to do the following: (a) seek all available facts about the problem; (b) describe these facts in clear and unambiguous terms; (c) distinguish relevant from irrelevant information and objective facts from unverified inferences, assumptions, and interpretations; (d) identify the factors and circumstances that actually make the situation a problem; and (e) set a series of realistic and attainable problem-solving goals (D'Zurilla & Nezu, 1982; Nezu, Nezu, & Perri, 1989).

Unlike the vast majority of nonretarded individuals seeking outpatient treatment for psychological problems, the individual with mental retardation and concomitant emotional difficulties will most likely be referred by someone else. People making referrals might include natural or foster parents, siblings, direct care staff, group home staff, or vocational rehabilitation staff. An initial clinical task is to determine who is the actual client for purposes of goal setting. To some degree, the nature of the presenting problem, as well as the mentally retarded person's age and/or guardianship status, will answer this question. For example, the natural parents of a 9-year-old, moderately retarded girl displaying self-injurious behavior would most likely be identified as the clients. These parents, as clients, would work with the therapist in determining goals. But what about the 29-year-old mildly retarded male who is his own guardian (no one having initiated proceedings to become his guardian) but is behaving aggressively in his semi-independent living arrangement? Who is the client in this case: the group home staff, who are concerned about this behavior, or the young man himself? What would be the goals of treatment? Who would be responsible for articulating and agreeing to them? The answers to these questions would depend on the specifics of the case. However, unlike nonretarded adults who are self-referred, mentally retarded persons with psychological problems bring with them ambiguity about personal goals. Legal and ethical concerns come into play more frequently with this population; there are more complexities and fewer concrete rules. These additional concerns further underscore the need for mental health professionals to view themselves as active problem solvers throughout the treatment process.

Generation of Alternative Solutions

The purpose of generating alternative solutions is to make available as many ideas as possible and to maximize the likelihood that the best one(s) will be among them. An effective solution is defined as one that (a) achieves the specified goal(s), (b) maximizes possible positive consequences, and (c) minimizes potential negative consequences. This aspect of problem solving is based on the brainstorming method of idea production, which uses two general principles: the quantity principle and the deferment-of-judgment principle. In addition, we also advocate the use of the strategies-tactics procedure (cf. D'Zurilla & Nezu, 1982).

According to the quantity principle, the more alternatives that people produce, the more likely they are to arrive at the best possible idea for a solution. The deferment-of-judgment principle states that more high quality ideas can be generated if critical evaluation of any particular alternative is suspended until after an exhaustive list of possible solutions and combinations of solutions has been compiled. During generation of ideas, consideration of the value or effectiveness of each alternative should be avoided completely. The only requirement should be that the idea be relevant to the problem at hand. The strategies–tactics approach consists of initially conceptualizing general means or strategies to solve a problem and then producing various tactics or specific ways in which the strategy might be implemented. This approach encourages production of a greater variety or range of ideas.

Decision Making

The decision-making component of problem solving is designed (a) to evaluate the alternative solutions generated and (b) to select the most effective alternative(s) for implementation. During this phase, each alternative is systematically evaluated with regard to its consequences.

To make the best decision possible, the problem solver should first assess the utility of each alternative and then choose the alternative (or group of alternatives) with the greatest utility. Utility, in our model, is a joint function both of the likelihood of that alternative's actually achieving a particular goal and of its value.

Estimates of the likelihood that a particular alternative will have a particular effect should take into account whether or not the alternative can actually meet the stated goals. In other words, will the solution work? It is equally important to assess the likelihood that the problem solver is in a position to actually implement the alternative in its optimal form. A given solution might theoretically be an excellent idea but have practical limitations. Thus, in addition to evaluating the effectiveness of a given treatment approach for a given client, the therapist must also assess his or her personal ability to optimally implement that particular treatment.

In making judgments about the value of an alternative, the therapist should consider four categories of consequences: short-term or immediate consequences, long-term consequences, personal consequences (effects on oneself), and social consequences (effects on others). Personal consequences might involve the time and effort required to implement the alternative, personal and emotional costs versus gains, consistency with one's ethical and moral standards, and the effect of the alternative on one's physical well-being. In the social category, specific consequences may include effects on one's family, friends, or community.

Because clients differ in their personal values, goals, and commitments for change, it is impossible to develop a standard set of criteria on which to evaluate consequences for each type of problem situation. For this reason it is important to brainstorm all the potential consequences and effects of a given alternative, especially when the situation is particularly novel.

In evaluating the costs and benefits associated with various alternatives, the problem solver can use a rating system to estimate the utility of each one and then compare all the ratings. It is important to assess the total picture rather than the valence of any specific outcome criterion. For example, a solution might be judged extremely favorably on two criteria but might be rejected because the overall expected costs outweighed the overall expected benefits. On the basis of this comparison, the therapist should then choose those alternatives for which the expected overall outcome most closely matches the problem-solving goals. If only a few ideas emerge as potentially satisfactory, it may be necessary to go back and repeat the previous problem-solving tasks.

Solution Implementation and Verification

In the final problem-solving task, solution implementation and verification, the anticipated and actual consequences of solution implementation are compared. Even though a problem may be solved hypothetically, the effectiveness of the solution cannot be assessed until the solution is actually carried out. The last step in the problem-solving process involves (a) implementation of the solution, (b) observation of the consequences that occur after the solution is carried out, and (c) evaluation of the effectiveness of the solution (D'Zurilla & Nezu, 1982).

Implementation involves the actual application of the chosen solution. However, depending on the nature of the problem, implementation may not necessarily involve an overt behavioral response; it may mean making a decision or identifying a choice. In clinical decision making, for example, the problem-solving process can be used to identify and select important client target behaviors. Implementation of the solution in this case does not entail any overt therapist response beyond the verification process.

Observing the effects of the implemented solution entails measuring outcome at varying levels, not simply attending to the overall consequences.

To obtain accurate information concerning the outcome, it is sometimes necessary to use an objective recording procedure. In a clinical situation, an example would be periodic measurement of a client's behavior or change in symptoms.

During evaluation, the therapist compares the observed outcome with the desired outcome as specified during problem definition and formulation (i.e., the problem-solving goal). If the match is satisfactory—that is, the discrepancy between the expected outcome and the actual outcome is small—then the problem can be considered resolved. If the match is not satisfactory, the therapist needs to discover the source of the discrepancy. The difficulty may lie in suboptimal implementation of the solution, misapplication of certain aspects of the problem-solving process itself, or both. In either case, it is wise to backtrack and repeat one or more of the problem-solving operations. The therapist may have failed to define the problem adequately or to identify mediating factors that interfered with treatment. It is also possible that not enough ideas were generated initially or that the consequences of the solution were not evaluated accurately. Any discrepancy between the expected outcome and the actual outcome is a signal to cycle through all or part of the problem-solving process again.

If the discrepancy is due to deficient performance, the therapist can either repeat the whole problem-solving process or attempt to improve on the solution implementation. Assessment of solution performance should focus on the performance of both therapist and client. For example, if social skills training does not appear effective in reducing a client's aggressive behavior, the clinician should first assess whether the client (and/or caretaker in certain cases) is implementing this solution correctly; the therapist should also determine whether he or she actually gave the client (and/or caretaker) adequate training in these skills.

Some readers may object that, although the model appears helpful, they lack the time to apply it in actual clinical situations. We understand this concern but wish to reassure the skeptics by stressing two points. First, not every clinical problem that arises is significant or difficult enough to require a complete problem-solving analysis. We do strongly advocate the general use of this approach in the development of treatment plans for dually diagnosed persons. With certain complex cases or difficult decisions, use of the entire model may be imperative. For others, however, a subset of the problem-solving model may suffice. Second, we have found that the more one uses this model, the more it is applied automatically. As with any other skill in a clinician's repertoire, applying the decision-making model will require less time and effort with greater use.

SUMMARY

Our problem-solving model, briefly described, encompasses five components: problem orientation, problem definition and formulation, generation of alternatives, decision making, and solution implementation and verification. Problem orientation is one's overall set or approach to problems. For the therapist, an important aspect of orientation is his or her worldview concerning normal and abnormal behavior, in particular with regard to persons with mental retardation. We advocate adopting a worldview that emphasizes multiple causation, recognizing that the pathogenesis of similar problems is potentially varied and that the path for a particular client needs to be idiographically assessed. Further, we recommend approaching clinical interventions as strategies, rather than as sets of techniques.

The four remaining components of the problem-solving process provide specific goal-directed guidelines for individuals in general (and therapists in particular) to use in solving problems of all types, including those encountered within the clinical arena. The problem-solving process is dynamic and synergistic, with each component making an important and unique contribution. Effective application of these problem-solving components across a multitude of clinical tasks reflects the essence of our clinical decision-making model.

Section II

Chapter 3

A Problem-Solving Approach to Clinical Interventions With Dually Diagnosed Persons: Focus on Assessment

INTRODUCTION

Clinical interventions viewed within a problem-solving framework encompass four major stages: (a) screening, (b) problem analysis and selection of focal target problems, (c) design of the overall intervention plan, and (d) evaluation of the treatment effects (Nezu & Nezu, 1989a). Within each stage, the clinician, as problem solver, faces a multitude of decisions that require active and effective attempts at resolution. These clinical tasks range from the decision about whether a particular therapist should treat a given patient to the judgment about the need for a long-term maintenance program to prevent relapse or recurrence of a problem behavior. The effectiveness and validity of the decisions reached in one stage have direct implications for the probable success of those reached during other stages of treatment.

To clarify the application of our model, we divide clinical interventions into two structural categories: assessment and treatment. This dichotomy is necessarily artificial in that both assessment and evaluation occur continuously throughout treatment (e.g., collection of data to evaluate client progress). Moreover, the very assessment process often has a beneficial therapeutic effect; thus, assessment can serve as treatment (e.g., improved self-control owing to self-monitoring of aggressive behavior and its impact on family members). However, in the interest of clarity, this chapter will focus on assessment of dually diagnosed clients. Assessment encompasses the first two stages of the therapeutic enterprise: (a) screening and (b) problem analysis and target problem selection.

SCREENING

Screening, the initial phase of therapy, should yield a broad overview of the client's problems. The therapist's main purpose is to pose and answer the general question: Given this client's characteristics and the specific presenting problems, will I be able to help the client achieve his or her goals? A comprehensive response at this point is obviously premature. However, the therapist needs to provide a preliminary answer instead of automatically assuming that he or she can help every client who comes to treatment (an error of overconfidence; see chapter 2).

In general, answering this question can be considered an initial screening procedure. Gathering preliminary information, the therapist can begin to answer this question and make informed and deliberate decisions about the fruitfulness of continuing into the next therapy stage. Blindly prescribing a treatment protocol at this point might produce harmful iatrogenic effects.

A variety of obstacles or impediments can interfere with the initial decisions. These have been labeled *initiation difficulties,* as their presence may impede further assessment and the initiation of formal treatment (Nezu & Nezu, 1989b). In general, three categories of initiation difficulties can be identified; those related to (a) the client, (b) significant others, and (c) the therapist. Individually or collectively, such difficulties can prevent successful continuation into the next clinical intervention phase.

Initiation Difficulties Related to the Client

An important initiation difficulty related to the client concerns the individual's level of motivation, cooperation, and commitment to therapy. A client who comes to treatment as a result of family coercion, court mandate, or threatened loss of vocational workshop placement may be generally uncooperative. Even a client who initially shows a high motivation may not be fully committed to spending the necessary time and effort in treatment to achieve meaningful behavior change.

The presence of severe medical or physical problems may also influence the clinician's decision making during this initial phase. It may be important to refer the client to another professional, such as a physician, for diagnostic evaluation before initiating any psychosocial treatment. For example, a client's aggressive behavior may be related to lack of effective medication for seizures; reevaluation of the client's medication regimen by a psychiatrist may be a necessary first step. The considerable complexities of psychopharmacological treatment of dually diagnosed patients are beyond the scope of this book. Readers may wish to consult Aman (1983), Breuning and Poling (1982), and Sovner (1988) for descriptions of behavioral psychopharmacology.

Initiation Difficulties Related to Significant Others

As indicated previously, most clients with mental retardation and psychological dysfunctions do not come to mental health professionals through self-referral. Clinicians working with this population often have trouble determining whose goals should be the focus of treatment. Often, the client may articulate objectives that are quite discrepant from those stated by the parents or direct care staff. An example is Tony, a 17-year-old moderately retarded male, referred by his parents for the problem of public masturbation. His parents felt that such behavior was "disgusting" and wanted the therapist to help him stop masturbating entirely—"He's just a boy, he doesn't know what he is doing. . . . He can't know anything about sex. . . . Can't you get him to stop?" Tony, on the other hand, simply wanted "to be left alone." The clinician needs to identify such disparate goal statements as an initiation impediment and attempt to resolve the problem before beginning treatment. Tony's initiation problem was resolved when all concerned agreed on the goal of having Tony masturbate only in his own room with the door closed.

Beyond differences in goals stated by the client and significant others, another set of initiation difficulties concerns problems that each caregiver might be experiencing independently. These might include emotional problems, marital difficulties, family problems, burnout, lack of parenting skills, and inadequate knowledge about mental retardation and developmental disabilities. (Chapter 5 addresses assessment issues regarding the caregiving system.) Any of these difficulties may impede initiation of treatment.

Initiation Difficulties Related to the Therapist

A final set of potential impediments to treatment initiation relates specifically to the therapist. Self-assessment of one's competence or experience with a particular clinical problem is a key to accurate decision making. For example, the therapist with little or no background in substance abuse who is referred a mentally retarded client with severe alcohol problems should conduct such a self-evaluation. We are not advocating that all clinicians practice only within a restrictive specialty. However, we believe that the mental health professional is ethically bound to assess whether he or she can, in fact, be as helpful to a particular client as another therapist with specialized training. Related issues can emerge when a client's presenting problems involve significant moral or religious dilemmas; such a client may be better served by a member of the clergy.

Another initiation difficulty concerns the therapist's emotional reaction to the client. Clinicians being only human, some clients and/or their presenting problems may elicit distracting affective responses in a given therapist. Examples may involve racial, cultural, or religious differences between therapist and client. Such reactions can be either prejudicial or overly solicitous in nature; in either case, they can impede goal attainment. Other emotional reactions in the therapist might involve anger (e.g., the client has been accused of sexual abuse), arousal (e.g., the client is sexually provocative), fear (e.g., the client has been physically harmful to others), or sympathy (e.g., the client is a victim of strong negative peer reactions). Again, we are not suggesting that a therapist's strong emotional reaction automatically precludes successful treatment; however, it can be an impediment.

The foregoing list of initiation difficulties is far from exhaustive, especially in light of the differences among clients, therapists, and care-takers and the various possible combinations among such individuals. Because it is hard to know exactly what to look for at the initial meeting with a client, it is important for the therapist to be alert and observant rather than to jump into a course of treatment prematurely or succumb to diagnostic overshadowing. In the terminology of our model, this means having an orientation of sensitivity to the existence of problems (Nezu, Nezu, & Perri, 1989). If initial impediments exist, the therapist's goal-related self-question then becomes, Given this particular impediment, will I be able to help this client attain his or her goals? Applying the various problem-solving strategies can help answer this question.

Screening: Applying the Problem-Solving Model

As for each clinical task that the mental health professional faces, we advocate using the problem-solving model described in chapter 2 to address initiation difficulties. This means that initiation concerns become the focus of problem-solving efforts as the therapist attempts to answer the general question, How can I minimize the effects of these initiation impediments?

Upon recognizing an obstacle to successful treatment during the screening stage, the therapist begins to define the specific initiation difficulties. The problem-solving activities here include (a) gathering relevant information, (b) separating facts from assumptions, (c) identifying the specific problem, (d) using clear language, and (e) stating a goal to direct further problem-solving efforts.

Because cases are often complex, several initiation problems may exist. If that is the situation, the therapist needs to articulate multiple goal statements and try to determine if the problems are interrelated. Goal statements should reflect the analysis of the problems. For example, a dually diagnosed client's uncooperativeness may be related to dysfunction in his or her family system. In that case, the therapist's goal should address both the client's participation difficulties and the family problems.

For each stated goal, we recommend that the therapist apply the remaining components of the problem-solving model: generation of alternatives, decision making, and solution implementation and verification. Brainstorming can be used to generate both a variety of strategies to address the initiation difficulties and criteria by which either to evaluate the utility of these possible solutions or to answer other screening questions such as, Should I refer this client to another professional? or How can I increase this client's motivation to participate actively in therapy?

After a list of alternative solutions has been compiled, the predicted outcome of each one should be evaluated according to both its likelihood and its inherent value. Then, on the basis of a systematic cost/benefit analysis, the therapist can choose the optimal plan. After the chosen solution is implemented, the therapist should monitor the actual consequences to determine how closely they match the predicted consequences. If a significant discrepancy occurs, recycling through the various problem-solving tasks may be required. If the discrepancy is small, the problems of screening can be considered resolved and the therapist can move on to the next therapy stage, problem analysis and selection of focal problem targets.

The following clinical example illustrates the systematic application of the problem-solving model to the decisions involved in the screening phase of therapy.

Frank, a 49-year-old male with mild retardation, was referred to an outpatient clinic by staff members at his vocational workshop. They noticed that during the past several weeks Frank had become increasingly withdrawn and socially isolated. Initial hypotheses concerning this newly developed depression involved the recent move of a favorite caseworker, Joanne, to another state. Frank had always appeared to get along quite well with Joanne and would look forward to her visits. His recent drastic change in mood severely affected his ability to function well at the workshop.

During the initial sessions with Frank, the therapist found him inattentive and uncooperative. Frank missed several appointments, and, on one occasion, the therapist found Frank lingering in the hall outside the therapist's office 20 minutes after the session was supposed to begin. Only with some encouragement did Frank reluctantly decide to continue.

The therapist identified Frank's overall lack of motivation and commitment to treatment as an important initiation problem to solve. In an attempt to better understand this impediment, he stated his concern to Frank and asked for feedback. Essentially, Frank's reply was, "You're not my friend and can't help me . . . not like Joanne could!" At that point, the therapist needed to pose the goal-oriented question, How can I get Frank to become more motivated and actively involved in treatment?

Through brainstorming, Frank's therapist generated the following alternative strategies: increase the reinforcing properties of the treatment process, ignore the problem, discontinue treatment, attempt to obtain minor clinical changes (i.e., improve Frank's mood) as a means of demonstrating the feasibility of treatment, improve the therapist-client relationship, and use paradoxical intention strategies (i.e., convey the attitude that Frank is supposed to remain uncooperative).

The therapist then generated a list of tactics related to the first strategy (to increase the reinforcing nature of the sessions): offer refreshments, play Frank's favorite music in the background, focus initially on discussions of superficial topics chosen by Frank (e.g., television shows, movies, sports), discuss potential positive consequences of behavioral change, play cards, shorten the sessions, watch movies together, conduct sessions outdoors if weather permits, and pay Frank for coming to treatment. Tactics for the remaining strategies were generated as well.

The therapist evaluated the utility of each of the various tactics generated for each strategy according to the criteria in the problem-solving model: (a) likelihood of goal attainment, (b) likelihood of optimal implementation, (c) personal consequences, (d) social consequences, (e) short-term effects, and (f) long-term effects. Each tactic received a rating on each criterion according to a simple rating system ($+3$ = very positive; -3 = very negative). The tactics receiving the highest overall ratings were chosen as a means of increasing Frank's initial motivation. Specifically, in attempting to solve Frank's initiation problem, the therapist decided to use four tactics: conduct sessions outdoors, talk about television shows for the first 10 minutes of each session, offer Frank a soft drink at the beginning of each session, and focus on the positive consequences associated with changes in Frank's depressive feelings.

After implementing these alternatives, Frank's therapist monitored their effects, systematically noting increases in Frank's punctuality, increases in his general attendance, increases in his overall attentiveness (as defined by increased eye contact and appropriate body posture), increases in the length of his answers to questions, increased frequency with which he supplied substantive information in answering questions, and decreased frequency of "I don't know" responses. Because such changes did in fact occur, the therapist was ready to proceed to the next therapy stage: treatment addressing Frank's depressed mood. However, if no changes had occurred, the therapist would have needed to recycle through the problem-solving process to identify a more effective plan. If repeated attempts had ended in failure, referral to another therapist would have been appropriate.

Obviously, not all problems of client motivation are resolved so positively. Moreover, initiation difficulties can rest not only with the client, but also with the client's family and caregiving system. Because lack of motivation and commitment are frequently encountered problems, we offer a list (Table 3.1, adapted from Kanfer and Schefft, 1988) of possible strategies for increasing a client's commitment to treatment. We also recommend Kanfer and Schefft's excellent discussion of this aspect of therapy.

In light of the changing and dynamic nature of the therapeutic enterprise, the initiation difficulties described earlier are not always identifiable during the first few sessions. Throughout treatment, certain events may occur or pieces of information emerge that change the nature of the therapist's overall plan. Thus, some of the difficulties that were described as initiation problems can and do occur in the various therapy phases. We suggest applying a procedure similar to that just described under these circumstances as well.

PROBLEM ANALYSIS AND SELECTION OF FOCAL TARGET PROBLEMS

In proceeding to the next stage of therapy, that of problem analysis and selection of focal target problems, we assume either that no initiation problems were identified or that such problems were solved. During this stage, the therapist seeks to obtain a detailed understanding of the client's problems as well as of factors or variables that are etiologically or functionally related to those problems. Specific, albeit tentative, goals for treatment must also be identified. The therapist's problem at this point can be summed up in the following goal-related questions: What are this client's specific difficulties? What factors or circumstances have resulted in these problems? and, What are the specific treatment goals?

During initial screening, the therapist need only obtain a global or general picture of the client's difficulties to make a determination concerning the initiation of further assessment and/or formal treatment. During problem analysis, a more concrete and in-depth scrutiny takes place. The initial global assessment provides clues for the therapist to follow later in specifying treatment goals and in idiographically designing an effective treatment. In the following section, we will describe the application and importance of each component of the problem-solving process in conducting these clinical tasks.

Problem Orientation

To better understand a client's problems, the therapist should begin to gather information about the problems in as comprehensive a manner

---

Table 3.1   Alternative Strategies to Enhance Client Motivation

1. Disrupt automatic thoughts.

2. Encourage use of self-regulation skills.

3. Make small demands.

4. Do something associated with a small task.

5. Do a task without fear of failure.

6. Associate outcome with previous reinforcers.

7. Reattribute causes.

8. Use role-plays.

9. Work toward self-generated goals.

10. Encourage positive self-statements.

11. Record progress.

12. Use environmental cues.

13. Require a prior commitment.

14. Promote a facilitative environment.

15. Make contracts.

16. Use the therapeutic alliance.

17. Encourage the client to dream new dreams.

Note. From *Guiding the Process of Therapeutic Change* by F. H. Kanfer and
B. K. Schefft (pp. 138–139), 1988, Champaign, IL: Research Press.
Copyright 1988 by the authors. Adapted by permission.

as possible. However, the methods of assessment as well as the content areas to be assessed depend to a large degree on the clinician's worldview. Thus, the therapist's own problem orientation can significantly affect the manner in which the client's problems are defined and analyzed. As discussed in chapter 2, we strongly advocate that the mental health professional working with dually diagnosed clients adopt a worldview that emphasizes the following: (a) a multiple causality framework, (b) a tripartite approach to assessment and treatment, (c) a general systems conceptualization, (d) a focus on developmental issues, and (e) a focus on key behaviors.

Multiple Causality

As argued earlier, a worldview that acknowledges the plurality of factors causally or functionally related to the presenting problems is an important aspect of the therapist's orientation. Multiple variables can cause and/or serve to maintain maladaptive behavior; hence a mono-symptomatic client description or a unitary target behavior is a misrepresentation of clinical reality (Nezu & Nezu, 1989a).

The actual scope or range of such variables should be expansive and based on evidence presented in the individual case. However, it should also be somewhat limited by empirical findings relevant to the client's problem(s). To distinguish this approach from one of addressing only target behaviors, we previously adopted the term *focal problems* or *focal problem areas.* This term reflects the variables or factors that represent the specific impediments to a particular client's goal attainment (Nezu & Nezu, 1989b).

Tripartite Approach

In keeping with a multiple causality viewpoint, we advocate that the search for meaningful focal problems be expanded to include areas beyond the individual. That is, in addition to focusing on the client, assessment and treatment should encompass the caregiving system and the environment as well. The caregiving system includes the members of a client's life space who have direct responsibility for providing support, care, and supervision to the individual on a daily and continuous basis. These people might include natural parents, foster parents, siblings, relatives, and direct care staff.

The broad category of environment encompasses the client's social and physical environments. Social variables include friends, coworkers, roommates, fellow residents, and other individuals who touch a client's life (e.g., bus driver, letter carrier, teacher, vocational supervisor, caseworker). Physical variables include immediate living quarters (e.g., client's own room, entire house, group residence, work area) and surrounding neighborhood (e.g., urban or suburban neighborhood).

Any or all variables in the three general categories—client, caregiving system, environment—might serve as causal or maintaining factors regarding the presenting problems. Given the importance of these variables, the bulk of this book focuses on assessment and treatment issues related to each of these three categories.

General Systems Conceptualization

A key to an effective problem analysis is the manner in which such variables, across the three categories of the tripartite model, do or do not interact with each other to produce the client's presenting problems.

We adopt a general systems framework that emphasizes the potential interplay among a variety of psychological, environmental, and biological events in a person's life. These variables do not exist in isolation; rather, they have reciprocal influence. Consider the example of a person with mental retardation who is socially anxious and withdrawn. The retardation itself might be genetically caused (e.g., Down syndrome), but the social phobia can result from a complex interplay among a variety of factors: psychological (e.g., cognitive limitations influencing accurate interpretation of the social world), environmental (e.g., strong negative peer reactions to a "retarded person"), and biological (e.g., heightened sensitivity to negative arousal sensations). Any one of these factors alone might not result in the emergence of the anxiety disorder. But in combination they might indeed engender such a phobia. Moreover, a family's good intentions can result in overprotection, further reinforcing the client's psychological problem. Within the systems conceptualization, the client is not socially anxious because he or she has retardation but rather because of an interaction among psychological, environmental, and biological variables. Thus, it is important, in addition to assessing variables in each of the three categories, to evaluate their intricate interplay within a system. It is precisely the differences in these system interactions from one client to another that necessitate an idiographic approach to assessment.

Such an approach also has implications for program design. Rather than relying on the hope that improvement in certain problem areas will automatically result in improvement in other areas, we advocate identifying several problems for which several treatment strategies can be implemented. We suggest attacking the overall set of problems from a number of different vantage points. This approach increases the likelihood of maintenance and generalization and is consistent with research that has shown dysynchrony among various response modes within a system (i.e., changes in affect may not be correlated highly with changes in behavior; cf. Lang, 1968). Treatment, like assessment, should be pluralistic and should take account of all three areas of the tripartite model. For instance, treatment for the socially anxious client described earlier might simultaneously involve client-specific strategies geared to address each of the contributing factors (e.g., social skills training and stress management) and an educational component for the parents as a means of decreasing their inadvertent reinforcement of the phobia.

Focus on Developmental Issues

Developmental antecedents of problems must also be assessed. Knowledge of significant historical events, or distal causes, can contribute to an understanding of the evolution of current problems. Identification of specific developmental delays also sheds light on a client's abilities and limitations. This information is particularly important in the case of a client with mental retardation.

In addition, treatment strategies, although focused on future goals, may at times need to be adapted in recognition of a client's previous treatment successes or failures. For example, in working with younger mentally retarded children and their families, we have often seen parents react negatively to suggestions that they use positive reinforcement principles because of previous failure with token programs. Closer scrutiny usually indicates that the contingency management protocol was poorly conceived or implemented. However, the therapist needs to take history into account in order to develop an effective treatment plan.

Focus on Key Behaviors

Kanfer (1985), in advocating a systems approach to therapy, emphasizes that treatment should be geared toward "intervening on those component processes or behaviors that hold a key position and can affect other events in a network-like system. . . . Preference is given to those elements which alter the system balance most quickly and widely" (pp. 11–12). In other words, assessment should aim to identify those areas that will have a clinically significant impact on the probability of goal attainment. The most relevant arena for change consists of the variables that can help the client move toward his or her goal state. This approach contrasts somewhat with the isolation of hypothesized causative factors. For example, social skills training procedures might be chosen to remedy skill deficits identified as causally related to a client's aggressive behavior. Conceptually, this procedure is based on the assumption that social skill deficits in some way "caused" the aggression, and treatment is designed to alleviate these deficits. In our model, however, social skills training would be complemented by additional treatment geared toward increasing the client's adaptability to new and stressful life situations. Coping skills training or social problem-solving therapy may be appropriate alternatives to incorporate later in the decision-making process (Nezu et al., 1991). The emphasis is on enhancing the client's future functioning, in addition to helping him or her overcome some of the present obstacles to goal attainment (Kanfer, 1985).

In summary, we strongly suggest expanding the arena of relevant problems beyond simple unitary target behaviors. Instead, we urge the therapist to identify a wide range of focal problem areas that may be causally or functionally related to the presenting complaints. These problem areas are situated within a systems model that accommodates a wide variety of possible variables and their interrelationships. Such variables can be grouped into three general categories related to the client, the caregiving system, and the environment.

Within this system, boundaries are defined by the empirical findings reported in the literature that are related to a particular disorder or problem. However, given the paucity of research specific to the assessment and treatment of mental health problems of persons with mental retardation, the therapist working with such clients should also consult the literature on specific psychological disorders of nonretarded persons. Further, a problem-solving approach to clinical intervention implies that treatment should use strategies that improve the client's chances of actually achieving his or her goals, even if a particular strategy does not focus on removing certain factors causing the presenting problems. Finally, we suggest that the therapist complete the remaining four problem-solving tasks within the context of this particular problem orientation.

Problem Definition and Formulation

In problem definition and formulation, the therapist gathers all relevant information about the problem(s); separates facts from assumptions; identifies the factors that actually are linked, causally or functionally, to the client's problems; and identifies realistic problem-solving goals. To minimize biases inherent in this process, the therapist should use language that is unambiguous and concrete.

At this point, the mental health professional confronts two specific clinical questions: Which areas of the client's life space should be assessed? and, Which assessment procedures are optimal for this assessment? Although these questions are interrelated, the therapist should take care to avoid letting the answer to the first dictate the answer to the second. At times, it may be tempting to choose assessment procedures that are similar in modality to the problem area being measured. For example, if the presenting complaints involve depressive symptoms, the therapist must guard against using measures (self-reported or clinician-rated) that are geared to assess only the severity of depressive affect. Additional assessment procedures (role-plays, behavioral observation, frequency count of missed work days, perceptions of family members) might also be important for accurate evaluation of treatment concerning related problems and overall goal attainment. The selection of assessment procedures is especially crucial given the lack of proven assessment tools for evaluating the emotional problems of individuals with mental retardation.

In searching for the optimal assessment tools, the therapist may need to apply the overall problem-solving model. The search is somewhat restricted by the types of assessment procedures currently available. And at times, the therapist will need to be creative and use the problem-solving method to develop assessment procedures unique to a given case.

With regard to the first clinical question—which specific problem areas should be addressed—we recommend that postscreening assessment involve a broad-based investigation of possible focal problem areas in each category of the tripartite model (client, caregiving system, and environment). Chapters 4, 5, and 6, respectively, discuss the many variables that should be addressed in each of these three areas. Figure 3.1 depicts a three-dimensional, tripartite framework that can guide the

Figure 3.1 Three-Dimensional, Tripartite Model for Assessment, Treatment, and Therapy Evaluation

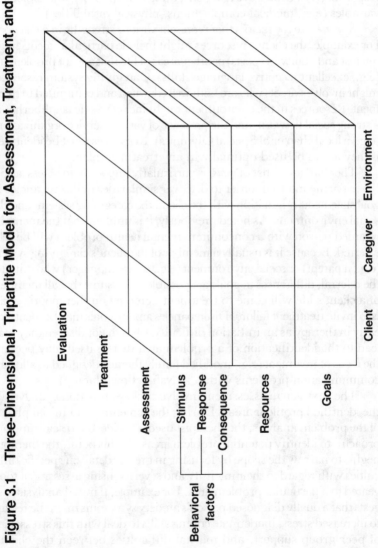

therapist in conducting this assessment. The problem-solving model also provides guidelines for the selection of treatment strategies and therapy evaluation targets.

According to the tripartite model, assessment should focus on variables related to behavioral factors, resources, and goals in each of the three categories. *Behavioral factors* include a variety of individual response modalities such as overt behavior (e.g., aggressive behavior, communication difficulties, self-injurious behavior); cognitive factors (e.g., cognitive distortions, misattributions, poor information processing); affective responses (e.g., depressive reactions, anxiety responses); and biological variables (e.g., medical complications, physical disabilities).

Resources are the factors that represent various strengths in a category. For example, the client's resources might include particular talents (e.g., interest and ability in sports) or other areas of life that are not problematic (e.g., excellent receptive language skills). Caregiving system resources might involve parents who are both well educated and committed to treatment. Resources in the environment might include a safe neighborhood, a strong social network, and the presence of various service organizations (e.g., a local chapter of Special Olympics). Resources must be identified if they are to be used optimally in any treatment plan.

The third area, that of *goals,* is particularly important to assess across the tripartite model in order to discover similarities or discrepancies in goal statements originating with the client, the caregiving system, and the social environment. As noted previously, it is unlikely that the mentally retarded person with a concomitant mental health problem will be self-referred. Because it is usually a member of the client's caregiving system (e.g., a parent) or social environment (e.g., a case manager) who initiates the referral, differences in goals are possible. To assume that all members of a client's life will come to treatment agreeing on therapeutic goals is to invite treatment failure. Discrepancies among goals may be identified early in therapy as an initiation difficulty. Or a major discrepancy may lead to the identification of a problem area that in itself may become the focus of treatment (e.g., modified family therapy designed to alleviate communication problems within a dysfunctional family).

The next step in assessment involves a closer functional analysis of the identified problem areas. During the screening and initial phases of the problem analysis, the therapist used a "wide-band scanning approach" to identify potential problem areas. At this point, the therapist begins to narrow the scope by focusing in greater detail on specific difficulties with regard to their intensity and severity, using assessment tools geared to a particular problem area. For example, if initial analysis suggests that a dually diagnosed person's anxiety symptoms might be related to increased stress, inadequate coping skills to deal with this stress, lack of peer group support, and marital difficulties between the client's parents, the therapist may need to assess each of these areas using specific tests or evaluation procedures.

In keeping with a systems approach to problem solving, the next level of assessment concerns the function of each of the variables with regard to the identified problem area. As Figure 3.1 depicts, for each of the three areas—namely, client, caregiving system, and environment— each variable in the behavioral factors category (i.e., overt behavior, cognitive factors, affective reactions, biological/physical variables) can be identified as a stimulus (S), response (R), or consequence (C). Although one can argue that a consequence can actually be a stimulus for another response (which can act as a stimulus for a third response, etc.), it is generally useful to identify the presenting problem as the response. Assessment can then be geared toward analyzing which variables, within this three-dimensional model, actually serve as antecedents and consequences of the response.

In conducting such an analysis, the therapist can recall the acronym S-O-R-K-C to indicate the relationships among these variables, where S = stimulus (individual or environmental antecedent), O = organismic variable that might mediate the stimulus (e.g., biological, emotional, or cognitive state of the individual), R = response, K = ratio of consequence frequency to response, and C = consequence. This acronym was first proposed by Kanfer and Phillips (1970) to summarize the major variables that influence the probability of the occurrence of a response. In problem-solving terminology, this sequence, or behavior chain, helps to identify the variables that are major impediments to goal attainment, as well as their interrelationships. Depicting relationships among variables in this three-dimensional manner generates valuable information that helps the therapist designate focal problem areas. Theoretically, interventions can be developed to address each variable within the chain. In other words, treatment can focus on changing aspects of the stimulus, the response, the consequence, the organism, and/or the operant relationship between the response and the consequence. Again, we advocate including several therapeutic strategies that address various aspects of this chain in the overall treatment protocol.

The case of a hypothetical client, Eric, illustrates the behavior chain and a microanalysis of his aggressive behavior. Eric responds aggressively (response) when faced with stressful or frustrating situations such as provocation from peers or parental denial of a request (stimulus), and he becomes angry and unable to cope adequately with the situation (organismic state). The aggressive reaction usually involves feelings of anger, poor impulse control, cursing, throwing of objects, and various tantrum behaviors (topography of response). When Eric begins to feel angry, it becomes difficult for him to respond appropriately because he lacks effective coping skills. Often, his aggressive behavior engenders increased social attention and parental acquiescence to his demands (consequence). Given that this pattern has recurred frequently during the past 3 months (ratio of consequence to response), it is probable that Eric, when confronted in the future with a frustrating situation, will react with overt aggression.

In considering treatment alternatives, Eric's therapist can identify intervention strategies that address each of the variables in this behavioral chain. For example, attempts can be made to decrease Eric's unreasonable demands on his parents (focus on stimulus); teach Eric stress management skills to reduce the intensity of his anger (focus on organism); provide training in self-control or problem-solving skills to develop Eric's ability to identify alternative ways of reacting when he feels angry (focus on response); and/or teach Eric's parents certain behavior management skills, such as extinction and contingency management, to minimize the reinforcing quality of his aggressive behavior (focus on consequence and on ratio of consequence to response).

In addition to the focal problem areas and intervening variables highlighted in chapters 4, 5, and 6 of this assessment section, we offer three general guidelines to help the clinician identify potential variables in each of the three areas of the tripartite model.

First, the clinician can look to the literature for theories, models, and research findings concerning a particular disorder in both populations with mental retardation and general populations. This nomothetical information then can serve as a data base from which to assess the idiographic applicability of a model, theory, or analysis to the problems of the dually diagnosed individual. In using the literature, it is important to avoid focusing on one's preferred theory or set of data. As with the influence of judgmental errors on clinical decision making (see chapter 2), biased search strategies can distort the reading process. To minimize judgmental errors during the problem analysis phase, it is important to assess potential variables across all three areas of the tripartite model. By doing so, the therapist can obtain both confirming and disconfirming evidence concerning the variables that may be causally related to the identified problems.

Kanfer and his colleagues (Kanfer & Grimm, 1977; Kanfer & Schefft, 1988) provide another useful set of assessment guidelines. They suggest that many psychological problems fall into one or more of the following five categories: behavioral deficits (e.g., lack of knowledge in a particular area, self-control deficit, inadequate coping skills); behavioral excesses (e.g., excessive anxiety, excessive aggressive responses); inappropriate environmental stimulus control (e.g., milieu restrictions on personal goals, failure to meet environmental demands); inappropriate self-generated stimulus control (e.g., mislabeling of internal cues, inappropriate self-labeling); and inappropriate reinforcement contingencies (e.g., lack of support for appropriate behaviors, social support for undesirable behaviors, noncontingent reinforcement). Attending to each of these areas with respect to various psychological difficulties can generate information of considerable value to the clinician.

A second approach to categorizing referral problems uses psychiatric diagnoses as delineated in the most recent *Diagnostic and Statistical Manual of Mental Disorders* (DSM-III-R; American Psychiatric Association, 1987). Although it is beyond the scope of this book to debate the merits or limitations of such taxonomies (see Haynes & O'Brien, 1988; Hersen, 1988, and chapter 4 of this book), we would like to address two important points.

On the one hand, we believe that diagnostic classifications can provide a useful context for understanding response constellations, behavior clusters, and their covariations (Kazdin, 1982). Covariations are the correlations among various responses that tend to be reliable over time. Understanding the types of covariations that occur within a particular diagnostic category can help the clinician identify variables that might be causally or functionally related to the client's difficulties within our three-dimensional, tripartite assessment framework (Figure 3.1). Diagnostic categories also serve as umbrellas under which various research findings can be grouped. Research data, thus situated, are more easily applied to a particular client's case. This time- and labor-saving step also saves having to "reinvent the wheel" with each new client.

On the other hand, diagnostic categories can function as labels that may lead to substantial judgmental errors and biased search strategies that compromise problem analysis, selection of focal problem targets, and treatment design. We therefore advocate the use of taxonomic systems such as DSM-III-R, but only as an initial step toward identifying focal problem areas idiographically relevant to a given client.

Thus far, we have proposed that, during problem analysis and focal problem selection, the therapist apply the problem definition and formulation process in the following manner: (a) gather data in each category of the tripartite model (i.e., client, caregiving system, environment) with regard to the host of behavioral factors, resources, and goals; (b) use the problem-solving model to identify appropriate assessment procedures (e.g., tests, observational techniques) that will aid in this search; (c) gather data within the three-dimensional framework to obtain both confirming and disconfirming evidence regarding hypotheses about the presenting problems; and (d) utilize the S-O-R-K-C formula to examine how these variables functionally or causally relate to one another.

Through the process just described, hypotheses are formulated concerning the etiology and maintenance of the client's problems. As a final step in this stage of therapy, we recommend developing a Clinical Pathogenesis Map (CPM), a graphic depiction of those hypotheses (Nezu & Nezu, 1989b). The CPM is a useful means of education when shared with the client (if appropriate) and/or with members of the caregiving system. In addition, the CPM provides an important basis for treatment design. Finally, the CPM is a concrete statement of the clinician's hypotheses against which alternative ones can continually be tested. For example, a CPM can be compared to the three-dimensional assessment grid (Figure 3.1) to determine whether vital information may have been overlooked.

Important information not obtained during initial assessment should be incorporated into the CPM and not ignored. The original CPM, as a working idiographic model of a client's difficulties, can help the therapist answer the question, How does this new development fit into my existing formulation? At times, the CPM may need to be substantially revised, or a new one constructed, if it is to represent the client's problems accurately. As emphasized throughout the discussion of problem solving, the mental health professional must be quite flexible and willing to change the original plan in order to respond to the fluid exigencies of therapy.

Figure 3.2 is a sample CPM constructed around the problem of aggression. In addition to focusing on the client's current dysfunctional system, the CPM also shows both distal and proximal causal variables. Relationships among the elements of the CPM are reciprocal: For example, the consequences of aggressive behavior (e.g., inconsistent reinforcement) can in turn engender increased anger and aggression, reinforcement of the client's demands and aggressive reactions, and a general "vicious cycle" pattern (Nezu & Nezu, 1989b).

After developing an individualized CPM, the therapist proceeds to the next problem-solving tasks—generation of alternatives and decision making—to select focal problem areas to target for change.

Generation of Alternatives and Decision Making

In developing a preliminary list of problems to target for intervention, the clinician draws on the pool of potential problem areas across the three-dimensional, tripartite assessment model. Specifically, this means brainstorming a list of variables that appear, on the basis of a S-O-R-K-C analysis, to be functionally related to the identified problems. Once a list of potential target problems is generated, the next step is to select those that will be the initial targets of intervention. By applying the decision-making guidelines, the clinician can systematically identify the variables most in need of change. Table 3.2 lists decision-making criteria in the form of questions to ask when considering both the likelihood of positive effects and the value of choosing a given problem as an intervention target. Because even patients who experience similar problems can differ vastly in their unique CPM profiles, the therapist, in addition to applying those criteria, may need to generate a list of all possible consequences of selecting certain target problems for a given client.

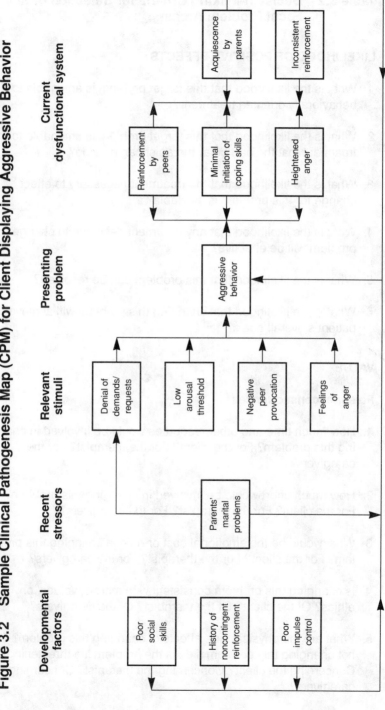

Figure 3.2 Sample Clinical Pathogenesis Map (CPM) for Client Displaying Aggressive Behavior

Table 3.2 Decision-Making Criteria for Selection of Key Focal Problem Areas

LIKELIHOOD OF POSITIVE EFFECTS

1. What is the likelihood that this target problem is amenable to behaviorally oriented treatment?

2. What is the likelihood that this target problem is amenable to the treatment that the particular therapist can provide?

3. What is the likelihood that the treatment necessary to effect change for this problem is available?

4. What is the likelihood that any treatment designed to change this problem will be effective?

5. What is the likelihood that this problem can be resolved?

6. What is the likelihood that changing this problem will achieve the patient's overall goals?

VALUE

Personal consequences

1. How much time and other resources would be involved in changing this problem? For the client? For the therapist? For the caregivers?

2. How much effort would be involved in changing this problem? For the client? For the therapist? For the caregivers?

3. What would be the emotional cost or gain in changing this problem? For the client? For the therapist? For the caregivers?

4. Is changing this problem consistent with morals, values, or ethics? Of the client? Of the therapist? Of the caregivers?

5. What are the physical side effects of changing this problem? Of not changing this problem (i.e., is the problem life threatening)? Concerning the client? Concerning the therapist? Concerning the caregivers?

6. What is the impact on the client's personal growth if this problem is changed?

7. What are the effects on other client problem areas if this problem is changed? On other caregiver problems?

Social consequences

1. What are the effects on other people if this problem is changed? On family? On friends? On the community?

2. Is changing this problem consistent with the values of others?

3. Will changing this problem engender support or antagonism from others?

SHORT-TERM CONSEQUENCES

1. Will changing this problem have a positive or negative effect on the client's motivation? On that of caregivers?

2. Will changing this problem have an immediate positive or negative impact on the client's other problems? On those of caregivers?

3. Are there any immediate short-term iatrogenic effects even though the long-term consequences are predicted to be positive?

LONG-TERM CONSEQUENCES

1. What are the long-range consequences of changing this problem?

2. Will the long-term effects of changing this problem achieve the client's goals? Those of the caregivers?

3. Will changing this problem obviate or minimize the need for future psychological intervention?

Using the criteria given in Table 3.2 (and any others appropriate in a particular case), the therapist then evaluates the overall cost-benefit profile for each problem area on the list of potential targets. The highly rated items (i.e., the targets that are assessed as having a high likelihood of overall positive effects and minimal negative effects) are then chosen as initial target areas. We suggest choosing several highly rated target areas to maximize the potential for overall goal attainment.

While identifying focal target problems, the therapist should work with the client (if appropriate) and members of the caregiving system to develop a parallel list of their potential goals and should articulate subgoals that represent ways to attain the larger goals. For instance, in addition to goals that the client and/or caregivers may have brought to therapy (e.g., to reduce anxiety), the therapist, using the problem analysis, specifies subgoals (e.g., build problem-solving and coping skills, improve impulse control) that the client must meet in order to attain the ultimate goals.

As in selecting focal target problems, the clinician also applies the problem-solving process in identifying realistic therapy goals. This would mean generating (via brainstorming) a list of possible goals and objectives; evaluating and rating each possibility on the major decision-making criteria; and selecting, in cooperation with the client and caregivers, the goals that appear to have the highest utility (positive likelihood and value ratings). Questions previously posed in the evaluation of potential target problems would be raised again in the selection of therapy goals.

We have found it useful to construct a Goal Attainment Map (GAM; Nezu & Nezu, 1989b) as a visual representation of progress from point A (presenting problems) to point B (goal attainment). The GAM, discussed in chapter 7 and illustrated in Figure 7.2, is analogous to the CPM depicting the client's difficulties and includes both treatment subgoals and ultimate goals, as well as the intervention strategies (to be identified during the next therapy stage, treatment design) that will be implemented as a means of facilitating goal attainment. However, before proceeding to that stage, the therapist subjects the list of target problem areas and potential goals to the last problem-solving step, solution implementation and verification.

Solution Implementation and Verification

Construction of a client's CPM represents the implementation component of the problem-solving process. For the verification component, in which the clinician monitors the effects of the decisions to compare the predicted consequences with the actual ones, two sources of useful feedback exist. One source is the client and significant members of his or her caregiving system. Although the therapist should have been discussing the case regularly with these people, a formal presentation of the

CPM and the GAM (without the intervention analysis) will help elicit specific feedback, especially with regard to goal statements. Although the client's and/or caregivers' perceptions may be biased and the resulting feedback inconclusive, successful treatment is unlikely in the absence of mutual agreement. (Discrepancies in goal statements may need to be treated as initiation difficulties.)

A second source of feedback is suggested by Turkat and Maisto (1985) with regard to the testing of specific hypotheses that arise from behavioral case formulation. In a case formulation model, several predictions about current or future behavior can be made on the basis of one's problem analysis. For example, if the therapist hypothesizes according to a CPM analysis that a major presenting problem of anxiety is related to interpersonal difficulties and fears of rejection by others, one prediction might involve high scores on self-report measures of social avoidance and distress. A second prediction might be that, during a structured role-play portraying a move to a new community residence (and a need to meet new people), the client would display visible signs of anxiety and report feelings of distress. Given the confirmations and disconfirmations provided by such tests, the therapist can begin to evaluate the accuracy of the original problem analysis.

Using data from these two sources, the therapist continues with verification by evaluating the match between the predictions and the actual consequences (i.e., feedback from client and caregivers about proposed goals and subgoals). If the match is unsatisfactory, the clinician cycles through the various problem-solving operations once again. If the comparison is positive (i.e., all parties agree that the specified treatment goals are appropriate), he or she proceeds to the next therapy stage, the design of a treatment plan.

SUMMARY

We conceptualize treatment for dually diagnosed persons as involving a series of clinical decisions that are prerequisite to successful therapy. Clinical intervention encompasses major clinical tasks that can be grouped into four stages: screening, problem analysis and focal problem selection, treatment design, and treatment implementation and evaluation. This chapter focused on the first two stages, broadly covering tasks associated with assessment. Across these assessment stages, we advocate applying each of the five problem-solving operations: problem orientation, problem definition and formulation, generation of alternatives, decision making, and solution implementation and verification.

In the screening stage of treatment planning, various kinds of initiation difficulties can stand in the way of successful treatment. Such difficulties involve factors relating to the client, the therapist, and significant others (e.g., parents, direct care staff), as well as the appropriateness of given psychological interventions for the particular client.

Application of the problem-solving model during the second assessment stage, problem analysis and focal problem selection, is geared to (a) yield a comprehensive understanding of the client's problems, (b) identify the variables that are causally or functionally related to these problems, and (c) delineate realistic goals and subgoals for treatment. To assist in these tasks, we offer a three-dimensional framework that guides the therapist in gathering information across three problem-related areas (behavioral factors, resources, and goals) with respect to the components of the tripartite model (client, caregivers, and environment).

This broad-based assessment across a variety of potentially important areas reflects our worldview, which emphasizes (a) a multiple causality framework, (b) a tripartite approach to assessment and treatment, (c) a general systems conceptualization, (d) a focus on developmental factors, and (e) a focus on key behaviors.

To graphically depict a conceptualization of the client's problems, the therapist can construct a Clinical Pathogenesis Map (CPM). The CPM represents the therapist's clinical hypotheses regarding the major factors underlying the initiation and maintenance of the problems. (Our sample CPM concerned the presenting problem of aggression.) By sharing the CPM with all parties concerned in a case (client, caregivers, significant others), the therapist can elicit feedback about its appropriateness. Assuming that all agree, the therapist then moves to the next therapy stage—treatment design. If there is significant disagreement among the concerned parties, the therapist needs to cycle through the problem-solving operations once more in an attempt to solve the new problem.

Chapters 4, 5, and 6, reflecting our tripartite model, will focus on specific assessment issues regarding the dually diagnosed client, the caregiving system, and the environment. In Section III, we will return to treatment design and evaluation and will describe the application of the problem-solving model to this stage of therapy.

Chapter 4

Assessment of the Individual

INTRODUCTION

Evaluation of comorbidity involving mental retardation and mental illness in one individual can be a challenge for the mental health professional. The diagnosis of dual disabilities calls for both the presence of mental retardation (established through formal assessment of intellectual and adaptive functioning level) and the presence of specific additional symptoms that warrant a psychiatric diagnosis. As noted in chapter 1, obtaining a valid psychiatric diagnosis for a nonretarded individual can be difficult. Because deficiency in adaptive behavior is a partial criterion for mental retardation itself, this process is even more complex for a person with retardation. The presenting symptoms of deficient adaptation must be severe enough and sufficiently intense, frequent, and/or disruptive to justify an additional psychiatric diagnosis (Jakab, 1982).

Behavioral difficulties and subjective distress (e.g., severe aggression, withdrawal, suicidal intention) are indicators of the need for therapeutic intervention and may be considered symptoms. There are several ways to approach the assessment of these symptoms. One method involves formal diagnosis, which is important for organization of clinical information, research on homogeneous patient populations, communication among professionals, and prediction of an individual's clinical course. However, the clinical utility of any diagnostic category depends on its reliability and whether it leads to important information concerning etiology, prognosis, and treatment. Proponents of formal diagnosis see an accurate diagnosis as the key to understanding the etiology of behavioral symptoms. In practice, however, the formal diagnostic process too often results in little more than labeling of an individual and may lead to the assumption that knowledge of diagnosis alone will result in effective treatment.

71

An alternative approach to assessment focuses on a behavioral analysis of discrete target problems. This approach uses a variety of behavioral assessment procedures, focusing less on diagnostic classification and more on a data-based formulation of current maintaining variables associated with each target problem.

We view both diagnosis and behavioral analysis as parts of the overall assessment process; these two need not be viewed as incompatible. Within a clinical decision-making framework, combining accurate diagnosis and sound behavioral assessment procedures yields a more comprehensive picture.

THE NEED FOR A MULTIMATRIX ASSESSMENT MODEL

An empirical, multimatrix assessment would include an evaluation of the individual's strengths and weaknesses on biological, neurological, intellectual, developmental, adaptive, physiological, psychosocial, and behavioral dimensions. Each client brings a universe of possible difficulties that may contribute to the original referral problems. Such contributing difficulties may be developmental (e.g., reduced mental age), psychological (e.g., low self-esteem), biological (e.g., presence of seizure disorder or other brain dysfunction), social (e.g., community rejection), and/or environmental (e.g., past and current learning environments, family systems issues).

Particularly with a client who has multiple disabilities, viewing the individual as monosymptomatic can be clinically naive and a gross misrepresentation of clinical reality. Effective empirical analysis entails investigating the interactions among problem areas that engender the client's presenting symptoms and complaints. We believe that the systems framework outlined in the previous chapter is helpful in understanding such interactions. A systems approach (Kanfer, 1985) emphasizes the functional relationships among various target mechanisms, such as organic deficits, environmental inputs, behavioral sequences, and cognitive/emotional components. We have found that summarizing pertinent information within the three focal areas of the client, the caregiving system, and the environment—and analyzing the reciprocal impact among these areas—provides a structure for integrating all important sources of information. In addition, significant historical events, early learning experiences, and other more distal occurrences can provide a useful context for understanding how current problems developed.

In summary, assessment of persons with dual disabilities is a challenge to clinicians. We have found that a multifaceted assessment process, which includes both differential diagnosis and behavioral assessment, is needed for accurate definition of presenting problems and development of efficacious treatment plans. The following sections will describe assessment problems and strategies that we have found helpful.

ISSUES CONCERNING DIFFERENTIAL DIAGNOSIS

The presence of phenomena commonly associated with intellectual deficiencies makes differentiation of psychiatric symptoms difficult. Obstacles to an accurate psychiatric evaluation of a developmentally disabled person often include (a) the diagnosis of mental retardation itself, (b) the client's own cognitive or developmental limitations, (c) the phenomenon of diagnostic overshadowing, and (d) the presence of multiple etiological factors. These impediments to diagnostic clarity are discussed in the following sections.

Diagnostic Issues Regarding Mental Retardation

In order to be dually diagnosed, an individual must first present a history of mental retardation. In other words, the cognitive impairments and deficits in adaptive functioning that characterize developmental disabilities must exist prior to the psychiatric symptomatology (Eaton & Menolascino, 1982).

According to the *Diagnostic and Statistical Manual of Mental Disorders* (DSM-III-R; American Psychiatric Association, 1987), an individual with mental retardation must demonstrate significantly subaverage intellectual functioning; in addition, concurrent deficits and impairments in adaptive behavior must be evident. Adaptive behavior refers to the individual's effectiveness in meeting the standards of personal independence, self-care, and social responsibility appropriate for his or her age or cultural group. Significantly subaverage intellectual performance is typically defined by attainment on a standardized intelligence test of a score two or more standard deviations below the mean (IQ of approximately 70 or below, depending on the test used). According to the 1973 revision of the American Association on Mental Deficiency's classification schema (Grossman, 1973), the four levels of mental retardation and the associated approximate IQ ranges are as follows:

Level of Mental Retardation	IQ score
Mild	56–70
Moderate	41–55
Severe	26–40
Profound	25 and below

Moreover, these deficits must be manifested before age 18. (This definition refers to delayed or deficient behavioral performance without reference to presumed causes.)

Instances of unidentified mental retardation as well as falsely identified mental retardation often occur. It is not uncommon for clients to carry
inaccurate and vague diagnostic labels of "mental retardation" or
"organic brain syndrome" in their psychiatric records and reports. These
labels, however, are often of little value to the client or family seeking clinical services. One of the authors recently interviewed a 29-year-old woman
with a 15-year diagnosis of mental retardation. That diagnosis was the
result of a psychosocial history summary conducted at a psychiatric hospital when the client was 14 years old. The report stated that she had a "subaverage IQ of 65" but did not indicate what tests were administered,
who conducted the testing, or where the testing took place. Furthermore,
none of the woman's previous reports included a valid estimate of her
adaptive functioning. This situation dramatizes the need, during the
assessment process, to avoid assumptions based solely on previous evaluations. Unless a valid, recent intellectual evaluation can be documented,
such an evaluation may be an essential first step in the diagnostic process.
Some clients with significant developmental disabilities have never received such evaluation, and the extent of their developmental impairment may have gone unrecognized. As a result, they may be missing
opportunities for clinical services and vocational or rehabilitative training
designed specifically for persons with a diagnosis of mental retardation.

Although intellectual performance continues to be the most salient
criterion used to diagnose mental retardation, the criterion of adaptive
behavior may be more salient to the professional who is responsible for
treatment. This is evident in the case of the woman just described. On
completion of standardized testing she achieved a full-scale IQ score
(Wechsler Adult Intelligence Scale–Revised) of 72, which placed her in
the category of borderline intellectual functioning. However, a rating
of her adaptive behavior, as measured by the American Association on
Mental Retardation (AAMD) Adaptive Behavior Scale (Nihira, Foster,
Shellhaas, & Leland, 1975), yielded a profile of significant adaptive
deficits, with scores on more than half the profile scales well below the
40th percentile for her norm group (496 institutionalized clients with
levels of intellectual impairment ranging from mild to profound). Rather
than the IQ score alone, what became important for the clinician
evaluating this woman was the presence of severe adaptive deficits that
could not be explained by her present intellectual deficits. This indicated
a need for intervention aimed at factors other than intellectual functioning. At the same time, the woman's strengths and deficits as revealed
through her intellectual evaluation provided an extremely useful
framework for weighing the potential effectiveness of intervention alternatives. In this case, the client's demonstrated verbal strengths suggested
a positive outcome of several psychotherapy alternatives requiring a certain degree of verbal skill and an ability to learn specific verbal concepts.
In addition to providing information necessary for a diagnosis of mental
retardation, measures of both intellectual and adaptive functioning may

provide extremely useful points of orientation for the analysis of possible therapeutic target areas for a given client.

We suggest that the current DSM-III-R criteria for a diagnosis of mental retardation (intellectual and adaptive deficits) be used as an aid in diagnosis of dual disability as well. Beyond the IQ scores and level of adaptive functioning, assessment on either of these dimensions yields an abundance of clinical information that may enhance the effectiveness of therapy. As described by Leland (1983), adaptive behavior measures can contribute to a client's quality of life by indicating where the person's strengths lie and what he or she can do that is consistent with society's demands. The overall picture of strengths, as opposed to deficiencies, can help define the least restrictive environment for the client.

Measurement of adaptive functioning usually requires the cooperation of a significant person in the client's life, as ratings are based on reports of the client's daily functioning in his or her environment. The person doing the reporting must have the opportunity to observe the client across most waking-hour activities and in multiple settings—for example, at home and in a school or day program environment. Of rating instruments that have been developed systematically, the AAMD Adaptive Behavior Scale–Revised (Nihira et al., 1975) and the Vineland Adaptive Behavior Scales (Sparrow, Balla, & Cicchetti, 1984) appear to be the most widely used. Both scales provide indices of an individual's functioning across various behavioral domains considered important to adaptive, independent functioning. In addition, both scales provide a measure of current maladaptive behavior that might interfere with a person's ability to benefit from education or rehabilitation.

The use of both standardized intelligence scales and adaptive behavior scales can be helpful not only in making a clear diagnosis of the level of mental retardation, but also in making an initial functional analysis of individual strengths and weaknesses.

Although an exhaustive review of available intelligence scales and adaptive behavior measures is beyond the scope of this chapter, we list the most frequently used instruments in Table 4.1. The list also includes measures for persons with severe and profound intellectual impairment and with multiple disabilities.

As Morgenstern (1983) points out, establishing a client's actual scores on any of these measures is a relatively technical but simple procedure. However, interpreting the pattern in a way that recognizes strengths and weaknesses and applying this assessment to the client's therapeutic plan is much more difficult. In describing the complexities involved in interpreting performance on a "simple" task of object manipulation, for example, Morgenstern notes that

> this skill also implicitly involves comprehension of the task, direction of attention, control of movement and other voluntary actions, form perception and discrimination, spatial relations

Table 4.1   Measures of Intellectual and Adaptive Functioning

INTELLIGENCE SCALES

Stanford-Binet Intelligence Scales
(4th ed.; Thorndike, Hagen, & Sattler, 1986)

Wechsler scales

Wechsler Adult Intelligence Scale–Revised
(Wechsler, 1981)

Weschsler Intelligence Scale for Children–Revised
(Wechsler, 1974)

Wechsler Preschool and Primary Scale of Intelligence–Revised
(Wechsler, 1989)

Developmental scales

Bayley Scales of Infant Development
(Bayley, 1969)

Cattell Infant Intelligence Scale
(Cattell, 1960)

Tests for special populations

Columbia Mental Maturity Scale
(Burgemeister, Blum, & Lorge, 1972)

Leiter International Performance Scale
(Leiter, 1980)

Peabody Picture Vocabulary Test
(Dunn, 1965)

Slosson Intelligence Test
(Slosson, 1963)

ADAPTIVE BEHAVIOR SCALES

AAMD Adaptive Behavior Scale–Revised
(Nihira et al., 1975)

Vineland Adaptive Behavior Scales
(Sparrow, Balla, & Cicchetti, 1984)

and visual memory. Moreover, all these functions and processes are subject to the influence of behavioral factors. . . . Thus, test results represent the interplay of maturation, cognitive and perceptual functions, sociocultural influences, emotional factors, and psychological/physiological processes. (p. 209)

Therefore, regardless of the testing measure used, it is extremely important for the clinician analyzing intelligence testing results to focus on the *functions* assessed by various test items. We have found, for example, that the Wechsler Scales (Wechsler, 1974, 1981) are useful, via a scatter analysis (if differences are statistically significant), in providing information about one's strengths and weaknesses. In addition, score clusters, determined by factorial analysis, can be helpful in assessing an individual's learned methods of approaching a task, attentional problems, and estimated tolerance of frustration.

Because the lower limit of the Wechsler Scales' range does not meet that of individuals with severe and profound deficits, and because it may be inappropriate for individuals with multiple physical disabilities (e.g., deafness, blindness, cerebral palsy), other measures may better assess some clients' functional areas. These measures include developmental scales, such as those designed by Cattell (1960) and Bayley (1969), which may provide a good indication of development in the areas of language, motor, social, and adaptive functions. Instruments that can be used with clients who have severe language problems or physical handicaps include the Peabody Picture Vocabulary Test (Dunn, 1965), the Columbia Mental Maturity Scale (Burgemeister et al., 1972), the Leiter International Performance Scale (Leiter, 1980), and the Slosson Intelligence Test (Slosson, 1963).

Diagnostic Issues Regarding Cognitive/Developmental Limitations

Clinical evaluations of clients with developmental disabilities are often conducted without the luxury of a verbally expressive or articulate subject, an adequate history of previous treatment, or an accurate account of previous institutional experiences. Concrete thinking, expressive language delays, lack of time concept, displays of stereotypic motor behaviors, and impaired ability to communicate emotions pose major obstacles to efficient clinical interviews. To identify what is significant or pathological, the examiner must be familiar with predictable adaptive deficits associated with various age ranges and levels of intellectual functioning. In fact, several authors have suggested that the diagnostic criteria of the DSM-III-R may not be appropriate for individuals with developmental disabilities. This may be due to poor reliability of diagnostic categories and the lack of rigorous evaluation of this system. We have found that the existing diagnostic systems are not necessarily inappropriate but that using those systems requires an awareness that developmentally disabled persons may exhibit modified clinical presentations of the various categories of symptoms. Moreover, it is important in considering various diagnostic possibilities to look for disconfirming evidence to clinical hypotheses and to explore fully the context in which symptoms occur. Consider the following case example.

Larry, a 34-year-old man with moderate mental retardation and a history of congenital syphilis, had been referred for complaints of seeing "monsters," "scary faces," and "the bogeyman." He initially appeared paranoid and delusional, describing the feared bogeyman in detail. An assessment of possible neurochemical or physical factors that might help explain the recent onset of these symptoms yielded no significant diagnostic information; a behavioral assessment was then conducted. Larry's perception of monsters was specific to certain situations, such as being alone in a dark room. In an assessment session, the clinician accompanied Larry to specific locations where he feared being alone; in other words, part of the interview was conducted in vivo. After seeking both confirming and disconfirming evidence regarding specific diagnostic categories of symptoms, the clinician found that Larry had been attempting to describe his fear of descending the dark stairwell at his group home to carry out his assigned chore of taking down the trash. A careful assessment of Larry's symptoms yielded the differential diagnosis of a phobic disorder. Larry's monsters could be attributed to his limited means of communicating his fear of being alone in the dark. A treatment aimed at teaching him fear reduction strategies included several desensitization sessions in which the therapist initially accompanied him to the basement. The treatment resulted in the disappearance of Larry's symptoms.

For a psychiatric diagnosis to be justified, there must be certainty regarding the presence of serious symptoms (e.g., delusions, hallucinations, depression, anxiety) that are not the result of communication difficulties resulting from mental retardation. Because of the time required for careful interpretation of overt psychiatric symptoms in persons with mental retardation, the use of current standard diagnostic tools, such as the DSM-III-R, has received some criticism. Indeed, reliability and validity studies regarding the DSM-III-R that are specific to this population are lacking (Szymanski, 1988). It would appear premature, however, to discount DSM-III-R as a valid diagnostic and classification tool. Russell (1988) has endorsed its use, citing its multiaxial structure as a strength in capturing the complexity involved in many cases of dual diagnosis. Yet what is clinically required is a respect for this complexity and a familiarity with a client's idiographic means of communication and expression. Conversely, symptoms of subjective distress, frequent and/or intense behavioral disturbance, mood alteration, or changes in an individual's characteristic way of responding to the world given his or her developmental level should not be ignored as the "typical" behavior of persons with mental retardation.

Issues Concerning Diagnostic Overshadowing

Although symptoms such as withdrawal, aggression, disorganization, and self-damaging or destructive acts warrant hospital admission among clients of average intellectual functioning, similar symptoms in persons with mental retardation are often viewed, erroneously, as untreatable. The phenomenon of diagnostic overshadowing (Reiss, Levitan, & Szyszko, 1982), described in chapter 1, may cause clinicians to take these problems less seriously. In other words, maladaptive behavior is seen as an associated feature of mental retardation rather than as a symptom of diagnostic importance. Although some behaviors are more commonly observed in individuals with mental retardation (e.g., stereotypic motor behaviors, expressive speech difficulties, perseverative approaches to tasks, disturbance of motor functioning associated with concomitant neurological diseases), these behaviors should not be confused with specific psychiatric syndromes operationalized within the various diagnostic categories. Moreover, as discussed in chapter 1, people with developmental and organic deficits are as vulnerable to the full range of psychiatric, psychological, and emotional disorders as the population at large. In fact, their limitations often make learning positive coping patterns and understanding their own emotions even more difficult.

This phenomenon is exemplified in the case of Daniel, a 32-year-old man with mild mental retardation and a history of emotional outbursts, exaggerated responses to any perceived rejection, and loud, silly attempts at comedy in inappropriate situations. Previous counselors and work supervisors had always viewed Daniel's behavior as examples of poor inhibition and immaturity that "would be expected" for someone with his disabilities. Daniel's therapist, however, through a comprehensive psychiatric evaluation coupled with behavioral assessment, recognized symptoms consistent with an anxiety disorder. These included excessive worry over several current stressful life circumstances, motor tension, autonomic hyperactivity, and an exaggerated startle response. Historical information about Daniel's early social learning experiences supported the therapist's hypotheses concerning salient etiological factors and current symptoms. Daniel's developmental disabilities had been identified only after several years of frustrating educational experiences. Daniel's mother, who ignored recommendations from educational specialists, would force him to sit for hours in front of school assignments and would scold him continually for his inability to complete the tasks. One means Daniel had discovered for gaining positive recognition from peers and family was to exhibit his skills as a clown and a mimic. At the same time, he was perpetually fearful that others would discover his failure to read or write competently. Unfortunately, for years Daniel had been regarded as a funny character, who sometimes became overly aggressive and "too sensitive." He had been periodically prescribed neuroleptic medication following various incidents of aggression. Many professionals with whom Daniel came into contact saw this practice as customary for an individual with mental retardation.

Multiple Etiological Factors

Etiology of symptoms frequently involves a combination of organic and environmental causes. For example, aggressive behavior may be associated with partial complex (temporal lobe) seizure activity; communication of an affective state (e.g., pain, frustration, anger, depression); iatrogenic effects of specific medications (Sovner & Hurley, 1981); learned behavior (e.g., exposure to aggressive models, reinforcement of aggressive responses); or skill deficits (e.g., poor social skills or impulse control). It may represent one aspect of a constellation of symptoms that form a psychiatric syndrome (e.g., bipolar disorder, schizophrenia). In addition, an individual described as aggressive may be exhibiting problem behavior that results from a combination of these etiological factors. This is often true regarding many referral problems or target behaviors, as the following case illustrates.

Bonnie, a 34-year-old woman with severe mental retardation, exhibited symptoms consistent with a diagnosis of bipolar disorder. These included cyclical periods of extreme withdrawal, isolation, and motor retardation, along with episodic periods of manic behavior, accelerated motor activity, sleeplessness, and weight loss. She also frequently engaged in high-risk behavior, such as running out to make a store purchase in the middle of the night. In addition, the family history indicated a presence of affective disorder. Bonnie's parents, who had been diagnosed with psychiatric illnesses, were unable to care for her. Although she resided in a community group home at the time of referral, her paternal uncle, who visited her often, had been responsible for most of her previous care. Bonnie's uncle was a sympathetic and caring individual who believed that her deficits were irremediable and attempted to help her by immediately gratifying all of her demands. Although many of Bonnie's symptoms could be associated with her psychiatric disorder, several additional problems, such as minimal gratification delay, frequent refusal of rehabilitative tasks, and screeching demands could be understood in terms of social learning and previous environmental contingencies.

As in Bonnie's case, the diagnosis of a person with multiple disorders often requires the skills of more than one specialist and should address variables in the following areas: medical (e.g., presence of seizure disorders, metabolic abnormalities), psychological (e.g., intellectual functioning, coping resources), familial (e.g., history of mental illness), social (e.g., interpersonal functioning), emotional (e.g., presence of anxiety, dysphoria), and educational (e.g., learning history, attention span). Further, assessment in each area requires the use of reliable and valid diagnostic tools, such as pertinent history records, evaluation forms, checklists, behavioral recording forms, and standardized tests.

COMPONENTS OF CLIENT ASSESSMENT

Given the difficulty of making accurate diagnoses, we recommend using a clinical decision-making model for clients with a dual diagnosis. As stated previously, assessing the client's intellectual/cognitive level (with a focus on functional abilities and deficits) as well as evaluating his or her adaptive functioning will provide both a diagnostic criterion for mental retardation and initial information regarding important clinical problem areas.

The following procedures outline important assessment components. We emphasize component areas rather than prescribing a sequence because the order in which areas are assessed may vary according to individual client characteristics, previous records or information obtained, or the availability of appropriate personnel to conduct the assessment tasks. Table 4.2 summarizes the assessment components.

Component I: Initial Consultation

This assessment component is designed to define major referral problems, obtain a history of the client's present difficulties, and gather information about previous evaluations, rehabilitative programs, and treatments. Before this visit, it may be useful to obtain consent from the client (and the legal guardian, if appropriate) so that the interviewer has access to previous psychological testing reports, accounts of the client's progress in educational or rehabilitative settings, and thorough records of previous medications or treatments as well as the client's responses to these past treatments. This component may also serve as a starting point for observing the client's current behavior patterns in his or her present environment; this may entail instructing caregivers in observation methods or arranging for the interviewer or a member of the diagnostic team to make several visits.

Component II: Evaluation of Strengths and Deficits

If valid test results or adaptive behavioral profiles are not already available, psychological testing and assessment of the client's adaptive behavior will serve multiple diagnostic purposes. In addition to yielding a valid diagnosis concerning the client's developmental disability, these procedures will also provide important profiles of strengths and weaknesses,

Table 4.2   Components of Assessment

Component I: Initial consultation

Define referral problems
Obtain history of difficulties
Obtain treatment history
Obtain initial sample of behavior
Obtain appropriate consents

Component II: Evaluation of strengths and deficits

Complete psychological testing
Obtain adaptive behavior profile
Define roles of significant caregivers
Conduct reinforcer survey

Component III: Neuromedical assessment

Obtain medical and developmental history
Conduct physical exam and review of physical systems
Conduct neurological exam
Conduct laboratory tests
   (blood work, electroencephalogram, tomography if indicated)

Component IV: Observational analysis

Obtain mental status information through clinical interview
Conduct functional analysis of behavior
   (based on learning principles)

permit observation of the client's approach to tasks, and aid the clinician in forming a collaborative relationship with the client's caregivers. Because an assessment of the client's adaptive behavior depends on the cooperation of significant individuals in the caregiving system, ideally they will work with the clinician as team members from the outset. This may not be possible if the caregivers themselves exhibit symptoms of cognitive, physical, environmental, or emotional disability. Thus, an aspect of this assessment component involves defining the roles of members of the client's caregiving system (see chapter 5).

This component should also include a systematic survey of the most salient, identifiable reinforcers for the client through a combination of self-report, ratings by others, and direct observation. We cannot overemphasize the importance of this step and the value of this information for later behavioral procedures. Although identification of client-specific motivational features has been clearly stressed as crucial for effective behavioral therapy (Gardner, 1988), we are disheartened by the infrequency with which systematic surveys of reinforcers are conducted by "behavioral" program providers. We have seen clients for whom, according to day programming or residential support staff, behavioral procedures were ineffective in remediating behavioral difficulties, only to learn that programming had come from a "cookbook" menu. In such cases token economies were based on lists of common reinforcers and on social activities that were simply assumed to have some significance for the clients.

Particularly with adolescent and young adult clients, we have seen mental health professionals overlook peer approval, increased responsibility, or a sense of control over one's environment as important sources of positive reinforcement. Staff members using prepared token economies based on edibles such as ice cream or hamburgers and tangible items such as makeup or magazines have been surprised when asked, "What leads you to believe these items represent reinforcement for this client?" Unfortunately, the answers to such questions frequently betray a careless approach to behavioral technology with no attempt to discover what will motivate a given client. We believe that a careful, step-by-step, *individualized* reinforcement survey can provide some of the most powerful information for a comprehensive picture of the client's difficulties as well as for later therapeutic endeavors.

The importance of an individualized reinforcement survey is clear in the case of Richard, a 29-year-old man with severe mental retardation, referred for chronic and extensive public masturbation. Our initial survey failed to identify potential reinforcers that could compete with Richard's masturbatory activity. During 93% of the sampled time, he was observed engaging in genital self-stimulation. Although we gave him access to a huge variety of other possible reinforcers (intrinsic, social, edible, tangible, and self-stimulatory), he displayed a preference, in any free choice situation, for masturbation. Finally, after exhaustive interviews with several significant people in his environment, we heard a former teaching aide at Richard's day program say, "At least he can't rip papers anymore, because we don't let him have any." It turned out that the client, several years earlier, had annoyed program staff by continually ripping up pieces of available paper. However, they had broken this habit by rigorously blocking access to newspapers and magazines.

When Richard was given several reinforcement choice trials, in which he was seated at a table and told that he could either "touch himself" or "rip the papers," he chose paper ripping as the preferred activity! Armed with a competing reinforcer that the therapists could control (i.e., paper ripping), we were able to develop a procedure using differential reinforcement of incompatible behavior (DRI) that led to a significant decrease in the public masturbation (Nezu, Cannon, &

Petronko, 1987). Richard's on-task work at his day program was also significantly increased through use of paper ripping as a reinforcing activity. Eventually, using a reinforcer displacement procedure in which the opportunity to rip paper was paired with presentation of an edible reinforcer, we were able to phase out the paper ripping and maintain adaptive behavioral changes using edible reinforcers. This kind of procedure will be discussed in more detail in the chapters on treatment. The point here is that, in the assessment phase, a dogged search for meaningful reinforcers and careful evaluation of the behavioral effects of contingent events provided crucial information regarding the client's overall difficulties.

Component III: Neuromedical Assessment

The third component of assessment is a series of medical procedures that reveal the contribution of the client's physical, metabolic, and neurologic conditions to his or her current problem areas. These procedures include a comprehensive physical exam, a neurologic exam, blood tests as determined by the examining physician(s), a medical and developmental history, and an electroencephalogram (and tomography if indicated). The neuromedical assessment will likely require several visits to the appropriate professionals, though this will depend on the individual case and the facility where the assessment takes place. For example, a client referred for a psychiatric diagnosis may, through agency support, have received a recent and comprehensive neurologic and medical evaluation. Consultation with the relevant professionals may provide sufficient diagnostic information that further tests are not immediately required. However, it is crucial that a competent neuropsychiatrist (or a group of consulting neurologists and psychiatrists) be present on the clinical diagnostic team. Severe and chronic brain disorders—such as epilepsy, irreversible dementias, closed head injuries, and encephalopathies due to multiple causes—may all have psychiatric consequences. Neurobehavioral symptoms can include aggression and withdrawal, hyperactivity and anergia, psychosis, and self-injurious behavior (Gualtieri, 1988). A competent neuropsychiatric professional can monitor required anticonvulsant therapy, measure drug toxicity, and determine the etiology of the various dyskinesia symptoms (for example, anticonvulsant dyskinesia versus tardive dyskinesia).

Component IV: Observational Analysis

The final assessment component incorporates the following: (a) a complete family and social history, (b) a formal clinical interview, and (c) observations of the client's interactions with other members of the milieu and of his or her current behavior on operant (reinforcement), respondent, cognitive-behavioral, and/or social learning dimensions. This component can also incorporate initial diagnostic screening measures, such as the Psychopathology Instrument for Mentally Retarded Adults (Matson, Kazdin, & Senatore, 1984) or the Reiss Screen for Maladaptive Behavior (Reiss, 1988).

The Clinical Interview and Mental Status Examination

One of the most valuable tools for assessing a person with dual disabilities rests in the examiner's observational skills. At present, one's clinical interviewing skills and judgment may be more effective and reliable than structured interview instruments (Anthony et al., 1985; Helzer et al., 1985). From the moment a client is introduced to the examiner, observations of even the most minor experiences may provide important pieces of diagnostic information. What is the adaptive level of the client's response to the interpersonal introduction? What is the discrepancy between chronological and mental age? What impressions are conveyed concerning general appearance, level of grooming, self-care, orientation to the environment, speech, general mood, and motor behavior? How interested is the client in the examiner? How is the client interacting with the examining room environment? Are there any stimuli of interest present, such as toys, games, desk items, food, drink, artwork? Are other people present?

The examiner obtains mental status information by both direct questioning and careful observation of the client. Almost every instructional book in neuropsychology, neurology, and psychiatry contains guidelines for conducting a mental status examination. Mental status scales and clinical interview instruments by different authors may vary in their organization and emphasis, but all variations include assessments of the following areas, as reported by Lezak (1983).

1. *Appearance.* This includes observation of the client's grooming, facial expressions, carriage, eye contact, mannerisms, and general movements.

2. *Orientation.* The client's awareness of person, place, time, and present situation is assessed.

3. *Speech.* This includes observations of both delivery and content of speech. Behaviors of particular importance include rate of speech, tone quality, articulation, use of phrases, and mode of verbal delivery.

4. *Thinking.* This area of assessment may be particularly problematic because of the difficulty of distinguishing between speech and thought disorders in clients with verbal dysfunctions. However, it is important to evaluate speech separately from such characteristics as mental confusion, appropriateness of associations, developmentally appropriate logic, rate of thought production,

and specific thinking disorders such as blocking, confabulation, and tangentiality.

5. *Attention, concentration, and memory.* This area includes attention span as well as immediate, recent, and remote memory. Frequently used strategies include assessing the client's recollection of personal history, performance on visual memory tasks, digit span, and reversed digit span.

6. *Intellectual functioning.* This involves an estimation of general intellectual functioning based on vocabulary, reasoning, judgment, general fund of knowledge, performance on simple arithmetic tasks, responses to questions about similarities and differences between objects and concepts, and simple drawing and copying tasks.

7. *Emotional state.* This includes an evaluation of both mood (the client's overall or prevailing subjective emotional state) and affect (the range, intensity, and appropriateness of emotional reactions during the interview).

8. *Special preoccupations and perceptual experiences.* This includes an assessment of reports of somatic concerns, distortions of self-concept, delusions, hallucinations, phobias, obsessive-compulsive characteristics, paranoid ideation, suicidal thoughts or intentions, or dissociative reactions such as fugue states, depersonalization, and reality testing.

9. *Insight.* This evaluation addresses the client's understanding of himself or herself, awareness of disabilities, expectations, and goals.

Data obtained from mental status examinations are often phenomenologic and impressionistic. Observations at this stage should not be tied to a particular theoretical orientation but rather should constitute an initial screening of intellectual and social behavior. During the evaluation process, the examiner must consciously analyze many client responses to which he or she would ordinarily react without thinking. This sort of subjectivity creates a vulnerability to distortion and errors of bias. Observations, therefore, need to be clearly distinguished from interpretation and facts clearly distinguished from assumptions. Conclusions require observational evidence, and disconfirming as well as confirming evidence of pathology should be sought.

Finally, the examiner may be alerted to areas requiring a more intensive assessment focus. These may include psychotic symptoms, such as hallucinations or delusions; evidence of dyskinesias or other motor disabilities; and other relevant psychiatric symptoms.

Although the agenda for any assessment session may be focused on particular tasks such as conducting psychological testing, obtaining a medical history, conducting a behavioral analysis, or completing self-report measures, each interaction with the client and the caregivers provides a brief sample of the individual's social interactions, level of compliance, and coping skills, as well as insight into dynamics of the caregiving or family system. As assessment methods are described, it is important to remember that continued clinical observation throughout the assessment process remains a rich source of data to integrate into the differential diagnosis.

The Psychopathology Instrument for Mentally Retarded Adults

The Psychopathology Instrument for Mentally Retarded Adults (PIMRA; Matson et al., 1984) is a self-report inventory of psychopathology symptoms in adults with mental retardation, designed as a measure of symptom severity and as an aid to differential diagnosis with this population. The eight diagnostic scales (schizophrenia, affective disorder, psychosexual disorder, adjustment disorder, anxiety disorder, somatoform disorder, personality disorder, inappropriate adjustment) include 57 items based on the DSM-III. Investigations by Matson et al. (1984) have shown this measure to evidence moderate to high levels of internal consistency and test-retest reliability. Preliminary findings regarding the validity of the PIMRA are quite promising (Senatore, Matson, & Kazdin, 1985). The PIMRA consists of a pair of structured interviews: One interview is based on self-report and the other on an interview with an informant who has the opportunity to interact with the client daily.

The Reiss Screen for Maladaptive Behavior

The Reiss Screen for Maladaptive Behavior (Reiss, 1988) is completed by an informant and assesses the likelihood that an adolescent or adult with mental retardation has a significant mental health problem. The test is designed for use with persons functioning in the mild, moderate, and severe ranges of mental retardation; it is not intended for use with children under 12. Its purpose is to facilitate the identification of persons with dual diagnoses by structuring an objective interview with the client's caregiver. The instrument is supported by research concerning norms, reliability, and validity.

Other Measures

In addition to the initial clinical interview and mental status exam, the PIMRA, and the Reiss Screen for Maladaptive Behavior, other measures may be used for further diagnostic clarity. However, most additional instruments likely to be employed were not developed specifically for a population of developmentally disabled individuals and therefore should be used with caution and sensitivity. These instruments include measures that are specific to diagnostic categories such as anxiety disorders, affective disorders, schizophrenic disorders, disorders of impulse control, adjustment disorders, psychosexual disorders, somatic disorders, and personality disorders. Many instruments useful in diagnosis of attentional deficit and hyperactivity, as well as conduct disorder, are geared toward assessment of children and have not been validated with regard to adults who have developmental disabilities. However, such instruments may be useful with this population.

We have found psychiatric symptom screening measures, such as the Brief Symptom Inventory (BSI; Derogatis & Spencer, 1982) useful in providing further diagnostic information. The BSI is a 53-item self-report inventory of point-in-time, psychological symptom status that yields three global indices and nine dimensional scales. The General Symptom Severity Index (GSI), the most sensitive of the global scales, proved sensitive to improvement as a function of treatment regarding a sample of adult outpatients with dual diagnoses (Nezu et al., 1991). However, items frequently need to be read and explained to clients; consideration of biased response patterns (e.g., "yes" answers to all questions) is also necessary. Our practice is to question caregivers regarding information received in order to have some consensual validation of client responses.

Behavioral Assessment

A behavioral assessment involves observation of behavioral phenomena through systematic recording of response parameters (Rojahn & Schroeder, 1983). Although the other assessment procedures discussed thus far also involve observation, it is the conceptualization of behavioral observations according to principles of learning that distinguishes behavioral assessment. Contemporary behavior therapists are aware of the complexity of problems evident in clients with dual disabilities. As stated by Gardner (1988), the objectives of behavioral assessment are (a) to describe the internal and external conditions under which problems are likely to occur, (b) to develop hypotheses concerning the functions served by problem behaviors, and (c) to discover the client-specific, or organismic, characteristics that contribute to current difficulties. Gardner further stresses that a clinical understanding of client-specific characteristics is required if treatment is to bring about effective and durable changes. This is a particularly important point in that a limitation of many studies documenting the efficacy of behavioral procedures concerns problems with maintenance and generalization of behavior change.

A comprehensive approach to behavioral assessment, therefore, does not focus exclusively on operant analyses of overt behavioral sequences but takes into account associative learning processes, social learning models, and cognitive-behavioral or self-management learning models as well.

Particularly with persons who function in the mild range of mental retardation, analysis of antecedent and consequent events associated with referral problems and overt behavior constitutes only one portion of the assessment process. Other models of learning (e.g., social learning; Bandura, 1977b) view the individual as an active participant in his or her own development. A cognitive-behavioral assessment would additionally focus on self-regulation and self-control skills (Kanfer & Phillips, 1970). When conducting a behavioral assessment, it is important to view the client as an individual who possesses a unique set of subjective characteristics, such as physical and affective states, social learning history, motivational characteristics, and idiopathic coping skills. Assessment should incorporate the perspectives associated with several different learning models: respondent, operant, social learning, and cognitive-behavioral (Gardner, 1988). Behavioral assessment should occur not in isolation but in keeping with a multidimensional model and should be integrated with a biomedical understanding of the individual. This view recognizes that various neuromedical and behavioral factors may each contribute in a major or minor way to a client's current difficulties (Sovner & Hurley, 1986).

Observation of overt behavioral sequences entails recording the client's behavior in different settings, with different individuals, and at different times. Depending on the referral or the target behavior under analysis, a microanalysis using particular observation strategies may be indicated—for instance, observing events antecedent and consequent to the behavior; assessing the frequency, intensity, or duration of the behavior; or sampling the behavior at intervals. Recording of social interactions may involve using role-play situations or assessing actual interactions in the client's milieu. The latter task often involves systematic observation of caregivers, described in the following chapter.

Objectivity of behavioral assessment procedures depends on the quality of observation strategies, especially the level of agreement among observers. Use of videotapes can ease time pressure for a two-person observation team. It can also provide data that different members of the clinical team can review for various purposes, such as assessing interobserver agreement or sampling baseline behavior. For instance, videotaped behavior gives the physician associated with the clinical team a baseline for comparison in the event that movement disorders, such as withdrawal dyskinesias, emerge.

The behavioral assessment also provides an opportunity to separate facts from assumptions concerning target problems, to test hypotheses, and to construct a baseline against which to measure effectiveness of subsequent intervention strategies.

SPECIFIC CATEGORIES OF DISORDERS

Remembering the caveat that people with mental retardation are vulnerable to the same disorders as members of the general population, we have compiled assessment considerations and strategies for certain psychiatric disorders that have been useful in our experiences with dually diagnosed clients. The following sections concern some of the major diagnostic categories.

Organic Brain Syndromes

Persons with mental retardation, in the moderate to profound range in particular, have usually sustained some form of brain disturbance (Gualtieri, 1988). However, the presence of retardation, perhaps with an additional condition such as epilepsy, does not warrant an "organic" diagnosis. In other words, individuals with mental disabilities of organic origin are still vulnerable to problems not associated with organic deficits. A neurological exam and laboratory results can be useful in determining how many of the client's problems can be attributed to organic damage. Recent advances in neurochemical challenge studies, studies of receptor binding, brain imaging techniques, and amino acid screening permit more precise measures of cognitive functioning, brain pathology, and neurochemical processes (Hunt & Cohen, 1988). The relationship between brain deficits and behavioral sequelae associated with selective deficits may lead to more precise psychopharmacological treatments; for example, an individual's particular strengths and weaknesses may be associated with specific impairments in information processing. However, sound methodological studies in these areas have only recently begun, and definitive conclusions concerning brain-behavior relationships are sparse.

One helpful assessment strategy involves investigating the situational specificity of the identified problems. For example, if problems of discriminatory attention or behavioral inhibition are evident, are they consistent across situations or tasks? Problems of inattention, perseveration, or dyscontrol that are specific to certain environmental contingencies may in fact indicate the presence of learned behavior.

When organic factors are suspected as a major etiological or maintaining variable in behavioral or emotional disruption, a neuromedical evaluation is essential. Conversely, a loosely defined diagnosis of "organic disorder" does little more than confirm a cognitive disability.

Neuropsychological testing can also be helpful in isolating specific areas of function and dysfunction. Information gleaned from such assessment may guide the therapist in focusing learning strategies. For example, we obtained a neuropsychological consultation regarding a 45-year-old deinstitutionalized female who had recently begun living in a group residence. Her referral problems included aggression associated with terminating an activity in which she was engaged (e.g., ironing, washing dishes, listening to the radio). Neuropsychological testing revealed that the client had sustained a loss of frontal lobe functioning, which had severely impaired her ability to initiate and terminate activities. The intervention plan included providing clear and concrete cues in the woman's home milieu that would help her comply with time limitations for various activities. Her aggression decreased when she was better able to understand and predict her daily routine.

Schizophrenia

Although psychotic disturbances have been grossly overdiagnosed among persons with cognitive, perceptual, and/or sensory disabilities, symptoms of gross disorganization, presence of hallucinations, hebephrenia, flat affect, and a positive family history are all significant indications of a possible schizophrenic disturbance. Measures such as the PIMRA may be helpful in both confirming these symptoms and disconfirming the presence of competing disorders.

Although persons with mild mental retardation may be evaluated on the current DSM-III-R criteria, it is crucial to conduct the assessment with a focus on developmentally appropriate behavior. For example, we assessed a client whom staff had observed talking to himself and telling others that he "was returned from heaven by the angels." We found that the client was exhibiting a developmentally and culturally appropriate coping response following the death of his grandmother, though he had previously been diagnosed as exhibiting a psychotic manic episode. We obtained independent psychiatric evaluations by a clinical psychologist and a neuropsychiatrist, both clinically familiar with a developmentally disabled population. They sought and found disconfirming evidence regarding the previous diagnosis, including information about the client's overall degree of organization, sleep habits, and appetite; his previous functioning and family history; and the familial and cultural context in which he lived. The client, raised in a deeply religious home, had, as mentioned earlier, recently experienced the death of his lifelong primary caretaker, his maternal grandmother. Following a time of initial sadness, anxiety, and dysphoria, his symptoms provided him with a means of expressing to himself and others that his grandmother was safe in heaven and that he must continue on earth without her and return to his work and previous level of productivity.

Affective Disorders

Unipolar depression often goes unrecognized in persons with mental retardation because behaviors of passivity, isolation, and anhedonia are often viewed as part of the expected repertoire of such persons. Because most researchers support a diathesis/stress model of depression, knowledge of current stressors may be helpful in assessing depression. Depressed persons functioning in the mild range of retardation may be expected to exhibit symptoms similar to those of depressed persons in general—for instance, sad mood, low self-esteem, and somatic or neurovegetative symptoms. Chronic behavior difficulties, such as poor impulse control, hyperactivity, aggression, and self-stimulatory behaviors, may increase in intensity.

Rating scales designed to measure depression among the general population have recently been used with some success for mentally retarded adults. Kazdin, Matson, and Senatore (1983), for example, found significant correlations between the Beck Depression Inventory (Beck, Ward, Mendelson, Mock, & Erbaugh, 1961), the Zung Self-Rating Depression Scale (Zung, 1965), and their revised adaptations of these scales for a mentally retarded population. In addition, both self-report instruments showed positive correlations with clinical diagnoses for this population.

Measures of depression-related cognitive and coping deficits—such as frequency of automatic negative statements about the self (Hollon & Kendall, 1980), lack of reinforcing activities, and cognitive distortions (Dysfunctional Attitude Scale; Weissman, 1979)—can also be used with mentally retarded persons, albeit with caution because few measures have been validated with reference to this population. One exception is the Problem-Solving Role-Play Task (Nezu et al., 1991), which helps to evaluate use of relevant problem-solving skills in particular situations. This measure consists of five interpersonal problem situations (e.g., making new friends, resolving conflicts) commonly experienced by people with mental retardation. The examiner reads the problem description to the subject and, to control for individual preferences, specifies the goal for each problem (e.g., "Your goal is to make a new friend"). The subject then responds verbally to a series of questions concerning his or her means of problem resolution (e.g., "What is the actual problem?" "What are some things you can do to solve this problem?"). All answers are audiotaped and later rated by two independent coders. This measure proved sensitive to changes in social problem-solving skills with a dually diagnosed adult population (Nezu et al., 1991). However, although problem-solving deficits have been empirically linked to unipolar depression in other populations (Nezu, Nezu, & Perri, 1989), no studies have directly investigated problem-solving skill deficits as a predisposing factor for depression in a sample of developmentally disabled adults.

Individuals with more severe cognitive impairment may exhibit withdrawal and hypomotility, manifesting a symptom pattern similar to that described in the DSM-III-R for a reactive attachment disorder of infancy.

Presence of neurovegetative changes and the melancholic features of weight loss, sleep disturbance, and poor appetite, along with a positive family history and a positive dexamethasone suppression test (DST), may strengthen the hypothesis of biological vulnerability.

Anxiety Disorders

In view of the environmental obstacles faced by people with developmental disabilities, it is probable that chronic frustration with tasks, social labeling and ridicule, low expectations from significant others, and fear of novel situations all contribute to the high prevalence of anxiety disorders. Various self-report rating scales and fear inventories can provide a baseline against which to measure symptom severity.

Physiological assessment can also shed light on anxiety disorders. Although measurement of heart rate, muscle tension, and skin conductance may meet with resistance from a client unfamiliar with the equipment being used, evaluation of physiologic indices of anxiety and correlation with cognitive symptoms can provide insight into the maintenance of symptoms and offer guidance in the choice of treatment alternatives. For example, a client's ease in adjusting to the use of physiologic measures may suggest that he or she will be able to work with a biofeedback protocol.

With less verbal clients, observation of the individual's exposure to stimuli associated with reactive or avoidant behavior can reveal patterns of anxiety-provoking antecedent situations.

Personality Disorders

It is not surprising that, in an outpatient clinic sample of developmentally disabled adults, we found approximately 35% with personality disorders (Nezu, Miescher, & Solgan, 1989). It is possible that the combination of deficits (e.g., cognitive, physical, social) common in individuals with mental retardation results in a predisposition to personality disorders. For people with limited intellectual resources, the harmful effects of institutional or rejecting environments—where individuals have only minimal opportunities to understand their environment, form positive self-concepts, or cope in interpersonal situations—may be exacerbated.

When a referral is based on behavior patterns that appear self-defeating, tend to undercut positive relationships, and reflect a generalized way of interpreting social experiences (and when other diagnostic considerations are ruled out), a diagnosis of personality disorder may be likely. The individual with this type of disturbance is frequently attempting to integrate into a society without the benefit of early structure, support, or intervention. The clinician should focus on evaluating realistic goals, assessing skill deficits as well as strengths, and establishing a collaborative therapeutic relationship.

Substance abuse, which may result from attempted self-medication for distress or peer group influence, may be present and require a separate assessment focus.

Psychosexual Disorders

In a sample of 543 cases of dual diagnosis at the Nebraska Psychiatric Institute, including equal numbers of males and females across the lifespan, approximately 6% of the patients were found to exhibit psychosexual disorders (Menolascino, 1988). The investigators posited years of societal segregation, institutionalization, and lack of sex education as possible etiological factors. Important areas of assessment with such individuals would be social skill deficits, deficits in sex education, and availability of alternatives for sexual satisfaction.

Although psychosexual dysfunction is a relatively infrequent diagnosis among dually diagnosed clients, it merits attention. The AIDS epidemic has created a significant health risk for anyone who engages in sexual behavior without adequate AIDS prevention training.

Aggressive/Destructive Behavior Disorders

Aggressive behavior, in which the focus of aggression may be other people, property, or the client himself or herself (self-injurious behavior), is one of the most common reasons for mental health referral. Aggression may be one symptom in a more inclusive disorder or syndrome; thus, symptoms of aggression may provide evidence for almost any diagnosis. In addition, aggression may be a learned manner of coping with the environment or communicating unpleasant affective states, or it may indicate a neurologic condition, including partial complex seizure activity or toxic delirium. For certain psychiatric diagnostic categories, however, aggressive behavior is a chief defining characteristic. These categories include disruptive behavior disorders (e.g., conduct disorder), disorders of impulse control (e.g., intermittent explosive disorder), and personality disorders (e.g., antisocial personality disorder, borderline personality disorder). In the case of such a disorder, it is likely that the aggressive behavior itself will be a focus of direct intervention. Although individuals with aggressive disorders are often referred under crisis circumstances (e.g., emergency hospitalization following an escalation of behavior), it is extremely important to follow the guidelines outlined previously for a comprehensive assessment of the behavior. In the absence of careful assessment, arbitrary trials of neuroleptic medication and crisis behavior management strategies usually do little to remedy behavioral difficulties; in fact, they may actually exacerbate the problems. For example, neuroleptic medication can have untoward side effects and reduce cognitive functioning; arbitrary behavior modification plans may confuse and frustrate a client.

INITIAL CLINICAL DIAGNOSTIC FORMULATION

When the four assessment components have been completed in a clinical decision-making framework, the data may be summarized and integrated into a comprehensive problem analysis. The information obtained from history, interview, observation, screening, psychological testing, and laboratory work may be used to separate facts from assumptions, confirm or disconfirm initial hypotheses, and examine the client's strengths and deficits. A list of the important variables contributing to the client's difficulties, including those requiring further assessment, may be compiled. At the point of diagnostic formulation, hypotheses concerning functional or causal relationships among these variables are generated. As a final step in initial assessment, we have found it useful to depict this formulation with a Clinical Pathogenesis Map (CPM; cf. Nezu & Nezu, 1989b). A sample CPM is presented as Figure 3.2. This procedure integrates a visual representation of the functional relationship among the client's characteristics (including biological/genetic makeup, physical condition, developmental and social learning history, current resources and deficits, motivational or reinforcement characteristics, and potential for learning social and coping skills) with an assessment of the client's physical and psychosocial environment and caregiving system. The latter two areas are covered in the following chapters.

SUMMARY

In this chapter we presented a multimatrix assessment strategy for clients with mental retardation and symptoms of mental illness. We suggested an approach to evaluation that combines the use of a formal differential diagnostic method with behavior analysis. These historically divergent paths to assessment may provide the most comprehensive clinical mapping of individual difficulties, thus contributing to efficacious treatment plans.

We also underscored the importance of assessing functional relationships as key to understanding a wide variety of behavioral disorders. Indeed, research based upon functional analysis has indicated that many different variables can control or maintain target behavior problems. For example, maladaptive behavioral responses can be reinforced with positive attention, access to tangible materials or activities, or client-specific sensory stimulation. In addition, aberrant behavior can be contingently reinforced through escape from task demands and avoidance of aversive stimuli, or socially learned by observation of other clients. Finally, specific stimulus conditions or organic states can provide a triggering mechanism for various pathological behaviors.

We advocated that all available information from medical, developmental, psychological, and intellectual spheres be considered as important sources of data when conducting an assessment of the individual client. Specific suggestions for synthesizing these various sources of data with regard to different diagnostic groups was also provided.

Chapter 5

Assessment of the Caregiving System

INTRODUCTION

John, a 39-year-old man with concomitant diagnoses of autism and mental retardation, was referred to an outpatient psychiatric clinic following an explosive episode at his group residence. The incident involved a staff member who had been injured and hospitalized as a result of the client's attack. John was labeled hostile and aggressive following the attack. The staff incident report stated that he was uncontrollable and dangerous to others and had been referred for psychiatric evaluation. His placement in the group residence became tenuous. It was later discovered that John had maintained a history of compliance and hard work at the residence, whereas the staff member had been dismissed for stealing money from residents, being physically aggressive toward them, and abusing drugs and alcohol. Our clinical team wanted to know why the resident had been referred for evaluation instead of the staff member.

Although John's situation was highly unusual, it does underscore the importance of carefully assessing the client's caregiving system. This means examining competencies, weaknesses, and systemic issues that may be operationally involved in the client's initial referral problems.

Clinical service to persons with mental retardation and concomitant psychiatric difficulties often involves simultaneous, collaborative, or even therapeutic work with their caregivers. This treatment focus is especially important given the national deinstitutionalization movement, in which efforts have been directed at maintaining developmentally disabled persons in community settings.

Effective therapeutic intervention requires a sensitivity to the clinical issues that may result from living with and caring for a person with mental retardation. For example, unique adaptation is required of parents rearing a child who remains dependent, engages in stereotypic or self-injurious behaviors, and exhibits multiple delays in adaptive skills or severe communication deficits. Frequently, entire family systems evolve around the stresses of intensive medical care, shock, guilt, and overwhelming demands on family resources. The clinician must often make difficult diagnostic discriminations—for instance, assessing whether a family's current interactional system represents a helpful adaptation to stress or a dysfunctional core needing therapeutic restructuring that will also help the client to function better.

Over the past two decades, increasing numbers of researchers have begun to study the stressors faced by families and caregivers of persons with mental retardation (Cameron & Orr, 1989; Nihira, Myers, & Mink, 1980; Orr, Cameron, & Day, 1991; Wikler, 1986). Their studies have examined factors that may improve a family's ability to cope with the stress of caring for a developmentally disabled child, as well as factors that may exacerbate a family's difficulties. A recent study by Orr et al. (1991), for example, showed that the effectiveness of external resources in reducing harmful stress within the family appears to depend on the way the caregivers define and interpret the child's needs, level of functioning, problem behaviors, and other individual characteristics. In addition, Cameron and Orr (1989) found that some caregivers appear capable of reframing their child's disability in a positive context, thus reducing distress within the caregiving system. Successful intervention with families of clients with dual disabilities, then, is often related to the way the disability is perceived and the way therapeutic resources are used.

Many issues regarding assessment of family systems may be generalized to community caregiving systems as well. For instance, in line with a stress/coping model proposed by Zeitlin, Williamson, and Rosenblatt (1987), issues of burnout, feelings of incompetence, bureaucracy problems, and staff turnover may be affected by the beliefs, expectations, and values that serve as a filter through which stressors are processed. Such attitudinal factors may have significant impact on specific interventions, such as behavioral treatment plans.

This chapter will offer guidelines for assessment strategies that view the dually diagnosed client as part of an interactional system. There are two overall parts to the assessment: (a) a systems evaluation of the extended family and/or agency, including a "reality check" regarding the expectations, attributions, emotions, and behaviors of the system's members as well as a stress/coping evaluation of those who most often interact with the client and (b) an assessment of the caregivers' competency in behavior management skills. These two approaches are used to identify elements in the caregiving system that require change for the greater therapeutic benefit of the patient.

EVALUATION OF THE CAREGIVING SYSTEM

We define *caregivers* to include persons in the client's environment or natural milieu who are responsible for supervising, training, making resources available, delivering reinforcement, and providing social interaction. Because a client may be involved with many caregivers at any one time (e.g., at home or in a group residence, day treatment setting, workshop, or recreational center), we define the *caregiving system* as the constellation of active caregiving participants in the client's life.

The Need for Assessment of Caregivers

Before the national deinstitutionalization movement, the major alternative available to caregivers of dually diagnosed individuals was residential placement (institutionalization). However, with the national trend toward keeping persons with mental retardation in the community, it is not surprising that research has focused on ways to prevent such persons from returning to institutions. Research examining caregivers' decisions about residential placement alternatives appears related to two points. First, client characteristics, such as intelligence and adaptive functioning, are highly associated with the decision to seek placement (Sherman & Joseph, 1984). Because of the presence of adaptive behavioral problems, the client with dual diagnosis would seem to be at increased risk for being unable to integrate into a community setting. However, other research indicates that client characteristics alone do not fully explain why some individuals are institutionalized whereas others successfully remain in the community (Sexton, 1980). In a recent review of the literature on the effects of stress in families of developmentally disabled persons and these families' decisions regarding institutional placement, Sherman and Joseph (1984) conclude that the caregivers' ultimate decision to institutionalize a family member is a function of a complex set of interrelationships among factors. In addition to the client's intelligence and adaptive functioning, such factors include the quality of the caregivers' family and marital relationships, the kind and degree of social support available, and the caregivers' use of available support services. We believe that any assessment of the dually diagnosed client that neglects these factors is incomplete and will likely lead to ineffective treatment planning.

The Goal of Assessment

The goal of assessing the caregiving system is to aid in the development of the least restrictive (Turnbull, 1981) therapeutic milieu for the person with a dual diagnosis. This development is crucial to facilitate reinforcement of newly developed coping resources and prevention of relapse following treatment. There are many advantages to assessing the caregiving system as part of a multicomponent evaluation: (a) the transferring of therapeutic gains from the clinic to the home may be facilitated; (b) caregivers can be potent reinforcers of adaptive behavior changes and can provide ongoing follow-up to treatment; (c) caregivers may themselves need treatment, and assessment improves their access to therapeutic resources; (d) fewer professional staff members may be needed for treatment if caregivers become actively involved; and (e) many caregivers can be taught to apply principles of behavior change effectively.

Potential Problem Areas

Specific problems within many caregiving systems may be obstacles to effective treatment and are thus important to target during assessment. These problems include (a) poor integration of multiple systems; (b) deficits in caregivers' behavior management skills; (c) coping skills deficits that result in the caregivers' feelings of burnout, anxiety, depression, and inadequacy; (d) frequent staff turnover in community residential facilities; and (e) difficulties inherent in navigating government and private service systems. The presence of such problems is often related to confusion about the roles of different members of the caregiving system.

Confusion Regarding Caregiver Roles

Any professional who has worked with developmentally disabled clients and their families can attest to the unique experiences shared by such families.

> They are people who share the impact of the disability. . . .
> They experience the same stigma, the same celebrations of
> accomplishment, and many of the same stresses as the
> person with the disability, in addition to the stresses unique
> to themselves. . . . Families share the sorrows and the
> triumphs that disabilities bring. Thus, service providers are
> gradually broadening their definition of client to include the
> whole family. (Summers, 1988, p. 79)

Different mental health professionals, however, have held conflicting views of dually diagnosed clients' caregiving systems. In one view, the caregiving system is part of the problem or a source of the client's difficulties. In another view, the family are victims who are in need of resources and help themselves. Still other professionals view the family as a source of love and attention crucial to the client's learning of adaptive skills and adjustment to the environment. Finally, family and staff members may be viewed as part of the clinical team. In this view, caregivers are paraprofessionals who can provide continual therapeutic resources for the client. With professional service providers holding so many different views, it is hardly surprising that caregivers experience confusion over their own roles.

We have seen all of these attributed roles operational at different times, in different caregiving systems. An important task during assessment of any caregiving system, therefore, is a determination of the roles that are most appropriate within that system. Some caregivers may best be seen as clients themselves, and treatment may focus on increasing their adaptation to the disability. Other caregivers may exhibit strengths that would allow them to serve as significant paraprofessional resources. Treatments for members of caregiving systems may be largely educational and involve training in specific behavior management skills. In the clinical decision-making framework outlined earlier, the clinician's perception of a caregiver's role represents a problem to be solved. We will provide guidelines for assessment of caregivers in the context of some of their roles.

Caregivers and Problem Etiology

Integrating concepts from Engel's (1977) biopsychosocial model and from critical theory (Riegel, 1975), Levitas and Gilson (1990) explain how the caregiving system itself may at times contribute to the client's psychological problems. These authors describe a

> developmental pathway in which the primary psychosocial deficit of mental retardation interacts with familial-cultural variables over time to produce a secondary psychosocial deficit characterized by an atypical sense of self, deficits in self-regulation, extreme ambivalence toward autonomy and other related features. (p. 72)

Levitas and Gilson underscore the important influence of caregivers in the life of a developmentally disabled child—an influence often greater than it would be for a nondisabled peer. The child with mental retardation often needs caregivers not only to guide experiences of events, but also to guide his or her feelings about these experiences. Because of this relationship, evaluation should address caregivers' thoughts, feelings, and perceptions regarding the client's symptoms and behavioral difficulties. Beliefs and attributions within the caregiving system can affect the way an individual learns to cope with his or her own behavioral strengths and limitations, as well as the way he or she views others. When the beliefs and behaviors of individual caregivers are discrepant (e.g., an overprotective parent versus an emotionally distant sibling) or whole systems themselves are discrepant (e.g., a treating physician who views the client's behavioral dyscontrol as neurologically based versus group home staff who view the difficulties as manipulative), the client's distress is likely to increase. In such a case, the caregiving system may be viewed as part of the client's problem.

As therapists for dually diagnosed clients, we have experienced such distress ourselves when facing cognitive, behavioral, or emotional discrepancies among multiple caregiving systems. Consider the following case example of a referral to our outpatient clinic.

Laura, a 27-year-old woman with moderate mental retardation, had become a battleground for control between her mother and sister. Each believed she was protecting the client from the controlling influences of the other. Further, staff members at Laura's group residence were investing their energies in protecting Laura from both family members. Laura's anxiety was often overwhelming. Her symptoms included hypervigilance, paranoid ideation, obsessive-compulsive behavior, and aggression. We were very frustrated in attempting to develop therapeutic targets that would be meaningful to all caregivers. Two important goals of intervention were increasing the family members' motivation to change and orienting the group home staff to work with rather than to punish or avoid the family.

Functional Systems Assessment Strategies

In functional assessments of caregiving systems, we have found it helpful to use assessment procedures from functional family therapy approaches (Alexander & Parsons, 1982). Functional family assessment, based on the family systems literature, focuses on the interaction of the system's members. Two of its strategies are (a) evaluating interactions in the here and now, during both office visits and milieu observations, and (b) identifying functions of the client's behavior for each system member as well as for the client. In Laura's case, for example, the client's aggression toward her mother during home visits served different functions for the various caregivers. For Laura's sister, the aggression confirmed the validity of her own anger toward their mother and reinforced her attempts to separate Laura and herself from the parent. The sister frequently supported Laura's aggressive behavior as "understandable." For the mother, the aggression reinforced a belief that Laura was indeed too sick to live at home and allayed feelings of guilt at having placed her daughter in a group residence. For the residence staff, the aggression reinforced a notion that Laura's home visits were too upsetting and that they should be dropped from the client's treatment plan. Staff members also anticipated that our treatment team would support their decision to limit family contact. Even though Laura missed her family very much, her behavior had come to provide a means by which she could simultaneously separate from her mother, maintain a relationship with her sister, and live with some autonomy. Further, members of her various caregiving systems could maintain their own fixed beliefs and attributions and invest little energy in their own change processes, while still pursuing the goal of Laura's independence from her family.

Functional systems assessment often involves examining the behavioral, affective, and cognitive means by which members of the system try to reach their goals for relationships with other members. Each individual's behaviors, affects, and cognitive functions combine with those of other members to engender specific relational sequences with predictable payoffs for each member (Alexander, Barton, Waldron, & Mas, 1982). Payoffs take a variety of forms, but all represent some blend of attempts at closeness (or merging) and distance (or separating). They represent the psychological space a person tries to create in a relationship with another. Behavioral sequences that help an individual reach his or her goals may have positive or negative consequences for the client or other family members. In Laura's case, for example, learning job skills and fighting with her mother could both be considered attempts at separating; however, the second alternative has obvious negative consequences.

A third strategy in functional systems assessment is identifying all relationships involved in problematic behavior sequences. Laura, for example, had become the scapegoat for her fellow residents' behavioral difficulties. When other residents were questioned regarding their own acts of impulsivity or aggression, they would frequently respond, "Laura was acting out and got me upset."

To conduct a functional systems analysis, the therapist needs to enter the system in a way that both establishes rapport and elicits information. This requires observation of interactive behavior in both the treatment context and the natural setting.

Tactics of Functional Systems Assessment

To enter a family or staff's frame of reference, the interviewer needs to appear both empathic and credible. The problems of caregivers' resistance to change, discrepancies between systems, and conflicting expectations regarding treatment should be understood in terms of their *functions*, not merely viewed as troublesome hindrances. The therapist's approach to such difficulties can have a decisive impact on the assessment process. A warm, nonjudgmental style and a sense of humor will help the therapist join with a family group or reframe a caregiver's behavior in a more positive light.

In assessing the caregiving system, the therapist looks at the stages of the system's development; its structure, size, and economic resources; its ethnicity; and the individual characteristics of its members (e.g., age, sex, race, religious values, history, intellectual/emotional status). After taking a history, the therapist can use various self-report measures to identify the strengths and weaknesses of system members regarding such areas as emotional distress (e.g., anxiety, depression), marital and other relationship problems, degree of burnout, sense of hopelessness, problem-solving and other cognitive coping skills, use of available resources, and understanding of mental retardation as well as concomitant diagnoses. For example, we recently worked with a mother who was mature and intelligent, with highly adaptive coping skills. Although she was well educated about her son's developmental disability, she was relatively naive about his secondary diagnosis of schizophrenia. This lack of knowledge left her confused, and she became frightened by his symptoms and need for medication.

Several instruments designed to assess emotional distress, marital and family adjustment, level of current life stress, and coping skills within the general population are also helpful in evaluating members of care-giving systems. Measures focused on marital relationships include the Dyadic Adjustment Scale (Spanier, 1976), the Marital Satisfaction Inventory (Snyder, 1979), and the Relationship Beliefs Inventory (Eidelson & Epstein, 1982). For individuals, measures such as the Anxiety Disorders Interview Schedule–Revised (DiNardo et al., 1985) and the Beck Depression Inventory (Beck et al., 1961) may corroborate specific distress symptoms observed by the interviewer. To assess general life stress, an instrument such as the Life Experiences Survey (Sarason, Johnson, & Siegel, 1978) could be used. We cannot list all instruments currently available to assess all possible symptoms of emotional or rela-tionship distress among family or staff caregivers. However, we can emphasize the importance of examining the caregivers' individual and collective abilities to contribute to a therapeutic milieu for the dually diagnosed client. The caregivers may have multiple roles that are impli-cated in the client's disability. They may be contributing to the client's difficulties through their interactions with him or her. They may even need treatment themselves, individually or collectively.

We have found it useful for the interviewer to understand each sys-tem member's problem orientation and learn how each one views the client's difficulties. People with maladaptive problem orientations tend to (a) deny or avoid problems; (b) attribute problems to general, global, and stable personal defects; (c) appraise problems as a serious threat to well-being; (d) appraise problematic situations as unchangeable; (e) ap-praise their own problem-solving or coping abilities negatively; and (f) almost exclusively defer to others for finding solutions to problems. On the other hand, people with facilitative problem orientations tend to (a) recognize problems when they occur; (b) accurately attribute prob-lems to a combination of factors, some of which are changeable; (c) ap-praise problems as challenges or opportunities for benefit; (d) appraise their own problem-solving skills positively; and (e) commit time and energy to the problem-solving process (Nezu & D'Zurilla, 1989; Nezu & Nezu, 1991). One useful self-report method for assessing problem orientation, as well as other problem-solving skills, is the Social Problem-Solving Inventory (SPSI; D'Zurilla & Nezu, 1990).

In addition to individual members of the caregiving system, caregivers' interactions among themselves, as well as with the client, need to be assessed. For example, the literature on marital relationships indicates increased vulnerability to marital conflict and divorce in families of children with disabilities (Kazak & Marvin, 1984). Featherstone (1980) reported on the increased likelihood of marital distress in such families. Specifically, a child's disability may excite powerful emotional reactions in the parents, eliciting a shared view of failure. Siblings are likely to experience added stress as well. Family organization may be reshaped and vulnerability to conflict heightened. Observation of each caregiver's contribution to the system in terms of behavioral, affective, and cognitive processes is essential.

Cognitive processes include belief systems, values, expectations, and personal goals. Affective processes are an individual's emotional reactions. The caregivers' cognitive and affective processes, and their resulting behaviors toward the client and one another, may be linked with the payoffs inherent in certain interactional sequences. In other words, an individual's behavior is likely to be functionally related to his or her personal goals for the relationship. This notion is illustrated by the following case example.

Dave, a 30-year-old male with mild mental retardation, came to an outpatient clinic for evaluation. He was accompanied by his mother, who continued to arrange and finance his leisure activities, do his laundry, and complete his required chores at his supervised apartment despite his assessed capability to live independently. Although Dave was physically robust and adaptively capable, his mother's goals of support and caring were difficult to translate into support for her son's autonomy after years of commitment to his care. Dave's family came to therapy because of his mother's complaint that he "never did anything for himself." Despite his obvious strengths and potential for independent functioning, Dave would frequently complain of feeling "sick" or "tired" and call his mother for help when expected to take care of his own needs.

Simultaneously with Dave's recent move to a supervised apartment, his mother had begun a job that she enjoyed and, for the first time in over 30 years, was actively engaged outside the home. Dave's father, although verbally supportive, had always been responsible for the family income, leaving most of the details of his son's care to his wife. Dave's mother was now trying to maintain her employment while still investing significant energy in Dave's care. This effort often caused her to leave or miss work and feel defeated and less than competent both at home and on the job.

Initially, Dave's mother did not see the functional relationship between her own behavior and her son's "unmotivated" behavior. Challenging her or blaming her for Dave's behavior problem would have been likely to increase her sense of defeat, feelings of anger, and symptoms of burnout. Instead, the therapist reframed Dave's behavior as a metaphor for his mother's obvious feelings of being "tired" or "sick" of all the burdens of responsibility she was experiencing. Upon hearing this new interpretation, the mother responded, "You know, I never thought of it that way, but I never really told my husband how much I resent always being the one to get the calls from Dave at work." The therapist suggested that Dave call his mother for help on weekends and his father on weekdays; Dave's father agreed. Dave responded by saying, "Well, I guess now I'll have to wait until the weekends for help."

Although the therapist saw that the mother's behavior was functionally reinforcing the client's behavior, the choice of a strategic reframing placed Dave's behavior within a context that could prompt behavioral change on the part of Dave's mother. In this way the therapist empathized with her current stress rather than attacking her way of nurturing her son. This example highlights the importance of caregivers' willingness to change their own behavior—an area that needs to be assessed.

Turkewitz (1984) has outlined several key interview questions that can be helpful in clarifying problems within a family context. Although these questions were designed for assessment of family problems involving nonretarded children and adolescents, we have found them applicable in conceptualizing the developmentally disabled client's problem in a systems context. The following questions, adapted from Turkewitz's list, can help the therapist identify particularly important system variables.

1. Are the caregivers' report and understanding of the client's behavioral and emotional problems accurate?

2. Are all of the problems currently experienced in the caregiving system seen to result from the client's difficulties?

3. Is the client's behavior different from that of developmentally similar peers? If not, what are some of the caregivers' reasons for viewing the client as the "one with the problem"? For example, are caregiver expectations and attributions concerning the client unrealistic or overly critical?

4. What are the differences between the client's experiences and those of peers or siblings?

5. Do any family factors or characteristics contribute to the development of the client's problems?

6. Have caregivers treated this person differently than developmentally similar peers or siblings? Are they continuing to do so?

7. How do other individuals within this system react to family or system stress?

8. How do various members of the caregiving system cope with problems in general? Are ineffective or dysfunctional patterns

present? Will any family members experience significant losses (e.g., of responsibility, status, self-esteem, companionship) if the client's difficulties are resolved?

9. What is the quality of peer or sibling relationships? How do peers or siblings react to the client's problem behavior? Is the problem behavior precipitated or elicited by other members of the system?

10. How do system members communicate with one another? Are they clear and direct? Do they provide positive reinforcement concerning adaptive and social behavior? Do they attempt to engage the client in conflict or to defuse tension by focusing on the client? What are the client's reactions to conflict, if present?

11. What are the hierarchical arrangements within the caregiving system? Are caregivers supportive of one another?

12. Is the client exposed to anger or hostility among caregivers? Is the client often in the middle of these conflicts?

13. Are caregiver problems present (i.e., behavioral, cognitive, affective) that impede this system's provision of adaptive social learning experiences for the client?

If assessment reveals undesirable interactions between caregivers and client, it can be helpful to find ways of reframing client behavior that will (a) prompt caregiver behavior change and (b) be compatible with the involved caregiver's worldview and personal reality. This is particularly important when a caregiver's behavior directly impacts on the client's behavior. For example, it would be unrealistic to expect a direct care worker at a group home to set limits or extinguish a patient's troublesome behavior if the worker attributes the problem behavior to brain damage and thus sees it as uncontrollable.

Despite a 20-year trend toward training parents and community caregivers in behavior management skills, in practice there is often little attention to the type of systems assessment described. For example, a mother was recently referred to one of the authors for behavioral parent training after an unsuccessful attempt at such training in a large university-sponsored parent-training project. The woman was unable to follow the therapists' recommendations of behavioral strategies to use at home with regard to her 4-year-old developmentally disabled daughter's aggressive tantrums. What the project's clinical team had overlooked was that the mother had recently been diagnosed as HIV positive and thus faced a very poor health prognosis. This mother had attempted to comply with the team's instructions but was overwhelmed with guilt over her illness, worry about her daughter's future care, and anger at having to spend what she viewed as precious little time setting firm limits to her daughter's behavior. The behavior modification instructions could be seen as directly conflicting with the mother's agenda of achieving a close and eternal relationship with her daughter. Obviously, the lack of attention to these emotional issues was implicated in the failure of the previous intervention.

Summary of Functional Assessment

Although many theories situate an individual's behavioral difficulties within a family systems context, all systems theories share the basic tenet that the interpersonal context is critical in determining a client's behavior (Turkewitz, 1984). Evaluating the function of each individual's behavior within a caregiving system can help identify system changes that will result in a more therapeutic environment for the client. We have presented a general strategy for determining the personal goals and agendas of all members of the client's system and have suggested specific tactics for implementing this assessment strategy. Functional family assessment is particularly useful when other system members are seen as needing treatment themselves or as contributing to the client's target problems.

When caregivers are approached with a concern for the systemic issues just described, an initial evaluation may uncover unique strengths in the caregiving system. In such a case, caregivers may be considered valuable potential members of the clinical team. They may be asked to collaborate in developing treatment goals and to become involved in carrying out the actual treatment. At this point, the focus of assessment shifts to the caregivers' abilities to implement behavioral strategies. Even when an evaluation of the caregiving system shows that caregivers have mutual support, commitment to facilitating client progress, and the resources to positively reinforce adaptive behavior, they may lack the skills required to modify problem behavior. Because it is now commonly acknowledged that parents and caregivers can be effective agents in behavioral treatment (Harris, 1984), the following section will focus on this important assessment area of caregiver competency.

ASSESSMENT OF CAREGIVER COMPETENCY

Attempts by mental health professionals to train parents or caregivers in teaching, managing, and ameliorating behavior have gained momentum over the past few decades (Breiner & Beck, 1984; Graziano, 1977; Wells & Forehand, 1981). This application of behavior therapy, which includes the active and often direct participation of caregivers trained in paraprofessional roles, has been called one of the most important developments in child mental health (Graziano, 1977). The rationale for this form of treatment emphasizes the availability of natural caregivers (Griffin, 1979; Karlsruher, 1974), the effectiveness of the approach (Tavormina, 1975; Weitz, 1981), and its potential as a community prevention resource (Hanson, 1977; Petronko, Anesko, Nezu, & Pos, 1989; Weitz, 1981). Caregivers of persons with developmental disabilities seem to be a particularly important population to target for behavior modification training. Indeed, those caregivers have been trained to implement behavioral treatments for such problems as self-injury, self-stimulation, and aggression, as well as to teach new, adaptive behaviors (Harris, 1984).

Because maladaptive behaviors are so often present in clients with dual diagnoses, adequate training for caregivers could represent a critical resource for an individual's community adaptation. However, because many such clients present behavioral difficulties that challenge even trained professionals, some authors are troubled by inadequate assessment of caregivers' behavior management skills (Nezu & Petronko, 1985; Sapon-Shevin, 1982). Although past research has focused on developing effective ways to teach parents and caregivers the needed skills (cf. Graziano, 1977; Moreland, Schwebel, Beck, & Wells, 1982; O'Dell, 1974), the technology for assessing those skills has not kept pace with the training programs (Budd & Fabry, 1984; Sanders & James, 1983). There are few measurement tools for evaluating the appropriateness of a caregiver training "prescription." In addition, measurement strategies are needed for the clinical evaluation of caregivers who receive training in behavior management strategies.

Until recently, little attention has been paid to research involving systematic and direct observation of caregivers' change during their participation in behavioral training programs. In their review of the literature, Moreland et al. (1982) stated that approximately two-thirds of the reports in professional journals did not include information about actual changes in parent/caregiver behavior. More specifically, in a review concerning paraprofessional training, Balch and Solomon (1976) called for more research directed toward the development of behavioral criterion scales related to a variety of real-life situations. Although several structured observations have attempted to assess caregiver responses as a measure of training (cf. Budd, Riner, & Brockman, 1983), no observational system has empirically determined which criterion behaviors would constitute caregiver competency in implementing behavior management strategies. Moreover, no such attempts have been specifically directed toward caregivers of persons with mental retardation and concomitant behavior difficulties, even though previous authors have emphasized the need to develop the response content of assessment measures empirically before using them to evaluate treatment outcome (Goldfried & D'Zurilla, 1969; McFall, 1976; Sanders & James, 1983).

A Systematic Approach:
The Behavioral Role-Play Activities Test (BRAT)

Because of the dearth of appropriate assessment instruments, we will describe in detail one such measure: the Behavioral Role-Play Activities Test (BRAT; Nezu et al., 1990). The BRAT is an empirically derived measure of behavior management skills needed by caregivers of persons with developmental disabilities and concomitant behavioral disturbance. It was designed for maximum relevance to the population assessed, generalizability as an assessment device, and content validity. In addition, initial reliability and validity studies have addressed the BRAT's overall psychometric properties. Use of an observational instrument such as the BRAT provides a data-based measure of competency that lets the clinician pinpoint weaknesses in caregivers' "hands-on" behavior management skills.

Content of the BRAT

The BRAT, reproduced in the Appendix, consists of six structured role-play situations that assess a caregiver's competency in implementing particular behavioral management procedures to modify certain target behaviors. Each situation, or subtest, assesses a different behavioral strategy. The structured situations require the assistance of a collaborator, who portrays a developmentally disabled person in various situational contexts. The situations were scripted to represent common referral problems of persons with dual diagnoses (e.g., verbal and physical aggression, self-injurious behavior, poor self-help skills).

For each subtest, the caregiver receives a written description of the problem behavior, the situational context in which it occurs, and the intended goal. On the basis of this information, the caregiver is directed, within the structured role-play, to use a particular behavior management skill as a means of attaining the goal. Each subtest lasts 5 minutes and can be videotaped for later scoring, although initial results of a current investigation suggest that the measure may also be scored live as it is administered (Moore, Basquill, Nezu, & Nezu, 1991). The BRAT yields a score for each subtest, or skill area, as well as an overall score.

Development of the BRAT

Development of the BRAT was guided by the behavioral-analytic model of test construction (Goldfried & D'Zurilla, 1969). This model encompasses five steps: (a) situational analysis, (b) response enumeration, (c) response evaluation, (d) instrument construction and development of measurement format, and (e) psychometric evaluation. The behavioral-analytic model of test construction can be used to develop observational measures for many different assessment targets. For the benefit of readers who may wish to develop sorely needed instruments related to any area of concern discussed in the chapters on assessment, we will describe the development of the BRAT according to these five steps.

Step 1: Situational Analysis

This first step in construction of the instrument included two tasks: (a) identifying and selecting skill areas that represent behaviors of competent caregivers and (b) selecting typical client behaviors to be portrayed in specific stimulus contexts.

Selection of caregiver skill areas. The skill areas to be assessed were initially generated from two sources: research literature on parent and caregiver training, and published parent and staff training manuals. Although an exhaustive treatment of skills taught in caregiver training programs was beyond the scope of this project, we tried to include the skills that were consistently represented in both sources (e.g., Becker, 1971; Foxx, 1982; Patterson & Guillion, 1971; Rettig, 1973). The six skills chosen were (a) extinction, (b) shaping of new behavior through successive approximations, (c) differential reinforcement of incompatible behavior (DRI), (d) delivery of contingent positive reinforcement, (e) time-out, and (f) use of verbal cues and physical prompts.

Selection of client target behaviors. This task entailed constructing situational examples of behavioral problems typically encountered by caregivers of persons with dual diagnoses. In addition, each situation would include structured environmental antecedents to create equal opportunity for appropriate response across subjects. We reviewed behaviors identified by 150 caregivers of persons with mental retardation and coexisting behavioral or psychiatric disorders. These referral behaviors were derived from case summary information obtained over 4 years from a university-affiliated caregiver training program, Project Natural Setting Therapeutic Management (NSTM; Petronko et al., 1989).

Of the 150 behaviors, the most frequently occurring ones included aggression, tantruming, self-injurious behavior, noncompliance, and deficiencies in self-help skills (e.g., self-feeding, toileting, dressing). These behaviors are the prevalent referral behaviors of persons with developmental disabilities (Neisworth & Madle, 1982). This initial pool of target behaviors, incorporated in situational role-plays, would create relevant antecedents for competent caregiver responses. Therapists associated with the university-sponsored program rated these referral problems within various situational contexts to determine their relevance to real-life situations. This aided us in designing valid role-plays or vignettes: The target behaviors that occurred most frequently were embedded in situations that were rated most relevant by the project therapists.

Each proposed role-play was developed to provide a structured situation in which a caregiver could demonstrate a particular behavior management skill. Further, each skill could be implemented in the context of a common behavior problem. Each role-play vignette included the following components: (a) a description of the target behavior, (b) the purpose and description of the behavioral strategy to be implemented, and (c) the situational context or activity in which the behavior occurred. The situations were constructed to focus caregiver responses: A certain behavior might elicit a wide range of appropriate caregiver responses in different situational contexts.

Step 2: Response Enumeration

During the second step in instrument construction, empirically derived, operational definitions of caregiver skills were developed. The purpose of this step was to outline a combination of observable caregiver role-play responses that demonstrated each skill being assessed. This procedure was similar to a task analysis or an enumeration of all behavioral responses that would demonstrate competency in each skill. The procedure of developing a universe of possible desirable responses has been advocated for constructing observational systems in general (Haynes & Kerns, 1979). It is this developmental step in particular that distinguishes the BRAT from other recently designed observational assessments of caregiver training programs (cf. Budd, Riner, & Brockman, 1983; Forehand & McMahon, 1981; Weitz, 1981).

To develop this universe of responses, we gave a written description of each role-play scene and of each caregiver skill to be measured to seven therapists experienced in parent or staff training. All were asked to read each role-play description carefully, considering both the context of the client's behavior and the skill to be applied by the caregiver, and to generate a list of observable responses that would demonstrate the caregiver's competency in implementing the particular strategy. Specifically, the therapists were asked to imagine themselves in the situation and to generate all the possible responses that they might make in implementing that strategy. For example, the following responses might demonstrate the delivery of positive reinforcement: a pleasant tone of voice; immediate delivery of reinforcement following the desired behavior; and a clear, specific statement of the reason for providing the reinforcement. Finally, the therapists were reminded that each skill was being assessed separately and required a distinct list of caregiver responses. The number of responses generated was left to the discretion of each therapist. A list of responses enumerated for each of the six role-play scenes was compiled for each skill to be assessed.

Step 3: Response Evaluation

In this step of the behavioral-analytic model, the previously generated responses were evaluated for their relevance by a different group of professionals. We sent instructions explaining the purpose of the project to 20 professionals who met the criteria of doctoral level training in psychology and expertise in behavioral caregiver training demonstrated through either clinical practice with this population or scholarly publication in the area. Of the 20 contacted, 14 responded; they were asked to rate each caregiver response for each role-play scene on a 5-point Likert-type scale ranging from 1 (not very important response to demonstrate skill) to 5 (very important response to demonstrate skill). The responses with a mean rating of 3 or greater were selected as involving specific component behaviors of each skill as operationally defined. This procedure yielded the following final numbers of behaviors to be included for the various skills: extinction, 20; shaping, 16; DRI, 18; contingent positive reinforcement, 20; time-out, 20; and cues and prompts, 21. Thus, the total number of items was 115.

Step 4: Instrument Construction and Development of Measurement Format

Developing the instrument and measurement format involved two substeps: constructing standardized role-play scripts and devising a scoring system.

Role-play scripts. The client role-player's performance was standardized: The frequency and intensity of the target referral behavior was predetermined in each role-play script. Thus, each role-play situation contained a specific number of opportunities for the caretaker to demonstrate the skill being assessed.

We viewed several videotapes showing clinical assessment of the most common referral behaviors from Project NSTM (Petronko et al., 1989). Actual dialogue, verbalizations, and physical mannerisms from these videotapes were used to construct the client role-player's scripts. Examples of scripts depicting the various target behaviors were presented to five clinical therapists to be rated for authenticity and face validity. Scripts receiving an average rating of 7 or greater on a scale of 1 to 10 for authenticity (10 representing the most authentic) were randomly selected for inclusion.

Throughout initial evaluation of the BRAT, the same 10-year-old girl served as the role-play collaborator for all skills. This precluded the variance that would have resulted from the use of different actors. The child actor participated in 10 hours of training and practice sessions to achieve standardization and script adherence. Periodic random checks of the actor's adherence rate showed that her performance was highly reliable. For example, 10 videotaped BRAT tests were selected randomly from the psychometric studies and rated by two doctoral students trained for this purpose. The child actor's behavior was monitored at 1-minute intervals and scored for adherence to the scripts. Agreement between raters, interval by interval, was 100%. The role-player's level of accuracy in adhering to the script was found to exceed 97%.

Scoring system for the BRAT. Responses that had met the selection criteria used in the response evaluation phase of development were listed on a standardized scoring sheet for each role-play, together with instructions for scoring the test. When scoring the BRAT, the rater has a stopwatch, a description of each role-play scene, and the client role-player's script, along with the scoring sheet.

In scoring, the rater notes the occurrence (+) or absence (–) of each caregiver response listed on the scoring sheets. The number of (+) responses for each role-play, as well as for the total test, are summed and divided by the total number of possible responses. This yields a percentage score for each of the six skill subtests as well as a total. Percentage scores were used because the subtests contained different numbers of items. Thus, subtest scores are comparable across the BRAT, and the total score reflects an overall percentage (i.e., the number of behaviors actually observed divided by the total number of BRAT items). Higher scores reflect more competent caregiver behavior.

Step 5: Psychometric Evaluation of the BRAT

The last step in the behavioral-analytic model of test construction is an evaluation of the psychometric properties of the instrument. With regard to test-retest reliability, initial studies indicated that BRAT scores of a group of 22 caregivers of children with mental retardation were stable over a 2-month period. Reliability coefficients ranged between .70 and .91 across the BRAT subscales. Estimates of interrater reliability, a particularly important factor in observational procedures, were also high (intraclass coefficients of .94 and .95 for Time 1 and Time 2 of test-retest assessment points, respectively).

Reliability of the BRAT

Estimates of the BRAT's internal consistency indicated an overall high level of item homogeneity (Cronbach's alpha = .82). Item-subscale and item-total correlations (calculated on the second data set) ranged between .59 and .91 (mean of .73). Evaluation of the BRAT's construct, concurrent, and predictive validity was conducted in the context of a prospective treatment outcome study with a second sample of 27 caregivers of individuals with mental retardation.

Construct validity was assessed with specific regard to the BRAT's sensitivity to the effects of parent training. Theoretically, if caregivers are taught certain skills in a behavioral training program, improvement on those skills should be evident by their BRAT scores. Therefore, if the BRAT is a valid measure of competency as achieved through behavioral parent training, then a difference should emerge between a group of caregivers who have been trained and a similar group without benefit of such training. To examine this relationship, we randomly assigned the 27 subjects to one of two conditions: (a) behavioral caregiver training (BCT; n = 13) and (b) a waiting list control (WLC; n = 14). The BCT group participated in a 10-session (2 hours per session) caregiver training program that taught skills in the following areas: methods of defining and operationalizing behaviors, application of operant principles, and problem-solving strategies to aid in program development (Nezu & Petronko, 1985). In general, results indicated that (a) subjects in the BCT group significantly improved from pre- to posttraining, (b) WLC members showed no significant changes from pre- to post-BRAT scores, and (c) BCT subjects had significantly higher BRAT posttest scores than did their WLC counterparts. These results suggest that the BRAT can be a useful outcome measure for behavioral caregiver training, and they provide initial evidence of its construct validity.

In addition to the BRAT, two additional measures were administered at the pre- and posttraining assessment points. These included the Behavioral Vignettes Test–Revised (BVT; Heifetz, Baker, & Wickham-Searl, 1981) and the Behavior Problem Inventory (BPI). The BVT is a 20-item paper-and-pencil measure of one's knowledge of behavioral principles. The BPI, developed for the purpose of this study, rates the frequency, intensity, and resistance to change of the most prominent behavior difficulties experienced by a caregiver.

Although the BVT assesses knowledge of behavioral principles, it does not assess one's ability to implement those principles effectively. However, because it is one of the few tests used to evaluate caregiver change, the relation between the BVT and the BRAT does provide an initial indication of the BRAT's concurrent validity. The correlation between these two measures (based on posttraining scores) was .61, suggesting that the BRAT evidences good concurrent validity.

To address the issue of predictive validity, we hypothesized that changes in BRAT scores would be significantly related to changes in BPI scores. In other words, a caregiver's ability to implement behavioral management strategies competently should be predictive of his or her ratings of the frequency, intensity, and resistance to change of the client's behavior problems. In addition, we hypothesized that this relationship would be stronger than that between BVT and BPI scores. Results of a series of multiple regression analyses supported these hypotheses. Collectively, these results suggest that BRAT scores, which reflect caregiver competency in applying behavior management skills, are a useful predictor of client behavior change, whereas simple knowledge of principles is not.

Because behavioral caregiver training provides a limitless alternative for expanding community-based treatment for developmentally disabled persons with behavioral difficulties, empirically based, generalizable assessment tools are particularly important. Although the BRAT is limited in its assessment to six behavior management skills, it appears to be a promising measure of caregiver competency. We suggest that the BRAT may be useful not only in clinical assessment of strengths and weaknesses concerning the implementation of behavioral management strategies but also in outcome studies in cases where the treatment protocol includes caregiver training.

COMBINING A FUNCTIONAL SYSTEMS ASSESSMENT WITH EVALUATION OF NEED FOR CAREGIVER TRAINING

Although training caregivers in behavior management skills is one powerful means of improving treatment of the dually diagnosed client, several important variables derived from systems evaluation models must be considered before this approach is chosen. Four factors outlined by Gordon and Davidson (1981) exemplify the usefulness of a clinical decision-making model for caregivers of referred clients. First, it is important to assess the degree to which environmental control is possible. For example, in a group home that is poorly staffed, overcrowded, and under-funded, caregivers may not be in a position to alter a client's social environment significantly. In fact, needing relief from daily work burdens, they may have a hidden agenda to fail at such a task. In such a case, targeting the client's environmental characteristics (see chapter 6) for further assessment may be more fruitful.

Second, interpersonal problems among caregivers may preclude their working together. Thus, evaluation of all system members' interactions, discussed previously, is essential. Third, because caregivers are human, they too are vulnerable to various forms of dysfunctional behavior. Personal problems such as depression and anxiety may limit their ability to benefit from skills training. Finally, the client's resources and motivation may suggest different forms of intervention. Matching treatment to client on the basis of individualized assessment is the essence of effective clinical decision making.

SUMMARY

Because many individuals with developmental disabilities remain dependent in some way on caregivers in their community milieu, clinical service to dually diagnosed clients frequently involves assessment of the caregiving system. Such assessment may reveal that members of the caregiving system contribute to the client's difficulties, need treatment themselves, or can, with training, function in a paraprofessional role. We discussed potential advantages and limitations of including caregivers in clinical treatment, as well as specific strategies for clinical assessment of caregivers' skills. To identify the most effective treatments for individual clients, we proposed a comprehensive approach to assessment that takes account of both functional systems variables and caregiver competency in behavior management.

A useful resource for assessing caregiver competency is the Behavioral Role-Play Activities Test (BRAT). The process used in its development can be applied in the construction of other observational assessment measures.

Successful therapy rests on both a comprehensive functional systems analysis and an evaluation of caregivers' competency in behavior management.

Chapter 6

Assessment of the Environment

INTRODUCTION

In addition to the individual client and the caregivers, the environment must also be assessed. Both the physical and the social aspects of a setting can be important in determining functional relationships. The social environment is particularly critical. Often, the relationship between caregiver(s) and client is best understood through the social context in which a particular target behavior occurs. An understanding of the social environment also sheds light on the influences of other clients.

The effect of social environmental factors on client moods and behaviors is often stronger than it appears. Perhaps certain aspects of the environment create frustration; this may help to account for a client's aggression, which previously appeared to have no antecedents. Perhaps there are cliques of clients from which an individual is excluded; this may help to explain chronic dysphoria or low self-esteem.

The physical environment may also hold clues to client behavior. Perhaps the physical plant is uninspiring, deteriorated, or poorly laid out. Perhaps there are sources of physical discomfort. Space may be inadequate or poorly utilized. Such factors can increase frustration or annoyance for staff and clients alike.

A thorough assessment of the environment must also address programmatic variables. Tasks may be too easy or too difficult; methods of instruction may need to be changed. Boredom may be a factor if tasks are too repetitive or monotonous. It may be that schedules are too rigid. All such variables can create an unfavorable environment and trigger negative client reactions. The assessment of programmatic factors must take account of the interaction between the individual and the environment: A setting may not meet the needs of a particular client.

The extent to which treatment plans are tailored to each client in a setting is a key assessment issue.

Continuity across settings must also be examined. For example, are the rules of a day program different from the rules of the client's residence? Is the individual receiving consistent messages in all settings?

The case of Louie. Louie was a 27-year-old man with the diagnoses of moderate mental retardation and paranoid schizophrenia. Having attended a number of programs for individuals with developmental disabilities, Louie was referred to a new program because he was thought to need more structure and supervision.

For the first several days at the new program, Louie was quite friendly and jovial. He appeared to be in excellent spirits. He cooperated with staff, participated in program activities, and behaved appropriately. Staff conducted assessments of his skills for several weeks, then began to transition him into the workshop setting. Initially, Louie made a smooth transition; he seemed interested in the tasks and responded well to staff.

After a few days at the workshop, Louie's behavior changed. He began to have trouble concentrating on tasks and was easily distracted. He became less cooperative with staff. Louie also began to have interpersonal difficulties with peers. He would often complain about other program participants, saying, "He's making fun of me" or "I can't work with him here" and indicating a desire to work alone. Confused by this change in Louie's behavior, staff responded by attempting to calm him and by redirecting him to his work.

Louie's problem behavior continued to escalate. He began focusing on staff members in the room and grew increasingly paranoid and suspicious of both staff and other clients. He accused staff of "doing me in" or "calling me Bugs Bunny." When staff or clients were upsetting him, Louie would often try to make them leave the room. His tone at these times could be quite threatening. One day, during an agitated episode, he threw ceramic craft materials across the room, threatening to punch staff and other clients.

Louie presented a perplexing assessment question: What had been the antecedents of this outburst? What could explain his recent difficulties, especially given that his early adjustment had been problem-free? What environmental or programming variables could have contributed to these episodes?

Because Louie was so new to the setting, it seemed sensible to review records from his previous environment. Those records revealed several interesting pieces of information. The problem of targeting individuals as enemies was not new: Louie had a history of becoming sensitive to the presence of others. Unfamiliar figures were especially difficult for him to tolerate. At the previous program he had frequently become very upset with staff and peers, demanding that they leave the room. Records showed that Louie's former treatment team had often acceded to these demands in an effort to calm him. Staff at the new program, in fact, had been doing the opposite. Instead of complying with Louie's wishes, they were encouraging staff and peers to stay in the room. They reasoned that giving in to his demands would only reinforce his outbursts. In addition, they were beginning the process of desensitizing Louie to the presence of others.

Louie's records also showed that his workload in the previous setting had been minimal. Most of his day had been spent in self-initiated activities. Work demands were rarely made and never enforced. If Louie showed an unwillingness to work at a particular time, demands were lifted. In the new setting, however, Louie's day was organized around goals of productivity. This represented a serious change in daily routine and in level of demand.

This information about Louie's former environment led staff to question whether he needed more assistance in meeting the demands of his new program. Perhaps he needed to be shaped to this higher level of performance. Expectations, therefore, would have to be altered. Staff needed to scale down their immediate expectations of Louie's performance and focus on gradually building his skills. In other words, they needed to tailor the plan for Louie, recognizing his need for reduced demands and for the shaping of work behaviors.

The programmatic environmental assessment yielded much useful information about Louie. It explained some of his recent difficulties, and it produced ideas for treatment planning. To complement the programmatic assessment, staff conducted an assessment of the interpersonal realm and discovered that Louie's behavior was worse when he was working next to John. They recalled that John had lately been experiencing an increase in anxiety symptoms, talking to himself repeatedly and engaging in perseverative speech. He was also beginning to curse under his breath. Staff hypothesized that John's behavior might be exacerbating Louie's discomfort and contributing to his paranoid ideation.

In Louie's case, environmental assessments indicated several avenues of possible intervention. These included alterations in peer groupings and task demands, modified expectations for the present, and shaping of on-task behaviors. Staff members needed to appreciate the discrepancy in expectations for performance between Louie's two settings. They considered explaining some of the differences to him and involving him in the development of a new treatment plan. In this way, they might also increase Louie's sense of trust and support, as well as his understanding of the goals and the treatment plan.

The case of Billy. Billy was a 32-year-old man living in a group home in the community. He had a history of bipolar disorder, but his mood had been fairly stable over the past several years. He also was mildly retarded but had a number of excellent skills. In many ways, Billy was a model resident in his home, making steady progress.

Recently, however, Billy had been breaking windows in his group home. In the month before behavioral consultation, he had broken four windows at the residence. Typically, this occurred after an argument with a staff member about failure to complete a usual chore. According to staff, Billy had become considerably more obstinate and had begun refusing to comply with requests. This had happened frequently during the past 2 months. When staff had repeated requests or levied consequences for non-compliance, Billy had become agitated and, on several occasions, had broken windows.

Staff members were concerned about this perplexing new behavior. They were not able to identify any major changes for Billy during this time. The apparent antecedent of task demands was not new. Staff at Billy's day program reported no significant changes in his behavior, nor had there been changes in medication, treatment plan, primary caregivers, or program staff. The degree of Billy's contact with his family was unchanged, as was the nature of family interactions. In this case it was very difficult to identify antecedents to a behavior problem. The client himself gave no clues. Following an episode, when asked what was bothering him, he simply responded, "I don't know."

One day a staff member overheard Billy talking to himself in the hallway, saying, "Joe's wrong. I'm not ready to leave here." The staffer recalled that Joe was Billy's bus driver. Some questioning of Billy and Joe yielded interesting and useful information. Joe had been complimenting Billy on his progress. He would tease him, saying, "Soon they'll throw you out. You won't be needing to live there anymore. They'll give your bed to someone that can't make it on his own." Joe believed this to be a supportive comment. He had encouraged Billy for years, and he was proud and happy to see him moving toward independence. Billy, however, was terrified by such comments. To him they represented a real possibility of being moved out of his home and raised his anxiety level tremendously. Making further progress only heightened his anxiety, as it became associated with imminent discharge. When Billy misbehaved, on the other hand, he was no longer an "ideal" client. This relieved him because it seemed to make discharge less likely.

Although Joe was not a primary caregiver, he was a significant member of Billy's social environment. His interactions with Billy were thus a key to Billy's recent difficulties. The accidental discovery of this missing key clarified the issues and opened an avenue for intervention.

Staff are not always lucky enough to discover such hidden interpersonal nuances. It is thus important to explore the entire interpersonal realm when conducting an assessment. An apparently casual or insignificant variable may indeed be an integral piece of the puzzle. Minor players in an individual's life may exert influence and affect mood and behavior. As in Billy's case, social variables often influence behavior or contribute to behavioral changes.

The case of Fran. Fran was a 42-year-old woman diagnosed with moderate mental retardation and undifferentiated schizophrenia. Newly admitted to a community residence, she seemed to be having difficulty engaging in treatment. The staff requested a behavioral consultation on this issue.

Fran was extremely passive in her new home, where she spent much of the day lying in bed. She rarely emerged from her room and seemed content to do very little. The staff realized that this might be due to her history of prior institutionalization, but they were not sure how to change the situation. They also considered the possibility of an acute depressive episode, but Fran did not exhibit several of the associated characteristics. For example, her mood was euthymic, and her sleeping and eating patterns were normal. It was not evident that her behavior departed much from her baseline. It was also not clear whether her depression and passivity would diminish with environmental changes.

The consulting team first conducted an analysis of Fran's residential setting. It seemed to offer little stimulation. Though residents were allowed to have personal possessions and to decorate their rooms, Fran's room was bare and dreary, with an institutional appearance. The team advised changing the room to add brightness and stimulation. They also recommended that she spend more time out of the room to gain exposure to people, language, and activities.

To help improve Fran's motivation, the team conducted a reinforcer survey to identify potent primary and secondary rewards. This was difficult, as Fran did not respond positively to many of the reinforcers commonly used in the setting. Gradually, however, they developed a list of many appreciated foods and activities and made a plan to use these reinforcers as rewards for participatory, social, and goal-directed behaviors.

The team also worked closely with Fran's day program staff, who had for many years allowed Fran to remain marginal. They might inadvertently have reinforced her behavior as well. To ensure consistency among settings and service delivery professionals, Fran's plan was extended to her day program setting.

Fran's case shows how physical environment can affect behavior. A dreary, dull environment will not help to mobilize a passive, depressed client. In addition, the case underscores the need for consistency across settings to maximize the effectiveness of treatment and the generalization of treatment effects.

ASPECTS OF ENVIRONMENTAL ASSESSMENT

As the cases of Louie and Billy illustrate, social variables often have a strong influence on behavior or behavioral changes. As in Billy's case, the influential people are not just those who provide treatment or share living quarters; minor characters may have profound influences on individuals as well. Programmatic variables may also be key factors in the development or maintenance of problem behaviors. This was seen in Louie's case, where staff needed to reduce their expectations, shape work behaviors, and acknowledge the increased demands of the new setting. The physical environment likewise can influence behavior, especially when such factors as stimulation, comfort, and privacy are at issue. Fran's case illustrates the effects of a lack of stimulation, as well as the need for potent environmental reinforcers and consistency across settings. Environmental assessment is a complex, multifaceted process. A thorough assessment requires attention to the physical, social, and programmatic aspects of the setting.

Assessment of the Physical Environment

Various aspects of the physical environment can affect comfort and quality of life. A good deal of research has concluded that "institutionality" in living quarters can be detrimental to the satisfaction, mental health, and participation of clients. This was clearly the case with Fran. Dreary walls and bare rooms suggest deprivation. Stark physical surroundings create a poor atmosphere for anyone and are certainly not conducive to the development of a therapeutic setting or to the accomplishment of therapeutic goals. Stimulating, homelike, noninstitutional settings, in contrast, have been associated with improvements in self-help, communication, and social skills (Eyman, DeMaine, & Lei, 1979; Eyman, Silverstein, & McLain, 1975; Webb & Koller, 1979).

Overly stimulating surroundings can be problematic in a different way, increasing distractibility and agitation and even overwhelming certain individuals. According to Zentall and Zentall (1983), many developmentally disabled people can be overaroused by environmental stimuli. There is some evidence that limiting environmental stimulation can reduce behaviors that interfere with learning for certain individuals (Duker & Rasing, 1989); specifically, these authors found that inappropriate behaviors were reduced and that purposeful, on-task activity increased. An individual's susceptibility to overstimulation should be assessed and the need to alter the physical environment explored.

In addition to the appropriateness of the environment for each individual, global environmental features should be assessed. Is lighting adequate? Is the temperature comfortable? Are doors and windows in good working order? Is the area clean? Such basic qualities can directly affect client satisfaction, motivation, and behavior (Glass & Krantz, 1975; Proshansky, Ittleson, & Rivlin, 1976). Moreover, factors such as lighting and temperature can affect programming. In poor light, for example, it may be more difficult for clients to attend to tasks or to discriminate between objects. Uncomfortable temperatures can result in lethargy or negative mood states, which interfere with concentration, motivation, and satisfaction. Distress due to physical discomfort can cause irritability and can even predispose individuals to aggression (Baron, 1977).

Another potential environmental stressor is noise, especially unpredictable and uncontrollable noise. In settings for individuals with developmental disabilities, noise is typically somewhat unpredictable and difficult to control. Given the numbers of clients and staff and the amount of interaction among them, a high noise level is routine. In addition, clients sometimes become agitated, upset, or loud, adding to the ambient noise. There is some evidence that noise may stimulate interpersonal aggression (Donnerstein & Wilson, 1976), particularly when individuals are angry, annoyed, or irritated (Baron, 1977).

Excess noise can increase overall tension and can heighten frustration in clients and staff alike. It also tends to siphon staff members' attention away from clients. These factors in turn can heighten feelings of irritability and annoyance and may increase the likelihood of aggression. Clients must feel that they can seek out a quiet place when they need it. Quiet areas of a community residence may help to address this need and reduce potential stress.

Crowding is another source of environmental stress. There are mixed reports about the effects of crowding on aggression. Altman (1975) and Freedman (1975) could not find a strong link between population density and crime. Other research, however, has shown that crowding can lead to disruptive behavior and aggression (e.g., Freedman, Levy, Buchanan, & Price, 1972). It has, in extreme situations, even been linked to rioting (Baron, 1977). Like noise, crowding may intensify anger or irritability, thus increasing the likelihood of aggression.

Crowding certainly tends to impact negatively on the client's attitude toward the treatment environment. When people lack appropriate personal or private space, they often become disgruntled. Frustration sets in, and episodes of aggression may follow. Crowding usually creates an atmosphere that is conducive to interpersonal conflict as individuals become sensitive to violations of personal space. Often they feel that they lack control over the environment. This increases their sense of frustration vis-à-vis the environment and their sense of helplessness to effect change.

A critical variable in assessment of the physical environment is the extent to which individuals feel able to effect change. If they see themselves as having little control over their environment, they may experience distress in the cognitive, affective, and behavioral spheres. Thus, when clients feel unable to alter or escape from excess noise or crowding, negative feelings, thoughts, and behaviors may result.

When people feel helpless to alter or improve the environment, they will be less satisfied in the environment. They may also develop intense feelings of resignation and despair (like those associated with a learned helplessness model of depression) as a result of repeated lessons in the futility of their actions.

Assessment of the physical environment should be both quantitative and qualitative. Moos has developed several versions of the Community-Oriented Program Environment Scale (COPES; Insel & Moos, 1974; Moos, 1972) to measure the environmental characteristics of residential programs for individuals with psychiatric disorders. These scales assess the physical plant, the administrative structure of the program, the behavioral characteristics of program participants, the psychosocial (milieu) aspects of the residence, and the behavioral contingencies in effect (Moos, 1973). This measure can be used to obtain a quantitative analysis of the physical environment, as well as other aspects of the setting. Qualitative analysis is based on observation to determine whether the physical plant affords optimal access to residents and whether the level of stimulation is appropriate for each resident.

Assessment of the Social Environment

The social environment comprises all the individuals with whom a client interacts. Obviously, caregivers are part of this network; they may, in fact, exert the greatest social influence. Assessment of the caregivers' impact was discussed in chapter 5. However, it is important to assess the impact of other individuals as well. Relationships with peers, acquaintances, transportation workers, or cooks may seem irrelevant at first glance, yet these informal exchanges often have profound effects.

The Impact of Modeling

One of the most important mechanisms for acquisition of behavior is observational learning or modeling (Bandura, 1973, 1977a, 1986). Thus, an important aspect of the social environment to assess is the extent to which appropriate and salient models are available. It may be, for example, that staff members or other clients are modeling maladaptive or inappropriate behaviors. More appropriate models may not be as salient to the client. Also, other individuals in a client's social network may be good general models but be lacking as models of specific behavioral constellations. Paul's case illustrates this latter situation.

The case of Paul. Paul was a 32-year-old man with mild mental retardation who had been overweight his entire life. He recently had begun to develop symptoms of potential cardiac difficulties. His doctors had stated that he needed to lose weight or risk serious medical consequences.

Paul tried to follow the doctors' advice, but he frequently cheated on his diet. The housekeeper would sneak extra helpings, which Paul gladly took. This housekeeper also frequently advised Paul against obeying the doctors. "They're all alarmists. You only live once," he would say. In addition, Paul's uncle would sometimes visit and take him out to eat. The uncle had suffered several heart attacks and yet ate fatty, high-calorie foods.

Paul was exposed to two salient but poor models. Paul's uncle set a poor example for adapting one's diet to avert serious medical consequences. In addition, Paul received mixed messages from staff about the need to alter his behavior. His observations and interactions helped him play down the statements of his doctors and ignore the need to change his behavior.

Many other types of negative behavior can be modeled—for example, by staff members who reprimand clients by yelling or cursing. It is hardly appropriate to impose consequences on clients for such behavior when staff members engage in the behavior with impunity. Staff members also may talk about each other or about clients in disparaging tones. Although staff may describe such talk as "blowing off steam," they may not realize that their behavior has a powerful modeling impact.

Clients may also observe peers and model their behaviors—for instance, reactions to stressful situations. They may see another client throw a dish when dismissed from his work placement. They may see a client physically attack a staff member when denied a visit home. They may observe yelling and agitation prompted by a variety of circumstances. In addition to observing specific behaviors, they may also see positive consequences resulting from negative behaviors. A behavioral outburst may garner staff attention and peer admiration and may even be a way to evade housekeeping tasks.

Assessment of Social Support

Another important aspect of the social environment is social support, defined by Cobb (1976) as information leading the individual to believe that he or she is cared for, loved, esteemed, valued, and part of a network of mutual communication and obligation. According to Cobb, the primary feature of supportive relationships is the meeting of relational needs. Cohen and Wills (1985) have emphasized that the perceived availability of social support may be more critical than the actual receipt of that support.

Environmental assessment should examine the extent to which individuals have access to social support, as well as their perceptions about the availability of support. Do clients feel they have access to support when they need it? The Interpersonal Support Evaluation List (ISEL; Cohen & Hoberman, 1983) is a useful instrument for assessing the availability of support. In particular, the appraisal subscale of this inventory measures the perceived availability of someone with whom an individual can discuss problems.

Assessment of social support encompasses all levels: the environment, the client, and the caregivers. The extent to which a client perceives availability of support reflects the relationships with caregivers, the flexibility of the setting, and the responsiveness of the environment. The availability of social support can be described as an ecological or systems variable.

Assessment of Expressed Emotion

Expressed emotion on the part of others is an environmental/social variable that has been shown to affect the relapse rates of psychotic patients (Brown, Birley, & Wing, 1972; Koenigsberg & Handley, 1986; Vaughn & Leff, 1976). Although it has often been used in the assessment of family interaction, it is also a useful measure of certain social environmental characteristics.

Expressed emotion (EE) has three empirically derived components. The first and most significant component is the number of critical comments made by another person in reference to the client and his or her illness; the second component is hostility. Both components are indicated by manifestations of negative emotion: statements of disapproval, resentment, and rejection. The third component of EE is a marked emotional overinvolvement, indicated by excessive anxiety, intrusiveness, overconcern, and overprotectiveness. High-EE parents have been shown to exhibit more negatively charged verbal behavior, make more critical comments, and be more intrusive with their schizophrenic children than low-EE parents (Miklowitz, Goldstein, Falloon, & Doane, 1984).

Psychiatric patients have shown increased physiological arousal in the presence of high-EE relatives (Tarrier, Vaughn, & Lader, 1979), whereas low-EE relatives produced a soothing effect. In addition, individuals with high-EE relatives have significantly higher rates of relapse after hospital discharge than do individuals with low-EE relatives (Angemeyer, 1982; Vaughn & Leff, 1976). This predictive relationship has been found to be independent of a variety of other factors, including chronicity of disorder, severity of symptoms, and degree of occupational impairment. In addition, it has proven applicable to affective as well as psychotic disorders (Belsher & Costello, 1988).

The constellation of characteristics constituting EE may be important to address in an environmental assessment. In particular, criticism and hostility in the client's setting—whether from peers, staff, ancillary service providers, or custodial personnel—may have a deleterious effect.

Global Social Environmental Assessment

Other important aspects of the social atmosphere include the degree of cohesiveness or divisiveness and the extent to which individuals can communicate effectively. Several scales are useful indices of these variables. The Community-Oriented Program Environment Scale (COPES; Insel & Moos, 1974; Moos, 1972) measures the psychosocial/milieu aspects of settings. The Resident Management Practices Scale (RMPS; King & Raynes, 1968) and the Group Home Management Scale (GHMS; Pratt, Luszcz, & Brown, 1980), which assess the institutionality of settings, are useful as global environmental measures. These scales indicate the degree of social distance and depersonalization, important aspects of communication between caregivers and clients. These scales also provide general information about interpersonal relations in the setting (e.g., condescension versus respect, person-oriented versus object-oriented care).

Programmatic Assessment: The Behavioral Environment

Like aspects of the social environment, program-related conditions may encourage the development or maintenance of inappropriate behavior. In an earlier example, the client received staff and peer attention for a behavioral outburst. A client seeking attention may engage in maladaptive behavior toward this end. Individuals may receive, or expect to receive, rewards for unacceptable behavior. They may observe that clients who engage in aggression or other inappropriate behaviors are excused from certain tasks, or they may see negative behavior as a way to have demands eliminated.

An examination of the contingencies within the setting is crucial to a behavioral analysis of the environment. If negative behavior results in either positive rewards (e.g., increased staff attention) or negative reinforcement (e.g., lifting of task demands), contingencies need to be altered.

Assessment of Reinforcers

Perhaps the most critical aspect of the environment to assess is its reinforcing value. All other program variables are secondary to whether potent reinforcers are made available to program participants. Because reinforcers are highly individual and idiosyncratic, it is important to conduct a reinforcer survey. Potential reinforcers should be tested for their appeal before being incorporated in a behavioral treatment plan. It is not enough to assume that a particular item is reinforcing; its potency must be justified through observation, analysis of choices, and behavioral responses following the receipt of rewards. A variety of reinforcers should be available to ensure that the client has access to multiple rewards. Variety also alleviates the problem of satiation, as no single reward is overutilized.

Much recent attention has been given to the examination of preferences in reinforcers (Bannerman, Sheldon, Sherman, & Harchick, 1990; Parsons, Reid, Reynolds, & Bumgarner, 1990; Shevin & Klein, 1987). systematic behavioral assessment appears to be the best way to identify preferences (Green, Reid, White, Halford, Brittain, & Gardner, 1988). There is a good deal of evidence that individuals with severe disabilities often indicate preferred reinforcers different from those indicated by caregivers (Green et al., 1988; Wacker, Berg, Wiggins, Muldoon, & Cavanaugh, 1985). This information casts doubt on the efficacy of reinforcers that have not been identified directly through assessment of the individual's likes and dislikes.

Special Considerations for Dually Diagnosed Clients

Programs that serve clients with both mental retardation and mental illness contain different variables than programs addressing either mental retardation or mental illness alone. If a dually diagnosed client is in a program for mentally retarded individuals, there often is no means to address symptoms or behaviors stemming from psychiatric problems. The psychopathology of dually diagnosed individuals presents a major treatment challenge (Kazdin et al., 1983; Laman & Reiss, 1987; Matson & Barrett, 1982b) and is responsible for many failures in community placement (Jacobson & Schwartz, 1983). Likewise, programs designed to treat mental illness can be inappropriate, as they often fail to take into account the cognitive functioning level of the dually diagnosed individual. In assessing an environment for the dually diagnosed client, it is important to address some unique factors. A program for such a client must be designed to take into account the individual's cognitive deficits, repertoire of adaptive behaviors, and psychiatric symptomatology.

Assessing the Appropriateness of Expectations

The case of Leon. Leon was among a group of residents in a transitional facility for psychiatric patients. In addition to suffering periodic exacerbations of schizophrenia, Leon met the diagnostic criteria for severe mental retardation.

Leon was becoming a frustrating patient for staff. Each time he reported for activities of daily living inspection, he was wearing clothes belonging to other patients. Leon would be sent away with a reprimand and an instruction to find his own clothes. He would go to his room and choose more clothing from his closet. Typically, he returned to the staff with at least some clothing that was not his. The staff would repeat the instruction and send him back to his room. Often after several repetitions of this frustrating cycle, the staff would "fine" the patient for manipulative behavior.

In investigating the problem, the staff found Leon's closet full of other people's clothing. Further observation indicated that Leon often randomly chose clothing from the clean laundry pile when patients were told to retrieve their clothing. He did not understand how individuals identified their own clothing—this was a skill that he had never acquired. He needed to be taught to search for his name label when sorting through the clean laundry. In Leon's case, staff members were not aware of the full spectrum of skills necessary for compliance with their requests.

The case of Kelly. Kelly was a 22-year-old moderately mentally retarded woman with generalized anxiety symptoms. She was in a day program designed to teach individuals the skills to eventually obtain competitive employment. Her work skills were excellent, and she was highly motivated. She had recently been moved into a program designed for quick transition to work situations. The program was based on a complex token system with seven levels of classification. Each level was associated with different work demands, teacher assistance, pay, break times, and other rewards. Kelly suffered increased anxiety in this new environment and began to feel panic about her ability to function. She became distracted, confused, and upset. Her performance declined, and supervisors often found her crying rather than working. Supervisors and case managers attributed her behavior to an increase in anxiety symptoms and concluded that she might not be ready for the change.

One worker from Kelly's residence, however, speculated that she might need a simpler reinforcement system. When the system was scaled to a level more congruent with Kelly's ability to process information, she could perform much better. Intervals between rewards were lengthened as her functioning improved.

The case of Marie. Subtle skills may be absent even in high-functioning individuals with mental retardation. Marie was an inpatient who was responsible, stable, and eager to take on new challenges as she moved up the token economy ladder. She was especially looking forward to the privilege of signing in and out of the unit unaccompanied by staff. She lost the privilege the first week she had it, however, because she failed to sign back into the unit properly. This was confusing to staff, who wondered whether she might be ambivalent about the privilege or afraid of the increased responsibility. They wondered whether she was ready to move up the steps of the program and whether she was sabotaging her progress for an intrapsychic reason.

A staff member who recalled seeing Marie sign in and out, however, reported that she had given extraordinary time and attention to the procedure. The staffer recalled that she had painstakingly tracked her departure and arrival times and carefully studied the chart. He proposed that she might have been confused by the system.

Marie was then asked to perform the sign-in/sign-out task while staff assessed her ability to do so. She exhibited tremendous difficulty following the steps. She became confused by the sign-outs of other patients, and she had trouble concentrating on writing her name, her destination, her departure time, and her anticipated return time. She placed information in incorrect columns or beside the names of other patients. It was clear that the task demands were beyond the limits of Marie's comprehension and processing abilities. When staff understood this they devised an easier system for her, which simply involved moving a magnet to either an "in" or "out" column.

The programmatic assessment must evaluate the appropriateness of expectations for a client and their congruence with his or her abilities. This assessment may point to changes that should be made in consideration of individual needs. A client may need to learn a given task through demonstration, as did Leon. A client may respond better to visual cues and techniques (Fidora, Lindsey, & Walker, 1987) than to verbal ones. The task may need to be modified if the individual is to master a skill. This was evident in the case of Marie, who needed a simpler sign-out process. Staff may need to use more concrete or simpler language if the client's verbal processing skills are weak. A particular reinforcement system may be too abstract, too complex, or too lean for a particular client.

Clients need treatment plans that are developed in accordance with their levels of skill development and cognitive functioning. At times, these levels are difficult to assess or are not directly assessed, as when staff members are more familiar with a certain level of functioning and assume certain prerequisite skills. This situation can be highly frustrating for both client and staff. It can sometimes lead to repeated requests that a client function at a level beyond his or her capabilities, and behavioral difficulties may result.

If individual goals and expectations are to be in keeping with the client's abilities, environmental assessment information must be integrated with information from evaluation of the client and the caregiving system. Inappropriate expectations may be a prescription for failure. Changes in program variables can permit the shaping of behaviors toward the attainment of goals.

Assessing the Understanding of Psychiatric Symptoms

In addition to misjudging appropriate expectations for a client, staff members may not be fully aware of psychiatric symptoms and the ways in which they are experienced. Staff may ignore symptoms or give them too much attention. In general, staff may fail to respond in a way that helps the individual to cope with the symptoms or to function despite them. For example, psychiatric patients can learn to focus and attend to tasks and to pay less attention to hallucinations and delusional thoughts (Bellack, 1986); techniques then can help them be productive and coherent in the midst of psychosis.

The case of Tim. Tim was a moderately retarded man with the additional diagnosis of schizoaffective disorder. He was chronically psychotic, with prominent and intractable delusions and hallucinations. His affective symptoms tended to be depressive; he would appear sad, lose motivation for tasks, and express feelings of hopelessness.

Tim moved into a new residence and, after a few days, appeared to lose interest in performing daily chores. He needed prompting to attend to the details of task completion. His bed began to look sloppy, and he no longer folded his clothes neatly.

The residence staff considered Tim high functioning with regard to self-help tasks and knew he possessed many skills. Reports from Tim's previous program indicated that he was entirely independent in all activities of daily living skills and that he was, in fact, "somewhat compulsively neat" in completing tasks. Staff at the new program wondered whether Tim was becoming depressed, even though he was not expressing feelings of hopelessness. His mood appeared to be euthymic. His depressive symptoms did not seem to explain the deterioration in his functioning. His psychotic symptoms were unchanged.

Further examination showed that Tim faced inconsistent expectations. Whereas some staff members expected independence in self-care, others were more lenient. In addition, Tim had no peers with equivalent skills. The norm for his cohort at the residence was moderate independence and very modest attention to detail. Tim's own motivation to maintain previous standards of functioning declined. Both programmatic and social factors appeared to influence this outcome.

The staff reported that they had assumed Tim was not as high functioning as his records had indicated, largely because of the severity and chronicity of his psychiatric history. In this case, inappropriate expectations took the form of demands that were too low and obscured the actual abilities of the individual.

The case of Anna. Anna was a 32-year-old woman with mental retardation and paranoid schizophrenia. Most of the time she could function well. Occasionally, however, her paranoid ideation interfered with her ability to interact appropriately with others. She sometimes grew fearful of others when she became paranoid.

Anna's symptoms often increased during times of stress and change. She usually responded well to reassurances and reality-testing interventions, as well as to staff assistance in problem solving around her symptoms. She was usually greatly relieved when staff helped her refocus on reality, and she responded well when they helped her reframe her symptoms as indications of stress and reactions to change. In fact, she was sometimes able to make these interventions for herself.

One day, when Anna was feeling particularly stressed, she sought out staff members more than usual. This became stressful for them as well. She approached one staff member and asked if he was plotting against her. He lightheartedly responded, "Yes, Anna. I'm behind the whole plan." The well-meaning staff member sought to address some of her fear with humor. He did not realize the full extent of her inability to examine that fear realistically. The interaction engendered severe paranoia and genuine fear in the client.

Anna's case illustrates how inappropriate responses to psychotic symptoms can exacerbate those symptoms and increase agitation. One purpose of environmental assessment is to determine whether the environment and programming have taken an individual's psychiatric symptoms into account. This entails assessing how the environment responds to such symptoms and whether these responses are therapeutic for the individual. Others in the environment may need to learn more about symptoms and appropriate responses.

The goal in treatment planning is to develop a program and a setting in which both the cognitive and psychiatric impairments of the client are acknowledged. Staff should be trained to attend to cognitive limitations in their requests and interactions. In addition, they should be taught to identify psychiatric symptoms and intervene in a therapeutic manner at a level that respects the client's cognitive capacity.

THE ROLE OF FRUSTRATION

Frustration emerges as a common theme in discussions of all aspects of the environment. The extent to which an environment fosters frustration is a critical issue. Frustration is a major precursor for a number of individual and group behavior problems and produces a variety of negative emotions. It may result from aspects of the physical environment (e.g., crowding, noise) or from programmatic features such as inappropriate expectations.

The Frustration-Aggression Hypothesis (Berkowitz, 1969, 1978; Dollard, Doob, Miller, Mowrer, & Sears, 1939) suggests that the blocking of ongoing, goal-directed behavior results in the arousal of a drive to harm some person or object. In our context, frustration may result from the inability to find quiet in a noisy residence or the inability to master a task that is too difficult.

Although frustration can result in various emotions and attitudes such as resignation and despair, intense feelings of frustration can lead to aggression, especially when the situation appears to be arbitrary or illegitimate. For example, when a frustrated person sees the situation as unfair, aggression is more likely to ensue. This is often the case in a treatment context, where consequences are by definition often externally controlled. In addition, the person's ability to comprehend consequences may be impaired by limited cognitive abilities or psychiatric difficulties. It is important to keep these limitations in mind when explaining consequences. A situation is also more likely to be perceived as arbitrary or unfair if expectations are not appropriate. A client expected to function at a level beyond his or her capabilities will be compromised in completing tasks or earning rewards. Frustration is a likely result.

ASSESSING THE ENVIRONMENT FOR SUCCESS IN FOSTERING COMMUNITY INTEGRATION

Since 1960, there has been growing interest in creating normalized environments for people with developmental disabilities (Cuvo, Sievert, & Davis, 1988; Green, 1989; Nirje, 1969). As these people have been integrated into the community, their visibility has increased. The movement toward integration and independence has created a need for new and innovative treatment approaches. These changes have also altered the approach to environmental assessment.

Functionality and Generalization

Areas not previously addressed in assessment and treatment now merit more attention. For example, skills like money management and nutritional awareness are more critical for living semi-independently or independently in the community. Program assessment now must address the broad spectrum of self-care skills.

To what extent does the client's environment foster the development of skills needed for transition to the community? There has been a movement toward an ecological approach, focusing on identifying the skills most needed for effective functioning within a defined situation (Cuvo et al., 1988).

Functionality of skills is central to this approach as traditional teaching goals are modified to reflect life skills. Less emphasis is placed on standard academic skills and more on skills that will enhance autonomy. Goals are likely to concern independence in self-care, vocational skill development, and community integration. For example, whereas developmentally disabled adults might once have learned one-to-one correspondence by counting, they are now likely to learn it in a functional manner (e.g., in the context of table setting— each setting gets one glass, one plate, one fork, etc.) or as part of a vocational sorting program. Similarly, an individual may first learn to write his or her name rather than the alphabet.

A major focus in programmatic assessment is the functionality of skill training. Instructional goals should be relevant to community settings. In addition, community-related skills should be taught under relevant stimulus conditions (Cuvo et al., 1988). For example, if a client's ability to obey pedestrian traffic laws is in question, that ability should be evaluated in the actual settings, including controlled and uncontrolled intersections, and in situations of varying traffic volume. Similarly, if there is a question about a client's ability to manage money effectively, that skill should be evaluated in vivo—for example, at local delis and newsstands rather than through hypothetical mathematical problems.

It is critical to assess whether the environment is fostering the generalization of skills to the natural setting and to examine how generalization is encouraged. Generalization training should involve a variety of persons, situations, and settings. A client may know how to buy items at a local deli but not in a supermarket or cafeteria. Or a client may manipulate small sums of money successfully but run into trouble when handling more than 10 dollars. In short, the instruction must address the variety of situations likely to be encountered.

Assessing Leisure Availability

Communities still contain many barriers to leisure participation for individuals with developmental disabilities. These barriers force them to engage mostly in passive, solitary activity. In addition, there is still a great deal of stigmatization and stereotyping by individuals without developmental disabilities. As a result, developmentally disabled adults often lack skills and self-confidence (Chadsey-Rusch & Gonzalez, 1988). Some clinicians have suggested that focusing on leisure skills may address this problem. Leisure skill participation is one way to build self-confidence and to demonstrate commonality with nondisabled people (Bender, Brannan, & Verhoven, 1984). It is thus an area that should be addressed in the assessment of the therapeutic environment.

Assessing the Fostering of Normalization

The availability of leisure options is a normalization issue. Normalization has become a goal of many treatment programs (Jacobson & Schwartz, 1986; Walsh, 1989). Walsh has delineated a number of environmental characteristics that can foster normalization and integration of dually diagnosed clients. This milieu approach, designed to build client competency and autonomy, emphasizes extensive individualized treatment plans with specific goals. Treatment incorporates structured environments, a plethora of planned activities, and efforts at community integration. In addition, normalized contingencies and naturalistic rewards are used. Staff members work toward increasing client responsibility and encouraging client autonomy. The combination of individual care plans, planned and varied activities, and client autonomy has been associated with positive outcomes in residential settings (Eyman, Silverstein, McLain, & Miller, 1977; Walsh, 1989).

A number of instruments are available for assessing the quality of activities available to residential clients and the extent to which the facility applies principles of normalization. Some of these measures are described in Table 6.1. The Characteristics of the Treatment Environment scale (CTE; Jackson, 1964) assesses the extent to which clients can choose activities and measures two factors: autonomy and activity (Silverstein, McLain, Hubbell, & Brownlee, 1977). The extent to which a residence fosters autonomy and provides activity options has been linked to improvements in adaptive functioning (Mayeda, 1979).

The Program Analysis of Service Systems (PASS) inventories rate organizations in terms of normalization practices and administrative operations. The most commonly used PASS versions are PASS3 (Wolfensberger & Glenn, 1975) and PASSING (Program Analysis of Service Systems' Implementation of Normalization Goals; Wolfensberger & Thomas, 1983). Versions of PASS have been used to study community residences for developmentally disabled individuals (e.g., DeMaine, 1978; Eyman et al., 1979; Mayeda, 1979). The PASS index has proven a useful indicator of the degree to which a residence fosters normalization (Flynn, 1980; Jacobson & Schwartz, 1986).

The Rehabilitative Indicators–Activities Indicators scale (RI or RIAI; Diller, Fordyce, Jacobs, & Brown, 1978) assesses aspects of the environmental climate as well as client behavior. This scale examines the variable of client status (e.g., education, employment). It also measures activity, which is defined as access to self-care, leisure, and vocational or educational opportunities. The leisure dimension includes exposure to social, recreational, and cultural experiences. The scale identifies opportunities available daily, weekly, monthly, or less often.

Social Skills Training

To experience personal development and community integration, developmentally disabled individuals need to learn social skills in addition to productivity skills (Salzberg, Agran, & Lignugaris-Kraft, 1986; Salzberg, Lignugaris-Kraft, & McCuller, 1988; Salzberg, Likins, McConaughy, & Lignugaris-Kraft, 1986; Wehman & Hill, 1981). Assessment of the environment should take into account the scope of targeted behaviors and examine the degree of emphasis given to social skill development (Wacker & Berg, 1988). The degree to which the environment fosters the understanding of social rules, the development of specific interaction skills, and the process of communication is especially critical (Mesibov, 1984, 1986; Van Bourgondien & Mesibov, 1989).

Social validation is an important aspect of this type of environmental assessment. The ecological approach emphasizes that environmental assessments and task analyses should precede the development of goals. In addition, this approach stresses the direct observation of the client within the setting to determine the level of adaptive functioning. Validation checks are also encouraged. Parents, employment supervisors, or

Table 6.1 Environmental Assessment Measures

Scale	Environmental aspects assessed	References
Community-Oriented Program Environment Scale (COPES)	Physical plant Milieu aspects	Moos (1972) Insel and Moos (1974)
Family Environment Scale (FES)	Social aspects of family setting (communication, cohesion, etc.)	Moos and Moos (1976)
Characteristics of the Treatment Environment scale (CTE)	Client autonomy Client activity	Jackson (1964) Silverstein, McLain, Hubbell, and Brownlee (1977)
Rehabilitative Indicators—Activity Indicators (RI/RIAI)	Client goal attainment Client access to self-care, leisure, vocational activities	Diller, Fordyce, Jacobs, and Brown (1978)
PASS inventories		
Program Analysis of Service Systems 3 (PASS3)	Fostering of normalization Normalized treatment by caregivers	Wolfensberger and Glenn (1975)
Program Analysis of Service Systems' Implementation of Normalization Goals (PASSING)	Fostering of normalization Normalized treatment by caregivers	Wolfensberger and Thomas (1983)
Resident Management Practices Scale (RMPS)	Degree of institutionality Resident-oriented programming	King and Raynes (1968)
Group Home Management Scale (GHMS)	Degree of resident-oriented programming	Pratt, Luszcz, and Brown (1980)

other concerned community members are consulted about the appropriateness of targeted skills and progress in skill acquisition (Brown, Netupki, & Harme-Netupki, 1976; Cuvo et al., 1988).

The Concept of Meaningful Engagement

Several authors have emphasized the importance of meaningful engagement, or offering activities that foster the client's development and growth (Jones, Lattimore, Ulciny, & Risley, 1986). Engagement has been described as a context for teaching: An individual engaged in an activity can learn incidentally. This learning supplements available educational opportunities and reduces the need to rely on formalized teaching sessions. Engagement in activities is a normalizing way for staff to teach and for clients to learn. Use of normalization principles has been associated with improvements in adaptive functioning (Hull & Thompson, 1981).

Engagement can also help curb undesirable behavior. The amount of time spent in meaningful engagement is inversely related to the amount of time spent in inappropriate behavior (Akerly, 1984), a fact relevant to community integration and quality of life. Meaningful engagement means that an individual is exposed to activities, encouraged to learn, and freed of boredom and monotony. It also eases adaptation to the community by enhancing appropriate public behavior and developing new skills (Kraus, 1978; Mesibov, 1983).

Residential treatment designed to offer engagement and foster normalization reflects a philosophy of community integration. Normalization and engagement can be assessed through some of the instruments discussed earlier in this chapter. The Rehabilitative Indicators scale (RI; Diller et al., 1978) addresses engagement through an activities indicators rating, which measures access to self-care, recreational, and rehabilitative activities. Normalization practices can be assessed by the PASS inventories (DeMaine, 1978; Eyman et al., 1979; Flynn, 1980; Mayeda, 1979; Wolfensberger & Glenn, 1975). PASS ratings are useful indices of the extent to which program participants are treated as deviant. The Resident Management Practices Scale (RMPS; King & Raynes, 1968) was designed to assess management practices in residential settings. Pratt, Luszcz, and Brown (1980) used a version of this instrument, the Group Home Management Scale (GHMS), to assess management practices in community residences. These scales assess variables related to the "institutionality" of a setting; specifically, they examine the extent to which treatment is resident oriented. Four variables are rated: rigidity of routine, block treatment of residents, depersonalizing practices, and social distance between residents and staff members. The quality of the environment, therefore, is the main target of this measure. Individualization and flexibility are assessed, as well as communication between staff and clients, a variable related to normalization practices, client autonomy, and client participation in treatment.

ASSESSING QUALITATIVE ASPECTS OF THE ENVIRONMENT

A complete environmental assessment includes qualitative variables, global factors that span the social and programmatic realms. One example is the overall quality of communication among individuals in the setting: Is scathing criticism common, or do interactions tend to be supportive? Another qualitative variable is the overall atmosphere of the setting. Is there a feeling of cohesiveness? Is there a sense of purposeful-ness, or is chaos apparent? Is there evidence of cooperation among the members?

For developmentally disabled individuals living at home, the Family Environment Scale (FES; Moos & Moos, 1976) provides information about the social aspects of the home setting. This scale assesses the quality of relationships among family members and provides preliminary infor-mation on the family system. For individuals in community residences, the Community-Oriented Program Environment Scale (COPES; Insel & Moos, 1974; Moos, 1972) can be used. This instrument assesses rela-tionship, personal growth, and systems dimensions of the environment. Thus, it yields information on the way members treat one another, the extent to which individuals are encouraged to become autonomous, and the degree to which program participants understand rules and routines.

Jacobson and Schwartz (1986, 1991) have proposed an assessment that takes into account the variety of factors that can influence outcomes in a community residence. They propose that the occupants, the organi-zation, and the environment affect developmental progress, quality of life, and general ambiance.

ASSESSING RESOURCE MANAGEMENT

A final consideration in assessment of the environment is the allocation of environmental resources. Dellario and Crosby (1985) have proposed a system for evaluating this factor in residential settings for psychiatric patients. Their system addresses the extent to which client needs are understood, resources are available and accessible, and resources are used to promote skill acquisition.

SUMMARY

A comprehensive environmental assessment focuses on physical, social, and programmatic concerns. The physical environment should be evaluated in terms of comfort and stimulation. The social environment should be assessed for availability and salience of appropriate models and for adequacy of support; the overall social ambiance should be examined as well. Assessment of the programmatic aspects of the environment must address the suitability and potency of behavioral reinforcers, the appropriateness of expectations, and the staff's understanding of psychiatric symptoms. The entire environment should be assessed for its success in fostering clients' integration into the community. Numerous measures are available to aid in the assessment process.

The client, the caregivers, and the environment interact in complex ways that impact on treatment. An environmental assessment, therefore, must be done not in isolation but in conjunction with assessment of the caregiving system and of the individual.

Section III

Section III

Chapter 7

A Problem-Solving Approach to Clinical Interventions With Dually Diagnosed Persons: Focus on Treatment

INTRODUCTION

Previously, we suggested identifying four stages of clinical intervention in a problem-solving approach. These stages are (a) screening for initiation difficulties, (b) analyzing and selecting focal target problems, (c) designing an overall treatment plan, and (d) evaluating the effects of treatment (Nezu & Nezu, 1989b). Section II addressed the first two stages of clinical intervention for dually diagnosed clients and examined assessment issues related to the three members of our tripartite model: the client, the caregiving system, and the environment. In this chapter, we consider our problem-solving model as it applies to the other two stages of clinical intervention, designing and evaluating treatment. Chapters 8 through 10 will offer numerous treatment suggestions geared to address the client, the caregivers, and the environment, respectively.

DESIGNING TREATMENT

The third stage of clinical intervention involves designing an overall treatment plan that is individualized to help the client achieve his or her identified goals. In problem-solving terminology, this means that treatment should focus on helping the client overcome impediments to goal achievement as identified within the individualized Clinical Pathogenesis Map

(CPM; see chapter 3). In developing a treatment plan, the therapist needs to choose intervention strategies and identify appropriate training procedures.

During assessment, the therapist asked and answered the questions, What? (i.e., What problems need to change?) and, Why? (i.e., Why do these problems need to change? In what way do they relate to overall goals?). At this stage, there is a different set of questions: How? (i.e., How are these problems going to change?) and, Who? (i.e., Who is going to help change them?). In other words, the governing question is, Given this client's goals and focal target problems, what kind of intervention plan will help reach these goals and who should carry it out?

By applying the problem-solving model conscientiously during the initial stages, the therapist has minimized the likelihood of designing an ineffective treatment plan. He or she will probably have a valid picture or analysis of the client's difficulties, and treatment strategies aimed at the wrong targets are unlikely to be proposed. In practice, however, interventions rarely run smoothly. Often, additional problems occur, new information emerges that requires revision of the patient's CPM, or a treatment strategy proves to be ineffective with the particular client. We advocate applying the five problem-solving operations to address such common clinical exigencies related to treatment design.

Problem Orientation

Like other clinical tasks, the selection of treatment strategies to include in an intervention program can be influenced by one's worldview. We advocate that professionals designing treatment protocols for dually diagnosed persons adopt a worldview based on the following assumptions:

1. That psychosocial interventions are a viable approach to the treatment of psychiatric disorders experienced by persons with mental retardation

2. That such treatments should embody the idiographic application of nomothetic principles

3. That clinical interventions for such persons should comprise treatment strategies, not techniques

4. That multiple causality exists and that treatment should therefore include multiple strategies

5. That such multiple strategies should address focal problems related to each area of the tripartite model (client, caregiving system, and environment)

6. That treatment plans should be consistent with the philosophy of the least restrictive alternative

Further, we advocate that treatment protocols for dually diagnosed clients include clinical strategies to build general coping skills (Nezu & Nezu, 1989b). Examples might include training in problem-solving skills (Nezu & Nezu, 1991), relapse prevention techniques (Marlatt & Gordon, 1985), stress management strategies (D'Zurilla & Nezu, 1989), and/or self-control skills (Kanfer & Schefft, 1987). Such intervention components would be included in order to (a) increase the likelihood of attainment of treatment goals (Kanfer & Schefft, 1988), (b) enhance maintenance and generalization of treatment effects, and (c) strengthen the client's ability to cope with future problems or stressful circumstances.

In addition to increasing a client's overall coping ability (Nezu & Nezu, 1991)—making the individual better equipped to deal with difficult daily life circumstances—skill training can be used to address specific problem areas. For example, we have trained groups of dually diagnosed young adults with aggression difficulties to use problem solving as a means of identifying and reacting with more appropriate behavioral responses to stressful situations (Nezu et al., 1991).

Because much of the data needed for treatment design was previously obtained during problem analysis and target problem selection (i.e., development of a CPM), the first problem-solving task during treatment is the generation of alternatives. However, movement within the problem-solving model is not always uninterrupted, systematic, and unidirectional. It may be that, after careful construction of a CPM, new exigencies in the client's life occur, the caregiving system becomes altered, or environmental resources change. Such situations often call for a detour from the proposed CPM. Thus, the therapist needs to be flexible and sensitive to such occurrences.

Generation of Alternative Solutions

In addition to brainstorming a list of potentially effective intervention alternatives that address the client's CPM and specific goals, the clinician applies the strategies-tactics approach to idea production. That is, first a list of strategies for each focal problem area on the CPM is generated. Then, for each strategy, a list of specific treatment tactics is constructed. Sometimes, combining elements from different strategies can result in more effective treatment.

In addition to brainstorming different tactics for the same strategy (e.g., cognitive restructuring versus progressive muscle relaxation training as a means of anxiety reduction), the therapist may also need to generate different methods of implementing the same tactic. Depending on a variety of individual factors (e.g., chronological age, cognitive ability, receptive speech), a given treatment tactic may need to be implemented differently with different clients. For example, training in relaxation skills is likely to be substantially different for an 11-year-old boy with moderate retardation and a 52-year-old woman with borderline retardation. For the boy, the therapist needs to be very concrete and specific (e.g., modeling loose Raggedy Ann body postures to demonstrate the concept of relaxation), whereas the woman can understand more didactic instructions.

Results of the generation of alternatives are illustrated in Table 7.1, a list of potential strategies, tactics, and procedural methods for dealing with the problem of aggression.

Decision Making

After a list of potential treatment ideas has been developed, the clinician must systematically evaluate each one. This process constitutes the decision-making step. Table 7.2 lists decision-making criteria that can help the therapist rate alternatives in relation to identified goal(s) and to assess each alternative's utility. (Utility has been defined as a joint function of the likelihood of a given alternative's resulting in goal attainment and the alternative's value.)

Likelihood of Positive Effects

In applying these criteria, the therapist is basically concerned with the probability that a given treatment alternative will help achieve identified goals. He or she must assess (a) the likelihood that a particular alternative will have a specific impact with regard to a particular target problem and (b) the probability that the alternative will be implemented optimally.

The first assessment requires familiarity with the treatment literature. However, as noted earlier, psychosocially based treatment approaches have only recently received adequate testing with specific regard to the psychiatric problems of persons with mental retardation. Thus, the therapist working with dually diagnosed clients needs to be creative in applying treatment approaches that have proven effective with nonretarded individuals. For example, when treating anxiety in a person with mild retardation, the clinician can draw heavily on the research literature concerning anxiety problems of nonretarded persons. However, addressing those problems in the client with more severe retardation will require additional attention. In such a case, the problem-solving model can be especially helpful.

The second assessment, concerning the degree to which the treatment strategy can be implemented in its optimal form, entails evaluating the competency, motivation, and skills of all treatment participants, including the therapist (e.g., Can the clinician adequately train the client in anger management skills?), the client (e.g., Can the client learn such skills?), the caregivers (e.g., Are the client's parents willing to implement the anger management program at home?), and any significant others (e.g., Are the staff at the vocational workshop motivated to facilitate this program with the client?).

Table 7.1 Potential Strategies, Tactics, and Methods for Addressing Problems of Aggression

Overall goal: To decrease aggressive behavior

Potential strategies

1. Increase client's interpersonal skills

2. Reduce frustrating environmental stimuli

3. Increase negative consequences of aggressive behavior

4. Decrease positive consequences of aggressive behavior

5. Increase client's coping and stress management skills

6. Reduce instigating nature of aggression-related negative affective states

7. Reduce instigating nature of aggression-related physical/biological factors

8. Reduce instigating nature of aggression-related cognitive variables

9. Decrease likelihood of poor social behavior

Potential tactics (under Strategy 1)

1. Increase client's communication skills

2. Increase client's assertiveness skills

3. Increase client's social problem-solving skills

4. Increase client's social skills

Potential methods to implement tactic (under Tactic 1)

1. Use didactic instructions

2. Provide live modeling

3. Use role-playing

4. Provide modeling through videotapes

5. Reinforce appropriate communications

6. Punish inappropriate communications

Table 7.2 Decision-Making Criteria for Evaluation of Alternative Treatment Ideas

LIKELIHOOD OF POSITIVE EFFECTS

1. What is the likelihood that this particular treatment alternative will achieve the specified goal(s)?

2. What is the likelihood that this particular therapist can optimally implement this treatment?

3. What is the likelihood that this client will be able to follow this treatment in an optimal fashion?

4. What is the likelihood that the caregivers and paraprofessionals will be able to carry out this treatment in an optimal fashion?

5. What is the likelihood that the client's social and/or physical environment will be able to support implementation of this treatment?

6. What is the likelihood that this treatment will enhance the client's ability to cope with future problems or stressful situations?

7. What is the likelihood that this treatment will produce clinically meaningful change?

8. What is the likelihood that this treatment strategy will help achieve the client's overall goals?

9. What is the likelihood that this treatment will influence positive change in other problem areas?

VALUE OF TREATMENT EFFECTS

Personal consequences

1. How much time and other resources are required to implement this treatment? For the client? For the therapist? For the caregivers?

2. What will be the emotional cost or gain if this treatment alternative is implemented? With regard to the client? To the therapist? To the caregivers?

3. Is use of this intervention consistent with morals, values, or ethics? Concerning the client (e.g., least restrictive alternative)? The therapist? The caregivers?

4. Are there any negative physical side effects associated with this treatment? With regard to the client? The therapist? The caregivers?

5. What will be the impact of this treatment on related client problem areas?

Social consequences

1. What will be the effects on others in the client's social sphere if the treatment is implemented? On the client's family? On friends? On coworkers? On fellow residents? On the community?

2. Is this particular alternative seen as acceptable by significant others in the client's social environment?

3. Will this treatment alternative engender support or antagonism from significant others?

SHORT-TERM CONSEQUENCES

1. Will implementing this treatment strategy have a positive or negative effect on the client's motivation to continue in treatment? On the caregiver's motivation?

2. Will the impact of treatment be immediate? Is such impact positive or negative?

3. Are there any immediate negative side effects that might occur, even if the long-term outlook is positive?

LONG-TERM CONSEQUENCES

1. What will be the long-range effects of implementing this treatment? On the client? On the caregivers?

2. Will the long-term consequences of this treatment continue to be consistent with the client's overall goals? With those of the caregivers?

3. Will use of this treatment help prevent or minimize the need for future psychological intervention?

Value of Treatment Effects

As highlighted in Table 7.2, the therapist, in rating the value of each treatment alternative, addresses both the personal and the social consequences of its implementation. In general, such consequences involve investments of time and effort, as well as the potential for negative side effects. Consistency with ethical, legal, and philosophical principles is also considered. Potential treatment effects are assessed with regard to the therapist, as well as to those who would be represented within the tripartite model (i.e., client, caregivers, social environment).

Short-Term and Long-Term Consequences

Treatment alternatives are evaluated in light of their short-term effects (i.e., immediate consequences) and long-term effects (i.e., likelihood of maintenance and generalization of positive treatment effects).

The ideal treatment approach would meet all the following criteria:

1. Have a high likelihood of attaining treatment goals

2. Be relatively easy to implement in optimal fashion

3. Alleviate distress associated with the presenting problems

4. Be associated with many positive consequences and few negative consequences

5. Require very little time and effort to implement

6. Be cost-effective

7. Carry both short- and long-term benefits

8. Enhance the quality of the client's life

9. Engender positive reinforcement from all members of the client's social environment

10. Be ethically sound

Obviously, as concerned professionals, we would prefer that all our treatments meet these criteria. Given the state of clinical interventions in general, and for persons with mental retardation in particular, it is unlikely that any treatment protocol can fit all aspects of this ideal. However, the therapist's responsibility is to approximate this definition as closely as possible for a given client. Use of the decision-making criteria outlined in Table 7.2 can improve the quality of treatment design.

Figure 7.1 shows a form that can facilitate the application of these decision-making criteria. It lets the clinician list and then rate all alternatives generated with regard to a given focal problem. This formal

Figure 7.1 Evaluation Form for Treatment Alternatives

Rating Scale:
Positive (+1 to +3)
Neutral (0)
Negative (−1 to −3)

Target problem: _____

Goal(s): _____

TREATMENT ALTERNATIVES	Likelihood of achieving goals	Likelihood of optimal implementation	Overall goal attainment	Time resources	Effort	Emotional effects	Morals, values, and ethics	Physical side effects	Impact on other problems	Other personal effects	Effects on family	Other social effects	Short-term effects	Long-term effects	Other	Other	Other	TOTAL SCORE

Note. Adapted from *Clinical Decision Making in Behavior Therapy: A Problem-Solving Perspective* (p. 99) by A. M. Nezu & C. M. Nezu (Eds.), 1989, Champaign, IL: Research Press. Copyright 1989 by A. M. Nezu and C. M. Nezu.

approach can be helpful in two ways. First, it can reveal negative aspects of an alternative: Negative ratings on numerous criteria would likely place an alternative low on the list of choices. The second advantage to systematically evaluating each alternative in this manner is that it may help the therapist identify factors that might stand in the way of successful treatment. In other words, where a particular alternative might rate high overall, any criteria that engender a negative rating can point to possible difficulties concerning treatment implementation or the maintenance and generalization of positive treatment effects. Such difficulties can then be addressed through the problem-solving model as the therapist modifies the initial treatment protocol where appropriate.

Using the overall set of ratings, the therapist then selects the alternatives with the highest positive ratio of positive to negative ratings to include in the client's initial treatment plan. As noted previously, we advocate incorporating several alternatives in the treatment package to facilitate maintenance and generalization and to increase the probability of attaining multiple goals simultaneously. Once the initial plan is formulated, the therapist can apply the last problem-solving operation, that of solution implementation and verification.

Solution Implementation and Verification

Before implementing actual treatment, the clinician can verify his or her choices by eliciting feedback from all involved, including the client, the caregivers, and significant others who might have a part in treatment. We have found it very helpful when seeking feedback on a treatment plan to use the Goal Attainment Map (GAM). The GAM is a pictorial representation of the treatment plan and its relationship to the client's goals. The GAM corresponds to the CPM and serves as a kind of "road map" for treatment. The therapist completes the GAM by listing selected treatment components that serve as pathways for the journey from Point A (presence of problems) to Point B (goal attainment). Figure 7.2 shows a sample GAM, based on the hypothetical CPM presented in Figure 3.2.

The GAM should be discussed with all significant individuals in the client's life, including parents, siblings, caretakers, group home staff, vocational rehabilitation workers, and others. As noted previously, it is unlikely that a person with mental retardation and concomitant psychological difficulties will be self-referred. Thus, there might be some differences of opinion regarding the acceptability of various treatment alternatives. A client's parents, for example, might object to a treatment protocol with a reinforcement component on the grounds that they would be "bribing" their child—even though the client was in favor of the approach. On the basis of this initial feedback, the therapist could either choose to discard the approach or attempt to problem solve the discrepancy (e.g., encourage parents to get a second opinion or attempt to change their opinion).

Figure 7.2 Sample Goal Attainment Map (GAM)

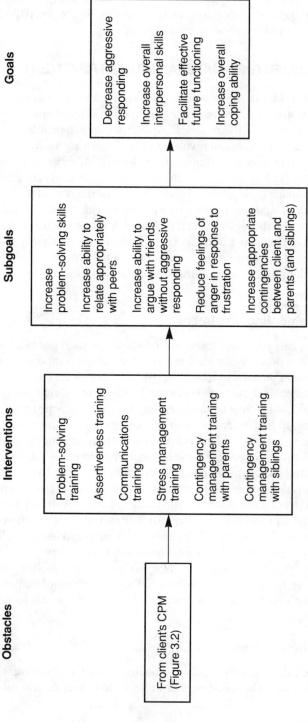

Obstacles

From client's CPM (Figure 3.2)

Interventions

Problem-solving training

Assertiveness training

Communications training

Stress management training

Contingency management training with parents

Contingency management training with siblings

Subgoals

Increase problem-solving skills

Increase ability to relate appropriately with peers

Increase ability to argue with friends without aggressive responding

Reduce feelings of anger in response to frustration

Increase appropriate contingencies between client and parents (and siblings)

Goals

Decrease aggressive responding

Increase overall interpersonal skills

Facilitate effective future functioning

Increase overall coping ability

When the therapist has secured initial agreement from all parties on the appropriateness and acceptability of the proposed GAM, implementation of the treatment plan can begin.

IMPLEMENTING AND EVALUATING TREATMENT

The last stage of the treatment process, implementation and evaluation, is very similar to the solution implementation and verification step in the problem-solving model. Like the final step in problem solving, this final stage in treatment involves (a) implementing a solution (i.e., carrying out a treatment protocol; (b) collecting information to monitor the effects of the solution (i.e., gathering both process and outcome data); (c) comparing the predicted and actual consequences of the implemented solution (i.e., determining if treatment is working and is helping to attain goals); (d) troubleshooting if the match is unsatisfactory (i.e., changing the treatment plan); and (e) exiting from the process if the match is satisfactory (i.e., terminating treatment). In the remainder of this chapter, we will highlight several important issues involved in the final therapy stage.

Implementing Treatment

Before carrying out a treatment protocol, the therapist needs to develop an initial timetable for implementing the various components of the intervention. The order in which treatment strategies are carried out depends on the details of the case. For example, if a client's parents appear to waver in their commitment to an intensive token economy program, the therapist might first carry out a minor contingency management plan for an easy-to-change problem as a means of strengthening their motivation.

A related issue concerns the amount of time that must elapse before the effects of treatment can be adequately assessed. In certain cases the research literature might be helpful, though few relevant studies exist. Moreover, individual circumstances (e.g., severity of symptoms or change in environmental resources) can affect the amount of time necessary for treatment to begin producing positive effects. Therefore, the clinician should continually monitor treatment progress (or lack thereof) to determine the need for further problem solving. In addition, we have found a need to be especially patient and tolerant when working with dually diagnosed persons because of the complexity of their cases.

Monitoring Treatment Effects

To best assess whether treatment is effective—that is, whether the solution is working—the therapist should begin to collect information across a variety of areas as soon as possible and should continue such assessment throughout the treatment. There should also be a plan for follow-up assessment (e.g., 3 months posttreatment).

Even in situations where a single problem is the focus of treatment, it is desirable to evaluate changes across a variety of areas. Obviously, in cases where multiple problems are being addressed simultaneously, it is crucial to evaluate changes in each area. In addition, measures not specifically addressing a targeted problem should also be included in order to screen for negative side effects. In keeping with our systems emphasis, this broad approach enables the therapist to monitor the effects of change in one targeted behavior on other components of the system and to identify emerging difficulties that may need to be addressed. In addition, such a comprehensive approach to assessment can uncover problems overlooked during previous stages of treatment. For example, after eliciting feedback from a mother undergoing behavioral parent training, the therapist may change the problem analysis from one of inappropriate external contingencies to one of unrealistic expectations on the part of the mother.

Appropriate assessment instruments are essential to a comprehensive evaluation of the effects of a treatment protocol. The problem-solving model can aid in the choice of assessment tools. In addition, we offer the following recommendations (adapted from Nezu & Nezu, 1989b):

1. Include several measures for each target problem area.

2. Select measures that are sensitive and relevant to the intervention being implemented.

3. Select measures that are psychometrically sound.

4. Choose less obtrusive, cumbersome, and inconvenient measures, if available and of high quality.

5. Include measures that assess areas not necessarily targeted for intervention.

6. Include measures that use varying data sources (e.g., client's self-report, family observation, in-session observation).

7. Focus on both outcome and process data (e.g., assess changes in the targeted problem area, such as severe anxiety, as well as changes in the hypothesized controlling variable, such as social skill deficits).

Matching Predicted and Actual Consequences of Treatment

Using the evaluation data, the therapist then compares the actual consequences (i.e., the observed effects of an intervention) with the predicted consequences (i.e., the effects that were projected during the decision analysis operation). Following are typical questions that might be posed at this point: "Did use of a contingency management protocol lead to a decrease in Dan's aggressive behavior?" "Did six sessions of role-playing increase Sonia's ability to make friends at her new group home?" "Did training Arden's parents in extinction procedures help reduce his negative attention-seeking behavior?" "Has the use of an exposure paradigm with Jenny helped her to overcome her fears of dark basements?" and "Has training Justin in relaxation skills improved his ability to cope with stressful interpersonal situations?"

Troubleshooting Versus Terminating

If the match between the actual and the predicted consequences is unsatisfactory (i.e., the intervention strategy is not leading to goal attainment), then the therapist, together with everyone involved (client, caregivers, siblings, etc.), should try to find out why the discrepancy exists. As noted in chapter 2, lack of goal attainment can be due to ineffective implementation of a strategy, ineffective clinical decision making, or both. In the former case, the therapist can problem solve alternative ways to implement the same strategy (i.e., different tactics or different methods of implementing the same tactic). In the latter case (i.e., ineffective clinical decision making), the therapist needs to recycle through the problem-solving process across each of the previous stages of treatment, especially the problem analysis and treatment design stages.

As an additional decision-making aid, we offer in Table 7.3 a series of questions, partly adapted from Nezu and Nezu (1989b), that the mental health professional can ask if treatment appears to be unsuccessful.

If repeated assessments over time yield a satisfactory match between the actual and the predicted consequences (i.e., treatment goals have been met), the therapist then addresses the issue of treatment termination. A positive termination experience involves a mutual agreement among all involved in a case (client, therapist, caregivers) that the specified goals have been satisfactorily attained. Not only have the presenting problems been alleviated, but positive consequences have been maximized and negative consequences minimized. Under these circumstances, particularly if treatment has been running smoothly and on schedule, all parties will be satisfied.

Even under such positive circumstances, the manner in which termination is handled is still an important clinical decision. We suggest that the therapist use the problem-solving model to plan the best way to terminate treatment in a given case. By this time, the clinician will have a rather detailed understanding of the client and his or her significant others and should be able to predict their reactions to termination. The termination phase can be structured in a variety of ways:

Table 7.3 Troubleshooting Questions to Ask If Treatment Appears to Be Ineffective

1. Is a psychosocial approach appropriate for this client?
2. Were any related problems overlooked?
3. Is the client/caregiver motivated to change?
4. Is the client/caregiver afraid to change?
5. Were any negative consequences overlooked?
6. Is this treatment generally effective for this problem?
7. Was this intervention implemented properly?
8. Does the client/caregiver understand this treatment?
9. Does the client/caregiver agree with the use of this treatment?
10. Is treatment too costly?
11. Is treatment taking too long?
12. Is there adequate social support for the client?
13. Was the problem analysis accurate?
14. Is this treatment engendering any negative effects?
15. Does this treatment conflict with the client's/caregiver's values?
16. Does the client/caregiver have unrealistic goals or expectations concerning therapy? Concerning this treatment?
17. Is the client/caregiver completing homework assignments?
18. Is the client/caregiver optimally practicing the technique(s) that are part of treatment (e.g., relaxation skills)?
19. Are any of the client's family members sabotaging the treatment?
20. Should a different treatment approach be used?
21. Should a different method be used to implement this treatment?
22. Am I sensitive to the client's feelings?
23. Is the implementation of this approach too mechanistic?
24. Is the use of this treatment premature?
25. Does the client/caregiver view me as invested in this treatment?
26. Does the client/caregiver trust me as a therapist?
27. Have the most salient reinforcers for this client been identified?
28. Are there problems or variables that serve to maintain the client's difficulties, thereby impeding a successful outcome?
29. Should treatment be terminated at this point?
30. Should I get opinions from other professionals?

1. Gradually extend the intervals between sessions to encourage increased independence from the therapist.

2. Plan for future "booster" sessions for the client and/or the caregivers.

3. Schedule future evaluation or follow-up sessions.

4. Set up future informal contacts (e.g., limited telephone calls, letters).

SUMMARY

The overall therapy enterprise comprises a series of clinical decisions that must be sound if treatment is to be successful. This chapter focused on the decisions involved in the last two stages of therapy: treatment design and treatment implementation and evaluation.

Regarding treatment design, we advocate a worldview incorporating the following beliefs: that (a) psychosocial interventions are a viable treatment approach, (b) treatment should involve the idiographic application of nomothetic principles, (c) treatment is composed of strategies rather than mere techniques, (d) multiple causes require multiple treatment strategies, (e) such strategies should address all components of the tripartite model (client, caregiver, environment), (f) the least restrictive treatment alternative should be sought, and (g) a treatment plan should include training in general coping skills.

Within this orientation, the therapist generates (through brainstorming) and evaluates (through systematic decision analysis) a variety of alternative treatment strategies that address specific goals. Alternatives are rated with regard to overall utility, and choices are made. On the basis of these choices, the clinician can construct a Goal Attainment Map (GAM) depicting the treatment pathways.

In the last stage of therapy, treatment implementation and evaluation, the clinician (a) attempts to carry out each of the clinical intervention strategies, (b) gathers data regarding the effects of each strategy, (c) compares actual and predicted effects, (d) evaluates the quality of this match, (e) terminates treatment if the goals are attained, or (f) recycles through the problem-solving operations to determine the source of a poor match. A final clinical decision concerns treatment termination.

The remaining chapters in this section address treatment concerns with respect to the three members of the tripartite model: individual, caregiver, and environment. Strategies described here should be seen as constituting a pool of possible treatment components, not a treatment manual per se. Choices in a given case should be made via the problem-solving model.

Chapter 8

Treatment Guidelines: Focus on the Individual Client

INTRODUCTION

Debates about the inherent worth of different treatment approaches (e.g., pharmacological versus behavioral treatments) often distract us from the more important question: For this individual with this particular set of problems, given this particular set of biological, developmental, family, learning, and environmental characteristics, which treatment—or combination of treatments—will most likely meet the therapeutic goals while minimizing negative side effects (Nezu & Nezu, 1989a)? We believe there are no shortcuts to an answer. As Gualtieri and Keppel (1985) note, "The fact that some problems might be psychiatric and others behavioral does not imply that drugs are inevitably indicated in the first category and behavioral treatments in the second, although this is frequently how treatment decisions are made" (p. 306). Rather, development of an overall treatment plan, especially for a dually diagnosed client, should proceed systematically as described in previous chapters.

As a starting point, this chapter will describe a variety of potentially relevant treatment approaches for the clinician to consider in the decision-making process. Clinical strategies centering on the client are grouped into the following categories: (a) behavioral approaches, including respondent learning approaches, reinforcement-based contingency management approaches, contingency management deceleration strategies, and social learning approaches, and (b) nonbehavioral approaches, including psychopharmacologic treatment, creative arts therapy, and other psychotherapy alternatives. These categories are not meant to represent mutually exclusive treatment protocols. Indeed, sound clinical decision making often indicates that a combination of strategies is best in a given

161

case. For each category, we provide a brief definition, a description of various clinical applications, a case example, and a discussion of special clinical considerations concerning the treatment of clients with multiple diagnoses.

BEHAVIORAL APPROACHES

Behavioral treatment approaches are clinical interventions that are based to a significant degree on principles of learning and that are methodologically sound and empirically validated. These approaches include respondent, operant, and cognitive-social learning models.

Respondent Learning Approaches

Definition

Approaches based on respondent or classical conditioning models are rooted in Ivan Pavlov's work early in this century. A *respondent* is a behavior that is reliably elicited by a particular *stimulus*. A classic example comes from Pavlov's more famous studies, which initially focused on a dog's behavior of salivation (the respondent) as elicited by the presentation of food (the stimulus). A human example might be a fear reaction elicited by the presence of a threatening dog. Such behaviors are considered *unconditioned responses* to *unconditioned stimuli*.

Respondent learning or conditioning occurs when, through the pairing of an unconditioned stimulus and a neutral stimulus, the neutral stimulus begins reliably to elicit a similar behavior, labeled now the *conditioned response*. For Pavlov's dogs, continual pairing of the ringing of a bell and the presentation of meat powder led to a situation where the bell alone elicited salivation.

Schwartz (1984) provides some common examples of Pavlovian conditioning involving humans:

> A man hears a song on the radio that was popular years
> ago, when he and his wife first fell in love. The long-absent
> feelings of new love come rushing back. . . . A woman
> leaves the hospital after recovering from a serious auto-
> mobile accident. As she is about to enter the taxi that will
> take her home, she is overwhelmed with terror. (p. 47)

Discontinuation of the association between the unconditioned and conditioned stimuli, or pairing of a different stimulus with the unconditioned stimulus, can result in *extinction,* or a reduced probability that the previously neutral stimulus will elicit the conditioned response. For example, if the traffic accident survivor is taught to associate a different reaction (e.g., a state of relaxation) with cars, then seeing an automobile will no longer elicit an anxiety response.

Professionals disagree as to what treatment strategies are based purely on respondent or classical conditioning paradigms. In the interest of clarity, however, we are including in that category treatments in which a response (e.g., anxiety) to a given stimulus (e.g., cars) is eliminated as a different behavior (e.g., relaxation) is elicited in the presence of that stimulus.

Clinical Strategies

Interventions based on classical conditioning paradigms include anxiety reduction strategies such as *systematic desensitization* and *exposure-based approaches.*

Systematic desensitization is aimed at gradually weakening anxiety responses associated with particular stimuli or situations (e.g., phobias) by teaching clients to substitute different responses that are competitive with or that reciprocally inhibit anxiety. Although several types of responses may help to inhibit anxiety, the most popular has been muscle relaxation (Wolpe, 1985). With this strategy, a client first learns how to relax, then is briefly exposed, either imaginally or in vivo, to a stimulus that arouses only minimal anxiety. During this brief period, the client attempts to relax in the presence of the stimulus; through repeated exposures, the stimulus eventually loses its power to evoke anxiety. The procedure is continually repeated for stronger or more anxiety-arousing stimuli. Systematic desensitization has proven effective for the treatment of various anxiety-related disorders, most notably phobias, in populations without disabilities (Masters, Burish, Hollon, & Rimm, 1987).

In an exposure-based approach the client is confronted with a stimulus that reliably elicits a negative emotional response (e.g., avoidance behavior, anxiety). Presentation, either imaginally or in vivo, of the feared stimulus continues until the unwanted behavioral and emotional responses begin to weaken. Over repeated and prolonged trials, the anxiety eventually dissipates through extinction. Exposure-based treatment strategies are often used in conjunction with other strategies, such as participant modeling, coping skills training, and contingency management programs. Exposure-based protocols have been effective in the treatment of simple phobias (Emmelkamp, 1982), obsessive-compulsive disorder (Masters et al., 1987), and agoraphobia (Emmelkamp, 1982) in nonretarded populations. Schloss, Smith, Santora, and Bryant (1989) successfully used a respondent conditioning approach to reduce anger responses of a dually diagnosed male.

Clinical Applications

Although systematic desensitization and exposure-based treatments have repeatedly proven effective with general populations (Masters et al., 1987), no large-scale, well-controlled outcome studies are available to document their efficacy in the outpatient treatment of clients with developmental disabilities. For example, although Peck (1977) found desensitization procedures effective for treating simple phobias (e.g., fear of rats and of heights) in adults with mild mental retardation, these results remain tentative because of the study's small sample size ($n = 4$ per condition). However, certain single-case studies do suggest that, under appropriate conditions, such strategies are effective (e.g., Guralnick, 1973; Luiselli, 1978).

Clinical Examples

Our first clinical example involves a client introduced in chapter 4, Larry, a 34-year-old man with moderate mental retardation. Larry, who had reported seeing "scary monsters" and "the bogeyman," was originally referred by his group home staff for possible psychotic-like delusions and hallucinations. After a neuromedical examination failed to identify physical or environmental factors that could explain such symptoms, a behavioral assessment was conducted. This assessment indicated that Larry's symptoms actually represented a phobic response to the dark. Specifically, when asked to go alone to any dark place, he became agitated, resisted, and made loud statements about monsters and scary faces. The most anxiety-provoking situation involved Larry's weekly chore of taking the trash to the basement at his group residence. Even if the residence staff excused him from this task, Larry would remain agitated because he believed that he was shirking an important responsibility.

Larry's treatment involved training in relaxation skills designed to produce a physiological state that was incompatible with his anxiety reaction. The training included progressive muscle relaxation exercises intended originally for children but adapted for a developmentally disabled population. The training was consistent with the client's developmental and cognitive levels. For example, rather than telling Larry to "make a tight fist, squeeze tight, then relax and let go," the therapist instructed him to "pretend that you have a whole lemon in your hand and squeeze all the juice out. . . . Now, let the lemon drop on the floor." In addition, Larry was taught to breathe deeply and to repeat verbal instructions to himself such as, "I'm very safe now . . . nothing is going to hurt me . . . this is a safe place . . . there are no monsters here."

After six sessions in which Larry practiced these strategies, therapist and client developed a hierarchy of "scary situations." The situation that was a "little scary" was a trip to the hospital basement with the therapist, lasting a few seconds. The "most scary" situation involved going alone to the basement of the group residence. Over repeated exposures, Larry mastered each step in the hierarchy by applying the relaxation strategies until he was able to stay relaxed and comfortable.

Our second clinical example involves Caroline, a 29-year-old woman with severe mental retardation associated with Down syndrome. Caroline had recently been deinstitutionalized and placed in foster care. However, her foster mother had referred her for treatment following the discovery that she was phobic of the foster family's pet dog. Upon seeing the animal, Caroline would scream and become violent and destructive as well as incontinent. The pet had been temporarily removed from the home pending a decision about another possible placement for Caroline.

A shaping procedure was developed with the caregiver's assistance. Caroline participated in a daily training session where she gradually increased her approach behavior to a "practice dog"—a small puppy. Caroline received various tangible reinforcers for tolerating increased exposure (i.e., more time and shorter distances between herself and the puppy). Relaxation training for Caroline would be extremely difficult because of her inability to follow verbal instructions. The therapist, therefore, applied the problem-solving model to find an alternative method of inducing a relaxed and comfortable state. The stimulus that was chosen to induce relaxation (and thus compete with the anxiety reaction) was music—Caroline's favorite song.

As Caroline succeeded with each step, she moved to the next level of "dog-approach behavior." In the final step, the actual family pet was introduced. The procedure was completed in 12 weeks, with treatment gains maintained at a 1-year follow-up (Nezu, O'Brien, & Nezu, 1982). Thanks to the intervention that alleviated her phobic response, Caroline was able to stay in foster care and thus remain in the community.

Special Considerations for Clients With Mental Retardation

At first glance, the techniques of systematic desensitization and exposure may appear deceptively easy. As with any treatment strategy, however, the effectiveness of these techniques depends on thorough and accurate assessment. It is possible, for instance, that the client's fears are justified because of significant skill deficits. One of our clients, Alex, suffered extreme social anxiety and would avoid all social activities. Alex had never received guidance in social or dating skills. His fears were realistic in that he literally did not know the first thing to say to a woman. Therefore, rather than addressing Alex's anxiety initially, we provided training in communication and dating skills. As a consequence, Alex experienced a significant increase in self-confidence. His anxiety became much easier to treat via relaxation training, which would probably not have been effective at the outset.

Another problem regarding anxiety reduction strategies is that a client may not appear openly anxious. For example, Larry, described earlier, appeared more psychotic than anxious at the initial referral. For other clients, anxiety may manifest itself in somatic symptoms. This was the case with Gloria, a 31-year-old woman with a dental phobia. She would often experience severe nausea and begin vomiting before a visit to the dentist. Some clients, like Caroline, may express anxiety by becoming destructive.

Caroline's case also illustrates the need to problem solve alternative methods of implementing a chosen strategy. Clients with mental retardation may exhibit deficient expressive and receptive speech. For such clients, the didactic instructions commonly used with the general population may not be appropriate, even when they include concrete examples and language. Thus, such a respondent conditioning approach may need to be implemented in conjunction with an operant approach (i.e., reinforcement of successive approaches to touching the dog).

Such a combination of approaches is consistent with our worldview, which advocates multiple treatment approaches as a means to goal attainment. In Caroline's case, strategies were aimed not only at treatment of the individual client but also at the other two aspects of the tripartite model: The caregiver learned to deliver exposure-based treatment in the client's natural environment as a means of facilitating generalization and maintenance.

Summary

Approaches based on respondent or classical conditioning paradigms, such as systematic desensitization and exposure-based interventions, represent one group of behavioral treatment alternatives. However, as illustrated by the case of Caroline, intervention protocols based exclusively on this type of learning tend to be uncommon. These methods have proven effective for nondisabled populations, but more research is needed concerning their effectiveness in the case of dually diagnosed clients.

When applying the problem-solving model to identify anxiety reduction treatments for a developmentally disabled client, the therapist should consider the following areas: (a) the possibility of actual skill deficits, (b) behavioral patterns of anxiety that are consistent with a less mature developmental level (e.g., crying, aggression, giggling, screaming, incontinence), and (c) novel uses or creative applications of previously documented theory-based strategies (e.g., the use of music to induce relaxation).

Contingency Management: Use of Reinforcement

Definition

A second learning-based approach involves *operant* or *instrumental conditioning* and is grounded in the law of effect, which states that behavior is governed by its consequences. Behavior is thus instrumental in obtaining rewards, and it *operates* or has an effect on the environment. Four types of behavior-consequence relationships can be identified.

1. Positive reinforcement (i.e., a positive consequence following behavior X leads to *increased* probability that X will recur)

2. Punishment (i.e., a negative or aversive consequence following behavior Y leads to a *decreased* probability that Y will recur)

3. Negative reinforcement or escape (i.e., elimination of an existing aversive stimulus leads to an *increase* in the behavior responsible for its removal)

4. Punishment II (i.e., removal of a positive stimulus leads to a *decrease* in the relevant behavior)

Contingency management procedures apply these basic operant principles by structuring the consistency of presentation of consequences relative to a given behavior. For instance, a supervisor, by providing positive feedback to an employee for a job well done, increases the probability that the person will continue to work diligently (positive reinforcement). Getting a speeding ticket may cause a driver to slow down (punishment). Getting up in the morning to turn off the irritating alarm clock leads one gradually to wake up on time (negative reinforcement). Removing a tantruming child from a favorite play area leads to a decrease in emotional outbursts (punishment II).

To understand the idiographic relationship between a client's behavior and various consequences, the therapist must analyze (a) the stimulus (antecedent) events, (b) the behavior under investigation, and (c) the pattern of consequences that follow the behavior. Consequences that may be reinforcing for one person may not be significant for another.

The goal of a reinforcement-based contingency management protocol is to increase a specific target behavior. One effective approach can be to address the matter indirectly, by increasing an alternative behavior—even when the clinical target involves a behavioral excess such as a client's screaming in public when lost. Rather than directly attempting to reduce the screaming behavior, a positive contingency management program might focus on increasing alternative behaviors such as relaxing, asking for directions, keeping a list of emergency phone numbers, or carrying extra change for phone calls. This type of procedure is known as *differential reinforcement*.

Differential reinforcement can be a powerful tool to reduce maladaptive behaviors by increasing appropriate ones. Foxx, McMorrow, Fenlon, and Bittle (1986) used such an approach to decrease the hard-to-treat behavior of public genital stimulation in a mentally retarded adult. Success with this intervention was replicated by Nezu et al. (1987) regarding a similar behavioral problem.

From both clinical and ethical viewpoints, reinforcement-based strategies aimed at increasing positive, prosocial behaviors (e.g., coping skills training) are preferable to punishment-based strategies aimed at decreasing maladaptive behaviors. In clinical terms, building new coping skills equips the client with strategies for interacting with the environment and often increases feelings of competence and self-esteem. Carr and Newsom (1985) have demonstrated that aggression can be decreased through the introduction of strongly preferred reinforcers for prosocial behaviors. The acquisition of prosocial behaviors can contribute to an individual's sense of competence. In such situations, reinforcement-based treatment not only reduces maladaptive behavior, but also develops adaptive behaviors that can result in more social reinforcement from the environment (e.g., appropriate interactions with peers can lead to new friendships).

From an ethical perspective, a behavioral intervention that teaches the client more effective ways of interacting with the environment also represents a least restrictive model of treatment. In reinforcement-based programs, behavior change is achieved with a minimum of restrictions or negative side effects—a fact that has important implications for clinical decision making. In contrast, decelerative or punishment-based strategies, as described in the next section, often fail to teach new skills and can have significant negative side effects.

The use of behavioral technology based on positive reinforcement to teach new or replacement behaviors, and thus to reduce problem behaviors, is an important treatment focus. This concept is not new, although recent advocates such as those describing "gentle teaching" (McGee, 1988) have presented it as such. We contend that gentle teaching is more accurately described as simply one form of a reinforcement-based behavioral treatment protocol (i.e., establishing a positive rapport with the client, extinguishing specific maladaptive target behaviors, redirecting the client toward more adaptive behaviors through cues and prompts, and finally providing social reinforcement for adaptive behavioral responses). Although this strategy may or may not be the optimal treatment for every client, it certainly represents a minimally restrictive form of treatment.

Clinical Strategies

Positive reinforcement can vary in complexity from occasional social praise to an extensive token economy system used in a residential program designed to develop daily living skills. Protocols can also differ in the type of reinforcement schedule used (e.g., ratio versus interval, fixed versus variable, intermittent versus continuous). Because a complete description of these approaches and their theoretical underpinnings is beyond the scope of this book, the reader is referred to two excellent resources (Kazdin, 1975; Matson, 1990).

Reinforcement-based contingency management procedures have been applied with success in a wide range of problem areas. These include eating disorders, fears and phobias, toilet training, speech skills, self-help skills, social skills, obesity, anxiety disorders, aggression and related conduct disorders, self-stimulation, self-injurious behavior, ruminative vomiting, personality disorders, symptoms of depression and schizophrenia, enuresis, encopresis, coprophagy, stripping, and specific behavioral deficits associated with autism (see Gardner, 1988; Gardner & Cole, 1984; Scibak, 1986; Whitman, Scibak, & Reid, 1983, for general reviews).

Special Considerations for Clients With Mental Retardation

Because reinforcement-based protocols have been documented as effective for clients with mental retardation, positive behavioral programming has become a popular and prevalent form of treatment for people with developmental disabilities. Most residents of supervised group homes receive some form of behavioral programming. However, whereas state regulations govern treatment of persons with mental retardation, there are no current legal or professional criteria for individuals who call themselves behavior specialists. Behavioral programs are often developed in the absence of adequate, comprehensive, and thoughtful behavioral assessment. As a result, although a specific behavior modification plan may be based on positive reinforcement and thus satisfy state regulations requiring least restrictive treatment, the plan may be poorly researched, conceived, constructed, and/or implemented. The client, failing to respond to the intervention, may be labeled "treatment resistant" and prescribed a more aggressive (and often aversive) form of treatment.

This was the situation of one patient we met, Roberta, who had been hospitalized after many attempts at behavioral programming in a group residence had "failed." Roberta's so-called token economy program could have been used as a *how not to* text. Some of the problems included the following.

1. Behavioral definitions were vague.

2. No functional analyses were offered (except that the author of the token economy program had concluded that Roberta was trying to get attention; however, no data backed up this claim).

3. There was no evidence of the reasons specific reinforcers were chosen.

4. There was evidence that Roberta could have free access to these reinforcers at times outside her programming; this lessened their reinforcement value.

5. No attempt was made to evaluate the residence staff's ability to implement the token program.

6. No attempt was made to monitor the effects of the intervention.

Such concerns are basic to the development and implementation of any contingency management protocol.

In addition to careful program development, another key to the development of contingency management approaches for dually diagnosed clients is recognition of individual skill level. Because many developmentally disabled clients exhibit skill deficits, it is important to set reasonable goals and to shape adaptive behavior by reinforcing successive approximations to these goals. Unfortunately, because many referrals occur under crisis conditions, this can sometimes be very hard to do. One client, Dawn, was referred to us after she had "become psychotic" and attacked a supervisor at her day treatment facility. Dawn had a long history of aggression, had been in three different psychiatric hospitals during the previous 2 years, was receiving large doses of antiseizure and neuroleptic medications, and had a list of previous psychiatric diagnoses. The referring agency said that if our treatment did not totally eliminate Dawn's aggression, she would lose all chances for future day programming. The agency was not pleased when we proposed establishing successive goals toward reduction of the aggressive outbursts.

Proposals for positive-reinforcement-based programming are often met with resistance by a staff or family member who is experiencing a crisis and/or has already developed a negative bias toward the client. It is important to avoid the temptation of pursuing an instant cure and to maintain objective and realistic goals. The therapists in the following case example wrestled with this problem.

Clinical Example

Billy was a 17-year-old boy with a history of brief psychiatric hospitalizations for impulsive, aggressive, and assaultive behaviors. He was referred to us during such a hospitalization. His attending psychiatrist desired a treatment consultation that might be helpful upon Billy's hospital discharge. Billy had recently been placed on an inpatient unit following an episode in which he had assaulted a peer and run away from his group residence. In addition, while on the inpatient unit, he had displayed problem behaviors like those mentioned.

The second of three children, Billy had first been hospitalized at age 9 for "attempting to kill" his newborn brother. At 15 he was admitted again for displays of "psychotic" and "agitated" behavior, the latter directed toward his mother. His reported symptoms included auditory hallucinations (although there was no evidence of these during the current hospitalization), paranoid ideas, and a pattern of running away from home. His assaultive behavior had been directed primarily toward his mother. Billy's parents shared a reportedly unstable marriage. His mother had a diagnosis of malignant hypertension and was described by others as high-strung. Billy's father had a history of alcohol abuse and was physically aggressive toward his wife.

Billy began living in a group residence after his second psychiatric hospitalization at age 15. He was treated with an antidepressant during that hospitalization and prescribed a major tranquilizer at discharge, although the rationale for these prescriptions was unclear. Since that time, Billy had continued to receive the tranquilizer and had participated in a small contingency management program in his group home (e.g., earning privileges for completing specific chores). On weekends, he visited his parents' home.

Billy's mother had a heart attack, and the family decided that Billy would spend several weekends with his aunt. When he returned home following his mother's recovery, he became especially aggressive toward her and attacked his younger brother when the brother tried to intervene. Billy was then admitted to a child-adolescent psychiatric inpatient unit.

The behavioral assessment conducted on this unit included staff descriptions of Billy's behavior and daily, 2-hour behavioral observations on the ward. Billy was observed during the unit's morning community meetings and at other random times throughout the day. Two independent observers recorded his behavior to maximize the likelihood of reliable assessment. Further, the patient was individually interviewed, and all past medical, neurological, and psychiatric records were reviewed.

Initial observations of Billy's behavior confirmed the earlier descriptions provided by the unit staff. Although he reported enjoying the community meetings on his unit, Billy invariably became loud and physically assaultive during the meetings. These incidents, which usually resulted in his removal, included verbal (e.g., cursing, insulting, and threatening) and/or attempted physical (e.g., punching or kicking) altercations with another adolescent on the unit. These episodes almost always occurred shortly after Billy had tried in an appropriate way—by raising his hand and waiting to be called on—to ask a question or bring up a point during the meeting. When Billy was called on, however, his comments or questions were often naive or poorly stated because of his expressive speech deficits. As a result, many of the patients laughed or giggled at his comments; this would often precipitate an outburst. Conversely, on the few occasions Billy was chosen to be the leader of the group, he behaved appropriately throughout the entire meeting, frequently asking for help from the staff to stay on track.

As part of the overall assessment, three staff members who knew and frequently interacted with Billy completed a Connors Rating Scale (Connors, 1969). Results indicated significant hyperactive tendencies and the presence of symptoms consistent with a DSM-III-R diagnosis of conduct disorder (American Psychiatric Association, 1987). Results of a reinforcer survey (Gelfand & Hartmann, 1984) indicated the following as particularly salient reinforcers for Billy: eating strawberry-flavored candies and cherry and grape popsicles, watching professional wrestling on television, watching action movies like *Teenage Mutant Ninja Turtles*, playing with action-hero dolls, playing video games, listening to rap and popular music, and playing card games. Direct behavioral observation during free-time periods indicated that Billy continually tried to get attention from those around him, particularly adults, and sought interpersonal interactions when provided with any opportunity. Finally, data indicated that Billy's behavior was not significantly altered by any medications that were trialed during his 2-month hospital stay. These included three different neuroleptics, a stimulant, and, finally, lithium.

Throughout the entire assessment period, we were continually told by many hospital staff members that Billy was psychotic and needed medication to calm him down. Others stated, "He has the mind of a 4-year-old; he needs to have limits set" and suggested that an appropriate behavioral contract should specify some punishments. On the positive side, two graduate students who served as objective behavior observers and an attending physician who was willing to select appropriate medications for empirical evaluation were helpful in the development of an appropriate plan.

The functional analysis resulting from this comprehensive assessment showed that Billy's assaultive behavior occurred when he was in the presence of other patients. Specific antecedents included giggles or remarks made by others. His difficulty expressing himself when agitated (he spoke more rapidly, less clearly, and with increased volume) also served as an antecedent. Before one explosive episode Billy was heard talking to himself, saying, "What are you doing to me? Why doesn't somebody help me?" as if trying to stop what was happening.

Billy's aggressive episodes usually resulted in his removal from the meetings. Although exclusionary time-out (i.e., placement in an area where the patient was unable to receive positive reinforcement) was the stated consequence of aggressive behavior on the hospital unit, it was observed that a staff member would actually accompany Billy to his room and stay with him until he calmed down. Although the extent of this social attention varied with different staff members, it intermittently reinforced, rather than punished, the aggressive episodes. Further, because the reinforcement was intermittent, it would likely make the aggressive behavior more difficult to extinguish. As a result, Billy would not be very motivated to learn alternative behaviors, as he was actually being reinforced for his aggressive behavior. The staff insisted, however, that they were indeed implementing time-out and that Billy was very sick and very resistant to treatment. They were becoming convinced that behavior modification was not working with this patient. Unfortunately, these hospital staff members were communicating their biases to Billy's direct care staff from the group home, who began to fear his discharge back to that residence. As a result, the group home staff were asking the attending psychiatrist at the hospital to prescribe a strong neuroleptic medication for Billy so that "we don't have to worry about him getting crazy."

To address Billy's referral target behaviors—aggression and assaultive behavior—a treatment plan would also need to address negative staff biases. Chapter 9 gives recommendations concerning caregiver interventions. In Billy's case, the group home staff were given the opportunity to discuss their concerns and were provided with a backup plan to use if their worst fears materialized. Seeing themselves as more in control of the situation, they were then willing to cooperate with the treatment plan despite the absence of the requested medication.

The therapeutic team developed a treatment plan by constructing a Clinical Pathogenesis Map (CPM; see chapter 3) and identifying the variables most in need of intervention. These problem areas, which influenced each other and appeared to have direct functional links to the patient's hospitalizations, included (a) vulnerability to stress (e.g., poor self-esteem, self-criticism, inadequate early role models, poor coping alternatives); (b) increased stress (i.e., negative social situations, being laughed at); (c) expressive deficits (loud, rapid, inarticulate speech under stress); (d) further increased stress; (e) exhibition of aggression (and limited alternatives); and, finally, (f) intermittent reinforcement of aggression.

The team specified two main behavioral goals for an operantly based intervention for Billy: (a) to reduce verbal and physical aggressive or assaultive incidents and (b) to increase appropriate coping behaviors under stress (e.g., breathing deeply, speaking slowly, asking for help, leaving the area for a few minutes). In generating alternatives, they listed all possible intervention strategies for both goals. Many alternatives were listed under each goal. Because the goals involved behavioral reduction, both positive reinforcement and punishment-based strategies were included.

The decision-making process involved rating each alternative on criteria including the likelihood of effectiveness; the likelihood of optimal implementation; the level of restrictiveness; the long- and short-term consequences for the patient, group home staff, family, and community; and the amount of time and effort required. Psychopharmacological alternatives received a low rating because those supported by the current psychiatric literature had largely been ruled out in trials conducted during Billy's hospitalization.

The behavioral intervention chosen for Billy involved a positive-reinforcement-based token economy that could be implemented at the group residence. Billy's appropriate behavior during group meetings was defined and included among his "earning" behaviors. He received tokens for practicing appropriate behaviors with a counselor at his group home each evening, as well as for exhibiting behavioral alternatives to aggression in vivo. The resident counselors were helped to develop a plan for teaching such alternative behaviors.

Reinforcers, chosen carefully, included activities identified on the basis of the Premack Principle (1959). This principle concerns the relationship between behaviors exhibited by an individual. It posits that, for any two behaviors, the rate of the less frequent behavior can be increased if access to the higher-rate behavior is made contingent on exhibition of the lower-rate behavior. For example, when Billy was given the opportunity to do whatever he chose, one high-frequency behavior involved playing a game with an adult; a low-frequency behavior involved practicing his "slow-motion speaking" and "quiet voice" exercise. Thus, in Billy's token economy, the opportunity to play a game with an adult was contingent on his earning tokens for practicing his speaking exercises.

Implementation of Billy's treatment plan over the course of 2 months resulted in a significant decrease—to near zero levels—in both verbal and physical aggressive behavior at the group home. A 3-month follow-up evaluation found continued maintenance of treatment effects, as well as an increase in prosocial behaviors and a concomitant decrease in expressive speech deficits.

Summary

Reinforcement-based contingency management approaches represent some of the most prevalent and valuable strategies for the treatment of clients with dual diagnoses. However, empirically based, creative strategies require a sound decision-making process. To generate as many reinforcement-based alternatives as possible, readers may want to expand their knowledge of operant treatment strategies. Several helpful texts are Cooper, Heron, and Heward (1987); Kazdin (1975); Masters et al. (1987); and Matson and Andrasik (1983).

The therapist facing clinical decisions concerning a client with developmental disabilities has two important concerns: First, dually diagnosed clients are often referred under crisis conditions, with caregiving staff and other professionals expressing both a negative bias toward the client and a sense of urgency. It is extremely important to remain objective and not be drawn into such a crisis situation; otherwise, there is a strong temptation to reach unrealistically for immediate solutions. The cooperation of a peer or colleague can be helpful in monitoring clinical decision making at this point. Second, when a reinforcement-based strategy is under consideration, it is imperative to remember that learning new skills takes time, especially for clients with developmental disabilities. Although the basic strategies useful for clients without developmental disabilities are useful for this population as well, learning may take longer, require perseverative sessions, and demand frequent task analysis (the breaking down of a task into small steps) for many simple tasks. For example, before a token system is implemented, a client who is very young or has severe cognitive impairment may need training to understand the concept of the token as reinforcer. Such training may require sessions devoted to repeatedly giving the client a token and immediately exchanging it for a reinforcer. Each repetition is accompanied by a statement such as "You can have a _____ when you have a chip!" Empirical evaluation would show when the client is ready to actually earn reinforcers—for example, when offered a choice of several objects, including a token chip, the client consistently chooses the chip.

Contingency Management: Use of Punishment Procedures

Definition

Operant strategies designed to decrease or decelerate the frequency and/or duration of target behaviors include response-contingent aversive stimulation (punishment) and withdrawal of reinforcers.

Clinical Strategies

Strategies based on the removal of reinforcement include *extinction* (removal of contingent positive reinforcement or attention—e.g., ignoring tantrum behavior), *response cost* (imposition of a fine or penalty—e.g., grounding a resident for missing a curfew), and *time-out* from positive reinforcement (removal from a reinforcing activity—e.g., removing a child from the television room for 5 minutes as a consequence of cursing). Strategies based on aversive consequences (punishment) include *primary punishment* (e.g., squirting lemon juice in a child's mouth to curb severe head banging), *restraint* (e.g., tying the hands of a violent patient), and *overcorrection* (e.g., having a resident turn a light off 25 times in succession for inappropriately leaving it on).

Because of potential risks, deceleration techniques are frequently categorized according to varying levels of restrictiveness. Extinction strategies, those involving some form of reinforcer withdrawal, are considered less restrictive. Most published treatment guidelines would recommend trying them first, before response-contingent aversive strategies (i.e., primary punishment) are attempted. We strongly concur with this view. Moreover, in the decision-making process we have outlined, the less restrictive procedures, having fewer associated risks, would be rated more favorably than primary punishment approaches.

Clinical Applications

Deceleration strategies using aversive consequences are commonly directed toward behavioral targets that represent significant threat to the client or others in the environment—for instance, severe self-mutilating behavior or extreme physical aggression toward others (Lennox, Miltenberger, Spengler, & Erfanian, 1988). Such behaviors may be life-threatening if permitted to continue. In some cases, deceleration techniques are useful to bring about an initial decrease in a harmful behavior so that a reinforcement-based strategy may be properly implemented later.

Unlike extinction or differential reinforcement procedures, primary punishment can be effective even if the therapist does not know which reinforcers are maintaining the troublesome behavior. In other words, contingent use of a potent aversive stimulus to decrease a behavior does not depend on an accurate functional analysis of this behavior, nor does it necessitate an assessment of prosocial or adaptive behaviors that could be targeted as positive alternative responses. However, use of punishment strategies without this knowledge would be highly irresponsible and unethical because the goal of any treatment should be improvement in the client's functioning and adaptive skills.

Punishment procedures have been effective in treating severe aggression problems (Birnbrauer, 1968) and self-injurious behavior (Lovaas & Simmons, 1969). The effectiveness of mild punishment has been increased by the inclusion of positive reinforcement strategies for adaptive behavior. Virtually all published treatment guidelines and training manuals regarding behavioral principles emphasize the guideline that *punishments should not be used without concomitant efforts to reinforce appropriate behaviors.* Use of response-contingent aversive stimulation has given rise to significant legal and ethical debates. This is not surprising, in that punishment has certain serious limitations and untoward side effects, which include, but are not limited to, the following iatrogenic problems.

1. Primary punishment procedures are effective only in suppressing behavior, not necessarily in eliminating it (e.g., a patient who is suicidal stops making suicidal statements but remains depressed and at risk).

2. Punishment procedures increase avoidance behavior, particularly concerning the punishing agent, in such a way that adaptive behavior and positive relations are hindered (e.g., a father slaps his son's face when the boy becomes verbally aggressive; the son learns to suppress the verbal aggression when his father is present and thus avoids his father).

3. Punishment procedures provide instruction in aggression by modeling aggressive action as a coping alternative.

4. Punitive consequences can help engender specific negative emotional symptoms such as anxiety, hostility, and fear.

5. Punishment strategies do not teach adaptive coping alternatives; the client's behavioral repertoire is therefore not enhanced with new coping skills.

In contrast, strategies using reinforcer withdrawal, such as extinction, carry much less risk of untoward side effects and, if based on a thorough assessment of a client's individual reinforcement profile, can be very effective (Feshbach, 1964; Martin & Foxx, 1973). Moreover, in contrast to the suppression of behavior that occurs with primary punishment strategies, extinction procedures may be more likely to result in actual elimination of the behavior.

Special Considerations for Clients With Mental Retardation

Although we would not totally negate the value of response-contingent aversive strategies (to do so would be counter to the notion of generating an inclusive list of possible alternatives), we believe that there has been an unfair focus in the literature on the efficacy of deceleration procedures, an emphasis possibly resulting in the temptation to use punishment strategies as a quick cure (Gardner, 1988). The following guidelines have been adapted from several sources (Favell, 1982; Gardner, 1988; Gardner & Cole, 1984; Nezu & Petronko, 1985) concerning the use of punishment-based alternatives. These guidelines should weigh heavily in the rating and evaluation of treatment strategies.

1. Like any treatment plan, the behavioral treatment should be based on a thorough and idiographic functional assessment of significant maintaining variables.

2. The behavior therapy strategies should reflect client-specific concerns, particularly with regard to the environmental context in which the behavior occurs, organismic (e.g., biological, genetic) variables, previous learning history, and current reinforcers.

3. The behavior therapy program should include procedures aimed at developing, strengthening, and maintaining specific prosocial and adaptive skills that will replace problem behaviors.

4. The behavior therapy program should reflect sound decision making; consideration of least restrictive procedures should precede a decision to use techniques of significant restrictiveness. (It may not always be possible to document that less restrictive procedures have been attempted, and it may actually be dangerous to the client or others to begin with strategies that a sound assessment indicates would not be effective.)

5. The behavior therapy program should be based on decisions that consider both long- and short-term benefits to the client.

6. When intrusive or aversive procedures are needed immediately to suppress dangerous, intense, or high-frequency behaviors, the selection of these procedures must be based on an empirical decision-making model—that is, on the clinician's best estimate of the factors influencing the problem behavior. This initial decision making should be considered temporary and a more thorough assessment conducted.

7. Aversive procedures should *never* be used in isolation but rather should be supplemented with strategies to limit possible negative side effects.

8. Although all behavioral (and other) treatments should be data based, programs using aversive procedures should be monitored particularly closely.

9. The aversive components of a program should be removed as soon as possible.

10. Punishment-based strategies should never be instituted as the result of caregivers' frustrations but only as the result of sound clinical decision making. We contend that protocols with a high degree of restrictiveness should be implemented only by those trained to do so effectively. For example, the practice current in some states of requiring a physician's referral for restraint equipment makes little sense if the physician has no competency in designing behavioral contingency programs or is unfamiliar with the foregoing guidelines.

Summary

Punishment-based deceleration treatment strategies are aimed at reducing a problem behavior. Because all punishment strategies restrict the client's freedom to some degree, professional and legal guidelines concerning such treatments have evolved. We have presented some of these. We strongly suggest that the use of a problem-solving framework further ensure that more restrictive strategies will be used only when they promise to provide maximum benefit to the client.

Social Learning Models of Treatment

Definition

Social learning theorists stress the importance of several causal determinants of behavior: person variables, environmental variables, and behavior variables. Each kind of variable both influences and is influenced by the other two. Bandura (1977b) termed this interacting system *reciprocal determinism*. Person variables are an individual's standards, values, beliefs, expectancies, self-evaluation, and repertoire of behaviors acquired through observational learning experiences (Mischel, 1973).

The following scenario illustrates reciprocal determinism: A young man with mental retardation favors Rambo movies with aggressive content (a person variable). He chooses to spent 5 evenings a week in front of his television set with rented Rambo movies (an environmental variable). While watching his hero attentively (a behavior variable), the young man learns new aggressive behaviors. He also learns that aggression is often reinforced and that tough, aggressive males often get attention from others. These newly acquired expectations (a person variable) may increase the likelihood that the young man will engage in these new aggressive behaviors. If these behaviors are reinforced—that is, he gets what he desires or obtains social attention—stable tendencies toward aggression may result.

Social learning theorists emphasize the self-regulation of behavior. Strategies that incorporate modeling, role-playing, and other cognitive-behavioral self-control techniques reflect social learning theory. Its concepts serve as rationales for treatments based on the teaching of new intrapersonal and interpersonal coping skills (Kanfer & Schefft, 1988).

Clinical Strategies

Social skills training programs usually include modeling, instruction, feedback, and role-playing. Self-control strategies incorporate training protocols derived from cognitive therapy (Beck, 1976), self-instruction (Whitman, Spence, & Maxwell, 1987), assertiveness training, problem-solving training (Nezu et al., 1991), and anger management training (Benson, 1986; Lochman, White, & Wayland, 1991).

Clinical Applications

Various social skills training packages have proven effective with dually diagnosed inpatients (Matson & Stephens, 1978; Matson & Zeiss, 1978). Cognitive-behavioral therapies based on self-control principles have also been shown to be effective with dually diagnosed populations. Many treatments have been adapted from programs demonstrated to be effective with nondisabled clients. An example is Benson's (Benson, Rice, & Miranti, 1986) anger-management treatment protocol, which involves a 12-week structured therapy and is based on Novaco's (1975) anger-management treatment for clients from the general population. This clinical intervention combines strategies including relaxation training, reinforcement, modeling, and behavioral rehearsal. Clients are taught to identify the situations that make them angry, the characteristics of their own responses to anger, and new ways of coping with their anger.

Nezu et al. (1991) have shown that a combination of assertiveness and problem-solving training is highly effective in reducing psychiatric symptoms, maladaptive behavior, and subjective distress in an outpatient sample of adults with mental retardation and various psychiatric disturbances. Gardner, Cole, Berry, and Nowinski (1983) reduced conduct problems in a sample of institutionalized adults with moderate cognitive impairment. Cole, Gardner, and Karan (1985) decreased aggression and increased work productivity with a self-management package that included self-monitoring, self-evaluation, and self-administration of consequences for behavior. Finally, current research indicates that self-instruction and self-control may be more effective than external contingency management systems for teaching new skills to individuals with mental retardation (Whitman, 1990; Whitman et al., 1987).

Special Considerations for Clients With Mental Retardation

Because many cognitive-behavioral strategies are based on clinical approaches developed for use with nonretarded individuals, it may be tempting to apply the same procedures with developmentally disabled clients. However, as noted previously, this translation is not simple. The following guidelines may be helpful.

1. Incorporate strategies for maintaining attention. Because attending to the stimulus to be learned is central to social learning, we have attempted to provide skill-building sessions that are entertaining. This effort has resulted in creative uses of video and audio technology, computer-assisted learning, role-plays, frequent client participation, and instructional games.

2. Because saliency of models is an important variable in social learning, we give careful consideration to the appropriateness of the model in each learning situation. In one instance, a young male with moderate mental retardation helped us develop a videotape that demonstrated specific self-control skills. Other clients later reported that watching a peer succeed at self-control was quite helpful.

3. For an individual with learning difficulties, we have found that repetition increases the likelihood that a skill will be learned. We have adopted the expectation that protocols may require many more sessions for persons with developmental disabilities than for others. Booster sessions may also be needed during follow-up periods.

4. Individuals vary greatly in their ability to generalize psychoeducational experiences. We have found, in implementing treatments based on self-control and self-regulatory strategies, that providing many concrete examples from a variety of situations can increase the likelihood that the client will actually apply the strategy.

5. Including specific reinforcement for use of newly learned skills seems to provide increased motivation to use new skills that are initially difficult to remember.

Clinical Example

Henry was a 28-year-old man with mild mental retardation and a concomitant diagnosis of schizophrenia. His group residence staff referred him because of behavior management difficulties—specifically, aggressiveness toward other residents and staff. Henry was described as "overreactive," "paranoid," and "explosive." For example, he had threatened another resident with a knife because the resident took a long time to finish his laundry. Henry blamed the circumstance on the notion that the other resident did not like him.

Following a thorough assessment and construction of a CPM, Henry's most salient focal problem was revealed to be impulsivity. The therapist's decision making led to a step-by-step program for shaping Henry's self-control behavior. The individualized program began with basic relaxation strategies and eventually introduced cognitive-behavioral self-control strategies.

Henry was first taught to think before reacting. Initially, he learned to breathe deeply to halt mounting anxiety and counter muscle tension. Next, Henry was taught to count to 10, then breathe deeply. Because this was difficult for him to learn, the therapist added an intermediate step to help Henry redirect himself toward better self-control. Henry would tell himself "Stop" and try to continue relaxation and deep breathing. He would then begin counting to 10 while continuing to breathe slowly and deeply.

Henry practiced this relaxation technique repeatedly during each session; he was also required to practice between sessions. Henry received an index card with pictorial reminders of the techniques, and staff members at his group residence were trained in coaching him to use them. In addition, the rationale for the techniques was explained at the residence so that the caregivers could supplement the treatment by reinforcing Henry's progress. Training the residence staff was also a strategic means of generalizing Henry's new skills, as they would be crucial in providing a positive therapeutic milieu for him in the group home.

When Henry demonstrated the ability to apply the self-control strategies, he was ready for structured role-plays where he could practice the new skills in situations that provoked intense anger. Some of the role-plays were based on actual circumstances. For others, therapist and client together invented scenarios that were likely to produce anger and resentment. Staff members were often included in these sessions, which provided a safe arena where Henry could practice behavioral responses to potentially anger-arousing situations.

Gradually, Henry began to apply these techniques outside of the therapy setting in actual situations that triggered resentment and anger.

Because staff members were included in the overall training, they were frequently available to help guide his behavior and reinforce approximations toward more effective self-control.

Several cognitive-behavioral interventions were introduced at this point. With some initial success in curbing Henry's tendency to act before thinking, the therapist was able to introduce new coping strategies and develop new cognitive skills. Social problem-solving training (Nezu & Nezu, 1991) was initiated. With this approach, for example, when Henry was feeling rejected, the therapist reviewed with him all possible ways that he could react. One alternative might be to become aggressive, as he had often done in the past. Another alternative might be going to his room, where he could calm down and use relaxation techniques. A third alternative might include talking to his counselor and asking for help in distracting himself, or thinking through the problem. Predictable consequences for each alternative were also reviewed. For example, aggressive acts would predictably be followed by physical restraint, loss of privileges, hospitalization, and shunning by other people.

Henry had initial difficulty learning to anticipate the consequences of his actions. One helpful strategy involved reviewing past incidents as a means of learning to predict possible consequences in the future. Gradually, Henry became quite adept at linking predictable consequences to concrete actions in hypothetical situations. This skill became part of Henry's cognitive-behavioral repertoire for reacting to stressful situations. After breathing deeply and counting to 10, he began to think through different possible actions and predict consequences. He was able to generate alternative courses of action, anticipate their consequences, and choose an alternative on the basis of this information.

Henry was also introduced to stress inoculation training. In this aspect of treatment, he was taught to (a) anticipate difficult situations, (b) picture himself coping in each situation, and (c) reinforce himself for actual attempts at coping with the situation. It was especially helpful for him to rehearse adaptive self-statements such as "I can handle this" when facing a stressful situation or feeling the onset of negative emotions.

Finally, changes were made in Henry's token reinforcement system. Several specific privileges were made contingent on his use of the new self-control skills. For example, by exhibiting self-control, Henry could now earn the opportunity to have his girlfriend visit. This was a potent reinforcer, as these visits had been arranged randomly in the past. Further, Henry met weekly with his primary counselor to review progress, solve new problems, and schedule his activity reinforcer for the week.

Summary

Cognitive-behavioral strategies based on social learning theories and aimed at increased self-regulation are a rich source of treatment alternatives for individuals with dual diagnoses. We have presented some of the alternatives. Because generalized self-control is a core characteristic of people who have adjusted to their environments, further research should explore the application of such treatments for people with mental retardation.

Many of these skill-building strategies are often more effectively implemented in group settings, as groups provide greater opportunities for peer involvement and social reinforcement. For this reason we will discuss them in greater detail in chapter 10, which offers treatment guidelines concerning environmental issues.

NONBEHAVIORAL APPROACHES

Psychopharmacological Treatment Approaches

Psychoactive drugs are often used to treat behavioral difficulties of individuals with mental retardation. However, our current knowledge about the efficacy of specific medications in relieving symptoms for dually diagnosed persons is inadequate. The application of psychopharmacological treatment for persons with mental retardation has been characterized as "abysmal" (Gualtieri, 1988). This is tragic because such treatment, when based on a careful assessment and the use of systematic decision making, can be an important and powerful source of help.

Clinical Strategies

Research with nonretarded populations indicates many problems that may be amenable to change via pharmacologic intervention. These include aggression and assaultive behavior, anorexia, anxiety, attentional disorders, depression, psychotic symptoms, enuresis, sleep disturbances, social withdrawal, and stereotypic behavior (Wilson, 1989). Further, goals of pharmacologic therapy may include reduction of arousal; positive changes in behavioral symptoms; and improvement in affective symptoms, perceptual functioning, verbal communication, and features of attention deficit disorder. Major drug groups include antipsychotic agents (phenothiazines, thioxanthenese, butyrophenones), stimulants, antidepressants, lithium, anxiolytics, and anticonvulsants (Aman, 1983). For each class of drug there are specific indications, particular risks of toxicity, and requirements for careful medical monitoring. The professional who manages the treatment plan for a dually diagnosed client needs to be familiar with these classes of drugs, their potential uses and contraindications, and symptoms of toxicity. Familiarizing the reader with all pharmacological alternatives is beyond the scope of this chapter; several good sources treat the subject in detail (Aman, 1983; Pirodsky, 1981; Sovner, 1988).

Special Considerations for Clients With Mental Retardation

Developmentally disabled clients are frequently prescribed potent medications that have no clear relation to a particular diagnosis. Often no treatment goals are specified and no rationale is provided for the use of one medication rather than another. Further, these clients are monitored infrequently, polypharmacy is often practiced, and medications are continued despite an absence of documented benefit to the individual. Finally, professionals responsible for behavioral programming often continue to develop treatment protocols in isolation without considering the client's current medication regimen and the way medication may enhance or inhibit treatment effects.

We have often received consultation requests from psychiatrists who, when asked about a client's diagnosis, would simply reply, "He's retarded and agitated." We know of situations where state regulations prohibit PRN prescribing of antipsychotic medication in an effort to curb neuroleptic abuse but where clients have, for years, had standing prescriptions for such drugs. Change is needed, and it can occur through sound decision making, ethical clinical practice, and more careful public policy planning.

In practice, psychopharmacological treatments are often nonspecific concerning a given psychiatric diagnosis. Moreover, potent antipsychotic drugs appear overly prescribed. For example, a study of drug use in community residences showed that 25.9% of a sample of 1,000 residents were receiving psychotropic medication (Hill, Balow, & Bruininks, 1985). A small minority of these drugs were given for a "psychiatric condition"; the great majority of them were prescribed for "overactive behavior." Aggregate data from studies in which medical files of persons with mental retardation were examined suggest that psychotropic medications were administered to about 35% to 50% of mentally retarded persons living in institutions (Sprague, 1982) and approximately 20% to 35% of mentally retarded persons living in the community (Lipman, 1986). Other surveys have indicated that 48% of persons with mental retardation received medication for behavioral control (Agran & Martin, 1985) and 86% of an institutionalized sample received such medications (Craig & Behar, 1980).

Such data support a characterization of developmentally disabled individuals as the most medicated people in society (Aman & Singh, 1983). We are not aware of any well-controlled psychopharmacological research on dually diagnosed outpatient adult clients. However, trends in the literature highlight the importance of such research. Pharmacological researchers (Poling, Picker, & Hall-Johnson, 1983) have suggested the kinds of information that would be most important to an understanding of drug-behavior interactions. These categories of information, which parallel the kinds of information essential to a case-by-case understanding of clients, include the following.

1. The type of drug administered and the reason for its administration

2. The dosage and the way it was determined

3. The route of administration

4. The time of drug administration in relation to the time of behavioral assessment

5. The length of exposure to drug treatment

6. Relevant characteristics of the client

7. All previous use of drugs (prescribed or leisure) by the client

Pending more controlled research on both the efficacy of various medications for specific disorders and the interaction of pharmacological and behavioral interventions, we advocate the evaluation of pharmacological treatment on a case-by-case basis, as illustrated by the following clinical example.

Clinical Example

John, at initial contact, was a 50-year-old white male with moderate mental retardation. His history of emotional and behavioral difficulties since childhood included aggression, hyperactivity, and stereotypic behaviors. He had been placed in a variety of institutional and residential care facilities. John was currently living in a community residence and had been referred to a psychiatric service that specialized in the treatment of persons with dual diagnoses.

Although the residence staff described John as exhibiting maladaptive and aggressive behavior that was unpredictable and unprovoked, subsequent interviews revealed that the group residence had recently undergone many staffing and administrative changes. In addition, the home had received a new resident, described as particularly assaultive and aggressive. Through independent interviews conducted by a psychologist and a psychiatrist, John was reliably diagnosed as meeting DSM-III-R criteria for Axis II diagnoses of autistic disorder and moderate to severe mental retardation.

Following a comprehensive evaluation, and in consultation with John's caregiving staff, we identified the following target behaviors: aggression (slapping and hitting others), pushing items off desk and table surfaces, rummaging through other clients' belongings and digging in garbage, excessive handwashing, and refusing to enter the van for the trip home from the day program. All behavioral data were collected by the group home staff, with several staff members making independent observations as a check for reliability.

The design of this $N = 1$ study was a modified version of a multiple baseline across behaviors format. Specifically, John's treatment included four phases: Phase 1 (4 weeks of baseline data collection across all target behaviors), Phase 2 (4 weeks of medication alone), Phase 3 (4 weeks of medication plus behavioral programming for only two of the target behaviors—rummaging and handwashing), and Phase 4 (4 weeks of medication plus behavioral programming for all five target behaviors). Data collection for all target behaviors continued across all treatment phases.

Medication consisted of the maximum daily dose of 240 mg of propranolol, administered orally in two doses. Propranolol, a beta adrenergic receptor blocker, has been evaluated in several open trials for use in treating violent and aggressive brain-injured patients (Yudofsky, Silver, & Schneider, 1987). As with much of our knowledge about drug-behavior relationships, there is some initial evidence that propranolol may be effective for treating aggressive or self-abusive behavior; however, methodologically sound studies are lacking. This lack may be due in part to the high degree of compliance required of clients' caregivers for the daily monitoring of vital signs (Boshes, 1987). In John's case, the residence staff's monitoring of the vital signs and administration of the medication was supervised by a board-certified psychiatrist.

John's behavioral programming involved a token system incorporating a differential reinforcement of other behavior (DRO) paradigm. Selection of reinforcers was based on a survey plus patient observation. We trained residence staff to optimally implement the token economy and provided hands-on supervision of the program.

The results in John's case support the utility of an approach integrating drug and behavioral treatment (Nezu, Nezu, & Miescher, 1989). Specifically, the drug regimen appeared to reduce aggression significantly but had no apparent impact on the other behaviors. The addition of a contingency management program during the last two treatment phases enhanced the overall treatment protocol. Figure 8.1 graphically represents the frequency of John's target behaviors across the phases of treatment.

Summary

Psychopharmacologic agents have a profound effect on both cognitive and behavioral functioning. The person with mental retardation and mental illness may significantly improve or seriously worsen, depending on the competency of those who are providing the psychopharmacologic intervention. Possible interactions of drugs and other treatment modalities must be assessed. In ethical terms, the goal of any psychopharmacologic treatment should be to maintain the client's maximum level of cognitive abilities while obtaining the most effective intervention.

Creative Arts Therapy

Some professionals believe that therapies based on art, dance, and other creative forms can help developmentally disabled individuals express

Figure 8.1 Target Behavior Frequency Across Treatment Phases for John

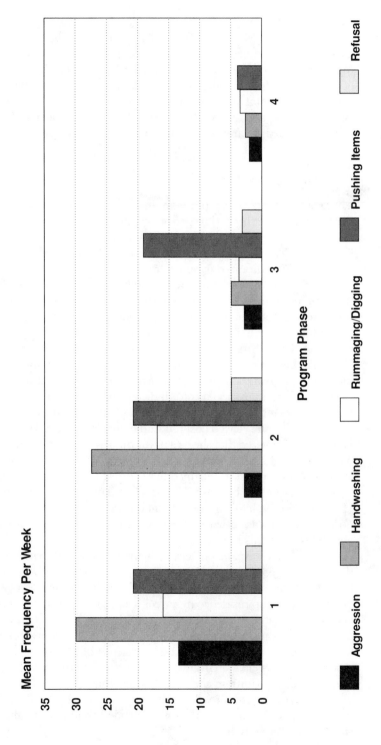

feelings, relate to one another through shared artistic experience, and gain self-esteem (Jakab, 1982). Rhythm and music therapy have been useful in structuring group interaction and improving motor functioning (Zagelbaum & Rubino, 1991). Recently, there has been advocacy of the position that "intelligence" itself is very limited and that an individual with mental retardation may not be delayed in such areas as rhythm, music, and dance (Burt, 1990). Recognition of an individual's talents in an artistic area would almost certainly enhance his or her self-esteem, as shown in the case example that follows.

Clinical Example

Doris was a 25-year-old woman with mental retardation and a second diagnosis of borderline personality disorder. Early years of parental rejection and abuse, in combination with multiple foster placements, had restricted her opportunities to develop effective emotional coping strategies. In addition, during several psychiatric hospitalizations, she had learned that violent, manipulative behavior was frequently followed by an increase in attention. When Doris met one of us for a consultation interview, she had recently experienced her fifth hospitalization following a threat to throw herself from the fourth-floor window of her group residence. Since her fourth hospitalization 8 months previously, Doris had been receiving antiseizure, antipsychotic, and antidepressant medications, with no improvement. She had undergone 2 years of individual psychotherapy, and records indicated that many different medications had been tried; her condition remained unchanged.

When we interviewed hospital staff members who had worked with Doris, we discovered that she had never missed the creative arts session on the unit. This level of appropriate interest was in direct contrast to her frequent disruptions during other activities. Consultation for Doris had been requested because she was viewed as "treatment resistant." However, no one had considered that the treatments offered, although possibly effective for other clients, might not have been idiographically appropriate for this individual.

Following a reevaluation period, all medications were removed except the antiseizure drug and Doris was given a structured creative arts therapy program with daily classes. Later, Doris was invited to lead her peers at the group residence in a weekly creative movement class. She was advised that, because she was now a "teacher," she had the responsibility of functioning as a model. Doris was paid 10 dollars for each class she instructed, and this heightened her sense of responsibility. Doris reported that participation in creative arts therapy made her feel important and helpful. In addition, she taught others that, when they were overwhelmed with "nasty or wild" feelings, dancing, beating a drum, or writing a speech about those feelings provided an important alternative to self-destructive behavior.

Other Forms of Psychotherapy

There are no studies examining the value and utility of treatment strategies based on either supportive or exploratory psychodynamic therapies for a mentally retarded population. This is unfortunate because those therapies might be beneficial for dually diagnosed adults who come to therapy because of emotional distress.

In discussing psychodynamic therapy for clients with dual diagnoses, Jakab (1982) cited the following treatment issues as basic to the double challenge of mental retardation and emotional disturbance.

1. A person with a developmental disability must adjust to the unchangeable consequences of that disability, including cognitive limitations, possible physical impairments, and a certain degree of social discrimination.

2. One aspect of treatment should involve motivating the client to use his or her assets to attain a higher level of social functioning.

3. In adapting treatment to the client's level of functioning, the therapist must find a balance regarding mental and chronological age, taking into account some predictable age-specific problems such as puberty, sexuality, end of schooling or education, menopause, and environmental crisis.

4. The method of therapy must be flexible and can range from nonverbal play therapy to dynamically oriented verbal therapy.

Jakab's points suggest how a therapy strategy not traditionally associated with clients with developmental disabilities may be adapted to the special needs of these clients. Certainly, the first three points could apply just as well to any form of psychosocially based treatment for this population.

Until studies of effective nonbehavioral treatment alternatives are sufficiently available to therapists in clinical practice, we are left with the alternative of creatively adapting, via the problem-solving model, procedures that have been successful with nondisabled populations.

SUMMARY

In this chapter, we grouped clinical intervention strategies that focus on the individual client into seven categories: Under the general heading of behavioral approaches are respondent learning approaches, reinforcement-based contingency management protocols, punishment-based contingency management approaches, and social learning approaches. Nonbehavioral approaches include psychopharmacologic treatments, creative arts therapy, and other forms of psychotherapy.

Although the behaviorally oriented strategies are the more data based, overall, a scientific foundation for clinical interventions with dually diagnosed clients is sorely lacking. Future research to address efficacy issues is crucial. Meanwhile, we strongly advocate use of the problem-solving model as one means of creatively adapting clinical interventions previously shown to be effective with nondisabled populations.

We remind the reader that the strategies discussed here should not be seen in isolation. Rather, the therapist needs to consider simultaneously a multitude of clinical strategies addressing focal problems related to the individual client, the caregiving system, and the environment.

Chapter 9

Treatment Guidelines: Focus on the Caregiving System

INTRODUCTION

Caregivers provide early learning experiences, serve as role models, and are often required to implement behavioral treatment plans in the home. For these reasons, in chapter 5 we emphasized the importance of evaluating the caregiving system. Assessment may suggest that the members of the caregiving system are part of the client's presenting problem. For example, parents of a developmentally disabled adult may have difficulty accepting their grown child's independent behavior. They may discourage or undermine his or her progress and advancement because of their own fears—for instance, fear of separation. As noted earlier, referral behaviors (e.g., aggressive outbursts) may actually serve a systemic function, such as enabling the client to continue living at home with the parents. In other situations, caregivers may themselves be viewed as the clients. Their emotional and/or physical resources may be depleted to the extent that they need individual treatment. They may suffer severe depression or anxiety that would certainly interfere with their ability to help the dually diagnosed individual. Finally, caregivers may possess unique strengths that allow them to function as part of the clinical team or even as cotherapists.

The therapist should assess the strengths, resources, possible pathology, and special needs of each family member or caregiver to determine if individual services or systemic interventions are required. As discussed in chapter 5, a functional systems analysis can yield information about these issues, focusing on interactions between individuals and identifying the functions of each person's behaviors in the system. In addition, assessment of each individual's resources, problem orientation, and general psychological well-being is important.

Even when the caregiving system is not part of the problem, it is often part of the solution. Caregivers are crucial in effecting behavioral change and providing continued support. Their roles with clients are more central than that of any consultant.

In this chapter, we will review areas of potential stress associated with caregiving and present models of coping as they apply to the treatment of family and staff members. Behavioral caregiver training and family systems interventions will be emphasized as treatment strategies. Finally, related issues such as social support, networking, and burnout will be discussed.

STRESS ASSOCIATED WITH CAREGIVING

As emphasized in chapter 5, the experience of parenting and/or caring for a developmentally disabled individual is inherently stressful. Families have difficulty coping with this experience for several reasons, including the lack of control over the stressor, the sense of loss associated with the stressor, the disruptions in family life created by the stressor, and the far-reaching emotional consequences of acknowledging the stressor (Figley, 1983; Sobotor, 1989). The impact of a family member's disability is never restricted to that member alone; immediate and extended family members are also affected (Figley, 1983; Lyon & Preis, 1983).

A family with a developmentally disabled child must cope with two sets of demands: those inherent in family living and those created by the presence of the child's disability (Harris, Boyle, Fong, Gill, & Stanger, 1987). The parents must deal with both the loss of an anticipated "normal" child and the heavy demands of their actual situation (Farran, Metzger, & Sparling, 1986). The social stressors demand both immediate and long-term responses. The need to cope with these additional stressors makes the family more vulnerable to dysfunction.

Certain factors interfere with successful coping by increasing the likelihood of family crisis and the consequent demand on family resources. These factors include (a) the ambiguity of the stressor, (b) the severity and duration of the stressor, and (c) the degree to which the stressor renders the individual incongruent with community norms (Bristol, 1984). In these terms, the presence of a developmentally disabled or dually diagnosed child is a severe stressor of long duration that sets the family apart from other families in the community. In addition, the child's learning potential and eventual placement are often difficult to predict, and thus the situation is high in ambiguity.

Effects on Mothers and Fathers

In response to the chronic stress of parenting a disabled child, both mothers and fathers have been found to be depressed, to have lowered self-esteem, and to be interpersonally dissatisfied. Mothers, however, experience the intense effects of stress to a significantly greater degree than do fathers (Bristol, 1984; Holroyd, 1974; Houser, 1987). Mothers describe themselves as being unable to pursue personal goals and having little free time (Holroyd, 1974), and they report ambivalence and grief over the amount of time devoted to the disabled child at their own expense and that of the family (DeMyer, 1979).

There is ample evidence that mothers of children with physical and developmental disabilities experience considerably more stress than do fathers. Mothers of such children report being more moody and prone to illness (Holroyd, 1974). They more acutely experience their child's acceptance or rejection by the community (Bristol, 1984; Holroyd, 1974), and they report considerably more family disharmony than do fathers (Holroyd, 1974).

Depressive Symptoms

Depressive symptomatology among mothers of children with disabilities has been documented in several studies (e.g., Cummings, Bayles, & Rie, 1966; Waisbren, 1980). In one study of mothers of autistic and dysphasic children, almost one-third reported depression associated with the stress of living with a disabled child (Cox, Rutter, Newman, & Bartak, 1975).

Some researchers have compared the rates of major depression in mothers of disabled and nondisabled children (Breslau & Davis, 1986). Experiencing chronic stress, the mothers of children with disabilities were found to suffer more dysphoria and more somatic symptoms than did other mothers. Over 30% of mothers of disabled children reported depressive symptoms, compared to 16% of mothers of other children. Nevertheless, the lifetime rates of major depressive disorders in the two samples were not significantly different. Thus, the difference between the two groups was in the experience of depressive symptoms, rather than in the presence of the complete syndrome of major depressive disorder. The mothers of disabled children, however, reported onset of the first depressive episode at an earlier age; this typically corresponded to the birth or first year of life of the child. Finally, depressed mothers of disabled children experienced more episodes of depressive symptoms than did depressed mothers of other children.

These findings suggest that the chronic stress experienced by mothers of children with disabilities may help precipitate episodes of depression. The implications concerning the design of treatment plans for dually diagnosed clients are significant. Specifically, treatment alternatives aimed at caregiver depression or somatic disorders may need to be considered in the decision-making process.

Marital Distress

The stress of having a developmentally disabled child can also affect the couple and marital harmony, although the effect is variable. Studies of couples who have children with Down syndrome indicate that some couples experience marital dissatisfaction associated with raising such a child, whereas others cope well, without significant marital disharmony (Gath, 1977, 1978).

A number of factors can affect a couple's ability to cope. The age of the child, the child's diagnosis, and the quality of the marital relationship before the child's birth all influence the adjustment of the couple (Crnic, Friedrich, & Greenberg, 1983). These factors help to explain some of the variability in different people's ability to cope effectively with similar situations. In addition, individual coping styles and available support systems significantly affect caregivers' adjustment and their ability to help rather than hinder the client's treatment.

Implications for Caregiver Treatment

Specific treatment alternatives based on stress-coping models address varying caregiver characteristics. The therapist working with caregivers thus has additional strategies to consider in the decision-making process.

MODELS OF COPING

Many models of coping and adaptation have been proposed (D'Zurilla & Nezu, 1989). Several of these are particularly useful in the treatment of caregivers, as they integrate individual and systemic factors.

According to the Stress Adaptation Model (Farran et al., 1986), the changes associated with stressors and the ability to make adaptive responses depend on both intrapersonal and interpersonal variables. Specifically, these authors note that adaptive capacity is shaped by prior coping experience, social support, and personal protective factors.

Locus of control is one personal protective factor that may be important in alleviating the effects of stress. For example, Farran et al. (1986) found that, among mothers of disabled infants, those with a high degree of internal control were judged to have better behavioral interactions with their children than mothers whose locus of control was more external. This result suggests that increasing a caregiver's internal locus of control may be an important treatment goal.

A model that identifies other personal variables as important in predicting coping ability is the "ABCX" Model (Hill, 1949, 1958; McCubbin & Patterson, 1983). This model attempts to explain the effect of a stressor on the family in terms of the family's crisis-meeting resources and their definition of the event. Crisis-meeting resources include formal supports, informal supports, and individual characteristics. The definition of the event is the subjective meaning given to the stressor (Wikler, 1986). Family members may, for example, view the presence of a disabled child as an opportunity to grow from a challenge. In such a family, members become active agents of adaptation. Treatment goals gleaned from this model may include changing a family's definition of the disability, enhancing their crisis-meeting resources, or strengthening each member's individual coping abilities.

Matheny, Aycock, Pugh, Curlette, and Canela (1986) have also presented a comprehensive model of coping. Their model emphasizes assessing the demands created by the disability, determining the coping resources of the family, and ascertaining the availability of various types of social support. Coping resources include specific familial values, familial beliefs, and the self-esteem of family members.

A line of recent research on the role of individual factors in moderating the effects of stress has concentrated on the personality attribute known as "hardiness" (Ganellen & Blaney, 1984; Kobasa, 1979; Maddi, Kobasa, & Hoover, 1979). After experiencing extreme stress, individuals with hardy personalities remain healthy as a function of a constellation of characteristics that differentiate them from people who are vulnerable to physical illness and other negative stress effects (Ganellen & Blaney, 1984). These characteristics include sense of control, commitment, and challenge. Hardy persons perceive their locus of control to be internal— that is, they believe they can influence events in their lives. A perceived external locus of control, in contrast, leads to feelings of helplessness. Commitment is a general sense of purposefulness and a tendency to be active and involved. The challenge dimension refers to the perception of events as challenges and opportunities.

In Ganellen and Blaney's (1984) model, personal vulnerability to stress is mediated by individual factors, such as hardiness, and situational factors, such as support networks. In a study designed to assess the roles of hardiness and social support in the alleviation of stress among mothers of autistic children, Gill and Harris (1991) found that the personality variable of hardiness increased the ability of some individuals to endure and cope under stressful circumstances.

All stress-coping models underscore the importance of a variety of coping styles. Cohen and Lazarus (1979) have examined coping in terms of instrumental and palliative strategies. They define instrumental strategies as those focused on implementing change directly, in persons or in the environment. Palliative coping strategies are focused on tolerating stress and minimizing its effects through internal mechanisms, such as finding alternative sources of satisfaction or holding a philosophically comforting view of life. Successful coping may involve the flexible use of both kinds of strategies.

More recently, D'Zurilla and Nezu (D'Zurilla & Nezu, 1989; Nezu & D'Zurilla, 1989) described a transactional/problem-solving model that focuses on social problem solving as a general coping strategy. In this model, stress is viewed as a function of the interaction among stressful life events, emotional states, and problem-solving coping. The latter is defined as a broad, versatile, and adaptive strategy. Problem-solving goals may be problem focused, emotion focused, or both, depending on the specific problem situation and how it is defined and appraised by the caregiver. When situational demands are appraised as changeable or controllable (e.g., a need to improve the client's compliance in taking medication), problem-focused goals can be adopted. If emotional stress is significant, emotion-focused goals (e.g., initial adjustment to a child's disability) may be more appropriate.

The transactional/problem-solving model provides a highly useful alternative for clinical stress management treatment of caregivers. Like the clinical decision-making model described throughout the book, this model presupposes an exhaustive search for the variables that can affect an individual caregiver's symptomatology.

When developing a list of potential treatment alternatives regarding clinical stress management for caregivers, we have found it useful to classify them as problem-focused strategies or emotion-focused strategies because assessment may indicate a greater need for one or the other focus. Some treatments would fall under both headings because they focus both on emotional or cognitive change and on concrete, instrumental skills (Nezu & Nezu, 1989a). As part of problem-solving therapy, the therapist and the caregiver attempt to discover or invent the best coping response or response combination, using the caregiver's existing response repertoire as defined by assessment. This procedure capitalizes on the individual's unique strengths and resources and determines the "best" coping response individually, using the caregiver's personal criteria for effectiveness (e.g., goals, values, feelings).

Table 9.1 lists stress-coping interventions under the headings of problem-focused and emotion-focused strategies. (The distinction is necessarily artificial with interventions such as problem-solving therapy, which focuses on multiple aspects of coping.)

Two strategies listed in Table 9.1, caregiver training (a problem-focused strategy) and family or systems therapy (a more emotion-focused strategy geared to changing caregiver perceptions) have proven very effective in the reduction of caregiver stress and in the overall treatment of individuals with dual diagnoses. We will discuss these two treatment strategies in more detail.

CAREGIVER TRAINING

Caregiver training programs have reduced stress by helping parents teach their children functional skills and appropriate behavior (Bristol, 1984; Harris, 1982, 1984). Parents can learn to modify their children's behaviors, including aggression, noncompliance (Patterson, Chamberlain, & Reid, 1982; Webster-Stratton, 1985), hyperactivity, disruptive behavior,

Table 9.1 Useful Coping Skills for Caregiver Stress Management

Common problem-focused strategies

Problem-solving training
Assertiveness training
Communication skills
Self-management skills
Time-management skills
Job skills
Financial management skills
Housekeeping skills
Sexual skills
Self-instructional skills
Covert rehearsal
Behavioral rehearsal
Role-playing
Self-advocacy skills
Caregiver training in behavior management

Common emotion-focused strategies

Problem-solving/coping therapy
Cognitive restructuring
Relaxation skills training
    Imagery and deep breathing
    Autogenic training
    Self-hypnosis
    Progressive muscle relaxation
    Meditation
Desensitization therapy
Exposure-based treatment
Catharsis (expressing feelings and emotions)
Seeking social support
Religious counseling, prayer
Distraction (increased leisure)
Thought stopping
Humor
Pleasant activities
Eating
Drinking
Anxiety medications, antidepressants
Physical exercise
Acceptance/resignation
Family therapy
Marital therapy

and self-stimulation (Johnson & Brown, 1969; Kurtz, Cook, & Failla, 1972). Several researchers have demonstrated that parents can alter their style of interacting with their child and can thus influence the child's behavior (e.g., Forehand & McMahon, 1981; Harris, 1983).

Caregiver training typically deals with attending to behavior, rewarding appropriate behavior or extinguishing inappropriate behavior, and requesting behaviors or issuing commands. Initially, emphasis is on developing positive exchanges between parent and child. Parents are often taught through modeling and coached role-play sessions. Play activities are often used to help parents behave more spontaneously with their child and to alert them to the possibility of more positive interaction (Berlin & Critchley, 1989). In later sessions, there is usually an emphasis on handling negative behaviors to prevent the development of a coercive pattern of interactions. Table 9.2 outlines a typical caregiver training program.

Caregiver training has been the primary mechanism for teaching family members techniques to change behaviors of developmentally disabled clients (Harris, Alessandri, & Gill, 1991). Such training may be considered an instrumental and problem-focused coping strategy, as it helps to change the situation concretely and immediately. At the same time, caregiver training requires commitment, motivation, and acceptance of the challenge; it often results in feelings of efficacy for the caregiver. The overall result usually includes improvements in behavior, more positive interactions between parents and children or staff and clients, and reduced stress. In this respect, caregiver training functions as an emotion-focused strategy.

Breiner (1989) has discussed some key concerns for the therapist conducting parent training. It is important to address the perception that a problem behavior results from developmental delays or disabilities and thus is not amenable to change. If parents see a behavior as unchangeable, it is unlikely that they will derive full benefit from training. In addition, it is important to assess the parents themselves, especially for the impact of behavior management difficulties on their self-esteem. Before engaging the caregivers in behavioral training, it may be appropriate to invoke other treatment strategies listed in Table 9.1. Parents who feel that they have failed with their child will need special attention. They may need reassurance about the frequency of behavior management problems among developmentally disabled individuals or about the need for specialized training in behavior management. They may also need encouragement, reinforcement, feedback, and additional means of managing stress throughout the training process.

Some caregiver training programs are information oriented, educating caregivers about symptoms and behavioral manifestations of psychiatric disorders. Helping caregivers understand management difficulties in the context of the disability can assist in reducing stress; it can

Table 9.2   Outline for Caregiver Behavioral Training

Session 1

A. Introduction of project staff and participants

B. Distribution of workshop outline

C. Statement of workshop goals

   1. Provide caretakers with training in behavior modification and social learning theory.

   2. Provide hands-on experience for caretakers through group exercises and use of strategies at home.

   3. Increase each caretaker's competency as a paraprofessional within the home.

D. Orientation to behavioral treatment approach

E. Group exercise

F. Assignments

   1. Read *The ABC's for Parents: An Educational Workshop in Behavioral Modification* (Rettig, 1973), chapters 1 and 2.

   2. Complete a list of 10 behaviors (handout). List behaviors in terms of excesses and deficits. Define behaviors in observable terms.

Session 2

A. Brief review on defining behavior in observable terms

B. Group exercise: Have participants share definitions from behavior lists to provide examples of well-defined behavior.

C. Observing and recording behavior—methods

   1. Frequency methods

   2. Interval methods

   3. Duration methods

   4. ABC method (antecedents, behavior, consequence)

D. Group exercise: Have participants role-play a behavior problem. Ask group to observe and construct an objective account of the scene via the ABC method of recording.

E. Deciding which behavior requires intervention

F. Group exercise: Use example from group to demonstrate the process of selecting two valid target behaviors.

G. Assignment

   1. Record observations of two selected target behaviors over a week.

   2. Read *ABC's for Parents,* chapter 3.

Table 9.2 (cont'd)

Session 3

A. Developing a behavior change strategy—the starting point

B. Introduction of basic learning principles

    1. Positive reinforcement

    2. Negative reinforcement

    3. Punishment (Type I)

    4. Punishment (Type II)

    5. Premack Principle

    6. Reinforcement of incompatible behavior

C. Group exercise: View videotape, *Behavioral Principles for Parents* (Baxley, 1979). Follow manual for instructions pertaining to film discussion.

D. Assignment

    1. Look for examples of principles involved in the behavior observed during the week.

    2. Continue to collect ABC data for two target behaviors.

    3. Read *ABC's for Parents,* chapters 4 and 6.

Session 4

A. Group exercise: Review participants' observations of learning principles they saw operating during week.

B. Group exercise: Review observation methods through the following exercise. Tell participants that you will portray a child who frequently bites his or her hand. In a 3-minute scene, a volunteer from the group will attempt to have you put a puzzle together. The scene will be played four times, giving participants the opportunity to use all four recording methods.

    1. Frequency method

    2. Interval method

    3. Duration method

    4. ABC method

Provide participants with appropriate sample data sheets prior to each role-play.

C. Choosing an observation method for collection of baseline data

    1. Use of initial ABC data

    2. Consideration of needed information versus practical considerations

D. Group exercise: Review several participants' ABC data from previous week. Have group engage in choosing an observation method for baseline data.

E. Assignment

    1. Begin baseline observation of target behavior.

Session 5

A. Reinforcement principle
   1. Shaping
   2. Premack Principle
   3. Token economy systems
B. Group exercise: Have group members practice delivering reinforcement to one another, taking the roles of caregiver and child. Ask other members to comment on the points stressed during the lecture.
C. Videotape presentation: Reinforcement.
D. Assignment
   1. Read *ABC's for Parents,* chapter 5.
   2. Continue to record baseline data on target behavior.
   3. Conduct reinforcer survey of child at home.

Session 6

A. Decreasing behavior—principles and strategies
   1. Punishment (Type I)
      a. Problematic side effects
      b. Necessary cost/benefit decision
      c. Types of punishment (Type I)
         (1) Reprimands
         (2) Overcorrection
         (3) Restraints
         (4) Painful stimuli (include discussion of legal/ethical considerations)
   2. Punishment (Type II)
      a. Types of punishment (Type II)
B. Group exercise: View and discuss project videotape demonstration on decreasing behavior.
C. Assignment
   1. Continue baseline data regarding target behavior.
   2. Read *ABC's for Parents,* chapter 9.
   3. Read handout explaining least restrictive treatment guidelines.

Session 7

A. Deciding on intervention strategy
   1. Use the least restrictive, yet most effective, method.
   2. Always include a component based on positive reinforcement. In this way, new adaptive behaviors are learned, and the child experiences successes.
   3. Assess your own environment and life-style.
   4. Assess your own capabilities. Begin with strategies that may be easier to implement.

Table 9.2 (cont'd)

B. Learning to solve problems systematically (provide handouts on the problem-solving model)

C. Group exercise: Choose behavior data from group volunteer and engage group in practice of using problem-solving guidelines to decide on intervention strategy.

D. Assignment

   1. Use problem-solving process to decide on an intervention strategy for modifying target behavior.

   2. Share program plans with family and plan to begin following next training session.

Session 8

A. Group exercise: Invite participants to share their intervention plans with the group and role-play portions of their strategies for group discussion.

B. Special training issues—cues and prompts

   1. View and discuss videotape presentation on cues and prompts.

C. Special training issues—self-injurious behavior and instructions for seeking additional professional consultation

D. Assignment

   1. Begin intervention strategy regarding target behavior.

   2. Keep accurate record of behavior throughout home strategy implementation.

Session 9

A. Review of participants' progress and group discussion of difficulties, using problem-solving model to generate solutions

B. Future directions—planning phase-out of the intervention strategy

   1. Monitoring progress through observation, recording, and graphing of behavior change

   2. Modifying methods of reinforcement

      a. Extending time between reinforcement periods

      b. Changing schedules of reinforcement

      c. Replacing tangible with social reinforcement

      d. Periodically taking future data to check for maintenance of progress

C. Assignment

   1. Continue intervention strategy regarding target behavior.

   2. Continue observing, recording, and graphing data.

Session 10

A. Review of participants' program progress and group discussion of difficulties

B. Completion of program evaluation and feedback form

C. Closing comments from workshop director

also aid them in depersonalizing the behavior problems or psychiatric symptoms. In one such situation, a mother, perplexed that her daughter refused to match socks at home when she frequently matched colors at school, became terribly frustrated and angry. She felt manipulated by the daughter, who randomly paired socks from a pile when instructed to match them. An explanation of this behavior came from the girl's teacher, who, in assessing the child's skills, determined that her learning had not generalized beyond matching colored blocks: She could not yet match papers, cups, beads, or socks. In other words, she had not yet reached the stage of instruction in which generalization had become a focus of teaching. When the mother heard this explanation and learned of a plan for gradually teaching generalization of the skill, she was relieved and realized that her daughter's behavior was not intentional. She also understood how she could help her daughter learn the skill.

Similarly, a caregiver in training once became very frustrated with a group home resident who asked for a repeated explanation of the day's events. The resident had hallucinated through the first explanation, hearing voices and responding to them. The trainee reprimanded the resident, saying, "If you can't listen the first time, you should not be told again." The caregiver failed to understand that psychiatric symptoms can interfere with the processing of information. When such symptoms are better understood, caregivers are less likely to interpret symptoms as willful behavior or as a manifestation of obstinacy or resistance to treatment.

Information about the ways in which symptoms affect interaction, attention, and behavior can alleviate feelings of futility, exhaustion, or frustration on the part of the caregiver. This is an important consideration for any professional working with caregivers, as these feelings often lead to a sense of hopelessness and burnout.

The parent training approach is often used with staff members who work with developmentally disabled individuals. Like family, professional staff can become frustrated and alienated. They may also feel inadequate and lose self-confidence if they are not effective with their clients. Like family members, they can benefit by learning techniques for managing problem behaviors and for fostering the development of positive behaviors.

Broadening the Focus of Staff Training

In addition to behavior management skills and understanding of symptoms, training should address other areas relevant to staff effectiveness. Staff members should be sensitized to the importance of environmental elements, both physical and social. The impact of modeling merits special attention: Staff members need to understand how clients can learn behavior from observing peers or caregivers. It is also important to address the issue of interactional styles and to educate staff in supportive, non-punitive, and normalizing ways to communicate with clients.

Staff members should be informed about the stress associated with caregiving and about typical reactions to this stress. By understanding the stress commonly experienced by others in caregiving roles, they may more readily recognize when their own frustration is impeding their ability to work effectively with clients.

In general, caregiver training programs seek to teach skills for assessing and addressing problem behaviors. The format typically evolves from a training model to a consultative one as training progresses. This progression is often empowering for the caregivers, as it enhances both their effectiveness and their independence.

Ensuring Staff Competency Through Assessment of Hands-On Skills

To ensure that staff members are competent in the skills that are the focus of training, it is not enough to lecture them about behavioral techniques. Rather, they need to demonstrate competency in applying these techniques.

The Behavioral Role-Play Activities Test (BRAT; Nezu et al., 1990) is one training tool that can be used to ensure staff competency. This measure, described in chapter 5 and presented in the Appendix, assesses competency in a variety of behavioral procedures: extinction, shaping, differential reinforcement, contingent positive reinforcement, time-out, and cues and prompts. These techniques constitute a core of behavioral interventions used with dually diagnosed clients.

The BRAT assesses competency through role-play scenarios that simulate treatment situations. Although the BRAT was designed as an assessment device, we have found it extremely useful as an actual treatment tool. It provides the caregiver with practice and feedback concerning frequently encountered problem situations. It also allows for considerable specific skill development outside of the treatment setting, in an arena where mistakes can be corrected at less cost to clients. Used as part of a clinical strategy, the BRAT role-plays have the benefit of active caregiver participation and are often rated as fun and realistic by trainees.

CAREGIVER SYSTEMS INTERVENTIONS

In certain situations, treatment may be focused on the relationships between family members, the roles of siblings, and other systemic issues. The life cycle of the family is one matter that has received attention (Harris, 1983). When working with a family, the therapist should be sensitive to the current stage of that family's life cycle (Harris, Gill, & Alessandri, 1991). At first, the family faces the difficulty of acknowledging the initial diagnosis of a child's disability and dealing with their sense of grief and loss. As the child approaches school age, the parents confront the increasing discrepancy between their child's progress and the developmental norm. Adolescence and young adulthood bring a number of difficult issues (Harris, Carpenter, & Gill, 1988). Parents become concerned about their child's social development, sense of self, and expression of sexuality. In addition, they must attend to pragmatic considerations, such as living accommodations, vocational training, financial provisions, and legal concerns (Chadsey-Rusch & Gonzalez, 1988). Dealing with these concerns and issues can cause distress for all family members.

It is helpful to examine how the life cycle of a family with a disabled child differs from that of other families. For couples with non-disabled children, marital satisfaction seems to diminish throughout the child-rearing years and to increase later in life. In families with disabled children, this pattern of diminished satisfaction may be intensified by continual caretaking demands. A family might be unable to bear the burdens associated with caring for the child, to modify goals and activities to include the child, and to alter familial patterns to minimize relationship strain (Patterson & McCubbin, 1983; Turnbull & Turnbull, 1986).

Within the family, flexibility in role assignment and sharing of power are associated with better coping and greater satisfaction. Pratt (1976) links successful coping with a lack of rigidity, the promotion of autonomy, and cohesion. According to Reiss and Oliveri (1980), families who cope have three important assets: configuration, coordination, and closure. Configuration is the ability of family members to work together in problem solving. Coordination refers to a shared perception of the world and an ability to communicate. Closure, the ability to delay decisions until sufficient data are gathered, reflects an openness to information. Family therapists try to build these skills and qualities in their client families through restructuring efforts, communication exercises, and problem-solving tasks. In addition, they may help the family to appreciate the differences among its members (Elman, 1991).

The case of Bob. Bob was a 29-year-old man with the dual diagnoses of undifferentiated schizophrenia and moderate mental retardation. Bob frequently got into arguments with other residents at his group home. In addition, he often disobeyed staff instructions, threatened staff with physical harm, and behaved aggressively toward other people. His behavior had escalated dramatically to the point where his placement was jeopardized.

Interviews with Bob's family helped therapists understand more about this recently observed escalation in noncompliance and aggression. Bob's mother, a widow, was planning to move to a neighboring state to live with her other son. Bob's possible placement disruption was delaying her departure. At the same time, a long-standing struggle between Bob's brother and mother was being fueled: The brother believed that their mother needed to be more removed from Bob. The mother now had a legitimate excuse to delay or even cancel the move, about which she had previously expressed significant ambivalence. In essence, Bob's behavior at the group residence kept his mother close to him and prevented her from becoming closer to his brother. The therapist developed a treatment plan that addressed the family's systemic problems.

Clearly, Bob's family lacked the skill to work together to solve problems. In fact, they had difficulty communicating clearly, even on issues that were not conflict-ridden. One intervention was focused on increasing the family's communication and problem-solving skills. Improvement in listening skills was especially helpful, as it permitted each family member to be heard. In addition, the family needed help in letting each member propose solutions. Each member was overinvested in his or her personal solution; often they were unaware of other possibilities or potential compromises.

This family was handicapped by maternal enmeshment and over-involvement. The overinvolvement common among parents of children who have disabilities had not lessened as the child grew older. In this case, the rigid boundaries of the mother-child unit prevented Bob from achieving more autonomy and independence and interfered with his mother's retirement plan. In addition to patterns of enmeshment, Bob's family also suffered from overprotectiveness. This was evident both in the mother's treatment of Bob and in the brother's treatment of the mother.

During the family's treatment, Bob's mother received the assignment to spend a weekend with friends, away from the family. Had she not been widowed, the assignment might have been to spend time with her spouse. The therapist reframed the assignment as giving her a vacation from the burdens of "caring" too much. Both the mother and Bob experienced the separation as frightening at first. However, they both learned that it was not catastrophic. In fact, there were positive consequences. Bob experienced increased freedom, and his mother eventually began to embrace a compromise position that included living near her other son. She looked forward to this move, as she could spend more time with her grandchildren.

She also bought a car so that she could visit Bob regularly without depending on his brother for transportation. Bob was helped to anticipate the change and to predict the frequency of his mother's visits.

Deciding When the System Needs Help

It is not always easy for the clinician to identify which families need systemic interventions. Leahey and Wright (1985) have specified several criteria. Intervention is indicated in the following circumstances.

1. When a family member's mental or physical condition is having an obviously adverse effect on another family member

2. When family members are contributing to the symptoms or problems of an individual

3. When one member's improvement leads to symptoms or deterioration in another family member

4. When an important individual or family developmental milestone is missed

The decision to intervene is always guided by the data gathered in the assessment process, including information about the client, the environment, the caregivers, and the caregiving system. Even when the decision-making process indicates that a systemic intervention is clinically warranted, it is important to consider several additional issues. For example, if environmental control is not possible, if interpersonal problems among caregivers are extremely severe, or if one or more caregivers is seriously dysfunctional, systemic intervention may be inappropriate (Gordon & Davidson, 1981). The therapist must carefully assess each element along decision-making guidelines and match the intervention to the client with the full circumstances of the client's situation in mind.

Having decided to conduct a systems intervention, the therapist should remember that families who report finding a "broader meaning" for interpreting the client's condition function better than those who do not (Venters, 1982). Helping caregivers to agree on this broader meaning can help the system cope with stress. Bristol (1986) has emphasized the role that one's personal definition of a stressor can play in coping with a crisis: An individual's appraisal of the situation affects the perception of his or her ability to cope with it (Lazarus, Kanner, & Folkman, 1980). Frequently, individuals coping successfully with the stress of caring for a developmentally disabled person express a view of the situation that redefines its meaning. This view may take the form of religious conviction (e.g., "God gives his greatest burdens to his closest friends"), or it may reflect a set of values stemming from and congruent with the situation. For example, family members may express a changed sense of what is most important in life, a revision in priorities, or an appreciation of gifts or skills previously taken for granted. Some families and individuals seem to focus on the positive aspects of parenting or caretaking; they comment on the rewards and joys specific to the situation. Finding a positive meaning in caring for an individual with disabilities contributes to successful coping.

Orr et al. (1991) have discussed several additional cognitive factors affecting a family's adaptation to the presence of a child with a disability. The ways in which that family member is perceived—for example, the definition and interpretation of his or her deficits, skills, and needs—

can be very influential. A positive focus on the assessment of strengths and the development of skills reinforces positive perceptions. In addition, the ability to reframe the disability in a positive context alleviates caregiver stress. Although this coping strategy is especially important for families, it can help other caregivers (e.g., direct care staff) as well.

Systemic assessment yields much information about individual and familial perceptions. Family therapists pay attention to these perceptions, interpretations, and understandings and often use reframing or normalizing to help a family attach positive meaning to a stressful situation (Elman, 1991). *Normalizing* entails helping the family understand that their problems are not as different from those of other families as they may believe. This allows the family to feel less alone in the struggle and closer to the normative experience of families in general. Of course, the therapist must convey an understanding of the family's unique difficulties, but helping them see that others face similar difficulties can lead them to view their problems as less catastrophic. *Reframing* changes the meaning of behavior. It often involves giving a behavior a benign or positive meaning, as opposed to a negative or malicious one. Reframing behaviors as changeable (as opposed to intractable) problems can reduce the feeling of helplessness among family members. Parental overinvolvement, for example, can be reframed as deep caring; the therapist may acknowledge how difficult it is to adapt this caring to the age of the child or the needs of the family (Harris, 1983). Reframing frees the family to work on skills, such as collaborative problem solving, more effectively.

Other Systems Characteristics and Resources

Several other variables have been associated with systems that successfully adapt to the stresses of living with a disabled child (Bristol, 1984). These variables, which provide additional treatment pathways for the caregiving system, include degree of cohesion, degree of expressiveness, and the presence of recreational opportunities. Bristol found that families high in mutual commitment and support more easily accepted and coped with a disabled child than did other families. Other researchers have found that cohesion and harmony within the family are conducive to the development of support among members (Mink, 1986; Mink, Nihira, & Myers, 1983; Nihira et al., 1980).

In addition, families with such resources as financial assets and physical health cope better with stress than those who lack these resources (McCubbin, 1979). Other relevant resources include social support, parental energy, morale, and problem-solving ability. Strategies aimed at increasing any of these resources can be important in family intervention.

THE RECIPROCITY OF ADAPTATION: INTEGRATING SYSTEMS PERSPECTIVES, CAREGIVER TRAINING, AND STRESS/COPING IN THE TREATMENT PLAN

The process of adaptation appears to be reciprocal. Whereas the parents' distress is related to the child's adaptive competency, the child's progress is affected by the parents' coping ability (Nihira et al., 1980). Thus, in families whose adaptation is difficult, distress may worsen over time. For example, when a caregiver's frustration increases and tolerance declines, there may be an increase in negative exchanges between caregiver and client. Their interactions may become increasingly negative and coercive (Patterson, 1982). As this occurs, opportunities for both positive interactions and teaching decrease.

It is very easy for caregivers and clients to enter into what Patterson describes as "circles of coercion" (1982). One family explained how their frustration had turned into helplessness. Their son, Jeremy, played the television at high volume and liked to change channels incessantly. As he did this, he often ran about the room. When his parents attempted to stop him, Jeremy would scream loudly. A power struggle would ensue, with the parents initially sticking to their decision to terminate this behavior. However, as Jeremy became increasingly disruptive they usually gave in, returning the remote control to him. At this point they often felt relieved—at least the screaming had stopped. In short, they had been negatively reinforced. A noxious behavior (screaming) was terminated through an action (returning the remote control to Jeremy). Jeremy in turn learned that screaming eventually led to a desired outcome. When a pattern like this one develops, the result tends to be resentment, increased coercion, and power struggles.

The situation in Jeremy's family highlights the need to assess the reciprocity involved in a behavior management problem. Caregivers may inadvertently be reinforcing maladaptive behavior, and they may themselves be reinforced for yielding control of the situation.

Because of such reciprocity, interventions that simultaneously target multiple areas are often the most effective. Some additional areas that may serve as treatment foci are discussed in the following sections.

THE ROLE OF SOCIAL SUPPORT

The central buffering role of a strong family system with good coping resources has been discussed. Family and marital relationships are intimate forms of social support, which is part of the reason why they serve as buffers against stress. Caregivers are also helped by other forms of social support (Holroyd, 1974), which has been defined as information leading the individual to believe he or she is cared for, loved, esteemed, valued, and part of a network of mutual communication and obligation (Cobb, 1976). Cobb emphasized the meeting of relational needs, rather than material needs, as the primary feature of supportive relationships. Cohen and Wills (1985) noted that the perception of the availability of social support may be more critical than the actual receipt of that social support.

Social support has been shown to have a buffering effect in families (Johnson & Sarason, 1978). Highly stressed families with high social support coped more effectively than similarly stressed families with low social support. Social support has been postulated as a major coping resource for families with disabled children (Byrne & Cunningham, 1985; McCubbin, 1979).

In a series of studies of mothers with autistic children, Bristol (1984) found that the mothers experiencing the least stress were receiving the most support, particularly from their spouses and relatives. The elements of such social support include encouragement, assistance, and feedback (Gallagher, Cross, & Scharfman, 1981). Pragmatic help in the completion of daily tasks is also a significant factor in coping (Wolfensberger, 1967).

Several researchers have examined specific components of social support that may be important to an understanding of its buffering function (e.g., Crnic, Greenberg, Ragozin, Robinson, & Basham, 1983). These researchers have identified three types of social support: intimate support, support from friends, and community support. They found that parents with the most social support exhibited the most positive attitudes and behaviors toward their children.

Treatment Considerations

Treatment approaches for increasing social support include (a) helping individuals in need of support to identify people in their environments who may provide such support, (b) helping caregivers identify new ways of seeking social support, (c) teaching caregivers perspective-taking skills and ways to help each other, and (d) helping caregivers identify and use available formal support services (e.g., respite care).

Formal Support Services

One important community resource is respite care, which provides trained workers to care for developmentally disabled individuals, relieving family members of responsibility either for a brief vacation or on a more regular basis. Respite care is increasingly recognized as helping families to sustain their efforts for longer periods (Joyce, Singer, & Isralowitz, 1983). Parents receiving respite care services report that their families get along better, experience less stress, and have more freedom. In part because of the availability of respite care and other community support programs, the age of placement of individuals with developmental disabilities outside of the home has increased. This type of professional support appears crucial for reducing stress and alleviating the burden of care.

Networking

We have discussed the strategy of normalizing a family's problems to help them cope. Some community programs facilitate networking by introducing parents of disabled children to other parents in similar situations. Parents usually report that they feel relieved to find others whose lives are similar. Many say that these interactions have made them better able to accept responsibility and to assess their child's future realistically (Meadow & Meadow, 1971). In addition, a national parent advocacy organization offers parent-to-parent support (Bristol, 1985). Networking may be valuable for direct care personnel as well. The opportunity to share problems and solutions for similar situations may help them set realistic goals and feel a more positive sense of responsibility.

Communication and Consistency Among Caregiving Systems

Related to issues of social support and networking are strategies that aim to increase communication among caregiving systems. Knowledge about problems encountered by other caregivers or systems can be useful in treatment planning and troubleshooting. Inconsistency in the approaches of different caregiving systems may cause the client to suffer. Communication and consistency among caregivers in different settings is especially important for the developmentally disabled individual, who may depend on a certain treatment approach to achieve certain goals and who may not generalize skills spontaneously.

Caregivers in a client's day setting may have methods for dealing with behavior problems that would alleviate stress at home. For example, one young girl had a terrible phobia of the bathroom. She screamed, threw herself on the floor, and howled loudly when in or entering that room. The staff at the girl's school began to desensitize her to the bathroom gradually. At first, they rewarded her for tolerating proximity to the bathroom. They also played music tapes for her when she was near the bathroom; this was a powerful reinforcer. She was gradually encouraged to enter the bathroom and then to stay there. Although these techniques began to effect change at school, toileting times at home remained very difficult. Eventually the parents learned the school staff's techniques, and the situation became more manageable. In this case, communication between settings alleviated stress in the home and made the parents feel more competent. Moreover, communication was critical for the transfer of the new skill to the home setting.

Communication between caregivers may be one avenue of intervention that can lessen a caregiver's vulnerability to burnout, discussed in the following section.

Burnout

Burnout has been described as a syndrome of emotional exhaustion, depersonalization, and diminished sense of accomplishment that can affect people who work with others (Maslach, 1982). Pines and Aronson (1981) have noted some consequences of burnout, including physical depletion, feelings of helplessness and hopelessness, and the development of a negative attitude toward work and other people. Burnout has also been described as a loss of idealism, purposefulness, and energy (Edelwich & Brodsky, 1980; Farber, 1983). This form of distress among human service providers appears to have a number of sources.

Algozzine (1987) estimated that burnout affects approximately 6% of special education teachers annually. Several factors have been found to contribute to this group's vulnerability. Strategies to address these factors can be beneficial for all caregivers. One factor found to exacerbate burnout is poor supervision and inadequate feedback (Fimian, 1986; Fimian & Santoro, 1983). The provision of feedback and supervision can reduce stress among direct care workers. Feedback from colleagues and supervisors may be especially important for caregivers working with clients who do not provide much feedback themselves.

In addition, professionals who work with developmentally disabled clients appear to experience less burnout when they use teaching techniques that are specific and focused. When teaching goals are specified, tasks to be taught are sequenced by difficulty, and lessons are highly structured, learning often proceeds more smoothly (Gersten, 1985; Snell & Fisher, 1988).

Also, when the learning criteria used are functional (based on skill development) rather than developmental (based on mental age), burnout rates tend to be lower (Brinker, 1985). Thus, a client care approach that stresses individualized assessment of skill deficits and goal setting tends to be associated with less burnout (Heal, Colson, & Gross, 1984). This may be true because progress is more visible with these methods. Staff may also more readily see the usefulness of their instruction, as it develops skills relevant to independent functioning.

Burnout appears to be less frequent among service providers who work in mainstreamed or integrated settings (Brown, Ford, Nisbet, Sweet, Donellan, & Grunewald, 1983; Stainback & Stainback, 1985). Teaching staff in mainstreamed settings have more positive attitudes and report more hopeful feelings. In this light, the trend toward increased integration of developmentally disabled individuals into the community may benefit staff members as well.

Some have speculated about how the use of certain behavioral techniques affects burnout. It is clear that a structured and focused instruction method is advantageous for the client and reduces burnout among staff members. The controversy centers on the use of punishment and its impact on treatment. This issue has rightfully received a great deal of attention from clinicians, administrators, and lawmakers as a balance between rights and responsibilities is sought. Debates have focused on instructional aspects of punishment, including efficacy, maintenance of behavioral change, and generalizability.

More recently, Harris, Handleman, Gill, and Fong (1991) investigated the impact on human service professionals of using aversive procedures. They speculated that professionals might feel discomfort with these techniques because of their inherently painful qualities and general public concern. The results of this study suggest that having access to a wide range of behavioral interventions in the treatment of developmentally disabled clients tended to reduce job-related stress for direct care personnel. In particular, feelings of personal accomplishment were greatest among staff members of programs allowing the use of a wide variety of techniques.

In sum, burnout appears to be less where feedback and supervision are adequate; where programs are structured, teaching functional skills and using goal-focused techniques; and where community integration is encouraged. It is also important that staff be educated about burnout. Understanding the syndrome can help them to recognize symptoms in themselves or in coworkers. Administrative flexibility is needed to respond to staff burnout when it occurs. Altering assignments or schedules, reducing workloads, or arranging for needed time off can revitalize staff members who are beginning to suffer burnout (Maslach, 1982). Supportive responses from colleagues and administrators help individuals who are feeling depleted to voice their difficulties and to break the cycle.

Supervisors can provide support in the work environment in ways that diminish the likelihood of burnout. Giving feedback, being available to employees, and challenging them to do their best are elements of supervision associated with reduced employee burnout (Pines, 1983). In particular, technical support and technical challenges appear to be helpful, perhaps because they involve troubleshooting and problem solving.

Any reader of this book can probably be identified as a caregiver—a provider of some sort of service to a dually diagnosed client. Recognizing the symptoms of burnout can alert readers to the necessity for additional supervision, peer consultation, or even a needed vacation.

SUMMARY

Family members and other caregivers need support to sustain their efforts. People who perceive the availability of support cope more effectively than those who do not. Therapists working with families and staff members should be available to provide support in the form of feedback, encouragement, or therapeutic assistance. Support may also take the form of technical aid or troubleshooting; in some cases, it may simply require the validation of feelings. The critical factor is to be available and responsive to these needs.

In addition to support, caregivers may also benefit from other interventions. Fostering hardy attitudes is likely to have a number of buffering effects. Enhancing one's sense of control is particularly important. An increased perception of efficacy fosters self-esteem, energy, and feelings of accomplishment. Caregivers who feel more effective are also less likely to experience burnout. Problem-focused as well as emotion-focused coping strategies should be taught to increase feelings of efficacy in caregivers. In particular, behavioral training programs should be used to ensure competency.

Caregivers who have a positive view of the problem and perceive a broader meaning in the disability cope more effectively. Systemic evaluations that detect problems in this area should lead to systemic interventions to address them. Reframing is one way to foster the development of positive meaning. A focus on skill building may help to maintain optimism among caregiving staff. Presenting behavioral difficulties as challenges rather than disasters can also foster an optimistic attitude.

In summary, clinical research findings consistently support the idea that a variety of factors help caregivers cope with an individual's disability. Although social support continues to receive a great deal of deserved recognition for its role in this process, the range of variables considered potentially important has broadened. Specific instrumental skills, ecological/contextual factors, individual/personality factors, and systemic issues may all be significant avenues for caregiver intervention. Many of these variables may interact with each other in helping caregivers cope. Because caregivers provide the primary relationship(s) in the life of the dually diagnosed person, their needs deserve careful attention.

Chapter 10

Treatment Guidelines: Focus on the Environment

INTRODUCTION

Aspects of the environment that require attention in treatment include physical, social, and programmatic components. We will discuss ways to design these components so that treatment is enhanced. In addressing environmental concerns, we frequently refer to staff and caregivers, the people most often responsible for implementing environmental changes. Although many environmental strategies are described in the context of community residences (e.g., group homes, supervised apartments), they are often applicable to clients residing at home with their families. The goal of all the strategies presented is to strengthen the client's environment in such a way that it is not only a living situation but an actual treatment milieu. Moreover, treatment goals concerning this milieu should be developed to increase the likelihood of normalization and autonomy.

THE PHYSICAL ENVIRONMENT

As noted in chapter 6, physical comfort is basic to the therapeutic environment. In particular, factors such as noise and crowding can impede treatment (e.g., Baron, 1977; Donnerstein & Wilson, 1976; Freedman, 1975). Although it may not be possible to control such factors, caregivers should find ways to minimize the extent to which they interfere with treatment. Perhaps most important, clients need to feel that they have some control over their exposure to noxious environmental stimuli.

The problem-solving process outlined earlier may be useful in determining environmental changes needed for a particular client or setting. For example, perhaps one room can be designated as a quiet area where someone can go to read or rest without fear of encountering others involved in noisy exchanges or interactive games. Perhaps group residence staff can plan field trips for half the clients on each of two weekend days to give those at home more space during their leisure time. For clients living at home, designation of quiet rooms and adjustment of family schedules can alleviate problems stemming from crowding or excessive stimulation.

Another aspect of a client's physical environment concerns appropriate stimulation in colors and furnishings. In general, group residence settings should be noninstitutional and homelike (Jacobson & Schwartz, 1986; Zigler & Williams, 1963). Optimal levels of stimulation should be assessed individually because different individuals respond differently to environmental stimuli (e.g., Zentall & Zentall, 1983). Clients should also exercise some choice in furnishing their own rooms because this involvement increases a sense of belonging to the setting.

The physical environment should also correspond to programmatic considerations. The environment should be structured to accommodate individualized programming, social exchange, leisure activities, and privacy needs. Creating different areas to meet these different needs helps to increase satisfaction and reduce confusion.

THE SOCIAL ENVIRONMENT

The social aspects of the treatment environment, including the presence of appropriate and salient models and the availability of opportunities for observational learning, are also crucial. When appropriate behavior is modeled—and skills can be acquired informally as well as formally—the opportunities for incidental learning increase dramatically. Such learning is also normalizing and supportive of autonomy. Family and staff members should understand the power of observational learning (e.g., Bandura, 1973, 1986). They should learn to utilize modeling in teaching skills and in encouraging appropriate behavior. They should also be sensitized to the possible negative impact of modeling on client functioning or behavior. In particular, the effects of observing the inappropriate behavior of siblings and peers should be emphasized. Caregivers can be encouraged to use strategies for reducing the impact of inappropriate behaviors—for example, utilizing extinction for misbehavior and differential reinforcement of appropriate behaviors on the part of the client and his or her peers. Differential reinforcement is an especially useful technique because it enables well-behaved clients to receive attention when other clients are behaving inappropriately.

Family and residence staff members should also be cautioned about the impact of their own behavior. Many have never considered themselves to be potential models for clients; increased sensitivity to this issue can avert difficulties. In addition, caregivers' interactions with a client have a wide-reaching impact on the overall atmosphere, the client's learning, and the client's satisfaction in the setting. Caregivers must avoid speaking in ways that are condescending or belittling, or that may invite power struggles. As much as possible, caregivers should convey support.

Readily available social support is another important component of the social environment. Clients should have access to social support whenever they need it. This support may take the form of informal encouragement from staff, problem solving focused on specific issues, or increased staff attention and availability. A comprehensive therapeutic environment fosters the perception that support is available and accessible (e.g., Cohen & Wills, 1985).

AID TO PROGRAMMATIC INTERVENTIONS

Programmatic considerations are a third crucial aspect of the environment. As emphasized in chapter 8, a behavioral program in which contingencies are not appropriate, tasks are not tailored to the client's level of functioning, or reinforcers are not potent will not succeed. The result of such programmatic mistakes is often frustration for client and caregivers alike. In addition, interventions must be goal oriented. Specific, individualized, and appropriate goals should be developed for each individual. Target behaviors should reflect a broad sampling of behavioral and functional domains (e.g., Tennessee Department of Mental Health and Mental Retardation, 1978).

The physical environment can be designed to enhance the efficacy of programmatic interventions. For instance, a program may utilize a "time-in" area where reinforcers are available and where access is contingent on appropriate behavior. In addition to providing a special place for reinforcement, a time-in area makes contingencies clearer and more concrete for the client. The focus of the time-in area is on appropriate behavior, reinforcement, and skill building. It is, of course, the opposite of the traditional time-out, which relies on the removal of rewards contingent on misbehavior.

QUALITATIVE ASPECTS OF THE ENVIRONMENT

Certain qualitative aspects of the environment—psychosocial or milieu variables—have an impact on clients' progress and satisfaction, as well as on the general social ambiance of the setting.

Access to opportunities is a crucial environmental variable. Clients need the opportunity to learn skills and to apply these skills in the community. Opportunity constraints limit the options of individuals with developmental disabilities and may cause them to be categorized as less capable than they are (Hill & Bruininks, 1981). Access to opportunities is an aspect of normalization, which is known to be related to positive

outcomes for clients (e.g., Hull & Thompson, 1981). Normalization pro-
motes individual development, responsibility, and autonomy, and pre-
pares the client for the ultimate goal of integration into the community.

Another qualitative aspect of the treatment environment is the nature
of interactions between clients and staff. Depersonalization, social
distance, and critical comments do not tend to foster progress (Brown
et al., 1972; Pratt et al., 1980). Interactions marked by these qualities
are "institutional," not client oriented (e.g., King & Raynes, 1968).

The treatment environment should be oriented toward normalization of clients and their integration into the community. Clients should
have a myriad of opportunities for participation in activities. Interactions
between clients and staff members should be characterized by respect
and support.

Our suggestions for interaction between caregivers and clients may
seem like mere idealized goals, but it is possible to program for this aspect
of the environment through education and training of family and staff
members. In addition, the feedback and reinforcement provided to caregivers can help effect changes in interactional styles.

A MODEL RESIDENCE FOR
DUALLY DIAGNOSED INDIVIDUALS

Group residences designed for dually diagnosed individuals hold a great
deal of promise for meeting the complex and unique needs of this population. The following is a description of one residence for 12 dually diagnosed individuals. For the purpose of illustration, we are presenting a
hypothetical residence that makes use of a combination of existing environmental treatment options. By describing this residence, we hope to
provide a feasible example of the advantages for client development
through such a model.

The 12 residents in our model varied considerably in level of functioning and degree of psychiatric symptomatology. All required highly individualized treatment plans and intense staff attention. Although there
were group activities and tasks such as preparing dinner or setting the
table, each member's contribution was specified exactly. Staff helped
each resident to pursue his or her own personal goal. The goals were
based on careful and thorough individual skill assessments and task
analyses. For example, one resident, Lori, was working on placing plates
and cups on placemats to complete two table settings. Joe worked on
pouring juice into glasses, while Harold cut vegetables for salad. Each
one earned tokens or other rewards for specified behaviors.

The specificity of individual goals was reflected in the specificity
of individual rewards. A reinforcer survey was conducted for each resident. Varied and potent reinforcers were made available, with access

to them contingent on the execution of appropriate behaviors and the completion of tasks. Residents were weaned to more normalized schedules of reinforcement as progress permitted. Additional motivators were provided for clients who had gained more independence.

Before working with clients, staff received thorough training in a number of areas, including counseling skills, professional communication skills, family systems factors, problem-solving strategies, cognitive-behavioral techniques, and behavior management. Behavior management training included instruction in behavioral assessment and behavioral interventions, as well as familiarization with specific plans developed for residents. In addition, staff members were introduced to symptoms associated with various forms of psychopathology and learned effective ways to intervene when those symptoms were manifested. Hands-on measures of competency (e.g., the BRAT; see chapter 5 and the Appendix) were used to assess staff members' behavior and, thus, the extent to which they had mastered behavioral training. This hands-on assessment allowed trainers to reinforce staff for specific behaviors and to provide positive feedback. It also enabled them to identify areas of weakness and to plan for additional training as needed.

Further, staff members were instructed to be good models of appropriate behavior and to reinforce appropriate modeling on the part of residents. They were cautioned against using tactics such as threats and intimidation that might undermine treatment effectiveness. They also learned about the harmful effects of interactions characterized by high degrees of expressed emotion (EE) (Brown et al., 1972; Vaughn & Leff, 1976). This portion of training was aimed at minimizing the likelihood that staff members would become critical of or overinvolved with clients.

EE training was made available to individuals who interacted with clients on a more casual basis as well. Transportation personnel, cooks, and other auxiliary staff were invited to these workshops, along with members of residents' families. In this way, coordination with other caregiving systems was built into the program model.

Some of the environmental management techniques mentioned earlier were used in this residence. One upstairs room was designated as a quiet area where residents could go to sit, rest, read, or otherwise quietly pass time. No loud talking or game playing was allowed in this room, which often provided an alternative to busier, more social leisure options. In addition, there was a "time-in" area to which access was earned through appropriate behavior and where many varied reinforcers were available.

Community meetings were held in the residence several times a week. These meetings allowed for the airing of grievances and for the development of solutions to community problems such as noise or other disruptions. Having a forum for airing such gripes, residents were less subject to the sense of helplessness typically surrounding such issues. Staff were helpful in facilitating these meetings and ensuring that scapegoating did not occur. They also followed through on suggestions from residents—an important step because it communicated a sense of respect to program participants.

Staff members led several groups, typically meeting in the evening, to facilitate communication and cooperation among the residents. Although evenings were used for structured leisure activities and self-care tasks, skill groups were always offered as well. The following sections describe the kinds of skill groups offered in our model residence.

THERAPEUTIC GROUPS

Therapy groups designed for people with developmental disabilities or dual diagnoses are rare. They can, however, be a helpful alternative to individual treatment, especially for addressing social and interpersonal issues (Monfils, 1989). Several topics are particularly amenable to a group therapy context and have special relevance for this population. All of the group treatments discussed here, particularly those focused on self-regulatory skills (e.g., social skills, problem solving, stress inoculation), can be effectively adapted to individual treatment. We include them under the heading of group treatments because of their potentially powerful effect on the group milieu.

Supportive Groups

Supportive group counseling provides a forum for airing frustrations, receiving feedback, and gaining support from peers. Support groups can be less structured than other types of skill groups.

One support group was designed to address problems encountered in the community. Group members were all clients experiencing a new level of visibility in and interaction with the community at large. Most were in the range of moderate retardation. In addition, they had psychiatric problems including affective illness, schizophrenia, and personality disorders.

Members of this group had previously lived in developmental centers or other segregated settings, where they were fairly isolated. As members of a group residence, they now lived in and traveled through the community. This increased exposure was a scary prospect for them.

During one session, which focused on feelings of rejection, isolation, and stigmatization, group members were able to share feelings about being labeled by others. Several indicated that they felt ostracized by others and "out of sync" with the community at large. Members discussed the frustration they felt when reminded of their disabilities by members of the community. These reminders could take very different forms. At times, community members treated them as more disabled than they were. At other times, they sensed that community members feared them or sought to avoid them. In the worst instances, people ridiculed them.

The group members offered one another support in facing these experiences of rejection. They helped one another struggle to accept their limitations. They also shared their profound sense of discrepancy from the norm and mourned the things they were unable to achieve. In addition, they shared their anger at those who rejected them and attempted to offer explanations for the rejections (e.g., fear, ignorance). These explanations sometimes made the rejections feel less personal and more comprehensible.

In another session, group members commented that they felt vulnerable, especially to crime. In many instances, they were traveling alone for the first time. Many were unused to being the only individual with a disability in a public situation; this heightened their sense of vulnerability. The members shared the perception that the symptoms of their illnesses, especially talking to themselves and appearing visibly upset, marked them as targets; they were able to share their feelings of vulnerability. They went on to discuss strategies for coping with these fears. Some members related the practice of going places with a friend, especially if the neighborhood was bad. Others told how they conquered anxiety by using relaxation procedures and coping statements when they became fearful.

Enriching the Structure of Group Interventions

When a group such as the one just described has few strategies available, direct care staff can be motivated to initiate new training procedures. In other words, the group itself can help guide treatment. Identified skill deficits can be targeted for intervention. The staff may prepare hypothetical problem situations and use a problem-solving format with the group members. Role-play exercises might be developed as an adjunct to discussions. Such creative responses to the group's needs enrich the treatment, broaden the focus of discussion, and increase the generalizability of the intervention. At the same time, the role of direct care staff is expanded, their participation in the development of treatment is enhanced, and their interaction with clients is encouraged. Finally, a rich treatment environment may minimize the need for individual treatment, which can be costly.

Social Skills Training

A potentially appropriate area for more structured group therapy with dually diagnosed clients is social or interpersonal skills (Matson & Fee, 1991). One way to organize such a group is to focus on a type of problem situation that involves dealing with other people. Components of social skills group training include instruction, modeling, role-playing, feedback, and social reinforcement (Hersen & Bellack, 1976; Matson & Fee, 1991). Initially, it can be helpful for group leaders to generate topics for the discussion. As time passes, however, staff should look to the group for suggestions.

One subject that received a great deal of attention in this residence was conversational skills. Two group members were asked to hold a conversation: They were to initiate a discussion, listen accurately, and ask relevant follow-up questions. Staff and other residents helped the key players determine if their contributions to the conversation were appropriate, relevant, and polite. The group eventually compiled a list of rules for good conversation. The list itemized basic social skills such as making eye contact and not interrupting. It also addressed some "poor habit" skills secondary to depression or psychosis and included suggestions such as being active and involved and remaining on the topic.

Group members also learned how to redirect one another to the topic. Instead of terminating a conversation when the partner made a bizarre statement, they often attempted to help the partner refocus. These efforts changed the nature of interactions to allow for the possibility of continued engagement.

An innovative way to enhance social skills in the dually diagnosed population is to use games as teaching tools. One advantage of this method is that it helps to maintain the interest of participants (Matson & Fee, 1991). A game developed by Foxx, McMorrow, and Schloss (1983) incorporates social skills training in areas such as giving and receiving compliments, handling criticism, and answering questions.

Training in Perspective-Taking Skills

When a group has mastered some basic social skills, it is time to introduce some of the more subtle aspects of interaction. One of the most interesting challenges can be to teach the participants perspective-taking skills. This was recently done in a skill group at the residence. The group leaders perceived that the members' interpersonal conflicts often centered around issues that could be clarified if one individual could see the perspective of the other party involved in the dispute. The challenge was to direct the group away from egocentricity and provide a broader focus for interpersonal conflict.

One member of the group, Michael, often complained bitterly about his roommate. Michael was irritated by the amount of staff attention routinely given to the roommate. He was also annoyed that his roommate had a separate set of rules to follow and was exempt from certain tasks expected of other residents—for instance, making his bed or doing his laundry. The group asked whether there were any reasons for the differential treatment and were told that Michael's roommate had a number of serious medical problems.

The group continued to listen to Michael's complaints and continued to offer him empathy for his feelings of annoyance. With staff assistance, however, they began to introduce the concept of individualized treatment plans. The group leaders began to ask other group members pointed questions such as "Why do you think the staff allow Michael's roommate to stay in his room during cleanup times?" The members of the group began pointing out to Michael that there were valid reasons behind these apparent inequities.

Staff members also began to introduce empathy for the roommate by asking group members to recall the last time they felt seriously ill. In this way, the group's attention began to shift from Michael and his anger to the situation of his roommate. Michael began to feel empathy for his roommate and to understand the position of the staff. This helped him to depersonalize the issue and to see it in context. Michael frequently slipped back into a more personalized view of the situation, but the group could then gently remind him to think more broadly.

Another opportunity for learning to adopt another's perspective arose when one group member lost a close friend to cancer. Loretta came in quite sad and expressed feelings of great loneliness. The group allowed her to talk about the loss but then refocused their attention on their individual issues (roommate problems, money worries, etc.). Loretta sat in a corner chair, slipping farther away from the group and becoming increasingly sad. A group leader commented, "Everyone look at Loretta. Why do you think she isn't involved in our discussion today?" This prompt helped focus the group's attention on Loretta. The group members were then better able to take care of Loretta and give her loss the attention it deserved. The leaders suggested that the group's minimal reaction to Loretta's loss might have increased her sadness. The members then expressed regret at having unintentionally hurt her feelings.

The group also served as a forum for problem solving, as members brought their interpersonal conflict issues to the meetings. The group reviewed the problem situation, critiqued the member's reaction, and generated alternative solutions. This was especially helpful for members who had difficulty with anger control. Group members helped one another to link consequences to behavior. Certain members who had made progress in anger control and in developing the capacity to reflect before acting were able to give advice to more impulsive peers and to speak more eloquently than staff on the rewards of enhanced self-control.

Problem-Solving and Assertiveness Training

Two other forms of therapy that lend themselves to a group format involve training in problem-solving and in assertiveness. Problem-solving therapy has been described as a learning process, a self-management technique, and a general coping strategy (D'Zurilla, 1988; Nezu & Nezu, 1989a). Different levels of problem-solving skills have been noted.

On a general level, problem orientation cognitions are an individual's overall orientation toward problems encountered in daily life (Butler & Meichenbaum, 1981; Meichenbaum & Asarnow, 1979). Factors such as an individual's locus of control and personal style help determine this orientation. Specific problem-solving skills include defining a problem, generating alternative solutions to the problem, and assessing the outcome of a solution (D'Zurilla & Goldfried, 1971). The ability to generalize specific problem-solving skills to more global issues and circumstances is also important.

Social problem-solving therapy aims to help people better understand their problems and to build skills for altering problem situations and/or for reacting to those situations (Nezu, 1987). This approach has proven effective for clients with a wide range of psychological disorders (Nezu & Nezu, 1989a) and for clients with developmental disabilities as well. Specifically, it has been shown to increase the social competence of adults with moderate and mild retardation (Castles & Glass, 1986) and to reduce their aggressive behaviors (Benson, Rice, & Miranti, 1986). The interventions have been demonstrated to be generalizable and socially valid (Foxx, Kyle, Faw, & Bittle, 1989).

Nezu et al. (1991) investigated the differential effectiveness of assertiveness training and problem-solving training for individuals with mild mental retardation and psychiatric diagnoses. Specific focus was on the effectiveness of these interventions in terms of adaptive social behavior, anger control, problem-solving ability, distress, and degree of psychiatric symptomatology. Underassertiveness and aggression have been identified as problems for dually diagnosed individuals. Some researchers have suggested that frustration and anxiety may interfere with these individuals' ability to cope effectively in situations that require an assertive or decisive response (Menolascino, 1977; Reiss & Benson, 1984).

The study by Nezu et al. (1991) was designed to examine the differential effects of general and specific levels of intervention. Problem solving has been described as a general coping strategy that gives the individual a variety of alternatives for responding to stressful events (Nezu, Nezu, & Perri, 1989). Assertiveness training is a more specific intervention that teaches the individual to behave and communicate assertively in situations that provoke anger; other alternative responses are typically not addressed in assertiveness training. The researchers found that an approach combining assertiveness training and problem-solving training was associated with self-reported improvements in distress and psychological symptoms. In addition, improvements were reflected in caregiver ratings of adaptive functioning. Positive outcomes were associated with both types of interventions, and no significant differences between treatment protocols were found. Results did indicate, however, that problem-solving training impacted on both problem-solving ability and assertiveness skills, whereas assertiveness training impacted on assertiveness alone. These findings suggest that the problem-solving intervention may have a greater impact in treatment and a wider scope of applicability.

Problem-solving training and assertiveness training have the merit of being self-regulatory interventions (Nezu et al., 1991). Such interventions are desirable because they increase client autonomy and efficacy (Meichenbaum, 1990; Whitman, 1990). They are especially desirable for developmentally disabled individuals, who are likely to have self-control problems (Benson, 1985).

At present, the choice of problem-solving therapy for use with developmentally disabled clients is often based on cognitive constructs like those applied to child and adolescent populations. For example, recent research has indicated significant deficiencies in social problem-solving abilities among aggressive children (Lochman, Meyer, Rabiner, & White, in press; Lochman et al., 1991). Aggressive children seem hypervigilant in their attention to hostile cues. They appear to expect hostility and to assign hostile, rather than benign, meanings to other people's behavior (Dodge, 1980; Dodge & Frame, 1982). Such an orientation suggests some cognitive distortions. In addition, highly aggressive children, when faced with problems, tend to consider fewer solutions (Lochman, Lampron, Burch, & Curry, 1985) and to generate fewer verbally assertive and more direct, action-oriented solutions (Asarnow & Callan, 1985; Lochman & Lampron, 1986) than do nonaggressive children.

These same types of cognitive distortions and problem-solving deficiencies may be present in adults with developmental disabilities. The impressive collection of studies by Lochman and his colleagues would support further investigation of social problem-solving therapy as a useful treatment for aggression in this adult population. In addition, assertiveness and problem solving can be taught as self-regulatory and self-control techniques that inherently enhance clients' efficacy and autonomy.

Furthermore, advances in self-control interventions may reduce the traditional reliance on aversive or punishment techniques (McGee, 1988) and neuroleptic drugs (Gualtieri & Keppel, 1985) with this population.

Applications of Problem-Solving Therapy

Problem-solving skills can be developed in a variety of contexts. A focus on interpersonal issues is especially helpful for dually diagnosed clients because it addresses social skills, behavioral control, and problem-solving ability. Redmond (1985) used a group format to improve decision-making skills in psychiatric patients, focusing on decisions about the use of unstructured time. Group members would generate ideas for filling empty hours; evaluate alternatives on the basis of availability of resources, practicality, and other factors; and identify potential problems. Later, they would evaluate the effectiveness of their planning and reinforce themselves for their efforts. A similar group format can be used for a variety of other issues relevant to community living.

Additional Cognitive Treatments

Stress inoculation training (Meichenbaum, 1986) can often complement problem-solving approaches. Stress inoculation training helps individuals to identify stressors and to prepare for the feeling of being overwhelmed by the stressor. It then focuses on developing and rehearsing techniques to cope with the anticipated stress. Self-instruction, or the use of self-statements, is especially heavily emphasized, and self-reinforcement is encouraged. Stress inoculation training can be coupled with problem-solving techniques to develop coping strategies and techniques for handling stressful situations.

Group Therapy and Empowerment

In addition to providing a useful teaching forum, group therapy can aid in reducing the distance between helpers and clients. Group therapy often empowers the members to help each other; this can indirectly address undesirable effects of prolonged involvement with professionals, such as dependency and low self-esteem. Group members feel more competent to handle problems and assist others in similar situations. As one group member put it, "It's good to know I can help someone else with what I know myself from experience."

KEY COMPONENTS OF RESIDENTIAL TREATMENT

Building feelings of competency in clients was an important goal of our model residence; it should be the goal of all therapeutic settings for the dually diagnosed. Staff should give as much assistance as needed while seeking to empower residents to accept as much responsibility as possible (Walsh, 1989). Clients who are capable of monitoring their own behavior should be encouraged to do so. In this way, they progress toward normalized means of behavioral control. In addition, they learn to attribute changes in their behavior to their own efforts rather than to the external influence of a treatment intervention or a staff member's response.

Walsh (1989) has described the essential components of a therapeutic environment for dually diagnosed clients. These environmental characteristics, discussed in chapter 6, contribute to the goal of reducing institutionalization, psychiatric hospitalization, and highly aversive behavioral intervention.

Residential environments should offer specific, intensive training in a wide variety of adaptive skills, with detailed, individualized plans for each resident. Individual attention should be complemented by scheduled, community-based activities. To increase clients' responsibility and autonomy, treatment should tend toward normalization. It should incorporate normalized contingencies and naturalistic rewards, as well as encouraging integration into the community at large.

There is evidence that environments emphasizing autonomy and offering a multitude of programmed activities foster positive changes in clients' functioning and behavior (Eyman et al., 1975; Eyman et al., 1977). In addition, settings that encourage normalization and integration have been linked to improvements in clients' adaptive skills (Eyman et al., 1979; Hull & Thompson, 1981).

Efforts to integrate clients into the community typically result in improved relations with community members as well. Neighbors who oppose the initial opening of a community residence are usually neutral or supportive 2 years later (Lubin, Schwartz, Zigman, & Janicki, 1982). A positive reception by the community opens the possibility for additional participation and interaction with community members.

ADDRESSING THE GOAL OF INCREASED VISIBILITY AND INTEGRATION

One increasingly important aspect of treatment is the provision of opportunities that increase the visibility and integration of individuals with developmental disabilities. The pursuit of this goal often means changes in the allocation of environmental resources. Such changes may affect the distribution of personnel and the development of new programs.

Many programs for dually diagnosed individuals are introducing supported employment in an effort to improve clients' functioning and facilitate their integration into the community. Rusch and Hughes (1989) have defined supportive employment as competitive work in an integrated work setting for individuals with severe handicaps for whom competitive employment has not occurred. McClannahan and Krantz (1990) have examined a number of important points concerning supported employment. Wehman and Hill (1981) have emphasized the importance of matching the individual to the job. Variables such as hours, physical limitations, dress codes, and skill requirements should be considered in this process. In addition, to the extent possible, personal interests should be incorporated into the analysis.

McDonnell, Nops, Hardman, and Chambless (1989) have shown that the intelligence level of the worker and the outcome in an employment setting are largely unrelated. In addition, employer evaluations do not vary with the functioning levels of the workers (Shafer, Kregel, Banks, & Hill, 1988). Workers who are intellectually low functioning are not necessarily judged by employers to be less effective employees, and their employment outcomes may equal those of higher functioning workers.

This information says much about the feasibility of placing individuals with severe disabilities in competitive employment positions. Supported employment programs have even been shown to be cost-effective (Conley, Rusch, McCaughrin, & Tines, 1989; Green, 1989; Hill et al., 1987; Kregel, Wehman, & Banks, 1989). In a supported employment situation, clients are actually earning income rather than drawing from public assistance funding for their day program requirements. Although there are obvious economic advantages for both the client and the social funding system in such an arrangement, the most important benefit to the client engaged in a normalized work setting is the opportunity to develop a sense of autonomy.

The goal of many treatment teams is to obtain jobs in the community for their clients. Such an undertaking involves good management of environmental resources. One way to approach the goal is to constitute the program as a transitional model with extensive support services. An example of such a program follows.

The Example of Project Job

The staff at a day program for developmentally disabled adults became concerned about the lack of appropriate job possibilities for their successful clients. They decided to develop a supported employment program— Project Job—to bring these clients to the next level of independence.

Staff members solicited cooperation from community employers and inquired about their willingness to employ workers with disabilities. Although many doors were closed, several businesses expressed some interest. Once interest on the part of an employer was ascertained, staff visited the potential job site and interviewed the employer about the nature of the work, the responsibilities of the employee, and other relevant matters. Staff members then began the process of job analysis, identifying the specific behaviors needed to successfully manage the demands of the job. Associated factors, such as stress level, time constraints, and interpersonal demands were also evaluated. This information helped the staff match individual clients to specific jobs. At times, some preliminary skills training was conducted at the day program. Clients then visited the work site, met the employer, and learned about the demands of the job.

Clients were thus slowly introduced into the job setting. Initially, they were accompanied to work by staff members, who served as job coaches. This support helped them generalize skills learned in the program to the job setting. Staff members also served as liaisons with the on-site supervisors, helping employers learn about the characteristics of each employee and discover the best methods for working with each one.

The case of Kathy. Kathy was a 23-year-old woman with a history of mild mental retardation and obsessive-compulsive disorder. She was very high functioning and was a star in the day program. She helped other clients, supervised the operation of the client-managed coffee shop, and had mastered the full range of skills at her workshop. Staff felt that she was a good candidate for Project Job.

Kathy's anxiety was a stumbling block, and staff realized they would have to work closely with her throughout the transition. They found Kathy a job at a local nursing home—an excellent choice because Kathy would continue to have a high level of contact with people. She would also be in a helping role, which she enjoyed.

Kathy's main job was to distribute meals to the patients. This process entailed assembling trays according to placed orders and delivering them to patients' rooms. She was also responsible for picking up the orders for the next day's meals.

The difficulty Kathy encountered was in adapting to situations in which something could interfere with the perfect completion of her job. Perhaps the kitchen was out of apple juice, and she needed to substitute on an order. Perhaps a cup of coffee spilled on the cart, necessitating a quick cleanup. Perhaps a patient was away from her room, and Kathy could not get the order for the next day's meals. Situations like these would send Kathy into a state of acute anxiety. She sometimes became so distressed that she was unable to solve the problem and complete her tasks in a timely fashion.

To address this difficulty, Kathy's coach used a stress inoculation approach (Meichenbaum, 1986). This training focused on helping Kathy identify and prepare for stressors, cope with the feeling of being overwhelmed by a stressor, use self-statements and relaxation procedures to meet the demands of the situation, and reinforce herself for attempts at coping. The coach also introduced a problem-solving approach, helping Kathy to identify alternative solutions for a variety of problem situations. This would alleviate her tendency to freeze in panic situations.

Kathy required many weeks of intensive coaching to successfully manage the transition to the world of work. Once her anxiety decreased, she enjoyed her job, and staff and patients at the nursing home considered her a real asset to their setting.

The case of Paul. Paul was a 29-year-old mentally retarded man with the additional diagnosis of paranoid schizophrenia. He worked best alone, in situations not requiring a high degree of interaction with others. He was able to follow complex instructions independently. In addition, he was able to travel on his own, and he knew his way around the city well. The staff found Paul a job as a messenger, which seemed to suit him.

Paul initially did very well on his job. However, after a few weeks, the employer reported that a delivery had not been completed. Discussing the situation with Paul, the coach learned that his client had seen two large dogs en route to the delivery site, had become frightened, and had turned back. The coach attempted to verbally intervene, to calm Paul's apprehensions about dogs, and to reassure him that he was capable of continuing with his assigned tasks.

The scenario was repeated the following week. The coach decided to address the phobia with a systematic desensitization technique. He accompanied Paul on a delivery to the site where dogs were often present and helped him use calming techniques as he approached the building. The coach accompanied Paul on several more deliveries, taking a less active role in the intervention each time. Eventually, Paul was able to manage the trip alone.

The Need for Intensive Treatment in Employment Settings

Extended one-to-one treatment in the job setting was critical for Paul's and Kathy's success. It prevented the kind of failure that might have undermined the employee's self-esteem and created hesitancy on the part of the employer.

McDonnell et al. (1989) have shown that intensive one-to-one training is necessary for positive outcomes. Frequent contact with the coach in the employment setting, detailed job analysis and training programs, and highly individualized support appear to create a situation favorable to success (McDonnell et al., 1989; Shafer et al., 1988). In fact, treatment and training appear to be more important to outcome than the employee's level of functioning (McClannahan & Krantz, 1990). The intensive treatment model bridges the transition from day program to employment: It helps orient the employer to the employee and provides a mechanism for problem solving, especially early in the transition.

The case of Raul. One of Project Job's first employees was Raul, a high-functioning developmentally disabled man with a number of skills. He was especially good at following instructions, and he could work independently for long periods. He was best at physical tasks that did not require a great deal of interpersonal interaction or negotiation. Raul was employed at a local supermarket, where he stacked and priced goods and kept track of inventories.

During his lunch breaks, Raul often sat with other workers watching television. At lunch the television was often tuned to reruns of "I Love Lucy," a program with which Raul was somewhat obsessed. He would become very excited while watching the show and would begin talking about it loudly to other employees. He would sometimes impersonate the show's characters in a falsetto voice. He would often continue these behaviors after lunch. His distraction level was high, and his interpersonal style became increasingly bizarre.

The job coach was consulted about this problem. The employer wondered whether Raul should be forbidden from watching television during lunch, as this would remove him from the problem situation. The coach considered this possibility and rejected it for several reasons. First, it would also segregate Raul and remove him from the other workers. Second, it would not teach him ways of handling the situation appropriately.

Instead, the coach used an approach that was both behavioral and cognitive. Attention was focused on generating alternative courses of action for the target situation and on predicting potential outcomes of these alternatives. The coach helped Raul to anticipate the consequences of various actions, pointing out that his actions had negative social consequences and created tension with his boss. This information helped motivate Raul to focus on coping effectively with the situation. The coach spent much time helping Raul to distinguish appropriate and inappropriate responses to the stimuli. Together they rehearsed appropriate behaviors and developed ways to inhibit the inappropriate, impulsive responses. Raul was able to curb his extreme silliness and to distract himself with other mental activities. He learned to rehearse coping statements when faced with the problem situation, and he began to reinforce himself for appropriate responses and efforts at self-control.

When his skills became more established, Raul began to self-monitor his behavior. He was able to keep track of the situations and his responses and to evaluate his own progress. He spontaneously generalized these skills to a number of other situations in which he had previously behaved inappropriately. For example, when he heard planes overhead, Raul frequently imagined that he was a pilot. At such times, he could get carried away with these fantasies, losing the ability to focus on his work and appearing bizarre to coworkers. Raul spontaneously began using some of his self-control techniques to govern this behavior. In fact, the problem behaviors themselves (distractibility, becoming lost in fantasies) served as cues to invoke self-control strategies. As a result of the generalization of these skills, Raul became better able to integrate into his job setting and to interact with coworkers.

The case of Jack. Jack was another client involved in Project Job. Jack worked in the mail room of a large insurance company. His sorting and sequencing skills were superior, and he needed no supervision to complete sorting tasks. Although Jack posed no significant behavior problems, his social deficits needed some attention. Jack's main problem in integrating into his work setting lay in a failure to comprehend nuances of interpersonal situations. For example, other workers sometimes teased him—not with vicious taunts, but with the mild, joking comments that were universal among the crew. Jack reacted by ignoring his coworkers' comments. Sometimes, however, his feelings would be hurt, and he would typically withdraw sullenly. When several of these events had occurred, he usually would respond angrily. The other workers began to see Jack as a "bad sport" without a sense of humor.

The coach began to address this problem as a skill deficit. She explained teasing and its meaning. More important, however, she began to tease Jack in a similar way. Together they rehearsed and role-played teasing exchanges. Jack was able to understand that the coach was kidding him, and he did not read ridicule into her comments. Their exchanges enabled him to learn and practice appropriate responses.

Eventually, Jack was able to transfer these skills to the workplace. At first, he was unsure which comments were teasing comments, but he continued to practice the skills learned with the coach and transferred these responses to the job setting. His coworkers responded positively to this change. Once Jack could respond to teasing, other avenues of interaction opened. For example, fellow employees began including him in lunch activities and softball games.

Social Skills Training for Employment

The examples of Raul and Jack point to the need for treatment of social skill deficits. Often, employment is jeopardized by social skill deficiencies when performance is otherwise satisfactory. Raul's blatantly inappropriate behavior and lack of social awareness created a troublesome situation on the job. He needed to learn to distinguish between appropriate and inappropriate social behaviors. In addition, he needed help in inhibiting inappropriate behaviors that interfered with his integration into the setting. Jack's social skill deficiencies likewise impacted on his ability to integrate into the environment. In addition, his lack of social understanding hampered his acceptance by coworkers.

It has been noted that job coaches need to focus on skills other than work and productivity skills (McClannahan & Krantz, 1990). This is true at every stage of employment. At the outset, job interview skills are needed. Kelly, Wildman, and Berier (1980) taught clients with developmental disabilities to present themselves positively to potential employers. In addition, the clients learned how to request more information about prospective jobs and to express enthusiasm about potential positions.

Some of the most common behavior problems in the work setting include bizarre behavior, excessive verbalization, and inappropriate interaction (Salzberg, Lignugaris-Kraft, & McCuller, 1988). It is important for the coach to address conversational skills, social behavior skills, and self-control skills (Salzberg, Likins, McConaughy, & Lignugaris-Kraft, 1986). Some have suggested that the best interventions are naturalistic and socially valid. LaGreca, Stone, and Bell (1983) designed a treatment incorporating modeling, coaching, and rehearsal to teach appropriate responses in difficult interpersonal situations. Results indicated that individuals thus taught had improved social competencies and better vocational outcomes. In addition, naturalistic consequences such as warnings and work suspensions have proven to be effective interventions for disruptive problem behaviors (Rusch & Menchetti, 1981; Schultz, Rusch, & Lamson, 1979).

Deficiencies in social awareness and comprehension, such as an inability to respond appropriately to teasing, must also be addressed (Chadsey-Rusch & Gonzalez, 1988). Skills training may be needed to develop comprehension of such interpersonal nuances (McClannahan & Krantz, 1990). In situations in which social skill deficits are a significant problem, the appropriate skills should be the object of direct intervention.

THE IMPORTANCE OF PROACTIVE INTERVENTION

Referrals for dually diagnosed individuals typically occur under crisis conditions. Often, there is an acute need to control severe maladaptive behaviors. Self-injury, property destruction, threatening behavior, and aggression are typical precursors of a referral for treatment. Such behaviors often pose significant risk for the individual, other clients, or staff members. In addition, they may jeopardize the individual's placement in a group home or employment setting. In these cases, the behaviors must be addressed immediately and specifically; intervention is necessarily reactive, guided by the severity of the presenting problems. The treatment goals are defined inherently by the fact that a crisis condition exists.

The existence of crisis situations, and the need to address crisis referrals quickly and directly, can obscure the need for proactive interventions. Proactive interventions emphasize skill acquisition. Coping skills programs and problem-solving training are proactive interventions that equip clients with skills to handle stressful situations effectively. In particular, they emphasize the assessment of situations, the examination of alternative response choices, and the evaluation of choices. Clients who are instructed in these techniques learn to inhibit impulsive or automatic responses to stressful stimuli. This ability can prevent the behavioral escalations that lead to crisis situations.

Social skills are also taught as part of proactive interventions. By learning prosocial behaviors, clients increase their communication abilities. In addition, clients with good social skills have more positive interactions with peers and with staff members. Reducing negative interactions can have a positive impact on client behavior and satisfaction.

There is evidence that skills training and participation in activities is associated with favorable outcomes for clients. Individuals who have failed in community residences have typically participated in few social activities and engaged in few skills training programs (Gollay, Freedman, Wyngaarden, & Kurtz, 1978; Seltzer, 1981).

In addition to offering programmatic instruction in a variety of skills, the environment can foster appropriate behavior in a variety of other ways. The environment itself, in other words, can be structured to be proactive. Reinforcement contingencies should encourage prosocial and appropriate behaviors. Some authors have suggested that settings should emphasize access to rewards as opposed to loss of rewards. The designation of a "time-in" area, discussed earlier, illustrates this principle.

SUMMARY

In our effort to provide the reader with guidelines for developing comprehensive and multicomponent clinical treatment plans, this chapter focused specifically on the environment as an important target for intervention. Although clinicians working with persons with dual diagnoses rarely have the administrative power to make decisions regarding the physical environment or residence in which clients live, in their role as consultants, they frequently are able to provide suggestions regarding environmental changes to those who are in such administrative positions. In some cases environmental changes can be viewed as prerequisites to effective clinical intervention. For example, development of a proactive treatment plan utilizing a "time-in" area for positive reinforcement cannot occur without the presence of the physical space required for such an area.

Interventions aimed at the social environment can be directly addressed by the clinician, but they require cooperation from the peer and caregiving systems in order to be successful. In this light, interventions aimed at either the physical or social environment should always be planned and executed with a sensitivity for those issues discussed in chapter 9 concerning possible caregiver resistance and system obstacles.

A hypothetical model residence drawing upon the authors' clinical observations and research was presented in order to provide some pragmatic and feasible guidelines for construction of a treatment milieu. The benefits of providing therapeutic groups within the context of a group or family residence was discussed. Efficacy of such groups was demonstrated through both clinical vignettes and initial outcome data regarding groups focusing on such areas as problem solving and assertiveness training. Psychotherapy groups can be cost-effective when offered either as part of the therapeutic milieu or as an outpatient treatment. Further, such groups provide a unique opportunity for clients to learn cooperative communication or perspective-taking skills. Finally, the benefits in terms of client autonomy inherent in job coaching and supported employment models was highlighted through several actual clinical case examples.

For persons with developmental disabilities, it is absolutely essential that the physical, social, and job training environments offer more than mere resources and opportunity: Clients must also have the training and instruction required to use these resources.

Appendix

The Behavioral Role-Play Activities Test (BRAT)

Administering the BRAT

Introduction and Role-Play Descriptions

Role-Play Scripts

Scoring Forms

Administering the BRAT

The Behavioral Role-Play Activities Test (BRAT; Nezu et al., 1990) is an instrument designed to assess, through scripted role-plays, the behavior management skills of parents or caregivers of individuals with developmental disabilities. Materials presented here include (a) role-play descriptions, intended to help orient the parent or caregiver to the role-play; (b) role-play scripts, to be used by the person playing the role of the developmentally disabled individual; and (c) scoring forms, including operational definitions for each caregiver skill.

The BRAT is intended to assess the behavior management skills of individuals 18 years or older. The role-play descriptions are written as they pertain to Ali, a 10-year-old female with moderate mental retardation. However, these role-play descriptions may be adapted as necessary so that a person of another age may role-play the part of the individual with developmental disabilities.

The examining team should consist of one examiner and one role-player. Prior to administration of the BRAT, the examiner and the individual serving as the role-player should be thoroughly familiar with the content, scripts, and scoring of the BRAT. Both should be so familiar with the materials that they do not require reference to the script or text during administration. The scoring forms are written with the assumption that the role-plays will be videotaped. If so, the examiner must be familiar and comfortable with the operation of all video equipment. If video equipment is not used, there should be two persons present who are thoroughly familiar with the scoring system and who may serve as in vivo raters. When training individuals who will later serve as in vivo raters, we have found it helpful first to establish a history of high interrater agreement by using videotaped practice BRAT tests. Raters should be given a copy of the description and script for each role-play along with the scoring forms.

The procedures described here for administration have been used to obtain data concerning the BRAT's psychometric properties (see chapter 5) and should be followed if comparisons with previous studies are to be meaningful.

Physical Conditions and Materials

The testing room should be well lit and ventilated, and relatively sound-proof. The room must be large enough to accommodate the following furniture: a folding table and two chairs, a sofa or freestanding chair, and a video camera or two in vivo raters (outside of the role-play area).

The following materials are required:

1. Folding table
2. Three chairs
3. Portable radio
4. Portable television
5. Stopwatch
6. Magazines or comic books
7. Crayons and drawing paper
8. Tokens (e.g., poker chips)
9. Cereal bowl and plastic spoons
10. Box of cereal
11. Sorting materials (two plastic containers and red and white pipe cleaners)
12. Pad and pencil
13. Various toys

Time of Administration

In most instances, completion of all six role-play sequences requires 60–90 minutes. This allows for introduction and explanation of the BRAT, as well as preparation time required between each role-play sequence. It is desirable to administer the entire BRAT in a single session; however, it is possible to use two or more sessions because the BRAT consists of discrete subtests.

General Directions

Before beginning the test, it is helpful to take a few moments to establish rapport by stimulating some interest in the BRAT, presenting the test in a businesslike but gentle manner, and describing what will happen next. It may be helpful to mention that the parent or caregiver is going to experience a group of short role-play tasks, that some may be more difficult than others, and that the person should simply "Try your best to follow directions."

Next, the parent or caregiver should be provided with the written introduction to the role-plays, given a moment to look it over, and asked if he or she has any questions. When answering questions, it is best to repeat or slightly reword the instructions for clarity but not to provide any teaching of skills or additional information regarding how the person should carry out the instructions.

After the parent or caregiver has read the introductory page, he or she should be given the written description for Role-Play 1. Tell the person that he or she may take a few moments to read the directions for the role-play and may keep the instructions during the role-play. Ask the person to let you know when he or she is ready to begin.

When the parent or caregiver has indicated readiness, say, "Begin the role-play" and start timing the role-play. If a videotape is being used, the taping should begin immediately. During each role-play sequence, you must keep an accurate and continuous record of time elapsed and provide subtle auditory cues (e.g., throat clearing or a slight cough) to the role-player to signal the various learned behavior sequences described in the role-play scripts. Doing so helps maintain a natural atmosphere during the role-play sequence. Repeat each role-play according to the preceding directions.

Special Instructions for the Role-Player

It is important to maintain reliable and standardized adherence to the role-play script provided. In other words, regardless of the parent or caregiver's responses during each role-play, the role-player's behavior must remain as scripted. The role-player may allow the parent or caregiver to provide physical guidance in a nonscripted task, if this is unavoidable, but should never become involved in a physical struggle or resistance. For example, if the script directs the role-player to throw an object on the floor, the parent or caregiver may insist that the role-player pick up the object. When the role-player adheres to the script and does not pick up the object, the parent or caregiver may take the role-player by the hand and guide him or her in picking up the item. In this case, the role-player should allow the parent or caregiver to provide physical guidance. However, as soon as possible, the role-player must resume behavior consistent with the script.

Introduction and Role-Play Descriptions

This role-play test is designed to give you the opportunity to put your behavior management skills into action. You will receive written descriptions of six role-play situations, each involving a parent or caregiver (P/C) and a child with a developmental disability. In each situation, the parent or caregiver is attempting to modify the child's inappropriate behavior. For each situation, the target behavior has been defined, and the strategy for parent or caregiver has been briefly outlined.

Each situation is the basis for a 5-minute role-play, with you in the parent/caregiver role. The child will be portrayed by a young person who has been trained to assist in the test.

Before each role-play, you will have a few minutes to read the description and think about how you will apply the strategy. When you are ready, you can notify the examiner to begin the scene.

The examiner will now give you the description for Role-Play 1. Thank you for participating in this assessment.

Role-Play 1

Extinction

Ali is a 10-year-old, moderately retarded female who often engages in verbal tantrums. A verbal tantrum is defined as screaming, name-calling, and use of obscenities. Important reinforcing consequences for Ali include social (attentional) reinforcement, as well as compliance with her demands that the family television be turned off. The strategy for this situation is *extinction*—ignoring any incidence of the target behavior throughout the role-play. In this role-play, you turn on the television shortly before dinner to watch the evening news. Ali is drawing with a pad and pencil in the same room.

Role-Play 2

Shaping

Ali, a 10-year-old, moderately retarded female, rarely plays with toys alone for more than 30 seconds. In the past, when given toys and told to play by herself, she would frequently scream and tug on her caregiver's clothing. This behavior would usually be followed by the caregiver's attempts to calm her with a back rub and a game of patty-cake.

The strategy for this role-play is *shaping*, to extend the time Ali will play "on task" with her toys. On-task behavior is defined as handling the toys provided (with one or both hands), without screaming or tugging at others' clothing.

In the role-play, you instruct Ali to play alone with her toys until "time is up" and tell her that you will play patty-cake with her if she succeeds. The first step in your shaping program is to reinforce Ali for playing on task for 30 seconds. If Ali stops her on-task activity (e.g., screams, tugs on your clothes) before 30 seconds have passed, you guide her back to the toys and remind her to play until time is up.

Patty-cake rhyme:

Patty-cake, patty-cake, bakerman,
Bake me a cake as fast as you can.
Roll it and roll it and mark it with B.
Put it in the oven for baby and me.

Role-Play 3

Differential Reinforcement of Incompatible Behavior (DRI)

Ali is a 10-year-old, moderately retarded female who frequently displays aggression toward others by pushing, slapping, grabbing hair, and pinching. The aggressive behavior commonly follows exposure to noise—for example, when a radio or dishwasher is turned on.

The strategy for this role-play is *differential reinforcement of incompatible behavior (DRI)*—attempting to reduce the aggressive behavior by reinforcing an incompatible behavior. The incompatible behavior to be reinforced in this role-play is color sorting, defined as any appropriate handling of the sorting materials provided.

In this role-play, you and Ali are both seated at a table. On the table are a pile of red and white pipe cleaners, as well as two plastic containers for sorting them by color. You turn on the radio and try to have Ali sort the colors, reinforcing her for that activity. At the same time, you are to extinguish (ignore) any aggression, as described in Role-Play 1.

Role-Play 4

Contingent Positive Reinforcement

Ali is a 10-year-old, moderately retarded female who has a habit of banging her head on the family television set. Head banging only occurs when the television is turned on and when Ali is seated on the floor within reach of the set.

The strategy for this role-play is *contingent positive reinforcement,* aimed at extending the time Ali sits in a chair out of reach of the television set while watching programs. You try to increase this behavior by reinforcing it with tokens. This strategy is an indirect way to reduce the head-banging behavior.

In the role-play, you tell Ali that, to earn tokens, she must stay in the chair while watching television. She receives a token for every full minute she stays seated in the chair. If she leaves her chair, you turn the television off and remind her of what she must do. You turn the television back on only when she is seated again.

Role-Play 5

Time-Out

Ali is a 10-year-old, moderately retarded female who engages in destructive behavior and spitting. Destructive behavior is defined as knocking objects off surfaces or picking objects up and throwing them. These behaviors commonly occur when Ali's demands for snacks such as soda or candy are not met.

The strategy for this role-play is *time-out*. You try to reduce the target behaviors by imposing time-out following any occurrence of spitting or destructive behavior. The time-out area is a chair in a corner of the room that is free of objects and other furniture.

In the role-play, you and Ali are looking at a magazine, an activity the child enjoys. Ali may periodically ask for a candy bar.

Role-Play 6

Cues and Prompts

Ali is a 10-year-old, moderately retarded female who refuses to eat with a spoon. She has occasionally demonstrated this skill at her day training program. At home, she usually eats with her fingers and whines when told to use a spoon.

The strategy for this role-play is verbal and physical *cuing and prompting*. In the role-play, you attempt to increase spoon-feeding behavior by cuing and prompting Ali through the process during her afternoon snack. You should first verbally cue Ali to pick up the spoon, then prompt her physically if necessary. Your goal is to complete the following sequence of steps as many times as possible in the time allowed.

Steps in spoon feeding:

1. Ali picks up the spoon.

2. Ali puts the spoon in the dish.

3. Ali scoops some food onto the spoon.

4. Ali puts the food in her mouth.

5. Ali puts the spoon down until she has swallowed the food.

Role-Play Scripts

Role-Play 1

Extinction

Materials: Pad, pencil, television set

Script (minutes)	Activity of Role-Player
0–1	Draw with pad and pencil until television is turned on. As soon as television is turned on, jump up and yell, "No noise! I hate this damn TV!" Approach P/C at close range and say, "Please turn it off" (three times) and cry loudly. Walk to the television and, while sitting down in front of it, say, "Damn it! I'm upset. Stupid damn TV!" Repeat this until next cue is given.
1–2	At examiner's cue, get up and stamp around the room, saying, "I hate this TV! Stupid! Stupid! Stupid!" (Repeat three times, more loudly each time.) Cry and sit on the floor until the next cue.
2–3	At examiner's cue, settle down and draw on the pad while looking occasionally at the television. Respond cooperatively to P/C.
3–5	At examiner's cue, begin second tantrum. Yell, "Now! I want it off, now! I'm very upset! Damn!" Cry for a few moments, then return to pad and pencil and continue drawing.

Role-Play 2

Shaping

Materials: Various toys scattered on the floor, stopwatch

Script (minutes)	Activity of Role-Player
0–3	Play appropriately with various toys. If P/C stops you to play patty-cake, respond cooperatively. After any sequence of patty-cake, return to playing with toys and await next cue.
3–4	At examiner's cue, stop playing and say, "No play—dance with me. La-la-la (sing)!" Continue repeating this, even if P/C attempts to guide you back, until next cue.
4–5	Return to appropriate toy play. Count silently to 20, then stop and say, "No more play." Attempt to play patty-cake sequence once. Return to appropriate play for remaining seconds of role-play.

Role-Play 3

Differential Reinforcement of Incompatible Behavior (DRI)

Materials: Table and chairs, radio, sorting materials (red and white pipe cleaners and two plastic containers)

Script (minutes)	Activity of Role-Player
0–1	As radio is turned on, begin bouncing in your seat and count to five. After counting, continually repeat, "No, Mommy, no!" Push sorting materials away and frequently slap at or pinch P/C. Continue this behavior until next cue.
1–5	At examiner's cue, sort one object and return to the above sequence for several seconds. Continue to alternate between sorting and aggressive sequence, gradually increasing number of objects sorted (one, two, three, and finally four objects) until the end of the role-play.

Role-Play 4

Contingent Positive Reinforcement

Materials: Tokens, television set, chair, stopwatch

Script (minutes)	Activity of Role-Player
0–1	Watch television from the chair, making several moves to leave the chair but continuing to stay seated until cue.
1–1.5	At examiner's cue, slide to the floor and remain seated there, rocking.
1.5–2	Whether or not P/C turns off the television, get up and pace floor saying, "I'll be good. I'll be good" in a whining tone (three times). Sit on the floor close to the television and continue to repeat the same statement until next cue.
2–5	At examiner's cue, take a seat and watch television appropriately until the end.

Time-Out

Materials: Magazines, stopwatch, time-out chair in corner of the room

Script (minutes)	Activity of Role-Player
0–1	Look through magazine with P/C, making appropriate comments.
1–5	See ad for snack and start to demand candy, saying, "I want some candy now!" Ask four times and begin to whine, getting louder and acting silly.

After fourth demand, spit twice and throw magazines. If P/C does not call time-out, repeat sequence two more times.

During any time-out, get up once at the start, grab a magazine, and begin to read. Go back to time-out if guided or told. Attempt to take magazine back with you to time-out chair unless P/C removes it.

After time-out is over, or if P/C did not call time-out after repeated spits and throws, return to looking at the magazine with P/C in appropriate manner.

Role-Play 6

Cues and Prompts

Materials: Bowl of cereal, spoon, table, chairs

Script (minutes)	Activity of Role-Player
0–1	Despite all attempts to prompt through feeding task, refuse to perform task and make three attempts to grab food with fingers.
1–2	Respond only to physical prompts for all steps.
2–3	Respond to verbal prompts for Steps 1 and 2 but only to physical prompts for all others.
3–4	Same as previous instruction, but make two attempts to grab food with fingers.
4–5	Respond to all verbal prompts. Perform all steps independently, in a slow and deliberate manner.

Scoring Forms

Subject _____

Date of test _____

Rater _____

GENERAL INSTRUCTIONS

You will be scoring the Behavioral Role-Play Activities Test (BRAT) as you view six videotaped role-play sequences. In each of the following scenes a parent or caregiver is attempting to modify the behavior of a child with developmental disabilities. The child's behavior has been scripted specifically for each role-play and remains consistent for each subject who is tested. Videotaping permits you to replay any or all of the sequences while scoring, thus maximizing scoring reliability.

You need to be familiar with the description and instructions for each scene, as well as instructions to the parent concerning the behavioral strategy to use. The description and script for each role-play are included with the scoring sheet. Each scoring sheet includes a list of defined parent/caregiver (P/C) responses, which are scored as present (+) or absent (0) during the role-play.

The scoring procedure for each role-play is as follows:

1. Read the role-play description for the scene.

2. Read the scoring sheet, which contains the expected P/C responses for the scene.

3. Score each P/C response in the space provided for the presence (+) or absence (0) of the response.

4. Add the number of (+) responses and enter that number in the lower right-hand corner of the scoring sheet, over the total number of (+) responses possible. Compute the ratio (total

responses divided by total possible responses × 100 = _____)
to obtain a percentage score for each role-play. Enter this score
in the space in the lower right-hand corner of the score sheet.

Special instructions are provided for each role-play. They are clearly
marked at the top of the scoring sheet. Please read these special instructions carefully before viewing each role-play.

SAMPLE SCORING

The following example shows completed portions of the score sheet for
Role-Play 1. The special instructions are as follows: Role-Play 1 contains
two discrete sequences of tantrum behavior. Items 1 through 9 describe
P/C behaviors scored as present (+) or absent (0) with regard to the first
tantrum. Items 10 through 18 are scored (+) or (0) for P/C behaviors
observed during the second tantrum. Items 19 and 20 are scored as
described in the general instructions.
    The following items are scored as if the P/C had successfully extin-
guished the first tantrum but had not demonstrated this skill during the
second tantrum. In other words, during the first verbal tantrum occurring during the role-play, the P/C made no verbal response (Item 1),
made no physical response (Item 2), made no eye contact (Item 3), maintained a neutral expression (Item 4), and so on. However, during the
second verbal tantrum, the P/C talked to the child, stroked her arm,
made direct eye contact, and smiled at the child.

P/C Responses	Tantrum I	Tantrum II
When defined tantrum behavior occurs:		
P/C makes no verbal response to child.	1 __+__	10 __O__
P/C makes no physical response to child.	2 __+__	11 __O__
P/C makes no eye contact with child.	3 __+__	12 __O__
P/C maintains neutral expression (i.e., "straight face") while ignoring tantrum.	4 __+__	13 __O__

After the entire list of P/C responses is rated, the total number of
(+) responses is summed. In this example, the P/C has been rated (+)
for half of the items. The total score would appear on the score sheet
as follows:

Total score: __10__ / 20

Percent correct: __50__ %

Role-Play 1

Extinction

Special instructions: Role-Play 1 contains two discrete sequences of tantrum behavior. Items 1 through 9 describe P/C behaviors scored as present (+) or absent (0) with regard to the first tantrum. Items 10 through 18 are scored (+) or (0) for P/C behaviors observed during the second tantrum. Items 19 and 20 are scored as described in the general instructions.

P/C Responses	Tantrum I	Tantrum II
When defined tantrum behavior occurs:		
P/C makes no verbal response to child.	1 _____	10 _____
P/C makes no physical response to child.	2 _____	11 _____
P/C makes no eye contact with child.	3 _____	12 _____
P/C maintains neutral expression (i.e., "straight face") while ignoring tantrum.	4 _____	13 _____
P/C provides no verbal response to demands for television to be turned off.	5 _____	14 _____
P/C attends to TV program rather than to child.	6 _____	15 _____
When defined tantrum behavior is absent for at least 15 seconds:		
P/C praises child for appropriate behavior (e.g., sitting quietly, drawing, watching television). This praise does not require a specific statement describing the behavior.	7 _____	16 _____
P/C uses verbal praise that is specific to the appropriate behavior.	8 _____	17 _____
P/C provides positive attention only during time in which child displays no tantrum behaviors.	9 _____	18 _____
Verbal praise is delivered in a warm, affectionate tone of voice.		19 _____
The television remains on throughout the entire role-play.		20 _____

Total score: _____ / 20

Percent correct: _____ %

Shaping

Special instructions: Although Role-Play 2 provides several trials for the P/C to exhibit the responses defined below, score for presence (+) or absence (0) of each response as described in the general instructions.

P/C Responses

P/C attempts to gain child's attention in order to state contingency by making eye contact and guiding face with hands, if necessary.   1 _____

While child is playing on task as defined:

P/C provides verbal reinforcement.   2 _____

P/C provides verbal reinforcement in a pleasant tone of voice.   3 _____

P/C maintains pleasant facial expression.   4 _____

P/C provides patty-cake game immediately (within 5 seconds) following 30 seconds of on-task play.   5 _____

P/C states clearly why patty-cake game is being played (because child played alone for 30 seconds).   6 _____

P/C states clearly when time is up and patty-cake reinforcement is about to be delivered.   7 _____

P/C pairs patty-cake game with social reinforcement and enthusiasm.   8 _____

When child stops playing on task before 30 seconds elapse and/or engages in screaming, laughing, or tugging at clothing:

Patty-cake game is not delivered.   9 _____

P/C verbally redirects child back to task.   10 _____

P/C delivers verbal redirection in neutral tone of voice at all times.   11 _____

P/C maintains neutral facial expression.   12 _____

P/C uses same verbal phrase for redirection back to task.   13 _____

P/C physically removes child in a neutral manner when she tugs at clothing.   14 _____

P/C makes no reinforcing statements and engages
in no pleasant social interactions.   15 _____

P/C attempts to stay out of child's reach.   16 _____

Total score: _____ / 16

Percent correct: _____ %

Role-Play 3

Differential Reinforcement of Incompatible Behavior (DRI)

Special instructions: Role-Play 3 contains three or more discrete trials for the caregiver to differentially reinforce a specific task (color sorting). In addition, three or more incidences of the target behavior (e.g., throwing objects, pinching) will be displayed. Please note that several P/C responses must be observed at least three times during the role-play to be scored as present (+). For each such response, there are three spaces below the P/C description (for example, see Item 4), to be scored as (+) each time the response occurs during the scene; all three spaces must be scored (+) in order for the item to be scored (+) overall. All other items are scored as described in the general instructions.

P/C Responses

At start of role-play, P/C states task in concrete terms
(e.g., "Put the red ones in here").   1 _____

P/C models task for child.   2 _____

P/C uses verbal statement to direct child to task.   3 _____

When child displays aggression toward P/C or materials:

P/C discontinues eye contact.
(three P/C responses required)   4 _____

_____ _____ _____

P/C turns attention away from child.
(three P/C responses required)   5 _____

_____ _____ _____

P/C confines all verbal exchange to a neutral cue to task.
(three P/C responses required)   6 _____

_____ _____ _____

P/C maintains a neutral facial expression.
(three P/C responses required)   7 _____

_____ _____ _____

P/C blocks child's aggression in a neutral manner when
it may cause harm or injury to P/C.   8 _____

P/C returns to table in a neutral manner any materials
that have been thrown.   9 _____

Any verbal reprimand made by P/C is brief and
immediately follows aggression.   10 _____

When child is attending to the task and not being aggressive:

P/C uses encouraging, directive tone of voice.
(three P/C responses required)   11 _____

_____   _____   _____

P/C verbally cues or models task for the child.
(three P/C responses required)   12 _____

_____   _____   _____

When child attempts any approximation of sorting task (e.g., touching
materials, reaching toward container with colored piece):

P/C provides verbal reinforcement.
(three P/C responses required)   13 _____

_____   _____   _____

P/C makes verbal reinforcement specific
(e.g., "Good, you're putting the red ones in here!").   14 _____

P/C uses physical reinforcement.   15 _____

When child sorts correctly, P/C intensifies verbal
reinforcement (e.g., clapping, exuberant tone of voice).
(three P/C responses required)   16 _____

_____   _____   _____

P/C orients face toward child.   17 _____

Noise stimulus remains on throughout role-play sequence.   18 _____

Total score: _____ / 18

Percent correct: _____ %

Role-Play 4

Contingent Positive Reinforcement

Special instructions: Role-Play 4 requires the P/C to dispense tokens for appropriate behavior (sitting in seat). The scene includes several trials for the P/C to exhibit this skill. Please note that for several P/C response items (for example, Item 4), the response must be observed at least twice during the role-play to be scored as (+) overall. For each such item, there are two spaces under the P/C description, to be scored as (+) when the response occurs during the scene. All other items are scored as described in the general instructions.

P/C Responses

P/C attempts to gain child's attention, physically
orienting face, if necessary. ⟶ 1 _____

P/C states contingency in clear, concrete terms
(e.g., "When you stay in your seat, you get a token"). 2 _____

P/C shows token to child to remind her of what she may earn. 3 _____

At the completion of each minute during which child has remained seated:

P/C provides immediate praise (within 5 seconds).
(two P/C responses required) 4 _____

_____ _____

P/C provides tokens immediately.
(two P/C responses required) 5 _____

_____ _____

P/C provides clear statement of why token is being given
(e.g., "You get a token because you stayed in your seat").
(two P/C responses required) 6 _____

_____ _____

P/C uses cue (e.g., "Time's up") to let child know when
1 minute has passed.
(two P/C responses required) 7 _____

_____ _____

P/C pairs dispensing of tokens with social praise.
(two P/C responses required) 8 _____

_____ _____

P/C delivers verbal reinforcement in enthusiastic,
warm tone of voice.
(two P/C responses required) 9 _____

_____ _____

P/C delivers verbal reinforcement with direct eye contact.
(two P/C responses required)   10 _____

_____   _____

Verbal reinforcement from P/C includes reminder that
token can be used later for other reinforcers.
(two P/C responses required)   11 _____

_____   _____

P/C verbally reinforces child during minute she stays seated.   12 _____

When child has left her seat:

P/C turns television off immediately (within 5 seconds).   13 _____

P/C states in neutral, firm tone why television is turned off. 14 _____

P/C reminds child, in positive terms, of what she must
do to earn tokens.   15 _____

P/C verbally redirects child back to seat in neutral
tone of voice.   16 _____

P/C does not provide any attention or social interaction
during any disruptive or resistive behavior.   17 _____

P/C does not scold or reprimand.   18 _____

P/C turns television on immediately following child's
return to seat (within 5 seconds).   19 _____

Total score: _____ / 19

Percent correct: _____ %

Time-Out

Special instructions: Although Role-Play 5 provides several trials for the P/C to exhibit the skill, score for the presence (+) or absence (0) of each response as described in the general instructions.

P/C Responses

While target behavior (spitting, aggression, destruction of property) is absent:

P/C provides reinforcement for appropriate behavior
(e.g., reading, sitting quietly). Verbal statement does
not require behavioral specificity.   1 _____

P/C praise for appropriate behavior is specific
(e.g., "You are sitting quietly, Ali. That's great!").   2 _____

When child makes demands for soda or snack:

P/C denies request in firm but neutral tone.   3 _____

P/C states when snacks are permitted.   4 _____

When child engages in spitting or knocking/throwing of objects:

P/C does not promise or negotiate snacks.   5 _____

P/C immediately guides child to time-out chair
(within 5 seconds).   6 _____

P/C immediately states reason for time-out
(e.g., "You have to go to time-out because you spit").   7 _____

P/C keeps verbal interactions with child brief and
to the point.   8 _____

P/C delivers verbal statements in a firm but neutral
tone of voice.   9 _____

P/C makes no social, tangible, or activity reinforcement
available to child while time-out is in effect.   10 _____

P/C does not talk to child, except to state needed
contingencies, while time-out is in effect.   11 _____

P/C remains physically distant from child (out of reach)
while time-out is in effect.   12 _____

P/C makes no eye contact with child while
time-out is in effect.   13 _____

262

P/C pursues own activity while time-out is in effect
(e.g., directs attention to reading or making notes).   14 _____

Time-out lasts at least 15 seconds, during which time
no target behavior occurs.   15 _____

When child attempts to leave time-out chair or engage in target behaviors
while time-out is in effect:

P/C guides child back to time-out chair.   16 _____

P/C neutrally restates contingency.   17 _____

P/C states that child will not be released from time-out
while exhibiting target behaviors.   18 _____

At conclusion of time-out:

P/C makes clear statement that time-out period has ended
(e.g., "OK, time-out is over").   19 _____

P/C guides child back to appropriate activity.   20 _____

Total score: _____ / 20

Percent correct: _____ %

Role-Play 6

Cues and Prompts

Special instructions: Role-Play 6 provides many trials to demonstrate verbal cues, physical prompts, and reinforcement during a five-step self-feeding task. Please note that many items involve scoring multiple P/C behavioral responses in order to score a given item as present (+). Refer to rating instructions for Role-Plays 3 and 4, if necessary, to review scoring for this type of item. All other items are scored as described in the general instructions.

P/C Responses

P/C begins by asking child, in firm but encouraging
tone of voice, to eat with her spoon.   1 _____

P/C begins procedure with verbal prompt
(e.g., "Ali, pick up the spoon").
(two P/C responses required)   2 _____

_____   _____

Verbal prompt is delivered in neutral tone of voice.   3 _____

P/C allows 3 seconds between verbal prompts.   4 _____

When child does not respond to verbal prompts, P/C provides physical prompt, guiding child's hand to hold spoon.
(two P/C responses required)   5 _____

_____   _____

Physical prompt is delivered in neutral rather than
punitive fashion.   6 _____

P/C allows 3 seconds between physical prompts.   7 _____

P/C continues prompts until child holds spoon.   8 _____

When child attempts to eat with fingers:

P/C states firmly, "No."   9 _____

P/C successfully blocks child's attempts to eat with fingers.
(two P/C responses required)   10 _____

_____   _____

P/C continues to prompt and does not provide social
attention (e.g., smiling, laughing) for child's inappro-
priate behavior.   11 _____

When child completes a step following a verbal cue or physical prompt:

P/C delivers immediate verbal praise.   12 _____

P/C makes clear, specific statement of behavior being
praised (e.g., "Good! You're holding the spoon!").   13 _____

P/C uses enthusiastic, animated tone of voice, in
contrast to neutral prompts.   14 _____

P/C exhibits smiling, pleased expression.   15 _____

P/C delivers physical reinforcement
(e.g., clapping, stroking, etc.).   16 _____

P/C provides immediate reinforcement (within
5 seconds) following completion of each step.
(five P/C responses required)   17 _____

_____ _____ _____ _____ _____

P/C does not use physical prompt when child has
responded to a verbal prompt.   18 _____

P/C does not allow any steps to be skipped over, ensuring completion of each step. If P/C allows any step to be
skipped at any time, the response is scored as (0).   19 _____

When child completes any step independently, P/C states
specifically which step has been completed independently.   20 _____

P/C reinforcement for independent steps is delivered
with more intensity and enthusiasm than reinforcement
for steps requiring cues and prompts.   21 _____

Total score: _____ / 21

Percent correct: _____ %

References

Abramowicz, H. K., & Richardson, S. A. (1975). Epidemiology of severe mental retardation in children: Community studies. *American Journal of Mental Deficiency, 80,* 18–39.

Agran, M., & Martin, J. E. (1985). Establishing socially validated drug research in community settings. *Psychopharmacology Bulletin, 21,* 285–290.

Akerly, M. (1984). Developmental changes in families with autistic children: A parent's perspective. In E. Schopler & G. Mesibov (Eds.), *The effects of autism on the family.* New York: Plenum.

Alexander, J., Barton, C., Waldron, H., & Mas, C. H. (1982, March). *Beyond the technology of family therapy: The anatomy of intervention model.* Invited address presented to the Fourteenth Annual Banff International Conference on Behavior Modification, Banff, Canada.

Alexander, J., & Parsons, B. V. (1982). *Functional family therapy.* Monterey, CA: Brooks/Cole.

Alford, J. D., & Locke, B. J. (1984). Clinical responses to psychopathology of mentally retarded persons. *American Journal of Mental Deficiency, 89,* 195–197.

Algozzine, R. (1987). Issues in personnel preparation. In J. Yesseldyke & R. Algozzine (Eds.), *Issues in special and remedial education.* Boston: Houghton Mifflin.

Altman, I. (1975). *The environment and social behavior.* Monterey, CA: Brooks/Cole.

Aman, M. G. (1983). Psychoactive drugs in mental retardation. In J. L. Matson & F. Andrasik (Eds.), *Treatment issues and innovation in mental retardation.* New York: Plenum.

Aman, M. G., & Singh, N. (1983). Pharmacological intervention. In J. Matson & J. A. Mulick (Eds.), *Handbook of mental retardation.* New York: Pergamon.

American Psychiatric Association (1952). *Diagnostic and statistical manual of mental disorders.* Washington, DC: Author.

American Psychiatric Association (1968). *Diagnostic and statistical manual of mental disorders* (2nd ed.). Washington, DC: Author.

American Psychiatric Association (1980). *Diagnostic and statistical manual of mental disorders* (3rd ed.). Washington, DC: Author.

American Psychiatric Association (1987). *Diagnostic and statistical manual of mental disorders* (3rd ed. rev.). Washington, DC: Author.

Ando, H., & Yoshimura, I. (1978). Prevalence of maladaptive behavior in retarded children as a function of IQ and age. *Journal of Abnormal Child Psychology, 6,* 345–349.

Angemeyer, M. C. (1982). The association between family atmosphere and the hospital career of schizophrenic patients. *British Journal of Psychiatry, 141,* 1–11.

Angus, L. R. (1948). Schizophrenia and schizoid conditions in students in a special school. *American Journal of Mental Deficiency, 53,* 227–238.

Anthony, J. C., Folstein, M., Romanoski, A. J., Vonkorft, M. R., Nestadt, G. R., Chahel, R., Merchant, A., Brown, C. H., Shapiro, S., Kramer, M., and Gruenberg, E. M. (1985). Comparison of the lay interview schedule and a standardized psychiatric diagnosis. *Archives of General Psychiatry, 42,* 667–675.

Arkes, H. R. (1981). Impediments to accurate clinical judgement and possible ways to minimize their impact. *Journal of Consulting and Clinical Psychology, 49,* 323–330.

Asarnow, J. R., & Callan, J. W. (1985). Boys with peer adjustment problems: Social cognitive processes. *Journal of Consulting and Clinical Psychology, 53,* 80–87.

Balch, P., & Solomon, R. (1976). The training of paraprofessionals as behavior modifiers: A review. *American Journal of Community Psychology, 4,* 167–177.

Balthazar, E. E., & English, G. E. (1969). A system for the social classification of the more severely mentally retarded. *American Journal of Mental Deficiency, 74,* 361–368.

Bandura, A. (1973). *Aggression: A social learning analysis.* Englewood Cliffs, NJ: Prentice-Hall.

Bandura, A. (1977a). Effecting change through participant modeling. In J. D. Crumbolts & C. E. Thoresen (Eds.), *Counseling methods.* New York: Holt, Rinehart, & Winston.

Bandura, A. (1977b). *Social learning theory.* Englewood Cliffs, NJ: Prentice-Hall.

Bandura, A. (1986). *Social foundations of thought and action: A social cognitive theory.* Englewood Cliffs, NJ: Prentice-Hall.

Bannerman, D. J., Sheldon, J. B., Sherman, J. A., & Harchick, A. E. (1990). Balancing the right to habilitation with the right to personal liberties: The right of people with developmental disabilities to eat too many donuts and take a nap. *Journal of Applied Behavior Analysis, 23,* 79–89.

Baron, R. A. (1977). *Human aggression.* New York: Plenum.

Baumeister, A. A. (1988). The new morbidity: Implications for prevention. In J. A. Stark, F. J. Menolascino, M. H. Albarelli, & V. C. Gray (Eds.), *Mental retardation and mental health: Classification, diagnosis, treatment, services.* New York: Springer.

Baumeister, A. A., & MacLean, W. E., Jr. (1979). Brain damage and mental retardation. In N. R. Ellis (Ed.), *Handbook of mental deficiency* (2nd ed.). Hillsdale, NJ: Lawrence Erlbaum.

Baxley, N. (Producer). (1979). R. Forehand (consultant). *Behavioral principles for parents* (Videotape). Champaign, IL: Research Press.

Bayley, N. (1969). *Bayley scale of infant development.* San Antonio, TX: Psychological Corporation.

Beck, A. T. (1976). *Cognitive therapy and the emotional disorders.* New York: International Universities Press.

Beck, A. T., Ward, C. H., Mendelson, M., Mock, J., & Erbaugh, J. (1961). An inventory for measuring depression. *Archives of General Psychiatry, 5,* 462–467.

Becker, W. C. (1971). *Parents are teachers.* Champaign, IL: Research Press.

Bellack, A. S. (1986). Schizophrenia: Behavior therapy's forgotten child. *Behavior Therapy, 17,* 199–214.

Belsher, G., & Costello, C. J. (1988). Relapse after recovery from unipolar depression: A critical review. *Psychological Bulletin, 104,* 84–96.

Bender, M., Brannan, S. A., & Verhoven, P. J. (1984). *Leisure education for the handicapped: Curriculum, goals, activities, and resources.* San Diego, CA: College-Hill.

Benson, B. A. (1985). Behavior disorders and mental retardation: Associations with age, sex, and level of functioning in an outpatient clinic sample. *Applied Research in Mental Retardation, 6,* 79–85.

Benson, B. A. (1986). Anger management training. *Psychiatric Aspects of Mental Retardation Reviews, 5,* 51-55.

Benson, B. A., Reiss, S., Smith, D. C., & Laman, D. S. (1985). Psychosocial correlates of depression in mentally retarded adults: II. Poor social skills. *American Journal of Mental Deficiency, 89,* 657–659.

Benson, B. A., Rice, C. J., & Miranti, S. V. (1986). Effects of anger management training with mentally retarded adults in group treatment. *Journal of Consulting and Clinical Psychology, 54,* 728–729.

Berkowitz, L. (1969). The frustration-aggression hypothesis revisited. In L. Berkowitz (Ed.), *Roots of aggression.* New York: Atherton.

Berkowitz, L. (1978). Whatever happened to the frustration-aggression hypothesis? *American Behavioral Scientist, 21,* 691–708.

Berlin, I. N., & Critchley, D. L. (1989). The therapeutic use of play for mentally ill children and their parents. In C. E. Schaefer & J. M. Briesmeister (Eds.), *Handbook of parent training: Parents as co-therapists for children's behavior problems.* New York: Wiley.

Billings, A. G., & Moos, R. H. (1982). Psychosocial theory and research on depression: An integrative framework. *Clinical Psychology Review, 2,* 213–237.

Birch, H. G., Richardson, S. A., Baird, D., Horobin, G., & Illsley, R. (1970). *Mental subnormality in the community: A clinical and epidemiological study.* Baltimore: Williams & Wilkins.

Birnbrauer, J. S. (1968). Generalization of punishment effects: A case study. *Journal of Applied Behavior Analysis, 1,* 201–211.

Borthwick-Duffy, S., & Eyman, R. K. (1990). Who are the dually diagnosed? *American Journal on Mental Retardation, 94,* 586–595.

Boshes, R. A. (1987). Pharmacotherapy for patients with mental retardation and mental illness. *Psychiatric Annals, 17,* 627–632.

Breiner, J. (1989). Training parents as agents of change for their developmentally disabled children. In C. E. Schaefer & J. M. Briesmeister (Eds.), *Handbook of parent training: Parents as co-therapists for children's behavior problems.* New York: Wiley.

Breiner, J., & Beck, S. (1984). Parents as change agents in the management of their developmentally disabled children's noncompliant behaviors: A critical review. *Applied Research in Mental Retardation, 5,* 259–278.

Breslau, N., & Davis, G. C. (1986). Chronic stress and major depression. *Archives of General Psychiatry, 43,* 309–314.

Breuning, S. E., & Poling, A. D. (1982). Pharmacotherapy. In J. L. Matson & R. P. Barrett (Eds.), *Psychopathology in the mentally retarded.* Orlando, FL: Gruen & Stratton.

Brinker, R. P. (1985). Curricula without recipes: A challenge to teachers and a promise to severely mentally retarded students. In D. Bricker & J. Filler (Eds.), *Severe mental retardation: From theory to practice.* Reston, VA: Council for Exceptional Children.

Bristol, M. (1984). Family resources and successful adaptation to autistic children. In E. Schopler & G. B. Mesibov (Eds.), *The effects of autism on the family.* New York: Plenum.

Bristol, M. (1985). Designing programs for young developmentally disabled children: A family systems approach to autism. *RASE, 6,* 46–53.

Bristol, M. (1986). The home care of developmentally disabled children: Empirical support for a model of successful family coping with stress. In S. Landesman-Dwyer & P. Vietze (Eds.), *Living with mentally retarded persons.* Washington, DC: American Association of Mental Deficiency.

Brown, G. W., Birley, J. T. L., & Wing, J. K. (1972). Influence of family life on the course of schizophrenic disorders. *British Journal of Psychiatry, 121,* 241–258.

Brown, L., Ford, A., Nisbet, J., Sweet, M., Donellan, A., & Gruenewald, L. (1983). Opportunities available when severely handicapped students attend chronological age-appropriate regular schools. *Journal of the Association for the Severely Handicapped, 8,* 16–24.

Brown, L., Netupki, J., & Harme-Netupki, S. (1976). The criterion of ultimate functioning and public school success for the severely handicapped student. In A. Thomas (Ed.), *Hey, don't you forget about me: Education's investment in the severely, profoundly, and multiply handicapped.* Reston, VA: Council for Exceptional Children.

Budd, K. S., & Fabry, P. L. (1984). Behavioral assessment in applied parent training: Use of a structured observation system. In R. F. Dangel & R. A. Polster (Eds.), *Parent training: Foundations of research and practice.* New York: Guilford.

Budd, K. S., Riner, L. S., & Brockman, M. P. (1983). A structural observation system for clinical evaluation of parent training. *Behavioral Assessment, 5,* 373–393.

Burgemeister, B. B., Blum, L. H., & Lorge, I. (1972). *Columbia Mental Maturity Scale.* San Antonio, TX: Psychological Corporation.

Burt, J. (1990). *Effectiveness of creative arts therapy for mentally retarded workers.* Colloquium presentation at the Philadelphia Developmental Disabilities Corporation, Philadelphia.

Butler, L., & Meichenbaum, D. (1981). The assessment of interpersonal problem-solving skills. In P. C. Kendall & S. D. Hollon (Eds.), *Assessment strategies for cognitive-behavioral interventions.* New York: Academic.

Byrne, E. A., & Cunningham, C. C. (1985). The effects of mentally handicapped children on families. A conceptual review. *Journal of Child Psychology and Psychiatry, 26,* 847–864.

Cameron, S. J., & Orr, R. R. (1989). Stress in families of school-aged children with delayed mental development. *Canadian Journal of Rehabilitation, 2*(3), 137–144.

Carr, E. G., & Newsom, C. (1985). Demand-related tantrums: Conceptualization and treatment. *Behavior Modification, 9,* 403–426.

Castles, E. E., & Glass, C. R. (1986). Training in social and interpersonal problem-solving skills for mildly and moderately retarded adults. *American Journal of Mental Deficiency, 91,* 35–42.

Cattell, P. (1960). *Infant Intelligence Scale.* San Antonio, TX: Psychological Corporation.

Chadsey-Rusch, J., & Gonzalez, P. (1988). Social ecology of the workplace: Employers' perceptions versus direct observation. *Research in Developmental Disabilities, 9,* 229–245.

Chess, S., & Hassibi, M. (1970). Behavior deviations in mentally retarded children. *Journal of the Academy of Child Psychiatry, 9,* 282–297.

Cobb, S. (1976). Social support as a moderator of life stress. *Psychosomatic Medicine, 38,* 300–314.

Cochran, I. L., & Cleland, C. C. (1963). Manifest anxiety of retardates and normals matched as to academic achievement. *American Journal of Mental Deficiency, 67,* 539–542.

Cohen, F., & Hoberman, H. (1983). Positive events and social support as buffers of life change stress. *Journal of Applied Social Psychology, 13,* 99–125.

Cohen, F., & Lazarus, R. (1979). Coping with the stress of illness. In G. C. Stone, F. Cohen, & N. Adler (Eds.), *Health psychology: A handbook.* San Francisco: Jossey-Bass.

Cohen, S., & Willis, T. A. (1985). Stress, social support, and the buffering hypotheses. *Psychological Bulletin, 98,* 310–357.

Cole, C. L., Gardner, W. I., & Karan, O. C. (1985). Self-management training of mentally retarded adults presenting severe conduct difficulties. *Applied Research in Mental Retardation, 6,* 337–347.

Conley, R. W., Rusch, F. R., McCaughrin, W. B., & Tines, J. (1989). Benefits and costs of supported employment: An analysis of the Illinois supported employment program. *Journal of Applied Behavior Analysis, 22,* 441–447.

Conners, C. K. (1969). A teacher rating scale for use in drug studies with children. *American Journal of Psychiatry, 126,* 884–888.

Cook, T. D. (1985). Post-positivist critical multiplism. In L. Shotland & M. M. Marks (Eds.), *Social science and social policy.* Beverly Hills, CA: Sage.

Cooper, J. O., Heron, T. E., & Heward, W. L. (1987). *Applied behavior analysis.* Columbus, OH: Merrill.

Corbett, J. A. (1979). Psychiatric morbidity and mental retardation. In F. E. James & R. P. Snaith (Eds.), *Psychiatric illness and mental handicap.* London: Gaskell.

Corbett, J. A., & Harris, R. (1974). *Epilepsy in children with severe mental handicap.* Paper presented at Symposium No. 16 of the Institute for Research into Mental and Multiple Handicap, London.

Cox, A., Rutter, M., Newman, S., & Bartak, L. (1975). A comparative study of infantile autism and specific developmental receptive language disorder: II. Parental characteristics. *British Journal of Psychiatry, 126,* 146–159.

Craft, M. (1959). Mental disorder in the defective: A psychiatric survey among inpatients. *American Journal of Mental Deficiency, 63,* 829–834.

Craft, M. (1960). Mental disorder in a series of English outpatient defectives. *American Journal of Mental Deficiency, 64,* 718–724.

Craig, T. J., & Behar, R. (1980). Trends in the prescription of psychotropic drugs in a state hospital. *Comprehensive Psychiatry, 21,* 336–345.

Craighead, W. E. (1980). Away from a unitary model of depression. *Behavior Therapy, 11,* 112–118.

Crnic, K. A., Friedrich, W. N., & Greenberg, M. T. (1983). Adaptation of families with mentally retarded children: A model of stress, coping, and family ecology. *American Journal of Mental Deficiency, 88,* 125–138.

Crnic, K. A., Greenberg, M. T., Ragozin, A. S., Robinson, N. M., & Basham, R. B. (1983). Effects of stress and social support on mothers of premature and full-term infants. *Child Development, 54,* 209–217.

Cummings, S. T., Bayles, H. C., & Rie, H. E. (1966). Effects of the child's deficiency on the mother: A study of mothers of mentally retarded, chronically ill, and neurotic children. *American Journal of Orthopsychiatry, 36,* 595–608.

Cuvo, A. J., Sievert, A. L., & Davis, P. K. (1988). Community living skills. In J. L. Matson & A. Marchetti (Eds.), *Developmental disabilities: A life-span perspective.* Philadelphia: Grune & Stratton.

Day, K. (1985). Psychiatric disorder in the middle-aged and elderly mentally handicapped. *British Journal of Psychiatry, 147,* 660–667.

Dellario, D. J., & Crosby, J. (1985). A system for evaluating community-based alternative living arrangements for the psychiatrically disabled. *International Journal of Partial Hospitalization, 3,* 49–58.

DeMaine, G. (1978). *Empirical validation of PASS 3: A first step in service evaluation through environmental assessment.* Pomona, CA: Individualized Data Base.

DeMyer, M. K. (1979). *Parents and children in autism.* New York: Wiley.

Derogatis, L. R., & Spencer, P. M. (1982). *The Brief Symptom Inventory (BSI): Administration, scoring, and procedures manual.* Baltimore, MD: Clinical Psychometric Research.

Dewan, J. G. (1948). Intelligence and emotional stability. *American Journal of Psychiatry, 104,* 548–554.

Diller, L., Fordyce, W., Jacobs, D., & Brown, M. (1978). *Postinstitutional placement project evaluation report.* New York University Medical Center, Rehabilitation Indicators Project.

DiNardo, P. A., Barlow, D. H., Cerny, J. A., Vermilyea, B. B., Vermilyea, J. A., Himadi, W. G., & Waddell, M. T. (1985). *Anxiety Disorders Interview Schedule—Revised* (ADIS-R). Albany, NY: State University of New York at Albany, Phobia and Anxiety Disorders Clinic.

Dodge, K. A. (1980). Social cognition and children's aggressive behavior. *Child Development, 51,* 162–170.

Dodge, K. A., & Frame, C. L. (1982). Social cognitive biases and deficits in aggressive boys. *Child Development, 53,* 620–635.

Dollard, J., Doob, L., Miller, N., Mowrer, O. H., & Sears, R. R. (1939). *Frustration and aggression.* New Haven, CT: Yale University Press.

Donnerstein, E., & Wilson, D. W. (1976). The effects of noise and perceived control upon ongoing and subsequent aggressive behavior. *Journal of Personality and Social Psychology, 34,* 774–781.

Donoghue, E. C., & Abbas, K. A. (1971). Unstable behavior in severely subnormal children. *Developmental Medicine and Child Neurology, 13,* 512–519.

Duff, R., LaRocca, J., Lizzet, A., Martin, P., Pearce, L., Williams, M., & Peck, C. (1981). A comparison of fears of mildly retarded adults with children of their mental age and chronological age matched controls. *Journal of Behavior Therapy and Experimental Psychiatry, 12,* 121–124.

Duker, P. C., & Rasing, E. (1989). Effects of redesigning the physical environment on self-stimulatory and on-task behavior in three autistic-type developmentally disabled individuals. *Journal of Autism and Developmental Disorders, 19,* 449–460.

Dunn, L. M. (1965). *Peabody Picture Vocabulary Test.* Circle Pines, MN: American Guidance Service.

Dupont, A. (1981). Medical results from registration of Danish mentally retarded persons. In P. Mittler (Ed.), *Proceedings of the Fifth Congress of the International Association for the Scientific Study of Mental Deficiency.* Baltimore: University Park Press.

D'Zurilla, T. J. (1986). *Problem-solving therapy.* New York: Springer.

D'Zurilla, T. J. (1988). Problem-solving therapies. In K. S. Dobson (Ed.), *Handbook of cognitive-behavioral therapies.* New York: Guilford.

D'Zurilla, T. J., & Goldfried, M. R. (1971). Problem-solving and behavior modification. *Journal of Abnormal Psychology, 78,* 107–126.

D'Zurilla, T. J., & Nezu, A. M. (1982). Social problem solving in adults. In P. C. Kendall (Ed.), *Advances in cognitive-behavioral research and therapy* (Vol. 1). New York: Academic.

D'Zurilla, T. J., & Nezu, A. M. (1989). Clinical stress management. In A. M. Nezu & C. M. Nezu (Eds.), *Clinical decision making in behavior therapy: A problem-solving perspective.* Champaign, IL: Research Press.

D'Zurilla, T. J., & Nezu, A. M. (1990). Development and preliminary evaluation of the Social Problem-Solving Inventory. *Psychological Assessment: A Journal of Consulting and Clinical Psychology, 2,* 156–163.

Eaton, L. F., & Menolascino, F. J. (1982). Psychiatric disorders in the mentally retarded: Types, problems, and challenges. *American Journal of Psychiatry, 139,* 1297–1303.

Edelwich, J., & Brodsky, A. (1980). *Burnout: Stages of disillusionment in the helping professions.* New York: Human Sciences Press.

Eidelson, R. J., & Epstein, N. (1982). Cognition and relationship maladjustment: Development of a measure of dysfunctional relationship belief. *Journal of Consulting and Clinical Psychology, 50,* 715–720.

Elman, N. S. (1991). Family therapy. In M. Seligman (Ed.), *The family with a handicapped child.* Boston: Allyn & Bacon.

Emmelkamp, P. M. G. (1982). In vivo treatment of agoraphobia. In D. L. Chambless & A. J. Goldstein (Eds.), *Agoraphobia: Multiple perspectives on theory and treatment.* New York: Wiley.

Engel, G. L. (1977). The need for a new medical model: A challenge for biomedicine. *Science, 196,* 129–136.

Evangelista, L. A. (1988). Comprehensive management of the mentally retarded/mentally ill individual. In J. A. Stark, F. J. Menolascino, M. H. Albarelli, & V. C. Gray (Eds.), *Mental retardation and mental health: Classification, diagnosis, treatment and services.* New York: Springer.

Eyman, R. K., & Call, T. (1977). Maladaptive behavior and community placement of mentally retarded persons. *American Journal of Mental Deficiency, 82,* 137–144.

Eyman, R. K., DeMaine, G. C., & Lei, T. (1979). Relationship between community environments and resident changes in adaptive behavior: A path model. *American Journal of Mental Deficiency, 83,* 330–338.

Eyman, R. K., Silverstein, A. B., & McLain, R. (1975). Effects of treatment programs on the acquisition of basic skills. *American Journal of Mental Deficiency, 79,* 573–582.

Eyman, R. K., Silverstein, A. B., McLain, R., & Miller, C. (1977). Effects of residential settings on development. In P. Mittler & J. deJong (Eds.), *Research to practice in mental retardation: Care and intervention.* Baltimore: University Park Press.

Farber, B. (1983). Introduction: A critical perspective on burnout. In B. Farber (Ed.), *Stress and burnout in the human service professions.* New York: Pergamon.

Farran, D. C., Metzger, J., & Sparling, J. (1986). Immediate and continuing adaptations in parents of handicapped children: A model and an illustration. In J. J. Gallagher & P. M. Vietze (Eds.), *Families of handicapped persons.* Baltimore: Brookes.

Favell, J. E. (1982). The treatment of self-injurious behavior. *Behavior Therapy, 13,* 529–554.

Featherstone, H. (1980). *A difference in the family.* New York: Basic Books.

Feldhausen, J. F., & Klausmeier, H. J. (1962). Anxiety, intelligence, and achievement in children of low, average, and high intelligence. *Child Development, 33,* 403–409.

Feshbach, S. (1964). The function of aggression and the regulation of aggressive drive. *Psychological Review, 71,* 257–272.

Fidora, J. G., Lindsey, E. R., & Walker, G. R. (1987). A special behavior unit for treatment of behavior problems of persons who are mentally retarded. *Mental Retardation, 25,* 107–111.

Figley, C. R. (1983). Catastrophes: An overview of family reactions. In C. R. Figley & H. I. McCubbin (Eds.), *Stress and the family: Coping with catastrophe.* New York: Brunner/Mazel.

Fimian, M. J. (1986). Social support and occupational stress in special education. *Exceptional Children, 52,* 436–442.

Fimian, M. J., & Santoro, T. M. (1983). Sources and manifestations of occupational stress as reported by full-time special education teachers. *Exceptional Children, 49,* 540–543.

Fletcher, R. J. (1988). A county systems model: Comprehensive services for the dually diagnosed. In J. A. Stark, F. J. Menolascino, M. H. Albarelli, & V. C. Gray (Eds.), *Mental retardation and mental health: Classification, diagnosis, treatment, services.* New York: Springer.

Floor, L., & Rosen, M. (1975). Investigating the phenomenon of helplessness in mentally retarded adults. *American Journal of Mental Deficiency, 79,* 565–572.

Flynn, R. J. (1980). Normalization, PASS, and service quality assessments: How normalizing are current human services? In R. J. Flynn & K. E. Nitsch (Eds.), *Normalization, social integration, and community services.* Baltimore: University Park Press.

Forehand, R., & McMahon, R. J. (1981). *Helping the noncompliant child: A clinician's guide to parent training*. New York: Guilford.

Foxx, R. M. (1982). *Increasing behaviors of severely retarded and autistic persons*. Champaign, IL: Research Press.

Foxx, R. M., Kyle, M. S., Faw, G. D., & Bittle, R. G. (1989). Problem-solving skills training: Social validation and generalization. *Behavioral Residential Treatment, 4,* 269–288.

Foxx, R. M., McMorrow, M. J., Fenlon, S., & Bittle, R. G. (1986). The reductive effects of reinforcement procedures on the genital stimulation and stereotyping of a mentally retarded adolescent male. *Analysis and Intervention in Developmental Disabilities, 6,* 239–248.

Foxx, R. M., McMorrow, M. J., & Schloss, P. (1983). Stacking the deck: Teaching social skills to adults with a modified table game: An analysis of generalization. *Journal of Applied Behavior Analysis, 17,* 343–352.

Freedman, J. L. (1975). *Crowding and behavior*. San Francisco: Freeman.

Freedman, J. L., Levy, A. S., Buchanan, R. W., & Price, J. (1972). Crowding and human aggressiveness. *Journal of Experimental Social Psychology, 8,* 528–548.

Gallagher, J. J., Cross, A., & Scharfman, W. (1981). Parental adaptation to a young handicapped child: The father's role. *Journal of the Division for Early Childhood, 1,* 3–14.

Ganellen, R. J., & Blaney, P. H. (1984). Hardiness and social support as moderators of life stress. *Journal of Personality and Social Psychology, 47,* 156–163.

Gardner, W. I. (1967). Occurrence of severe depressive reactions in the mentally retarded. *American Journal of Psychiatry, 124,* 142–144.

Gardner, W. I. (1988). Behavior therapies: Past, present and future. In J. A. Stark, F. J. Menolascino, M. H. Albarelli, & V. C. Gray (Eds.), *Mental retardation and mental illness: Classification, diagnosis, treatment, services*. New York: Springer.

Gardner, W. I., & Cole, C. L. (1984). Aggression and related conduct difficulties in the mentally retarded: A multicomponent behavioral model. In S. E. Breuning, J. L. Matson, & R. P. Barrett (Eds.), *Advances in mental retardation and developmental disabilities* (Vol. 2). Greenwich, CT: JAI.

Gardner, W. I., Cole, C. L., Berry, D. L., & Nowinski, J. M. (1983). Reduction of disruptive behaviors in mentally retarded adults—A self-management approach. *Behavior Modification, 7,* 73–96.

Gath, A. (1977). The impact of an abnormal child upon the parents. *British Journal of Psychiatry, 130,* 405–410.

Gath, A. (1978). *Down's syndrome and the family—The early years*. London: Academic.

Gelfand, D. M., & Hartmann, D. P. (1984). *Child behavior analysis and therapy* (2nd ed.). New York: Pergamon.

Gersten, R. (1985). Direct instruction with special education students: A review of evaluation research. *Journal of Special Education, 19,* 41–58.

Gettings, R. M. (1988). Barriers to and opportunities for cooperation between the aging and developmental disabilities services delivery systems [Special issue: Aging and disabilities]. *Educational Gerontology 14*(5), 419–429.

Gill, M. J., & Harris, S. L. (1991). Hardiness and social support as predictors of psychological discomfort in mothers of children with autism. *Journal of Autism and Developmental Disorders, 21,* 407-416.

Gillberg, C., Persson, E., Grufman, M., & Themner, U. (1986). Psychiatric disorders in mildly and severely mentally retarded urban children and adolescents: Epidemiological aspects. *British Journal of Psychiatry, 149,* 68–74.

Glass, D. C., & Krantz, D. S. (1975). Noise and behavior. In B. B. Wolman (Ed.), *International encyclopedia of neurology, psychiatry, psychoanalysis, and psychology.* New York: Springer.

Goldfried, M. R., & D'Zurilla, T. J. (1969). A behavioral-analytic model for assessing competence. In C. D. Spielberger (Ed.), *Current topics in clinical and community psychology* (Vol. 1). New York: Academic.

Gollay, E., Freedman, R., Wyngaarden, M., & Kurtz, N. R. (1978). *Coming back: The community experience of deinstitutionalized mentally retarded people.* Cambridge, MA: Abt.

Gordon, S. B., & Davidson, N. (1981). Behavioral parent training. In A. S. Gurman & D. P. Kniskern (Eds.), *Handbook of family therapy.* New York: Brunner/Mazel.

Gostason, R. (1985). Psychiatric illness among the mentally retarded: A Swedish population study. *Acta Psychiatrica Scandinavica, 71,* Supplementum 318.

Graziano, A. M. (1977). Parents as behavior therapists. In M. Hersen, R. M. Eisler, & P. M. Miller (Eds.), *Progress in behavior modification* (Vol. 14). New York: Academic.

Green, B. F. (1989). The integration of individuals with disabilities into the vocational mainstream. *Journal of Applied Behavior Analysis, 22,* 343-345.

Green, C. W., Reid, D. H., White, L. K., Halford, R. C., Brittain, D. P., & Gardner, S. M. (1988). Identifying reinforcers for persons with profound handicaps: Staff options versus systematic assessment of preference. *Journal of Applied Behavior Analysis, 22,* 31-43.

Griffin, M. W. (1979). Training parents of retarded children as behavior therapists: A review. *Australian Journal of Mental Retardation, 5*(5), 18-27.

Groden, G., Domingue, D., Pueschel, S. M., & Deignan, L. (1982). Behavioral/emotional problems in mentally retarded children and youths. *Psychological Reports, 51,* 143-146.

Grossman, H. (1983). *Manual on terminology and classification in mental retardation.* Washington, DC: American Association on Mental Deficiency.

Gualtieri, C. T. (1979). Psychiatry's disinterest in mental retardation. *Psychiatric Opinion, 16,* 26-30.

Gualtieri, C. T. (1988). Mental health of persons with mental retardation: A solution, obstacles to the solution, and resolution for the problem. In J. A. Stark, F. J. Menolascino, M. H. Albarelli, & V. C. Gray (Eds.), *Mental retardation and mental health: Classification, diagnosis, treatment, services.* New York: Springer.

Gualtieri, C. T., & Keppel, J. M. (1985). Psychopharmacology in the mentally retarded and a few related issues. *Psychopharmacology Bulletin, 21,* 304–309.

Guarnaccia, V. J., & Weiss, R. L. (1974). Factor structure of fears in the mentally retarded. *Journal of Clinical Psychology, 30,* 540–544.

Guralnick, M. J. (1973). Behavior therapy with an acrophobic mentally retarded young adult. *Journal of Behavior Therapy and Experimental Psychiatry, 4,* 263–265.

Hanson, M. (1977). *Training your Down's syndrome infant.* Eugene: University of Oregon Press.

Haracopos, D., & Kelstrup, A. (1978). Psychotic behavior in children under the institutions for the mentally retarded in Denmark. *Journal of Autism and Childhood Schizophrenia, 8,* 1–12.

Harris, S. L. (1982). A family systems approach to behavioral training with parents of autistic children. *Child and Family Behavior Therapy, 4,* 21–35.

Harris, S. L. (1983). *Families of developmentally disabled children: A guide to behavioral intervention.* New York: Pergamon.

Harris, S. L. (1984). The family and the autistic child: A behavioral perspective. *Family Practice, 33,* 127–134.

Harris, S. L., Alessandri, M., & Gill, M. J. (1991). Training parents of developmentally disabled children. In J. L. Matson & J. L. Mulick (Eds.), *Handbook of mental retardation* (2nd ed.). Elmsford, NY: Pergamon.

Harris, S. L., Boyle, T. D., Fong, P., Gill, M. J., & Stanger, C. (1987). Families of developmentally disabled children. In M. Wolraich & D. K. Routh (Eds.), *Advances in developmental and behavioral pediatrics.* Greenwich, CT: JAI.

Harris, S. L., Carpenter, L., & Gill, M. J. (1988). The family. In J. L. Matson & A. Marchetti (Eds.), *Developmental disabilities: A life-span perspective.* Philadelphia: Grune & Stratton.

Harris, S. L., Gill, M. J., & Alessandri, M. (1991). The family with an autistic child. In M. Seligman (Ed.), *The family with a handicapped child* (2nd ed). Boston: Allyn & Bacon.

Harris, S. L., Handleman, J. S., Gill, M. J., & Fong, P. L. (1991). Does punishment hurt? The impact of aversives on the clinician. *Research in Developmental Disabilities, 12,* 17–24.

Hayman, M. (1939). The interrelations of mental defect and mental disorder. *Journal of Mental Science, 85,* 1183–1193.

Haynes, S. N., & Kerns, R. D. (1979). Validation of a behavioral observation system. *Journal of Consulting and Clinical Psychology, 47,* 397–400.

Haynes, S. N., & O'Brien, W. H. (1988). The Gordian knot of DSM-III-R use: Integrating principles of behavior classification and complex causal models. *Behavioral Assessment, 10,* 95–105.

Heal, L. W., Colson, L. S., & Gross, J. C. (1984). A true experiment evaluating adult skill training for severely mentally retarded students. *American Journal of Mental Deficiency, 89,* 146–155.

Heaton-Ward, A. (1977). Psychosis in mental handicap. *British Journal of Psychiatry, 130,* 525–533.

Heifetz, L. J., Baker, B. L., Wickham-Searl, P. (1981). *Behavioral Vignettes Test* (rev.). Cambridge, MA: Educational Projects.

Helsel, W. J., & Matson, J. L. (1988). The relationship of depression to social skills and intellectual functioning in mentally retarded adults. *Journal of Mental Deficiency Research, 32,* 411–418.

Helzer, J. E., Robins, L. N., McEvay, L. T., Spitznagel, E. L., Staltzman, R. K., Farmer, A., & Brockington, I. F. (1985). A comparison of clinical and diagnostic interview schedule diagnoses. *Archives of General Psychiatry, 42,* 657–666.

Hersen, M. (1981). Complex problems require complex solutions. *Behavior Therapy, 12,* 15–29.

Hersen, M. (1988). Behavioral assessment and psychiatric diagnosis. *Behavioral Assessment, 10,* 107–121.

Hersen, M., & Bellack, A. S. (1976). Social skills training for chronic psychiatric patients: Rationales, research findings, and future directions. *Comprehensive Psychiatry, 17,* 559–580.

Herskovitz, H. H., & Plesset, M. R. (1941). Psychosis in adult mental defectives. *Psychiatric Quarterly, 15,* 574–588.

Hill, B. K., Balow, E. A., & Bruininks, R. H. (1985). A national study of prescribed drugs in institutions and community residential facilities for mentally retarded people. *Psychopharmacology Bulletin, 21,* 279–284.

Hill, B. K., & Bruininks, R. H. (1981). *Physical and behavioral characteristics and maladaptive behavior of mentally retarded people in residential facilities* (Proj. Rep. No. 12). Minneapolis: University of Minnesota, Department of Psychoeducational Studies.

Hill, B. K., & Bruininks, R. H. (1984). Maladaptive behavior of mentally retarded individuals in residential facilities. *American Journal of Mental Deficiency, 88,* 380–387.

Hill, M. C., Banks, P. D., Handrich, R. R., Wehman, P. H., Hill, J. W., & Shafer, M. S. (1987). Benefit-cost analysis of supported competitive employment for persons with mental retardation. *Research in Developmental Disabilities, 8,* 71–89.

Hill, R. (1949). *Families under stress.* New York: Harper & Row.

Hill, R. (1958). Generic features of families under stress. *Social Case Work, 49,* 139–150.

Hollon, S. D., & Kendall, P. C. (1980). Cognitive self-statements in depression: Development of an automatic thoughts questionnaire. *Cognitive Therapy and Research, 4,* 383–395.

Holroyd, J. (1974). The questionnaire on resources and stress: An instrument to measure family response to a handicapped member. *Journal of Community Psychology, 2,* 92–94.

Houser, R. A. (1987). *A comparison of stress and coping by fathers of mentally retarded and non-retarded adolescents.* Unpublished doctoral dissertation, University of Pittsburgh.

Hull, J. T., & Thompson, J. C. (1981). Factors contributing to normalization in residential facilities for mentally retarded persons. *Mental Retardation, 19,* 69–73.

Hunt, R. D., & Cohen, D. J. (1988). Attentional and neurochemical components of mental retardation. New methods for an old problem. In J. A. Stark, F. J. Menolascino, M. H. Albarelli, & V. C. Gray (Eds.), *Mental retardation and mental health: Classification, diagnosis, treatment, services.* New York: Springer.

Insel, P. M. & Moos, R. H. (1974). Psychological environments: Expanding the scope of human ecology. *American Psychologist, 29,* 179–188.

Itard, J. M. G. (1801). *De éducation d'un homme sauvage.* Paris: Goujon.

Iverson, J. C., & Fox, R. A. (1989). Prevalence of psychopathology among mentally retarded adults. *Research in Developmental Disabilities, 10,* 77–83.

Jackson, J. (1964). Toward the comparative study of mental hospitals: Characteristics of the treatment environment. In A. F. Wesson (Ed.), *The psychiatric hospital as a social system.* Springfield, IL: Charles C Thomas.

Jacobson, J. W. (1982). Problem behavior and psychiatric impairment within a developmentally disabled population I: Behavior frequency. *Applied Research in Mental Retardation, 3,* 121–139.

Jacobson, J. W. (1990). Do some mental disorders occur less frequently among persons with mental retardation? *American Journal on Mental Retardation, 94,* 596–602.

Jacobson, J. W., & Schwartz, A. A. (1983). Personal and service characteristics affecting group home placement success: A prospective analysis. *Mental Retardation, 21,* 1–7.

Jacobson, J. W., & Schwartz, A. A. (1986). The evaluation of community living alternatives for developmentally disabled persons. In J. L. Matson & J. A. Mulick (Eds.), *Handbook of mental retardation.* New York: Pergamon.

Jacobson, J. W., & Schwartz, A. A. (1991). Evaluating living situations of people with developmental disabilities. In J. L. Matson & J. A. Mulick (Eds.), *Handbook of mental retardation* (2nd ed.). New York: Pergamon.

Jakab, I. (1982). Psychiatric disorders in mental retardation: Recognition, diagnosis, and treatment. In I. Jakab (Ed.), *Mental retardation.* New York: Kaiser.

James, D. H. (1986). Psychiatric and behavioral disorders amongst older severely mentally handicapped inpatients. *Journal of Mental Deficiency Research, 30,* 341–345.

Johnson, J. H., & Sarason, I. G. (1978). Life stress, depression, and anxiety: Internal-external control as a moderator variable. *Journal of Psychosomatic Research, 22,* 205–208.

Johnson, S. M., & Brown, R. A. (1969). Producing behavior change in parents of disturbed children. *Journal of Child Psychology and Psychiatry, 10,* 107–121.

Jones, M. L., Lattimore, J., Ulciny, G. R., & Risley, T. R. (1986). Ecobehavioral design: Programming for engagement. In R. P. Barrett (Ed.), *Severe behavioral disorders in the mentally retarded: Non-drug approaches to treatment.* New York: Plenum.

Joyce, K., Singer, M., & Isralowitz, R. (1983). Impact of respite care on parents' perceptions of quality of life. *Mental Retardation, 21,* 153–156.

Kahneman, D., & Tversky, A. (1973). On the psychology of prediction. *Psychological Review, 80,* 237–251.

Kanfer, F. H. (1985). Target selection for clinical change programs. *Behavioral Assessment, 7,* 7–20.

Kanfer, F. H., & Grimm, L. G. (1977). Behavior analysis: Selecting target behaviors in the interview. *Behavior Modification, 1,* 7–28.

Kanfer, F. H., & Phillips, J. S. (1970). *Learning foundations of behavior therapy.* New York: Wiley.

Kanfer, F. H., & Schefft, B. K. (1987). Self-management therapy in clinical practice. In N. S. Jacobson (Ed.), *Psychotherapists in clinical practice: Cognitive and behavioral perspectives.* New York: Guilford.

Kanfer, F. H., & Schefft, B. K. (1988). *Guiding the process of therapeutic change.* Champaign, IL: Research Press.

Karlsruher, A. E. (1974). The non-professional as a psychotherapeutic change agent. *American Journal of Community Psychology, 2,* 61–72.

Kazak, A. E., & Marvin, R. S. (1984). Differences, difficulties, and adaptation: Stress and social networks in families with a handicapped child. *Family Relations, 33,* 67–77.

Kazdin, A. E. (1975). *Behavior modification in applied settings.* Homewood, IL: Dorsey.

Kazdin, A. E. (1982). Symptom substitution, generalization, and response covariation: Implications for psychotherapy outcome. *Psychological Bulletin, 91,* 349–365.

Kazdin, A. E., Matson, J. L., & Senatore, V. (1983). Assessment of depression in mentally retarded adults. *American Journal of Psychiatry, 140,* 1040–1043.

Kelly, J. A., Wildman, B. G., & Berier, E. S. (1980). Small group behavioral training to improve job interview skills repertoire of mildly retarded adolescents. *Journal of Applied Behavior Analysis, 13,* 461–471.

King, R. D., & Raynes, N. V. (1968). An operational measure of inmate management in residential institutions. *Social Science and Medicine, 2,* 1–53.

Knights, R. M. (1963). Test anxiety and defensiveness in institutionalized and noninstitutionalized normal and retarded children. *Child Development, 34,* 1019–1026.

Kobasa, S. C. (1979). Stressful life events, personality, and health: An inquiry into hardiness. *Journal of Personality and Social Psychology, 37,* 1–11.

Koenigsberg, H. W., & Handley, R. (1986). Expressed emotion: From predictive index to clinical construct. *American Journal of Psychiatry, 143,* 1361–1373.

Koller, H., Richardson, S. A., Katz, M., & McLaren, J. (1983). Behavior disturbance since childhood among a 5-year cohort of all mentally retarded young adults in a city. *American Journal of Mental Deficiency, 87,* 386–395.

Koriat, A., Lichtenstein, S., & Fischhoff, B. (1980). Reasons for confidence. *Journal of Experimental Psychology: Human Learning and Memory, 6,* 107–118.

Kraus, R. (1978). *Therapeutic recreation services: Principles and practices.* Philadelphia: Saunders.

Kregel, J., Wehman, P., & Banks, P. D. (1989). The effects of consumer characteristics and type of employment model on individual outcomes in supported employment. *Journal of Applied Behavior Analysis, 22,* 407–415.

Kurtz, P. S., Cook, C., & Failla, J. (1972). Behavior management training for parents of the mentally retarded. *Michigan Mental Health Bulletin, 6,* 5–16.

LaGreca, A. M., Stone, W. L., & Bell, C. R. (1983). Facilitating the vocational-interpersonal skills of mentally retarded individuals. *American Journal of Mental Deficiency, 88,* 270–278.

Laman, D. S., & Reiss, S. (1987). Social skills deficiencies associated with depressed moods of mentally retarded adults. *American Journal of Mental Deficiency, 92,* 224–229.

Lang, P. J. (1968). Fear reduction and fear behavior: Problems in treating a construct. In J. M. Schlien (Ed.), *Research in psychotherapy* (Vol. 3). Washington, DC: American Psychological Association.

Larson, C. P., & LaPointe, Y. (1986). The health status of mild to moderate intellectually handicapped adolescents. *Journal of Mental Deficiency Research, 30,* 121–128.

Lazarus, R. S., Kanner, A., & Folkman, S. (1980). Emotions: A cognitive-phenomenological analysis. In R. Plutchik & H. Kellerman (Eds.), *Theories of emotion.* New York: Academic.

Leahey, M., & Wright, L. (1985). Intervening with families with chronic illness. *Family Systems Medicine, 3,* 60–69.

Leiter, R. G. (1980). *Leiter International Performance Scale.* Chicago: Staelting.

Leland, H. (1983). Adaptive behavior scales. In J. L. Matson & J. A. Mulick (Eds.), *Handbook of mental retardation.* New York: Pergamon.

Lennox, D. B., Miltenberger, R. G., Spengler, P., & Erfanian, N. (1988). Decelerative treatment practices with persons who have mental retardation: A review of five years of the literature. *American Journal on Mental Retardation, 92,* 492–501.

Levitan, G. W., & Reiss, S. (1983). Generality of diagnostic overshadowing across disciplines. *Applied Research in Mental Retardation, 4,* 59–64.

Levitas, A. S., & Gilson, S. F. (1989). Psychotherapy with mildly and moderately retarded patients. In F. J. Menolascino & R. Fletcher (Eds.), *Mental retardation and mental illness: Assessment, treatment, and service for the dually diagnosed.* Lexington, MA: Lexington Books.

Levitas, A., & Gilson, S. F. (1990). Toward the developmental understanding of the impact of mental retardation on the assessment of psychopathology. In *Assessment of behavior problems in persons with mental retardation living in the community.* Rockville, MD: National Institute of Mental Health (DHHS Publication No. ADM 90-1642).

Lewinsohn, P. M., Hoberman, H. M., Teri, L., & Hautzinger, M. (1985). An integrative theory of depression. In S. Reiss & R. Bootzin (Eds.), *Theoretical issues in behavior therapy.* New York: Academic.

Lezak, M. D. (1983). *Neuropsychological Assessment.* New York: Oxford University Press.

Linaker, O. M., & Nitter, R. (1990). Psychopathology in institutionalized mentally retarded adults. *British Journal of Psychiatry, 156,* 522–525.

Lipman, R. S. (1986). Overview of research in psychopharmacological treatment of the mentally ill/mentally retarded. *Psychopharmacology Bulletin, 22,* 1046–1054.

Lochman, J. E., & Lampron, L. B. (1986). Situational social problem-solving skills and self-esteem of aggressive and non-aggressive boys. *Journal of Abnormal Child Psychology, 14,* 605–617.

Lochman, J. E., Lampron, L. B., Burch, P. R., & Curry, J. F. (1985). Client characteristics associated with behavior change for treated and untreated boys. *Journal of Abnormal Child Psychology, 13,* 527–538.

Lochman, J. E., Meyer, B. L., Rabiner, D. L., & White, K. J. (in press). Parameters influencing social problem-solving of aggressive children. In R. Prinz (Ed.), *Advances in behavioral assessment of children and families* (Vol. 5). Greenwich, CT: JAI.

Lochman, J. E., White, K. J., & Wayland, K. K. (1991). Cognitive-behavioral assessment and treatment with aggressive children. In P. C. Kendall (Ed.), *Child and adolescent therapy: Cognitive-behavioral procedure.* New York: Guilford.

Lovaas, O. I., & Simmons, J. O. (1969). Manipulation of self-destruction in three retarded children. *Journal of Applied Behavior Analysis, 2,* 143–157.

Lubin, R. A., Schwartz, A. A., Zigman, W. B., & Janicki, M. P. (1982). Community acceptance of residential programs for developmentally disabled persons. *Applied Research in Mental Retardation, 3,* 191–200.

Luiselli, J. K. (1978). Treatment of an autistic child's fear of riding a school bus through exposure and reinforcement. *Journal of Behavior Therapy and Experimental Psychiatry, 9,* 169–172.

Lund, J. (1985). The prevalence of psychiatric morbidity in mentally retarded adults. *Acta Psychiatrica Scandinavica, 72,* 563–570.

Lyon, S., & Preis, A. (1983). Working with families of severely handicapped persons. In M. Seligman (Ed.), *The family with a handicapped child.* New York: Grune & Stratton.

Maddi, S. R., Kobasa, S. C., & Hoover, M. (1979). An alienation test. *Journal of Humanistic Psychology, 19,* 73–76.

Malpass, L. F., Mark, S., & Palermo, D. S. (1960). Responses of retarded children to the Children's Manifest Anxiety Scale. *Journal of Educational Psychology, 51,* 305–308.

Mann, A. H., Jenkins, R., Cutting, V. C., & Cowen, P. J. (1981). The development and use of a standardized assessment of abnormal personality. *Psychological Medicine, 11,* 839–847.

Marlatt, G. A., & Gordon, J. R. (Eds.). (1985). *Relapse prevention: Maintenance strategies in the treatment of addictive behaviors.* New York: Guilford.

Martin, P. L., & Foxx, R. M. (1973). Victim control of the aggression of an institutionalized retardate. *Journal of Behavior Therapy and Experimental Psychiatry, 4,* 161–165.

Maslach, C. (1982). *Burnout: The cost of caring.* New York: Prentice-Hall.

Masters, J. C., Burish, T. G., Hollon, S. D., Rimm, D. C. (1987). *Behavior therapy: Techniques and empirical findings.* San Diego: Harcourt Brace Jovanovich.

Matheny, K. B., Aycock, D. W., Pugh, J. L., Curlette, A., & Canela, K. S. (1986). Stress coping: A qualitative and quantitative synthesis with implications for treatment.*The Counseling Psychologist, 14,* 499–549.

Matson, J. L. (1985). Biosocial theory of psychopathology: A three by three factor model. *Applied Research in Mental Retardation, 6,* 199–227.

Matson, J. L. (1990). *Handbook of behavior modification with the mentally retarded.* New York: Plenum.

Matson, J. L., & Andrasik, F. (Eds.). (1983). *Treatment issues and innovation in mental retardation.* New York: Plenum.

Matson, J. L., & Barrett, R. P. (1982a). Affective disorders. In J. L. Matson & R. P. Barrett (Eds.), *Psychopathology in the mentally retarded.* Orlando, FL: Grune & Stratton.

Matson, J. L., & Barrett, R. P. (Eds.). (1982b). *Psychopathology in the mentally retarded.* Orlando, FL: Grune & Stratton.

Matson, J. L., Barrett, R. P., & Helsel, W. J. (1988). Depression in mentally retarded children. *Research in Developmental Disabilities, 9,* 39–46.

Matson, J. L., & Fee, V. E. (1991). Social skills difficulties among persons with mental retardation. In J. L. Matson & J. A. Mulick (Eds.), *Handbook of mental retardation* (2nd ed.). New York: Pergamon.

Matson, J. L., Kazdin, A. E., & Senatore, V. (1984). Psychometric properties of the Psychopathology Instrument for Mentally Retarded Adults. *Applied Research in Mental Retardation, 5,* 81–89.

Matson, J. L., & Stephens, R. M. (1978). Increasing appropriate behavior of explosive chronic psychiatric patients with a social-skills training package. *Behavior Modification, 2,* 61.

Matson, J. L., & Zeiss, R. A. (1978). Group training of social skills in chronically explosive, severely disturbed psychiatric patients. *Behavioral Engineering, 5,* 41–50.

Mayeda, T. (1979). The use of client data in program planning and analysis. In P. Sanofsky (Ed.), *Evaluating program effectiveness: The administrator's dilemma.* Watertown, MA: Social Planning Services.

McClannahan, L. E., & Krantz, P. J. (1990). Current issues in the behavioral treatment of adults with autism: Blending research and practice. *The Behavior Therapist, 13,* 151–154.

McCubbin, H. (1979). Integrating coping behavior in family stress theory. *Journal of Marriage and the Family, 41,* 237–244.

McCubbin, H., & Patterson, J. (1983). Family stress adaptation: A double ABCX model of family behavior. In H. McCubbin, M. Sussman, & J. Patterson (Eds.), *Social stresses and the family: Advances and developments in family stress theory and research.* New York: Haworth.

McDonnell, J., Nops, D., Hardman, M., & Chambless, C. (1989). An analysis of the procedural components of supported employment programs associated with employment outcomes. *Journal of Applied Behavior Analysis, 22,* 417–428.

McFall, R. M. (1976). Behavioral training: A skill acquisition approach to clinical problems. In J. T. Spence, R. C. Carson, & J. W. Thibaut (Eds.), *Behavioral approaches to therapy.* Morristown, NJ: General Learning.

McGee, J. J. (1988). Issues related to applied behavior analysis. In J. Stark, F. J. Menolascino, M. H. Albarelli, & V. C. Gray (Eds.), *Mental retardation and mental health: Classification, diagnosis, treatment, services.* New York: Springer.

McQueen, P. C., Spence, M. W., Garner, J. B., Pereira, L. H., & Winsor, E. J. T. (1987). Prevalence of major mental retardation and associated disabilities in the Canadian maritime provinces. *American Journal of Mental Deficiency, 91,* 460–466.

Meadow, K., & Meadow, L. (1971). Changing the perceptions for parents of handicapped children. *Exceptional Children, 38,* 21–27.

Meehl, P. E. (1960). The cognitive activity of the clinician. *American Psychologist, 15,* 19–27.

Meichenbaum, D. (1986). *Stress inoculation training.* New York: Pergamon.

Meichenbaum, D. (1990). Cognitive perspectives on teaching self-regulation. *American Journal of Mental Deficiency, 94,* 367–368.

Meichenbaum, D., & Asarnow, J. (1979). Cognitive-behavioral modification and metacognitive development: Implications for the classroom. In P. C. Kendall & S. D. Hollon (Eds.), *Cognitive-behavioral interventions: Theory, research, and procedures.* New York: Academic.

Menolascino, F. J. (1969). Emotional disturbances in mentally retarded children. *American Journal of Psychiatry, 126,* 54–62.

Menolascino, F. J. (1970). *Psychiatric approaches to mental retardation.* New York: Basic Books.

Menolascino, F. J. (1977). *Challenges in mental retardation: Progressive ideology and services.* New York: Human Sciences.

Menolascino, F. J. (1988). Clinical research and training. In J. A. Stark, F. J. Menolascino, M. H. Albarelli, & V. C. Gray (Eds.), *Mental retardation and mental health: Classification, diagnosis, treatment, services.* New York: Springer.

Menolascino, F. J., & McCann, B. (Eds.). (1983). *Mental health and mental retardation: Bridging the gap.* Baltimore: University Park Press.

Mesibov, G. B. (1983). Current perspectives and issues in autism and adolescence. In E. Schopler & G. B. Mesibov (Eds.), *Autism in adolescents and adults.* New York: Plenum.

Mesibov, G. B. (1984). Social skills training with verbal autistic adolescents and adults: A program model. *Journal of Autism and Developmental Disorders, 14,* 395–404.

Mesibov, G. B. (1986). A cognitive program for teaching social behaviors to verbal autistic adolescents and adults. In E. Schopler & G. B. Mesibov (Eds.), *Social behavior in autism.* New York: Plenum.

Miklowitz, D. J., Goldstein, M. J., Falloon, I. R. H., & Doane, J. A. (1984). Interactional correlates of expressed emotion in the families of schizophrenics. *British Journal of Psychiatry, 144,* 482–487.

Mink, I. T. (1986). Classification of families with mentally retarded children. In J. J. Gallagher & P. M. Vietze (Eds.), *Families of handicapped persons.* Baltimore: Brookes.

Mink, I. T., Nihira, K., & Myers, C. E. (1983). Taxonomy of family life styles: I. Homes with TMR children. *American Journal of Mental Deficiency, 87,* 484–497.

Mischel, W. (1973). Toward a cognitive social learning reconceptualization of personality. *Psychological Review, 80,* 252–283.

Monfils, M. (1989). Group psychotherapy. In R. Fletcher & F. Menolascino (Eds.), *Mental retardation and mental illness: Assessment, treatment, and service for the dually diagnosed.* Lexington, MA: Lexington.

Moore, S. J., Basquill, M., Nezu, C. M., & Nezu, A. M. (1991, November). *Psychometric properties of the Behavioral Role-Play Activities Test (BRAT) for assessing competency of residential treatment staff.* Paper presented at the annual convention of the Association for the Advancement of Behavior Therapy, New York.

Moos, R. H. (1972). Assessment of the psychosocial environments of community-oriented psychiatric treatment programs. *Journal of Abnormal Psychology, 79,* 9–18.

Moos, R. H. (1973). Conceptualizations of human environments. *American Psychologist, 28,* 652–655.

Moos, R. H., & Moos, B. S. (1976). A typology of family social environments. *Family Process, 15,* 357–371.

Moreland, J. R., Schwebel, A. I., Beck, S., & Wells, R. (1982). Parents as behavior therapists: A review of the behavior therapy parent training literature—1975 to 1981. *Behavior Modification, 2,* 250–276.

Morgenstern, M. (1983). Standard intelligence tests and related assessment techniques. In J. L. Matson & J. A. Mulick (Eds.), *Handbook of mental retardation.* New York: Pergamon.

Myers, B. A. (1986). Psychopathology in hospitalized developmentally disabled individuals. *Comprehensive Psychiatry, 27,* 115–126.

Neisworth, J. T., & Madle, R. A. (1982). Retardation. In A. S. Bellack, M. Hersen, and A. E. Kazdin (Eds.), *International handbook of behavior therapy.* New York: Plenum.

Neuer, H. (1947). The relationship between behavior disorders in children and the syndrome of mental deficiency. *American Journal of Mental Deficiency, 55,* 143–147.

Newell, A., & Simon, H. A. (1972). *Human problem solving.* Englewood Cliffs, NJ: Prentice-Hall.

Nezu, A. M. (1987). A problem-solving formulation of depression: A literature review and proposal of a pluralistic model. *Clinical Psychology Review, 7,* 121–144.

Nezu, A. M., & D'Zurilla, T. J. (1981a). Effects of problem definition and formulation on decision making in the social problem-solving process. *Behavior Therapy, 12,* 100–106.

Nezu, A. M., & D'Zurilla, T. J. (1981b). Effects of problem definition and formulation on the generation of alternatives in the social problem-solving process. *Cognitive Therapy and Research, 5,* 265–271.

Nezu, A. M., & D'Zurilla, T. J. (1989). Social problem solving and negative affective states. In P. C. Kendall & D. Watson (Eds.), *Anxiety and depression: Distinctive and overlapping features.* New York: Academic.

Nezu, A. M., & Nezu, C. M. (Eds.). (1989a). *Clinical decision making in behavior therapy: A problem-solving perspective.* Champaign, IL: Research Press.

Nezu, A. M., & Nezu, C. M. (1989b). Toward a problem-solving formulation of psychotherapy and clinical decision making. In A. M. Nezu & C. M. Nezu (Eds.), *Clinical decision making in behavior therapy: A problem-solving perspective.* Champaign, IL: Research Press.

Nezu, A. M., & Nezu, C. M. (1991). Problem-solving skills training. In V. E. Caballo (Ed.), *Handbook of behavior modification and behavior therapy techniques.* Madrid, Spain: Siglio Veintiuno de Espana Editores, S.A.

Nezu, A. M., Nezu, C. M., & Arean, P. (1991). Assertiveness and problem-solving therapy for mild mentally retarded persons with dual diagnoses. *Research in Developmental Disabilities, 12,* 371–386.

Nezu, A. M., Nezu, C. M., & Perri, M. J. (1989). *Problem-solving therapy for depression: Theory, research, and clinical guidelines.* New York: Wiley.

Nezu, A. M., Petronko, M. R., & Nezu, C. M. (1982). *Cognitive, behavioral, or cognitive-behavioral strategies? Using a problem-solving paradigm for clinical decision making in behavior therapy.* Paper presented at the annual convention of the Association for Advancement of Behavior Therapy, Los Angeles.

Nezu, A. M., Shenouda, N., & Taylor, J. D. (1984). *Causal attributions, behavior change strategies, and the label "mentally retarded."* Paper presented at the annual conference of the American Association on Mental Deficiency, Rehoboth Beach, DE.

Nezu, C. M., Cannon, J., & Petronko, M. R. (1987). *Reducing public masturbation in a severely retarded male: Replication of a novel DRO procedure.* Paper presented at the annual convention of the Association for the Advancement of Behavior Therapy, Boston.

Nezu, C. M., Miescher, A., & Solgan, J. (1989). *Psychiatric treatment for persons with a dual diagnosis.* Paper presented at the annual convention of the American Psychological Association, New Orleans.

Nezu, C. M., Nezu, A. M., & Meischer, A. (1989, November). *Drug treatment and behavior therapy.* Paper presented at the annual convention of the Association for the Advancement of Behavior Therapy, Washington, DC.

Nezu, C. M., O'Brien, J., & Nezu, A. M. (1982, October). *Community adjustment: Elimination of a dog phobia in a recently deinstitutionalized severely retarded female.* Paper presented at the annual conference of the American Association on Mental Deficiency, Mid-Eastern Region, Harrisburg, PA.

Nezu, C. M., & Petronko, M. R. (1985, May). *Behavioral parent-training: Paraprofessionals or non-licensed practitioners?* Paper presented at the annual conference of the American Association on Mental Deficiency, Minneapolis.

Nezu, C. M., Petronko, M. R., & Nezu, A. M. (1990). *Development of the Behavioral Role-Play Activities Test (BRAT): Assessment of caregiver competency.* Unpublished manuscript, Hahnemann University.

Nihira, K., Foster, R., Shellhaas, M., & Leland, H. (1975). *AAMD Adaptive Behavior Scale—Revised.* Washington, DC: American Association on Mental Deficiency.

Nihira, K., Myers, C. E., & Mink, I. (1980). Home environment, family adjustment, and the development of mentally retarded children. *Applied Research in Mental Retardation, 1,* 5–24.

Nirje, B. (1969). The normalization principle and its human management implications. In R. Kugel & W. Wolfensberger (Eds.), *Changing patterns in residential services for the mentally retarded.* Washington, DC: U.S. Government Printing Office.

Nisbett, R., & Ross, L. (1980). *Human inference: Strategies and shortcomings of social judgement.* Englewood Cliffs, NJ: Prentice-Hall.

Novaco, R. W. (1975). *Anger control: The development and evaluation of an experimental treatment.* Lexington, MA: D. C. Heath.

O'Dell, S. (1974). Training parents in behavior modification: A review. *Psychological Bulletin, 81,* 418–433.

Ollendick, T. H., Balla, D., & Zigler, E. (1971). Expectancy of success and the probability learning of retarded children. *Journal of Abnormal Behavior, 77,* 275–281.

Ollendick, T. H., & Ollendick, D. G. (1982). Anxiety disorders. In J. L. Matson & R. P. Barrett (Eds.), *Psychopathology in the mentally retarded.* Orlando, FL: Grune & Stratton.

Orr, R. R., Cameron, S. J., & Day, D. M. (1991). Coping with stress in families with children who have mental retardation: An evaluation of the double ABCX Model. *American Journal of Mental Retardation, 4,* 444–450.

Oskamp, S. (1965). Overconfidence in case-study judgements. *Journal of Consulting Psychology, 29,* 261–265.

Parsons, M. B., Reid, D. H., Reynolds, J., & Bumgarner, M. (1990). Effects of chosen versus assigned jobs on the work performance of persons with severe handicaps. *Journal of Applied Behavior Analysis, 23,* 253–258.

Patterson, G. R. (1982). *Coercive family process.* Eugene, OR: Castalia.

Patterson, G. R., Chamberlain, P., & Reid, J. B. (1982). A comparative evaluation of a parent training program. *Behavior Therapy, 13,* 638–650.

Patterson, G. R., & Guillion, M. E. (1971). *Living with children.* Champaign, IL: Research Press.

Patterson, J., & McCubbin, H. I. (1983). The impact of family life events and changes on the health of a chronically ill child. *Journal of Applied Family and Child Studies, 32,* 255–264.

Paul, G. L. (1969). Behavior modification research: Design and tactics. In C. M. Franks (Ed.), *Behavior therapy: Appraisal and status.* New York: McGraw-Hill.

Peck, C. L. (1977). Desensitization for the treatment of fear in the high level adult retardate. *Behavior Research and Therapy, 15,* 137–148.

Penrose, L. S. (1938). *A clinical and generic study of 1,280 cases of mental defect.* London: HMSO.

Penrose, L. S. (1944). *The biology of mental defect.* London: Sidgwich & Jackson.

Penrose, L. S. (1966). The contribution of mental deficiency research to psychiatry. *British Journal of Psychiatry, 112,* 747–755.

Pepper, S. C. (1942). *World hypotheses.* Berkeley, CA: University of California Press.

Petronko, M. R., Anesko, K. M., Nezu, A. M., & Pos, A. (1989). Natural Setting Therapeutic Management (NSTM): Training in the natural environment. In J. M. Levy, P. H. Levy, & B. Nivin (Eds.), *Strengthening families: New directions in providing programs and services to people with developmental disabilities and their families.* New York: Young Adult Institute.

Phelps, A. N., & Hammer, D. (1989). *Mental retardation training in psychology graduate programs*. Paper presented at the annual convention of the American Psychological Association, New Orleans.

Phelps, R. M. (1897). Imbecility as an element in insanity. *Northwestern Lancet*, 283–285.

Philips, I. (1967). Psychopathology and mental retardation. *American Journal of Psychiatry, 124,* 29–35.

Philips, I., & Williams, N. (1975). Psychopathology and mental retardation: A study of 100 mentally retarded children: I. Psychopathology. *American Journal of Psychiatry, 132,* 1265–1271.

Pines, A. (1983). On burnout and the buffering effects of social support. In B. Farber (Ed.), *Stress and burnout in the human service professions*. New York: Pergamon.

Pines, A., & Aronson, E. (1981). *Burnout: From tedium to personal growth*. New York: Free Press.

Pirodsky, D. M. (1981). *Primer of clinical psychopharmacology: A practical guide*. Garden City, NY: Medical Examination Publishing.

Poling, A., Picker, M., & Hall-Johnson, E. (1983). Human behavioral pharmacology. *Psychological Record, 33,* 473–493.

Pollock, H. M. (1944). Mental disease among mental defectives. *American Journal of Psychiatry, 101,* 361–363.

Potter, H. (1922). Personality in the mental defective with a method for its evaluation. *Mental Hygiene, 6,* 487–497.

Pratt, L. (1976). *Family structure and effective health behavior: The energized family*. Boston: Houghton Mifflin.

Pratt, M. W., Luszcz, M. A., & Brown, M. E. (1980). Measuring dimensions of quality of care in small community residences. *American Journal of Mental Deficiency, 85,* 188–194.

Premack, D. (1959). Toward empirical behavior laws: I. Positive reinforcement. *Psychological Review, 16,* 219–233.

President's Commission on Mental Health (1978). *Report of the Liaison Task Force on Mental Retardation and Mental Health* (Vol. 4, Appendix). Washington, DC: Author.

President's Committee on Mental Retardation (1985). *National Strategy Conference on Mental Retardation and Mental Health* [Proceedings]. Washington, DC: Author.

Proshansky, H. M., Ittleson, W. H., & Rivlin, L. G. (1976). *Environmental psychology: People and their physical settings*. New York: Holt, Rinehart, & Winston.

Quine, L. (1986). Behavior problems in severely mentally handicapped children. *Psychological Medicine, 16,* 895–907.

Redmond, G. R. (1985). Increasing self-care through improving decision making by long-term psychiatric clients. *International Journal of Partial Hospitalization, 3,* 65–72.

Reid, A. H. (1980). Psychiatric disorders in mentally handicapped children: A clinical and follow-up study. *Journal of Mental Deficiency Research, 24,* 287–298.

Reid, A. H., & Ballinger, B. R. (1987). Personality disorder in mental handicap. *Psychological Medicine, 17,* 983–987.

Reid, A. H., Ballinger, B. R., Heather, B. B., & Melvin, S. J. (1984). The natural history of behavioral symptoms among severely and profoundly mentally retarded patients. *British Journal of Psychiatry, 145,* 289–293.

Reiss, D., & Oliveri, M. (1980). Family paradigm and family coping: A proposal for linking the family's intrinsic adaptive capacities to its response to stress. *Family Relations, 29,* 431–444.

Reiss, S. (1982). Psychopathology and mental retardation: Survey of a developmental disabilities mental health program. *Mental Retardation, 20*(3), 128–132.

Reiss, S. (1985). The mentally retarded, emotionally disturbed adult. In M. Sigman (Ed.), *Children with dual diagnosis: Mental retardation and mental illness.* Orlando, FL: Grune & Stratton.

Reiss, S. (1988). A university-based demonstration program on outpatient mental health services for mentally retarded people. In J. A. Stark, F. J. Menolascino, M. H. Albarelli, & V. C. Gray (Eds.), *Mental retardation and mental health: Classification, diagnosis, treatment, services.* New York: Springer.

Reiss, S. (1990). Prevalence of dual diagnosis in community-based day programs in the Chicago metropolitan area. *American Journal on Mental Retardation, 94,* 578–585.

Reiss, S., & Benson, B. A. (1984). Awareness of negative social conditions among mentally retarded, emotionally disturbed outpatients. *American Journal of Psychiatry, 141,* 88–90.

Reiss, S., & Benson, B. A. (1985). Psychosocial correlates of depression in mentally retarded adults: I. Minimal social support and stigmatization. *American Journal of Mental Deficiency, 89,* 331–337.

Reiss, S., Levitan, G. W., & McNally, R. J. (1982). Emotionally disturbed mentally retarded people: An underserved population. *American Psychologist, 37*(4), 361–367.

Reiss, S., Levitan, G. W., & Szyszko, J. (1982). Emotional disturbance and mental retardation: Diagnostic overshadowing. *American Journal of Mental Deficiency, 86,* 567–574.

Reiss, S., & Szyszko, J. (1983). Diagnostic overshadowing and professional experience with mentally retarded persons. *American Journal of Mental Deficiency, 87,* 396–402.

Rettig, E. B. (1973). *The ABC's for parents.* Van Nuys, CA: Associates for Behavior Change.

Reynolds, W. M., & Miller, K. L. (1985). Depression and learned helplessness in mentally retarded and nonmentally retarded adolescents: An initial investigation. *Applied Research in Mental Retardation, 6,* 295–306.

Richardson, S. A., Katz, M., Koller, H., McLaren, J., & Rubinstein, B. (1979). Some characteristics of a population of mentally retarded young adults in a British city. A basis for estimating some service needs. *Journal of Mental Deficiency Research, 23,* 275–285.

Richardson, S. A., Koller, H., & Katz, M. (1985). Continuities and change in behavior disturbances: A follow-up study of mildly retarded young people. *American Journal of Orthopsychiatry, 55,* 220–229.

Riegel, K. F. (1975). Toward a dialectical theory of development. *Human Development, 18,* 50–64.

Rojahn, J., & Schroeder, S. R. (1983). Behavioral assessment. In J. L. Matson, & J. A. Mulick (Eds.), *Handbook of mental retardation.* New York: Plenum.

Rusch, F. R., & Hughes, C. (1989). Overview of supported employment. *Journal of Applied Behavior Analysis, 22,* 351–363.

Rusch, F. R., & Menchetti, B. M. (1981). Increasing compliant work behaviors in a non-sheltered work setting. *Mental Retardation, 19,* 107–111.

Russell, A. T. (1988). The association between mental retardation and psychiatric disorders: Epidemiological issues. In J. A. Stark, F. J. Menolascino, M. H. Albarelli, & V. C. Gray (Eds.), *Mental retardation and mental health: Classification, diagnosis, treatment, services.* New York: Springer.

Rutter, M., Tizard, J., Yule, W., Graham, P., & Whitmore, K. (1976). Isle of Wight studies, 1964–1974. *Psychological Medicine, 6,* 313–332.

Salzberg, C. L., Agran, M., & Lignugaris-Kraft, B. (1986). Behaviors that contribute to entry-level employment: A profile of five jobs. *Applied Research in Mental Retardation, 7,* 299–314.

Salzberg, C. L., Lignugaris-Kraft, B., & McCuller, G. L. (1988). Reasons for job loss: A review of employment termination studies of mentally retarded workers. *Research in Developmental Disabilities, 9,* 153–170.

Salzberg, C. L., Likins, M., McConaughy, E. R., & Lignugaris-Kraft, B. (1986). Social competence and employment of retarded persons. *International Review of Research in Mental Retardation, 14,* 225–257.

Sanders, M. R., & James, J. E. (1983). The modification of parent behavior: A review of generalization and maintenance. *Behavior Modification, 7,* 3–27.

Sapon-Shevin, M. (1982). Ethical issues in parent training programs. *The Journal of Special Education, 16,* 341–357.

Sarason, I. G., Johnson, J. H., & Siegel, J. M. (1978). Assessing the impact of life changes: Development of the Life Experiences Survey. *Journal of Consulting and Clinical Psychology, 46,* 932–946.

Schloss, P. J., Smith, M., Santora, C., & Bryant, R. (1989). A respondent conditioning approach to reducing anger responses of a dually diagnosed man with mild mental retardation. *Behavior Therapy, 20,* 459–464.

Schultz, R. P., Rusch, F. R., & Lamson, D. S. (1979). Eliminating unacceptable behavior: Evaluation of the employer's procedures to eliminate unacceptable behavior on the job. *Community Service Forum, 1,* 5–6.

Schwartz, B. (1984). *Psychology of learning and behavior.* New York: Norton.

Scibak, J. W. (1986). Behavioral treatment. In J. L. Matson & J. A. Mulick (Eds.), *Handbook of mental retardation.* New York: Pergamon.

Seligman, M. E. P. (1975). *Helplessness: On depression, development and death.* San Francisco: Freeman.

Seltzer, G. B. (1981). Community residential adjustment: The relationships among environment, performance, and satisfaction. *American Journal of Mental Deficiency, 85,* 624–630.

Senatore, V., Matson, J. L., & Kazdin, A. E. (1985). An inventory to assess psychopathology of mentally retarded adults. *American Journal of Mental Deficiency, 89,* 459–466.

Sexton, J. D. (1980). The influence of familial econodemographic status, characteristics of the retarded child, and placement situation on parental attitudes toward mental retardation. *Dissertation Abstracts International, 41*(2), 630-A.

Shadish, W. R. (1986). Planned critical multiplism: Some elaborations. *Behavioral Assessment, 8,* 75–103.

Shafer, M. S., Kregel, J., Banks, P. D., & Hill, M. L. (1988). An analysis of employer evaluations of workers with mental retardation. *Research in Developmental Disabilities, 9,* 377–391.

Sherman, B. R., & Joseph, C. J. (1984). Stress in families of the developmentally disabled: A literature review of factors affecting the decision to seek out-of-home placements. *Family Relations, 33,* 95–103.

Shevin, M., & Klein, N. (1987). The importance of choice-making skills for students with severe disabilities. *Journal of the Association for Persons With Severe Handicaps, 9,* 159–166.

Silverstein, A. B., McLain, R. E., Hubbell, M., & Brownlee, M. (1977). Characteristics of the treatment environment: A factor analytic study. *Educational and Psychological Measurement, 37,* 367–371.

Slosson, R. L. (1963). *Slosson Intelligence Test.* New York: Slosson Educational Publications.

Snell, M. E., & Fisher, M. M (1988). The school. In J. L. Matson & A. Marchetti (Eds.), *Developmental disabilities: A life-span perspective.* Philadelphia: Grune & Stratton.

Snyder, D. K. (1979). *Marital Satisfaction Inventory.* Los Angeles: Western Psychological Services.

Sobotor, W. J. (1989). Family coping with stressors: A theoretical approach. In S. C. Klagsbrun, G. W. Kilman, E. J. Clark, A. H. Kutscher, R. DeBellis, & C. A. Lambert (Eds.), *Preventive psychiatry: Early intervention and situational crisis management.* Philadelphia: Charles.

Sovner, R. (1988). Behavioral psychopharmacology: A new psychiatric specialty. In J. A. Stark, F. J. Menolascino, M. H. Albarelli, & V. C. Gray (Eds.), *Mental retardation and mental health: Classification, diagnosis, treatment, services.* New York: Springer.

Sovner, R., & Hurley, A. (1981). The management of chronic behavior disorders in mentally retarded adults with lithium carbonate. *Journal of Nervous and Mental Disease, 169,* 191.

Sovner, R., & Hurley, A. (1983). Do the mentally retarded suffer from affective illness? *Archives of General Psychiatry, 40,* 61–67.

Sovner, R., & Hurley, A. (1986). Managing aggressive behavior: A psychiatric approach. *Psychiatric Aspects of Mental Retardation Reviews, 5,* 16–21.

Spanier, G. B. (1976). Measuring dyadic adjustment: New scales for assessing the quality of marriage and similar dyads. *Journal of Marriage and the Family, 38,* 15–28.

Sparrow, S. S., Balla, D. A., & Cicchetti, D. V. (1984). *Vineland Adaptive Behavior Scales.* Circle Pines, MN: American Guidance Service.

Sprague, R. L. (1982). Litigation, laws, and regulations regarding psychoactive drug use. In S. E. Breuning and R. Poling (Eds.), *Drugs and mental retardation.* Springfield, IL: Charles C Thomas.

Stainback, S., & Stainback, W. (1985). *Integration of students with severe handicaps into regular schools.* Reston, VA: Council for Exceptional Children.

Stark, J. (1989). Mental illness in persons with mental retardation. *News and Notes: Quarterly Newsletter of the American Association on Mental Retardation, 2,* 1–2.

Stark, J. A., Menolascino, F. J., Albarelli, M. H., & Gray, V. C. (Eds.). (1988). *Mental retardation and mental health: Classification, diagnosis, treatment, services.* New York: Springer.

Summers, J. A. (1988). Family adjustment: Issues in research on families with developmentally disabled children. In V. B. Van Hasselt, P. S. Strain, & M. Hersen (Eds.), *Handbook of developmental and physical disabilities.* New York: Pergamon.

Szymanski, L. S. (1988). Integrative approach to diagnosis of mental disorders in retarded persons. In J. A. Stark, F. J. Menolascino, M. H. Albarelli, & V. C. Gray (Eds.), *Mental retardation and mental health: Classification, diagnosis, treatment, services.* New York: Springer.

Tarrier, N., Vaughn, C., & Lader, M. (1979). Bodily reaction to people and events in schizophrenics. *Archives of General Psychiatry, 36,* 311–315.

Tavormina, J. B. (1975). Relative effectiveness of behavioral and reflective group counseling with parents of mentally retarded children. *Journal of Consulting and Clinical Psychology, 43,* 22–31.

Tennessee Department of Mental Health and Mental Retardation. (1978). *Tennessee goal domain directory.* Nashville: Author.

Thorndike, R. L., Hagen, E. P., & Sattler, J. M. (1986). *The Stanford-Binet Intelligence Scale: Fourth Edition.* Chicago: Riverside.

Tredgold, A. F. (1908). *Mental deficiency.* London: Bailliere, Trindall, & Cox.

Turkat, I. D., & Maisto, S. A. (1985). Personality disorders: Application of the experimental method to the formulation and modification of personality disorders. In D. H. Barlow (Ed.), *Clinical handbook of psychological disorders.* New York: Guilford.

Turkewitz, H. (1984). Family systems: Conceptualizing child problems within the family context. In A. W. Meyers & W. E. Craighead (Eds.), *Cognitive behavior therapy with children.* New York: Plenum.

Turnbull, A. P., & Turnbull, H. R. (1986). *Families, professionals, and exceptionality.* Columbus, OH: Merrill.

Turnbull, H. R. (1981). *The least restrictive alternative: Principles and practices.* Washington, DC: American Association on Mental Deficiency.

Tversky, A., & Kahneman, D. (1974). Judgement under uncertainty: Heuristics and biases. *Science, 185,* 1124–1131.

Van Bourgondien, M. E., & Mesibov, G. B. (1989). Diagnosis and treatment of adolescents and adults with autism. In G. Dawson (Ed.), *Autism: Nature, diagnosis, and treatment.* New York: Guilford.

Vaughn, C. E., & Leff, J. P. (1976). The influence of family and social factors on the course of psychiatric illness. *British Journal of Psychiatry, 129,* 125–137.

Venters, M. (1982). Familial coping with chronic and severe illness: The case of cystic fibrosis. In H. McCubbin (Ed.), *Family stress, coping, and social support.* Springfield, IL: Charles C Thomas.

Wacker, D. P., & Berg, W. K. (1988). Behavioral habilitation of students with severe handicaps. In J. C. Witt, S. N. Elliott, & F. M. Gresham (Eds.), *Handbook of behavior therapy in education.* New York: Plenum.

Wacker, D. P., Berg, W. K., Wiggins, B., Muldoon, M., & Cavanaugh, J. (1985). Evaluation of reinforcer reference for profoundly handicapped students. *Journal of Applied Behavior Analysis, 18,* 173–178.

Waisbren, S. E. (1980). Parents' reactions after the birth of a developmentally disabled child. *American Journal of Mental Deficiency, 84,* 345–351.

Walsh, K. K. (1989). *A milieu approach for treating dually diagnosed clients in a community living setting.* Paper presented at the annual convention of the American Association on Mental Retardation, Chicago.

Wason, P. C. (1969). Regression in reasoning? *British Journal of Experimental Psychology, 60,* 471–480.

Weaver, T. R. (1946). The incidence of maladjustment among mental defectives in military environment. *American Journal of Mental Deficiency, 51,* 238–246.

Webb, R. C., & Koller, J. R. (1979). Effects of sensorimotor training on intellectual and adaptive skills of profoundly mentally retarded adults. *American Journal of Mental Deficiency, 83,* 490–496.

Webster, T. G. (1963). Problems of emotional development in young retarded children. *American Journal of Psychiatry, 120,* 37–43.

Webster-Stratton, C. (1985). Predictors of treatment outcome in parent training for conduct-disordered children. *Behavior Therapy, 16,* 223-243.

Wechsler, D. (1974). *Wechsler Intelligence Scale for Children—Revised.* San Antonio, TX: Psychological Corporation.

Wechsler, D. (1981). *Wechsler Adult Intelligence Scale—Revised.* San Antonio, TX: Psychological Corporation.

Wechsler, D. (1989). *Wechsler Preschool and Primary Scale of Intelligence—Revised.* San Antonio, TX: Psychological Corporation.

Wehman, P., & Hill, J. W. (1981). Competitive employment for moderately and severely handicapped individuals. *Exceptional Children, 47,* 338-345.

Weissman, A. N. (1979). The Dysfunctional Attitude Scale: A validation study. *Dissertation Abstracts International, 40,* 1389B-1390B.

Weisz, J. R. (1979). Perceived control and learned helplessness among mentally retarded and nonretarded children: A developmental analysis. *Developmental Psychology, 15,* 311-319.

Weisz, J. R. (1981a). Effects of the "mentally retarded" label on adult judgments about child failure. *Journal of Abnormal Psychology, 90,* 371-374.

Weisz, J. R. (1981b). Learned helplessness in black and white children identified as retarded and nonretarded: Performance determination in responses to failure. *Developmental Psychology, 17,* 499-508.

Weitz, S. E. (1981). A code for assessing teaching skills of parents of developmentally disabled children. *Journal of Autism and Developmental Disorders, 12*(1), 13-24.

Wells, K. G., & Forehand, R. (1981). Childhood behavior problems in the home. In S. M. Turner, K. S. Calhoun, & H. E. Adams (Eds.), *Handbook of clinical behavior therapy.* New York: Wiley.

Whitman, T. L. (1990). Self-regulation and mental retardation. *American Journal on Mental Retardation, 94,* 446-471.

Whitman, T. L., Sciback, J. W., & Reid, D. H. (1983). *Behavior modification with the severely and profoundly retarded: Research and application.* New York: Academic.

Whitman, T. L., Spence, B. H., & Maxwell, S. E. (1987). A comparison of external and self-instructional teaching formats with mentally retarded adults in a vocational training setting. *Research in Developmental Disabilities, 8,* 371-388.

Wikler, L. M. (1986). Family stress theory and research on families of children with mental retardation. In J. J. Vietze (Ed.), *Families of handicapped persons: Research, programs and policy issues.* Baltimore: Brookes.

Wilson, J. E. (1989, February). *Pharmacological treatment of the mentally retarded/mentally ill individual.* Special workshop sponsored by the American Association on Mental Retardation, Baltimore.

Wing, L. (1978). Social, behavioral, and cognitive characteristics: An epidemiological approach. In M. Rutter & E. Schopler (Eds.), *Autism: A reappraisal of concepts and treatment.* New York: Plenum.

Wolfensberger, W. (1967). Counseling the parents of retarded children. In A. A. Baumeister (Ed.), *Mental retardation: Appraisal, education, rehabilitation.* Chicago: Aldine.

Wolfensberger, W., & Glenn, L. (1975). *PASS 3: A method for the quantitative evaluation of human services.* Toronto, Ontario: National Institute on Mental Retardation.

Wolfensberger, W., & Thomas, S. (1983). *PASSING: Program Analysis of Service Systems' Implementation of Normalization Goals* (Normalization criteria and ratings manual, 2nd ed.). Downsview, Ontario: Canadian National Institute on Mental Retardation.

Wolpe, J. (1985). Systematic desensitization. In A. S. Bellack & M. Hersen. (Eds.), *Dictionary of behavior therapy techniques.* New York: Pergamon.

Wright, E. C. (1982). The presentation of mental illness in mentally retarded adults. *British Journal of Psychiatry, 141,* 496–502.

Yudofsky, S. C., Silver, J. M., & Schneider, S. E. (1987). Pharmacologic treatment of aggression. *Psychiatric Annals, 17,* 6.

Zagelbaum, V. N., & Rubino, M. A. (1991). Combined dance/movement, art, and music therapies with a developmentally delayed, psychiatric client in a day treatment setting. *Arts in Psychotherapy, 18,* 139–148.

Zeitlin, S., Williamson, G. G., & Rosenblatt, W. P. (1987). The coping with stress model: A counseling approach for families with a handicapped child. *Journal of Counseling and Development, 65,* 443–446.

Zentall, S. S., & Zentall, T. R. (1983). Optimal stimulation: A model of disordered activity and performance in normal and deviant children. *Psychological Bulletin, 94,* 446–471.

Zigler, E., & Williams, J. (1963). Institutionalization and the effectiveness of social reinforcement: A three-year follow-up study. *Journal of Abnormal and Social Psychology, 66,* 197–205.

Zung, W. W. (1965). A self-rating depression scale. *Archives of General Psychiatry, 29,* 328–337.

Author Index

Abbas, K. A., 9
Abramowicz, H. K., 25
Agran, M., 137, 184
Akerly, M., 139
Albarelli, M. H., xv
Alessandri, M., 198, 204
Alexander, J., 102, 103
Alford, J. D., 6
Algozzine, R., 212
Altman, I., 125
Aman, M. G., 49, 183, 184
Ando, H., 7, 8, 16
Andrasik, F., 174
Anesko, K. M., 109, 111, 113
Angemeyer, M. C., 128
Angus, L. R., 21
Anthony, J. C., 85
Arean, P., 24, 25, 38, 57, 88, 92, 147, 179, 180, 224, 225
Arkes, H. R., 30
Aronson, E., 212
Asarnow, J., 224, 225
Aycock, D. W., 195

Baird, D., 7, 8
Baker, B. L., 115
Balch, P., 109
Balla, D. A., 25, 75, 76
Ballinger, B. R., 13, 22
Balon, E. A., 184
Balthazar, E. E., 7, 8
Bandura, A., 89, 126, 179, 216
Banks, P. D., 227, 228, 230
Bannerman, D. J., 130
Barlow, D. H., 104
Baron, R. A., 125, 215
Barrett, R. P., xv, 20, 130
Bartak, L., 193

Barton, C., 103
Basham, R. B., 210
Basquill, M., 110
Baumeister, A. A., 25
Baxley, N., 200
Bayles, H. C., 193
Bayley, N., 76, 77
Beck, A. T., 92, 104, 179
Beck, S., 108, 109
Becker, W. C., 111
Behar, R., 184
Bell, C. R., 232
Bellack, A. S., 132, 222
Belsher, G., 128
Bender, M., 136
Benson, B. A., 7, 8, 19, 20, 24, 179, 224, 225
Berg, W. K., 130, 137
Berier, E. S, 232
Berkowitz, L., 134
Berlin, I. N., 198
Berry, D. L., 180
Billings, A. G., 24
Birbrauer, J. S., 176
Birch, H. G., 7, 8
Birley, J. T. L., 128, 218, 219
Bittle, R. G., 167, 224
Blaney, P. H., 195
Blum, L. H., 76, 77
Borthwick-Duffy, S., 7, 9
Boshes, R. A., 186
Boyle, T. D., 192
Brannan, S. A., 136
Breiner, J., 108, 198
Breslau, N., 193
Breuning, S. E., 49
Brinker, R. P., 212
Bristol, M., 192, 193, 196, 207, 210, 211

Brittain, D. P., 130
Brockington, I. F., 85
Brockman, M. P., 109, 112
Brodsky, A., 212
Brown, C. H., 85
Brown, G. W., 128, 218, 219
Brown, L., 139, 212
Brown, M., 137, 138, 139
Brown, M. E., 129, 138, 139, 218
Brown, R. A., 198
Brownlee, M., 137, 138
Bruininks, R. H., 11, 184, 217
Bryant, R., 163
Buchanan, R. W., 125
Budd, K. S., 109, 112
Bumgarner, M., 130
Burch, P. R., 225
Burgemeister, B. B., 76, 77
Burish, T. G., 163, 174
Burt, J., 188
Butler, L., 224
Byrne, E. A., 210

Call, T., 16, 25
Callan, J. W., 225
Cameron, S. J., 98, 207
Canela, K. S., 195
Cannon, J., 83, 167
Carpenter, L., 205
Carr, E. G., 168
Castles, E. E., 224
Cattell, P., 76, 77
Cavanaugh, J., 130
Cerny, J. A., 104
Chadsey-Rusch, J., 136, 205, 233
Chahel, R., 85
Chamberlain, P., 196
Chambless, C., 227, 230
Chess, S., 9
Cicchetti, D. V., 75, 76
Cleland, C. C., 18
Cobb, S., 127, 210
Cochran, I. L., 18
Cohen, D. J., 90
Cohen, F., 128, 195
Cohen, S., 127, 210, 217
Cole, C. L., 169, 177, 180
Colson, L. S., 212
Conley, R. W., 228
Connors, C. K., 171
Cook, C., 198
Cook, T. D., 37
Cooper, J. O., 174

Corbett, J. A., 9, 25
Costello, C. J., 128
Cowen, P. J., 23
Cox, A., 193
Craft, M., 9, 19
Craig, T. J., 184
Craighead, W. E., 37
Critchley, D. L., 198
Crnic, K. A., 194, 210
Crosby, J., 140
Cross, A., 210
Cummings, S. T., 193
Cunningham, C. C., 210
Curlette, A., 195
Curry, J. F., 225
Cutting, V. C., 23
Cuvo, A. J., 135, 139

Davidson, N., 116, 207
Davis, G. C., 193
Davis, P. K., 135, 139
Day, D. M., 98, 207
Day, K., 9, 22
Deignan, L., 11, 16
Dellario, D. J., 140
DeMaine, G. C., 124, 137, 139, 227
DeMyer, M. K., 193
Derogatis, L. R., 88
Dewan, J. G., 7, 9, 17
Diller, L., 137, 138, 139
DiNardo, P. A., 104
Doane, J. A., 128
Dodge, K. A., 225
Dollard, J., 134
Domingue, D., 11, 16
Donellan, A., 212
Donnerstein, E., 125, 215
Donoghue, E. C., 9
Doob, L., 134
Duff, R., 20
Duker, P. C., 124
Dunn, L. M., 76, 77
Dupont, A., 7, 10
D'Zurilla, T. J., 27, 32, 35, 38, 39,
        40, 41, 104, 109, 110, 147,
        194, 195, 223, 224

Eaton, L. F., xv, 10, 19, 21, 22, 73
Edelwich, J., 212
Eidelson, R. J., 104
Elman, N. S., 205, 208
Emmelkamp, P. M. G., 163
Engel, G. L., 101

English, G. E., 7, 8
Epstein, N., 104
Erbaugh, J., 92, 104
Erfanian, N., 176
Evangelista, L. A., xv
Eyman, R. K., 7, 9, 16, 25, 124, 136, 137, 139, 227

Fabry, P. L., 109
Failla, J., 198
Falloon, I. R. H., 128
Farber, B., 212
Farmer, A., 85
Farran, D. C., 192, 194
Favell, J. E., 177
Faw, G. D., 224
Featherstone, H., 105
Fee, V. E., 221, 222
Feldhausen, J. F., 18
Fenlon, S., 167
Feshbach, S., 177
Fidora, J. G., 132
Figley, C. R., 192
Fimian, M. J., 212
Fischhoff, B., 32
Fisher, M. M., 212
Fletcher, R. J., 4, 5
Floor, L., 24
Flynn, R. J., 137, 139
Folkman, S., 207
Folstein, M., 85
Fong, P., 192, 213
Ford, A., 212
Fordyce, W., 137, 138, 139
Forehand, R., 108, 112, 198
Foster, R., 74, 75, 76
Fox, R. A., 11, 20
Foxx, R. M., 111, 167, 177, 222, 224
Frame, C. L., 225
Freedman, J. L., 125, 215
Freedman, R., 233
Friedrich, W. N., 194

Gallagher, J. J., 210
Ganellen, R. J., 195
Gardner, S. M., 130
Gardner, W. I., 5, 83, 88, 89, 169, 177, 180
Garner, J. B., 13
Gath, A., 194
Gelfand, D. M., 172
Gersten, R., 212
Gettings, R. M., xvi

Gill, M. J., 192, 195, 198, 204, 205, 213
Gillberg, C., 10, 19, 20, 21
Gilson, S. F., 25, 101
Glass, C. R., 224
Glass, D. C., 125
Glenn, L., 137, 138, 139
Goldfried, M. R., 32, 109, 110, 224
Goldstein, M. J., 128
Gollay, E., 233
Gonzalez, P., 136, 205, 233
Gordon, J. R., 147
Gordon, S. B., 116, 207
Gostason, R., 7, 10, 17, 21, 22
Graham, P., 7, 14, 17, 25
Gray, V. C., xv
Graziano, A. M., 108, 109
Green, B. F., 135, 228
Green, C. W., 130
Greenberg, M. T., 194, 210
Griffin, M. W., 109
Grimm, L. G., 62
Groden, G., 11, 16
Gross, J. C., 212
Grossman, H., 7, 73
Gruenberg, E. M., 85
Grufman, M., 10, 19, 20, 21
Grunewald, L., 212
Gualtieri, C. T., 4, 84, 90, 161, 183, 225
Guarnaccia, V. J., 20
Guillion, M. E., 111
Guralnick, M. J., 164

Hagen, E. P., 76
Halford, R. C., 130
Hall-Johnson, E., 184
Hammer, D., 6
Handleman, J. S., 213
Handley, R., 128
Handrich, R. R., 228
Hanson, M., 109
Haracopos, D., 7, 11
Harchick, A. E., 130
Hardman, M., 227, 230
Harme-Netupki, S., 139
Harris, R., 25
Harris, S. L., 108, 109, 192, 195, 196, 198, 204, 205, 208, 213
Hartmann, D. P., 172
Hassibi, M., 9
Hautzinger, M., 24
Hayman, M., 21
Haynes, S. N., 63, 112
Heal, L. W., 212

Heather, B. B., 13
Heaton-Ward, A., 11
Heifetz, L. J., 115
Helsel, W. J., 20, 24
Helzer, J. E., 85
Heron, T. E., 174
Hersen, M., 37, 63, 222
Herskovitz, H. H., 4, 21
Heward, W. L., 174
Hill, B. K., 11, 184, 217
Hill, J. W., 137, 227, 228
Hill, M. C., 228
Hill, M. L., 227, 230
Hill, R., 194
Hoberman, H., 24, 128
Hollon, S. D., 92, 163, 174
Holroyd, J., 193, 209
Hoover, M., 195
Horobin, G., 7, 8
Houser, R. A., 193
Hubbell, M., 137, 138
Hughes, C., 227
Hull, J. T., 139, 218, 227
Hunt, R. D., 90
Hurley, A., 20, 80, 89

Illsley, R., 7, 8
Insel, P. M., 126, 129, 138, 140
Isralowitz, R., 210
Itard, J. M. G., 4
Ittleson, W. H., 125
Iverson, J. C., 11, 20

Jackson, J., 137, 138
Jacobs, D., 137, 138, 139
Jacobson, J. W., 7, 11, 130, 136, 137,
     140, 216
Jakab, I., 9, 12, 71, 188, 189
James, D. H., 12, 20
James, J. E., 109
Janicki, M. P., 227
Jenkins, R., 23
Johnson, J. H., 104, 210
Johnson, S. M., 198
Jones, M. L., 139
Joseph, C. J., 99
Joyce, K., 210

Kahneman, D., 30, 31
Kanfer, F. H., 53, 54, 57, 61, 62, 72,
     89, 147, 179
Kanner, A., 207
Karan, O. C., 180

Karlsruher, A. E., 109
Katz, M., 12, 17, 19, 20, 25
Kazak, A. E., 105
Kazdin, A. E., 63, 85, 87, 92, 130,
     168, 174
Kelly, J. A., 232
Kelstrup, A., 7, 11
Kendall, P. C., 92
Keppel, J. M., 161, 225
Kerns, R. D., 112
King, R. D., 129, 138, 139, 218
Klausmeier, H. J., 18
Klein, N., 130
Knights, R. M., 20
Kobasa, S. C., 195
Koenigsberg, H. W., 128
Koller, H., 12, 17, 19, 20, 25
Koller, J. R., 124
Koriat, A., 32
Kramer, M., 85
Krantz, D. S., 125
Krantz, P. J., 227, 230, 232, 233
Kraus, R., 139
Kregel, J., 227, 230
Kurtz, N. R., 233
Kurtz, P. S., 198
Kyle, M. S., 224

Lader, M., 128
LaGreca, A. M., 232
Laman, D. S., 20, 24, 130
Lampron, L. B., 225
Lamson, D. S., 233
Lang, P. J., 56
LaPointe, Y., 12, 25
LaRocca, J., 20
Larson, C. P., 12, 25
Lattimore, J., 139
Lazarus, R., 195, 207
Leahey, M., 206
Leff, J. P., 128, 219
Lei, T., 124, 137, 139, 227
Leiter, R. G., 76, 77
Leland, H., 74, 75, 76
Lennox, D. B., 176
Levitan, G. W., xv, 5, 6, 79
Levitas, A. S., 25, 101
Levy, A. S., 125
Lewisohn, P. M., 24
Lezak, M. D., 85
Lichtenstein, S., 32
Lignugaris-Kraft, B., 137, 232
Likins, M., 137, 232

Linaker, O. M., 12
Lindsey, E. R., 132
Lipman, R. S., 184
Lizzet, A., 20
Lochman, J. E., 179, 225
Locke, B. J., 6
Lorge, I., 76, 77
Lovaas, O. I., 176
Lubin, R. A., 227
Luiselli, J. K., 164
Lund, J., 13, 19, 20
Luszcz, M. A., 129, 138, 139, 218
Lyon, S., 192

MacLean, W. E., Jr., 25
Maddi, S. R., 195
Madle, R. A., 111
Maisto, S. A., 69
Malpass, L. F., 18
Mann, A. H., 23
Mark, S., 18
Marlatt, G. A., 147
Martin, J. E., 184
Martin, P., 20
Martin, P. L., 177
Marvin, R. S., 105
Mas, C. H., 103
Maslach, C., 212, 213
Masters, J. C., 163, 174
Matheny, K. B., 195
Matson, J. L., xv, 4, 20, 24, 85, 87, 92,
    130, 168, 174, 179, 221, 222
Maxwell, S. E., 179, 180
Mayeda, T., 137, 139
McCann, B., 4
McCaughrin, W. B., 228
McClannahan, L. E., 227, 230, 232, 233
McConaughy, E. R., 137, 232
McCubbin, H., 194, 205, 208, 210
McCuller, G. L., 137, 232
McDonnell, J., 227, 230
McEvay, L. T., 85
McFall, R. J., 109
McGee, J. J., 168, 225
McLain, R., 124, 136, 137, 138, 227
McLaren, J., 12, 17, 19, 20
McMahon, R. J., 112, 198
McMorrow, M. J., 167, 222
McNally, R. J., xv
McQueen, P. C., 13
Meadow, K., 211
Meadow, L., 211
Meehl, P. E., 31

Meichenbaum, D., 224, 225, 226, 229
Melvin, S. J., 13
Menchetti, B. M., 233
Mendelson, M., 92, 104
Menolascino, F. J., xv, 4, 10, 13, 19,
    21, 22, 73, 94, 224
Merchant, A., 85
Mesibov, G. B., 137, 139
Metzger, J., 192, 194
Meyer, B. L., 225
Miescher, A., 22, 93, 186
Miklowitz, D. J., 128
Miller, C., 136, 227
Miller, K. L., 21, 24
Miller, N., 134
Miltenberger, R. G., 176
Mink, I., 98, 208, 209
Miranti, S. V., 179, 224
Mischel, W., 179
Mock, J., 92, 104
Monfils, M., 220
Moore, S. J., 110
Moos, B. S., 138, 140
Moos, R. H., 24, 126, 129, 138, 140
Moreland, J. R., 109
Morgenstern, M., 75
Mowrer, O. H., 134
Muldoon, M., 130
Myers, B. A., 25
Myers, C. E., 98, 208, 209

Neisworth, J. T., 111
Nestadt, G. R., 85
Netupki, J., 139
Neuer, H., 19, 21
Newell, A., 30
Newman, S., 193
Newsom, C., 168
Nezu, A. M., xii, 24, 25, 26, 27, 29, 30,
    31, 32, 35, 36, 37, 38, 39, 40,
    41, 47, 48, 50, 55, 57, 63, 64,
    68, 88, 92, 95, 104, 109, 110,
    145, 147, 153, 157, 158, 161,
    165, 179, 180, 182, 186, 194,
    195, 196, 204, 223, 224, 225
Nezu, C. M., xii, 22, 24, 25, 26, 27, 29,
    30, 31, 32, 35, 36, 37, 38, 39,
    47, 48, 50, 55, 57, 63, 64,
    68, 83, 88, 92, 93, 95, 104,
    109, 110, 111, 113, 115, 145,
    147, 153, 157, 158, 161, 165,
    167, 177, 179, 180, 182, 186,
    196, 204, 223, 224, 225

Nihira, K., 74, 75, 76, 98, 208, 209
Nirje, B., 135
Nisbet, J., 212
Nisbett, R., 31
Nitter, R., 12
Nops, D., 227, 230
Novaco, R. W., 179
Nowinski, J. M., 180

O'Brien, J., 165
O'Brien, W. H., 63
O'Dell, S., 109
Oliveri, M., 205
Ollendick, D. G., 3
Ollendick, T. H., 3, 25
Orr, R. R., 98, 207
Oskamp, S., 31

Palermo, D. S., 18
Parsons, B. V., 102
Parsons, M. B., 130
Patterson, G. R., 111, 196, 209
Patterson, J., 194, 205
Paul, G. L., 27
Pearce, L., 20
Peck, C., 20, 164
Penrose, L. S., 4, 13, 19
Pepper, S. C., 36
Pereira, L. H., 13
Perri, M. J., 24, 32, 35, 37, 39, 50,
        92, 224
Persson, E., 10, 19, 20, 21
Petronko, M. R., xii, 32, 84, 109, 110,
        111, 113, 115, 167, 177, 204
Phelps, A. N., 6
Phelps, R. M., 4
Philips, I., 13, 16, 18, 19, 22
Phillips, J. S., 62, 89
Picker, M., 184
Pines, A., 212, 213
Pirodsky, D. M., 183
Plesset, M. R., 4, 21
Poling, A., 49, 184
Pollock, H. M., 4, 13, 19
Pos, A., 109, 111, 113
Potter, H., 4
Pratt, M. W., 129, 138, 139, 205, 218
Preis, A., 192
Premack, D., 174
Price, J., 125
Proshansky, H. M., 125
Pueschel, S. M., 11, 16

Pugh, J. L., 195

Quine, L., 25

Rabiner, D. L., 225
Ragozin, A. S., 210
Rasing, E., 124
Raynes, N. V., 129, 138, 139, 218
Redmond, G. R., 225
Reid, A. H., 13, 18, 19, 22
Reid, D. H., 130, 169
Reid, J. B., 196
Reiss, D., 205
Reiss, S., xv, 5, 6, 14, 16, 20, 21, 24,
        79, 85, 87, 130, 224
Rettig, E. B., 111, 199
Reynolds, J., 130
Reynolds, W. M., 21, 24
Rice, C. J., 179, 224
Richardson, S. A., 7, 8, 12, 17, 19, 20, 25
Rie, H. E., 193
Riegel, K. F., 101
Rimm, D. C., 163, 174
Riner, L. S., 109, 112
Risley, T. R., 139
Rivlin, L. G., 125
Robins, L. N., 85
Robinson, N. M., 210
Rojahn, J., 88
Romanoski, A. J., 85
Rosen, M., 24
Rosenblatt, W. P., 98
Ross, L., 31
Rubino, M. A., 188
Rubinstein, B., 19
Rusch, F. R., 227, 228, 233
Russell, A. T., 78
Rutter, M., 7, 14, 17, 25, 193

Salzberg, C. L., 137, 232
Sanders, M. R., 109
Santora, C., 163
Santoro, T. M., 212
Sapon-Shevin, M., 109
Sarason, I. G., 104, 210
Sattler, J. M., 76
Scharfman, W., 210
Schefft, B. K., 53, 54, 62, 147, 179
Schloss, P., 163, 222
Schneider, S. E., 186
Schroeder, S. R., 88
Schultz, R. P., 233

Schwartz, A. A., 130, 136, 137, 140, 216, 227
Schwartz, B., 162
Schwebel, A. I., 109
Scibak, J. W., 169
Sears, R. R., 134
Seligman, M. E. P., 24
Seltzer, G. B., 233
Senatore, V., 85, 87, 92, 130
Sexton, J. D., 99
Shadish, W. R., 37
Shafer, M. S., 227, 228, 230
Shapiro, S., 85
Sheldon, J. B., 130
Shellhaas, M., 74, 75, 76
Shenouda, N., 25
Sherman, B. R., 99
Sherman, J. A., 130
Shevin, M., 130
Siegel, J. M., 104
Sievert, A. L., 135, 139
Silver, J. M., 186
Silverstein, A. B., 124, 136, 137, 138, 227
Simmons, J. O., 176
Simon, H. A., 30
Singer, M., 210
Singh, N., 184
Slosson, R. L., 76, 77
Smith, D. C., 24
Smith, M., 163
Snell, M. E., 212
Snyder, D. K., 104
Sobotor, W. J., 192
Solgan, J., 22, 93
Solomon, R., 109
Sovner, R., 20, 49, 80, 89, 183
Spanier, G. B., 104
Sparling, J., 192, 194
Sparrow, S. S., 75, 76
Spence, B. H., 179, 180
Spence, M. W., 13
Spencer, P. M., 88
Spengler, P., 176
Spitznagel, E. L., 85
Sprague, R. L., 184
Stainback, S., 212
Stainback, W., 212
Staltzman, R. K., 85
Stanger, C., 192
Stark, J., xv, 17
Stephens, R. M., 179
Stone, W. L., 232

Summers, J. A., 100
Sweet, M., 212
Szyszko, J., 5, 6, 79

Tarrier, N., 128
Tavormina, J. B., 109
Taylor, J. D., 25
Teri, L., 24
Themner, U., 10, 19, 20, 21
Thomas, S., 137, 138
Thompson, J. C., 139, 218, 227
Thorndike, R. L., 76
Tines, J., 228
Tizard, J., 7, 14, 17, 25
Tredgold, A. F., 4
Turkat, I. D., 69
Turkewitz, H., 106, 108
Turnbull, A. P., 205
Turnbull, H. R., 36, 99, 205
Tversky, A., 30, 31

Ulciny, G. R., 139

Van Bourgondien, M. E., 137
Vaughn, C. E., 128, 219
Venters, M., 207
Verhoven, P. J., 136
Vermilyea, B. B., 104
Vonkorft, M. R., 85

Wacker, D. P., 130, 137
Waisbren, S. E., 193
Waldron, H., 103
Walker, G. R., 132
Walsh, K. K., 136, 226
Ward, C. H., 92, 104
Wason, P. C., 31
Wayland, K. K., 179, 225
Weaver, T. R., 15
Webb, R. C., 124
Webster, T. G., 15, 25
Webster-Stratton, C., 196
Wechsler, D., 76, 77
Wehman, P., 137, 227, 228
Weiss, R. L., 20
Weissman, A. N., 92
Weisz, J. R., 24, 25
Weitz, S. E., 109, 112
Wells, K. G., 108
Wells, R., 109
White, K. J., 179, 225
White, L. K., 130

Whitman, T. L., 37, 169, 179, 180, 225
Whitmore, K., 7, 14, 17, 25
Wickham-Searl, P., 115
Wiggins, B., 130
Wikler, L. M., 98, 194
Wildman, B. G., 232
Williams, J., 216
Williams, M., 20
Williams, N., 13, 16, 18, 19, 22
Williamson, G. G., 98
Wills, T. A., 127, 210, 217
Wilson, D. W., 125, 215
Wilson, J. E., 183
Wing, J. K., 128, 218, 219
Wing, L., 21
Winsor, E. J. T., 13
Wolfensberger, W., 137, 138, 139, 210

Wolpe, J., 163
Wright, E. C., 15
Wright, L., 206
Wyngaarden, M., 233

Yoshimura, I., 7, 8, 16
Yudofsky, S. C., 186
Yule, W., 7, 14, 17, 25

Zagelbaum, V. N., 188
Zeiss, R. A., 179
Zeitlin, S., 98
Zentall, S. S., 124, 216
Zentall, T. R., 124, 216
Zigler, E., 25, 216
Zigman, W. B., 227
Zung, W. W., 92

Subject Index

AAMD, *see* American Association on Mental Deficiency

"ABCX" Model, 194–195

Adaptation, *see also* Coping
reciprocity of, 209

Adaptive behavior
measurement of, 75–77
mental retardation and, diagnosis of, 73, 74–77

Adaptive Behavior Scale, 74

Adaptive Behavior Scale–Revised, 75

Adolescents, EMR, depression in, 21, 24

Affective disorders, *see also* Depression
assessment of, 91–93
prevalence of, 20–21

Affective processes of caregivers, 105

Aggressive behavior
assessment of, 94
etiology of, 80
frustration and, 134–135

AIDS, sexual behavior and, 94

Alternative solutions, *see* Solutions, alternative

American Association on Mental Deficiency (AAMD), 4
Adaptive Behavior Scale of, 74
Revised, 75
mental retardation classification of, 73
mental retardation definition of, 7

American Association on Mental Retardation, 7

American Psychiatric Association, 4

Anchoring heuristic, 31

Anger management training, 179, *see also* Social learning models of treatment

Antipsychotic drugs, *see* Psychopharmacology

Anxiety disorders
assessment of, 93
prevalence of, 18–20
reduction of, respondent learning approaches in, *see* Respondent learning approaches

Anxiety Disorders Interview Schedule–Revised, 104

Appearance, assessment of, 85

Arts, in therapy, 186, 188

Assertiveness training, 179, *see also* Social learning models of treatment
in group therapy, 223, 224–225

Assessment, 47–70, *see also* Treatment evaluation; *specific assessment instruments; specific disorders*
behavioral, 88–90
of caregiving system, 97–117, *see also* Caregiving system(s), assessment of
category of problem and, 62–63
environmental, 119–141, *see also* Environmental assessment
functional analysis of problem areas in, 60–62
generation of alternatives and decision making in, 64, 66–68
of hands-on skills, staff competency and, 204
hypothesis formulation in, 63–64
of impediments, 33–34
of individual, 71–96, *see also* Individual, assessment of
literature consultation in, 62

307

Assessment (cont'd)
  multimatrix, need for, 72–73
  in problem analysis and focal target
      problem selection, 53–69, *see
      also specific aspect, e.g.,* Prob-
      lem orientation
  screening and, 48–53, *see also*
      Screening
  solution implementation and
      verification and, 68–69
  of symptoms, 71
Assessment tools, *see also specific tools*
  selection of, 58
Association for Retarded Citizens, 4
Assumptions, orienting, 36–38
Attention, assessment of, 86
Autism, 21
Autonomy, emphasis on, 227
Availability heuristic, 31
Aversive consequences, *see* Punishment

Beck Depression Inventory, 92, 104
Behavior(s), *see also specific type*
  adaptive, *see* Adaptive behavior
  appropriate, environmental
      fostering of, 233–234
  key, 57–58
Behavioral-analytic model of test
      construction, 110
Behavioral assessment, 88–90
Behavioral case formulation, *see* Case
      formulation
Behavioral chain, 61–62
Behavioral deficits, 62
Behavioral environment, assessment
      of, *see* Programmatic vari-
      ables, in environmental
      assessment
Behavioral excesses, 62
Behavioral factors, assessment of, 60
Behavioral problems, *see also specific type*
  in employment setting, 232–233
  prevalence of, 17–18
Behavioral Role-Play Activities Test
      (BRAT), 110–116
  content of, 110
  development of, 110–114
  instrument construction of,
      measurement format
      development and, 113–114
  psychometric evaluation of, 114
  reliability of, 114–116
  response enumeration in, 112

response evaluation in, 112–113
  scoring system for, 114
  situational analysis in, 111–112
  staff competency and, 204
Behavioral training of caregivers,
      108–109, 196–204
  need for, 116
Behavioral treatment approaches,
      162–183
  contingency management
      using punishment, 175–178
      using reinforcement, 166–175
  respondent learning, 162–166
  social learning models, 178–183
  staff burnout and, 213
Behavioral Vignettes Test–Revised
      (BVT), 115
Behavior Problem Inventory (BPI), 115
Bias, in clinical judgments, 30–32
  planned multiplism and, 37–38
Biological events, in general systems
      framework, 56
Biopsychosocial framework, multiple
      causality perspective within,
      36–38
Bipolar disorder, *see* Affective disorders
Bounded rationality, clinical judgment
      and, 30
BPI (Behavior Problem Inventory), 115
Brain deficits, in organic brain
      syndromes, 90–91
Brainstorming
  in alternative solution generation, 147
  in goal identification, 68
BRAT, *see* Behavioral Role-Play
      Activities Test
Brief Symptom Inventory (BSI), 88
Burnout, 212–213
BVT (Behavioral Vignettes
      Test–Revised), 115

Caregivers, *see also* Caregiving system(s);
      Professionals; Significant
      others
  behavior of, impact of, 216–217
  competency of
      assessment of, 108–116, 204
      BRAT and, 110–116
  defined, 99
  respite care and, 210–211
  roles of, confusion about, 100–101
  stress in, 192–214
      effects on parents of, 192–194

staff information about, 204
treatment of, 191–214
    caregiver training in, 196–204
    coping models and, 194–196
    problem-focused versus emotion-
        focused strategies in, 196
    reciprocity of adaptation and, 209
    social support in, 209–213
    systems interventions in, 204–208
Caregiver training, 108–109, 196–204,
    see also Professionals,
        training of
    information orientation in, 198, 203
    integration of, with systems perspec-
        tives and stress coping, 209
    need for, 116
Caregiving system(s), *see also* Caregivers
    adaptations of
        cognitive factors affecting,
            207–208
        variables affecting, 208
    assessment of, 97–117
        BRAT in, 110–116
        caregiver competency in, 108–116
        functional, 102–108
        goal of, 99–100
        hands-on skills in, 204
        need for, 99
        need for caregiver training and,
            116, 207–208
        potential problem areas in, 100
        problem etiology and, 101–102
        role confusion and, 100–101
    communication among, 211–212
    consistency among, 211
    defined, 99
    interventions in, 204–208
        determination of need for,
            206–208
    relationships within, 104, 105
    in tripartite approach, 55
Case formulation, for clinical
        interventions
    feedback and, 69
    problem-solving model of, 29–43, *see
        also* Problem-solving model
Causal factors, assessment of, 33–34
Causality, multiple, 36–38
    assessment and, 55, 80–81
Characteristics of the Treatment Environ-
        ment Scale (CTE), 137
Children's Manifest Anxiety Scale
        (CMAS), 18

Circles of coercion, 209
Classical conditioning, 162–166
Client, *see* Individual
Clinical diagnostic formulation,
        initial, 95
Clinical interventions, *see also* Treatment
    problem-solving model for, 29–43,
        see also Problem-solving
        model
Clinical interview, 85–87
Clinical judgment, errors in, 30–32
    planned multiplism and, 37–38
Clinical Pathogenesis Map (CPM),
        63–64
    initial assessment and, 95
    treatment plan and, 145
        alternative solution generation
            in, 147
        flexibility of, 147
Closure, family, 205
CMAS (Children's Manifest Anxiety
        Scale), 18
Coercion, circles of, 209
Cognitive-behavioral assessment, 89
Cognitive-behavioral treatment
        strategies, *see* Social learning
        models of treatment
Cognitive deficits
    depression-related, 92
    problem-solving therapy and, 225
Cognitive factors, in family adapta-
        tion, 207–208
Cognitive limitations, diagnostic issues
        regarding, 77–79
Cognitive processes of caregivers, 105
Columbia Mental Maturity Scale, 77
Communication
    among caregiving systems, 211–212
    conversational skills and, in group
        therapy, 222
    difficulties in, diagnosis and, 78–79
Community integration
    fostering of
        environmental assessment for
            success in, 135–140
        in residential treatment
            program, 227
    increased, goal of, 227–233
Community meetings, in model
        residence, 219–220
Community-Oriented Program
        Environment Scale
        (COPES), 126, 129, 140

Community resources, social support and, 210–211

Comorbidity, evaluation of, 71–96, *see also* Individual, assessment of

Competency
    caregiver, assessment of, 108–116, 204
    feelings of, as goal in residential treatment, 226–227

Concentration, assessment of, 86

Conditioned response, 162–166

Conditioning, operant, *see* Contingency management

Conduct disorder, 94

Confidence, excessive, clinical judgment and, 31

Configuration, family, 205

Confirmatory search strategies, 31–32

Conflicts, perspective-taking skills and, 222–223

Consequences
    in behavior chain, 61, 62
    consideration of, in decision making, 40–41
    in contingency management, *see* Contingency management
    of treatment alternatives, 152–154
        predicted versus actual, 157–158

Construct validity, BRAT and, 114–115

Consultation, initial, in client assessment, 81

Contingency management
    using punishment
        clinical applications of, 175–177
        clinical strategies for, 175
        defined, 175
        mental retardation and, 177–178
        staff burnout and, 213
    using reinforcement, 166–175
        clinical example of, 170–174
        clinical strategies for, 168–169
        defined, 166–168
        mental retardation and, 169–170

Continuity, across settings, 120–123

Control, locus of, coping and, 194, 195

Conversational skills, in group therapy, 222

Coordination, family, 205

COPES (Community-Oriented Program Environment Scale), 126, 129, 140

Coping
    models of, 194–196
    reciprocity of adaptation and, 209
    strategies for, importance of variety in, 195
    with stress, *see also* Caregivers, stress in
        cognitive factors affecting, 207–208
        factors interfering with, 192

Coping skills
    depression and, 24
    in treatment plan, 147

Covariations, diagnostic classifications and, 63

CPM, *see* Clinical Pathogenesis Map

Creative arts therapy, 186, 188

Crisis-meeting resources, coping and, 194–195

Crowding, as environmental stressor, 125

CTE (Characteristics of the Treatment Environment Scale), 137

Data sources, *see also* Information gathering
    prevalence rates and, 17

Deceleration techniques, 175–176

Decision making
    assessment and, 64, 66–68
    clinical
        problem-solving model of, 29–43, *see also* Problem-solving model
    in treatment planning, 148–154
    process of, 40–41

Deferment-of-judgment principle, alternative solutions and, 40

Deficits, *see also specific type*
    strengths and, evaluation of, 81–84

Delivery systems, and gap between mental illness and mental retardation, 6–7

Depression
    assessment of, 91–93
    in parents, 193
    prevalence of, 20–21
    psychological constructs and, 24–25

Desensitization, systematic, 163

Destructive behavior, assessment of, 94

Determinism, reciprocal, 179

Developmental issues, focus on, in assessment, 56–57, 77–79

Developmental limitations, diagnostic issues regarding, 77–79

Developmental scales, 77

Diagnostic and Statistical Manual of Mental Disorders, 16, *see also* DSM-III-R
Diagnostic categorization, 62–63
Diagnostic criteria, epidemiological studies and, 7, 16
Diagnostic formulation, initial clinical, 95
Diagnostic issues, in differential diagnosis, 73–81
Diagnostic overshadowing, 5–6, 79–80
Differential diagnosis, issues in, 73–81
  regarding mental retardation, 73–77
Differential reinforcement, 167
Differential reinforcement of incompatible behavior (DRI), 83–84
Disruptive behavior disorders, 94
Drug treatment, 183–186
DSM-III-R, *see also Diagnostic and Statistical Manual of Mental Disorders*
  cognitive/developmental limitations and, 78
  mental retardation criteria of, 73
    dual diagnosis and, 75
  prevalence rates and, 17
  in problem categorization, 63
Dual diagnosis, *see also* Individual, assessment of; Mental illness, mental retardation and; *specific psychiatric disorders*
  clinical interventions in, decision making and case formulation for, 29–43, *see also* Problem-solving model
  pathogenic mechanisms of psychopathology and, 23–26
  prevalence of, 7–23
  special considerations with, in programmatic assessment, 130–134
Dyadic Adjustment Scale, 104
Dysfunctional Attitude Scale, 92

Educable mentally retarded (EMR) adolescents, depression in, 21, 24
EE, *see* Expressed emotion
Emotional reactions of therapist, initiation difficulties and, 50
Emotional state, assessment of, 86
Emotion-focused goals, stress and, 196
Empathy, perspective-taking skills and, 223

Employment
  intensive treatment and, need for, 230–232
  Project Job and, 228–230
  social skills training for, 232–233
  supported, 227–233
Empowerment, group therapy and, 226
EMR adolescents, *see* Educable mentally retarded adolescents
Engagement, meaningful, 139–140
Environment
  assessment of, *see* Environmental assessment
  burnout and, 212
  in general systems framework, 56
  physical
    in assessment, 124–126
    programmatic interventions and, 217
    in treatment, 215–216
  programmatic
    in assessment, 129–134
    in treatment, 217
  qualitative aspects of
    in assessment, 140
    in treatment, 217–218
  social
    in assessment, 126–129
    in treatment, 216–217
  in treatment, 215–234, *see also* Treatment, environmental focus in
  in tripartite approach, 55
Environmental assessment, 119–141
  community integration and, 135–140
  continuity across settings and, 120–123
  frustration and, 134–135
  physical, 124–126
  programmatic, 129–134
  qualitative, 140
  resource management in, 140
  social, 126–129
Environmental stimulus, inappropriate control of, 62
Epidemiological issues, 7–23
Escape, contingency management and, 167
Etiological factors
  caregiving system and, 101–102
  multiple, 80–81
Expectations, appropriateness of, assessment of, 130–132
Exposure-based approaches, 163

Expressed emotion (EE)
    assessment of, 128
    training in, 219
Extinction
    conditioning and, 162
    in contingency management, 175

Facilitative problem orientations, 104
Failure feedback, learned helplessness
        and, 24–25
Family, see also Caregivers; Caregiving
        system(s)
    life cycle of, 204–205
    systemic interventions in, 204–208
Family Environment Scale (FES), 140
Fathers, see Family
Fears, see also Anxiety disorders
    prevalence of, 20
Feedback
    burnout and, 213
    helplessness-inducing, 24–25
    for solution verification, 68–69,
        154–156
FES (Family Environment Scale), 140
Focal problem areas, 37, 55
    selection of, assessment in, 53–69,
        see also Assessment
    strategy versus tactics and, 38
Formal support services, 210–211
Frustration
    of caregivers, see also Caregivers,
        stress in
    information alleviating, 203
    environment and, 134–135
Frustration-Aggression Hypothesis, 134
Functional assessment
    of caregiving system
        need for caregiver training
            and, 116
        strategies for, 102–103
        tactics for, 103–108
    of identified problem areas, 60–62
Functionality, generalization and,
        135–136

GAM, see Goal Attainment Map
Games, in social skills training, 222
Generalization, functionality and,
        135–136
General Symptom Severity Index
        (GSI), 88
General systems conceptualization, see
        also Systems approach

in problem analysis, 55–56
GHMS (Group Home Management
        Scale), 129, 139
Global social environment, 119
    assessment of, 129
Goal(s)
    assessment of, 60
    changes in, 34–35
    of increased visibility and
        integration, 227–233
    problem-focused versus emotion-
        focused, stress and, 196
    referrals by others and, 39
        initiation difficulties and, 49
    specificity of, 218–219
    subgoals and, 68
Goal Attainment Map (GAM), 68
    in solution implementation and
        verification, 154–156
Group(s), therapeutic, 220–226
    assertiveness training in, 223,
        224–225
    empowerment and, 226
    perspective-taking skills training
        in, 222–223
    problem-solving training in, 223–226
    social skills training in, 221–222
    stress inoculation training in, 226
    structural enrichment of interven-
        tions using, 221
    supportive, 220–221
Group Home Management Scale
        (GHMS), 129, 139
Group residences, 218–220
GSI (General Symptom Severity
        Index), 88

Hands-on skills, assessment of, staff
        competency and, 204
Hardiness of personality, stress effects
        and, 195
Helplessness, learned, depression and,
        24–25
Heuristics, judgmental, 31
Hindsight bias, 31
Hypotheses
    formulation of, 63–64
    testing of, feedback through, 69

Idiographic approach, 30, see also
        Problem-solving model
Impediments, identification of, 33–34,
        see also Assessment

Impulse control, disorders of, 94
Inappropriate stimulus control, 62
Incompatible behavior, differential
    reinforcement of, 83–84
Individual
    assessment of, 71–96
        cognitive/developmental
            limitations and, 77–79
        components of, 81–90
        diagnostic overshadowing and,
            79–80
        differential diagnosis and, 73–81
        evaluation of strengths and
            deficits in, 81–84
        initial clinical diagnostic
            formulation based on, 95
        initial consultation in, 81
        multiple etiological factors in,
            80–81
        need for multimatrix model in,
            72–73
        neuromedical, 84
        observational analysis in, 84–90
        specific disorders and, 90–94
    interactions with staff, nature of, 218
    treatment of, 161–190, see also Treat-
        ment entries
        behavioral approaches to,
            162–183, see also Behavioral
            treatment approaches
        creative arts therapy in, 186, 188
        intensive training in job setting,
            230–232
        model residence for, 218–220
        nonbehavioral approaches to,
            183–189
        psychopharmacological
            approaches to, 183–186
        psychotherapy in, 189
Individual attention
    in job setting, 230–232
    in residential treatment, 226–227
Individual differences, lack of
        "treatment cookbook"
        and, 29–30
Infantile autism, 21
Information gathering, clinical judgment
        and, 31–32
Information orientation, in caregiver
        training, 198, 203
Information processing, clinical
        judgment and, 30
Initial clinical diagnostic formulation, 95

Initial consultation, in client
        assessment, 81
Initiation difficulties
    defined, 48
    related to client, 48–49
    related to significant others, 49
    related to therapist, 49–50
Insight, assessment of, 86
"Institutionality," environmental, 124
Institutionalization, caregivers and,
        need for assessment of, 99
Instrumental conditioning, 166–178
Integration, see also Normalization
    environmental assessment for
        fostering success in, 135–140
    goal of increasing, 227–233
    residential treatment and, 227
Intellectual functioning
    assessment of, 86
    significantly subaverage, 73
Intelligence scales, 75–77, see also IQ
Intensive training, need for, in job
        setting, 230–232
Interactions, see also Social skills
    between clients and staff, 218
Intermittent explosive disorder, 94
Interpersonal Support Evaluation List
        (ISEL), 128
Interventions, see also Treatment
    problem-solving model for, 29–43,
        see also Problem-solving
        model
Interview, clinical, 85–87
IQ, see also Intelligence scales
    CMAS scores and, 18
    mental retardation and, diagnosis
        of, 73
ISEL (Interpersonal Support
        Evaluation List), 128
Isle of Wight studies, 17

Job coaches, 230–232
    in social skills training, 232
Job setting, 227–233
Judgment
    clinical, errors in, 30–32
        planned multiplism and, 37–38
    deferment of, alternative solutions
        and, 40
Judgmental heuristics, 31

Key behaviors, problem orientation
        and, 57–58

Labeling, professionals' perceptions and, 6
Language problems, assessment instruments and, 77
Learned helplessness, depression and, 24-25
Learning
　observational, see Modeling
　respondent, 162-166
　social, 178-183
Learning criteria, burnout and, 212
Leisure, availability of, assessment of, 136
Leiter International Performance Scale, 77
Life cycle, family, 204-205
Life Experiences Survey, 104
Literature, consultation of, assessment and, 62
Locus of control, coping and, 194, 195
Louisville Fear Survey, 20

Maladaptive problem orientations, 104
Mania, see Affective disorders
Marital relationships
　assessment of, 104, 105
　stress effects on, 193-194
Marital Satisfaction Inventory, 104
Meaningful engagement, 139-140
Medical problems, initiation difficulties and, 48-49
Memory, assessment of, 86
Mental hygiene services, and gap between mental illness and mental retardation, 6-7
Mental illness, see also specific type
　cognitive/developmental limitations versus, 77-79
　complexity of cases, treatment approach and, 30
　mental retardation and, 3-27, see also Dual diagnosis
　gap between, 4, 5-7
　historical concepts of, 3-5
　pathogenic mechanisms in, 23-26
　types of, definitions of, 16
Mental retardation
　definition of, epidemiological studies and, 7
　diagnostic issues regarding, 73-77
　falsely identified, 74
　label of, professionals' perceptions and, 6

levels of, 73
mental illness and, 3-27, see also Mental illness
unidentified, 74
Mental status examination, 85-87
Milieu variables, 217-218
Modeling
　in group residence, 219
　impact of, social environment and, 126-127, 216-217
Model residence, 218-220
Monitoring of intervention effects, 34
Mothers, see Caregivers
Motivation, see also Reinforcement; Reinforcers
　client-specific, evaluation of, 82-84
　enhancement of, strategies for, 53
　initiation difficulties and, 48, see also Initiation difficulties
Multimatrix assessment model, need for, 72-73
Multiple causality perspective, 36-38
　assessment and, 55, 80-81
Multiplism, planned, 37-38

National Association for Retarded Children, 4
Negative reinforcement, 167, see also Punishment
Networking, in caregiver support, 211
Neuromedical assessment, 84
Neuropsychological testing, in organic brain syndromes, 90-91
Noise, environmental, 125
Normalization, see also Integration
　fostering of, 218
　assessment of, 136-137
Normalizing, in family intervention, 208
NSTM (Project Natural Setting Therapeutic Management), 111

Objectives, see Goal(s)
Objectivity, behavioral assessment and, 89
Observational analysis, 84-90
　behavioral assessment in, 88-90
　clinical interview in, 85-87
　mental status examination in, 85-87
　miscellaneous measures in, 87-88
　PIMRA in, 87
　Reiss Screen for Maladaptive Behavior in, 87

Observational learning, *see* Modeling
Obstacles, identification of, 33–34,
    see also Assessment
One-to-one treatment, intensive, in job
    setting, 230–232
Operant conditioning, 166–178
Opportunities, access to, 217–218
    increased visibility and integration
        and, 227
Organic brain syndromes, assessment
    of, 90–91
Organismic variable, in behavior
    chain, 61, 62
Orientation
    assessment of, 85
    problem, *see* Problem orientation
Outcome measurement, solution imple-
    mentation and, 41–42
Overconfidence, clinical judgment
    and, 31
Overcorrection, 175

Parents, *see also* Caregivers
    stress effects on, 192–194
PASS (Program Analysis of Service
        Systems) inventories, 137, 139
PASSING (Program Analysis of Service
        Systems' Implementation of
        Normalization Goals), 137
Pavlovian conditioning, 162–166
Peabody Picture Vocabulary Test, 77
Peers, behaviors of, modeling of, 127
Perceptions, family, 208
Perceptual experiences, assessment of, 86
Personal consequences, 40–41
Personality, hardiness of, stress effects
        and, 195
Personality disorders
    aggression and, 94
    assessment of, 93–94
    prevalence of, 22–23
Perspective-taking skills, training in,
        in group therapy, 222–223
Pharmacologic intervention, 183–186
Philosophical framework, and problem
        orientation, 36–37
Physical environment, 119, see also
        Environment
    in assessment, 124–126
    programmatic interventions and, 217
    in treatment, 215–216
Physical handicaps, assessment
        instruments and, 77

PIMRA (Psychopathology Instrument
        for Mentally Retarded
        Adults), 87
Planned critical multiplism, 37–38
Positive reinforcement, 167
Power
    in family system, 205
    group therapy and, 226
Predictive validity, BRAT and, 115
Premack Principle, 174
Preoccupations, assessment of, 86
Prevalence rates, 7–23, 26
Primary punishment, 175, *see also*
        Punishment
Proactive intervention, importance of,
        233–234
Problem analysis, focal target problem
        selection and, assessment in,
        53–69, *see also* Assessment
Problem categories, in assessment, 62–63
Problem definition and formulation,
        38–39, 58–64
Problem-focused goals, stress and, 196
Problem orientation, 36–38, 53–58
    of caregiving system members, 104
    developmental issues in, 56–57
    general systems conceptualization
        of, 55–56
    key behaviors and, 57–58
    multiple causality and, 55
    treatment strategies and, 146–147
    tripartite approach to, 55
Problem-solving coping, with stress,
        195–196
Problem-solving model, 29–43
    assessment in, 47–70, *see also*
        Assessment
    components of process in, 35–43, *see
        also* Problem-solving process
    conceptualization of interventions
        in, 32–35
    desirability of, premises for, 29–32
    screening and, 50–53
    treatment in, 145–160, *see also*
        Treatment
Problem-solving process, 35–43, *see
        also* Problem-solving model;
        specific component
    alternative solution generation in,
        39–40
    decision making in, 40–41
    problem definition and formulation
        in, 38–39

Problem-solving process (cont'd)
  problem orientation in, 36–38
  solution implementation and
    verification in, 41–42
Problem-Solving Role-Play Task, 92
Problem-solving training, 179, see also
    Social learning models of
    treatment
  applications of, 225–226
  in group therapy, 223–225
Professionals, see also Caregivers; Care-
    giver training
  behaviors of, modeling of, 126–127,
    216–217, 219
  burnout in, 212–213
  competency of, hands-on skills
    and, 204
  initiation difficulties related to, 49–50
  interactions with clients, nature of, 218
  perceptions of, mental retardation
    label and, 6
  training of
    broadening focus of, 203–204
    deficiencies in, 6
    in model residence, 219
    parent training approach in, 203
  and understanding of psychiatric
    symptoms, 132–134
  worldview of, in problem orienta-
    tion, 36–37
Program Analysis of Service Systems
    (PASS) inventories, 137, 139
Program Analysis of Service Systems'
    Implementation of
    Normalization Goals
    (PASSING), 137
Program design, general systems
    approach and, 56
Programmatic variables, in environ-
    mental assessment, 119–120,
    129–134, see also Environ-
    mental assessment
  appropriateness of expectations
    and, 130–132
  functionality of skills training and,
    135–136
  reinforcers, 129–130
  treatment and, 217
  understanding of psychiatric
    symptoms and, 132–134
Progress, monitoring of, 34
Project Job, 228–230
  job coach and, 230–232

Project Natural Setting Therapeutic
    Management (NSTM), 111
Psychiatric disorders, see Mental illness;
    specific disorder
Psychiatric symptoms, see also Symptoms
    understanding of, assessment of,
    132–134
Psychodynamic therapy, 189
Psychological constructs, depression
    and, 24–25
Psychological events, in general
    systems framework, 56
Psychometric evaluation, of BRAT, 114
Psychopathology Instrument for
    Mentally Retarded Adults
    (PIMRA), 87
Psychopharmacology, 183–186
  clinical example of, 185–186, 187
  clinical strategies using, 183
  mental retardation and, special
    considerations with, 184–185
Psychoses, see also specific type
  prevalence of, 21–22
Psychosexual disorders, assessment of, 94
Psychosocial variables, 217–218
Psychotherapy, 189
Punishment, 167
  contingency management using,
    175–177
  staff burnout and, 213

Qualitative variables, in environmental
    assessment, 140
  treatment and, 217–218
Quantity principle, alternative solutions
    and, 40

Rating scales, see Assessment; specific
    scale or type of scale
Rationality, bounded, clinical judgment
    and, 30
Reciprocal determinism, 179
Reciprocity of adaptation, 209
Referrals, goals and, 39
Reframing, in family intervention, 208
Rehabilitative Indicators–Activities
    Indicators scale (RIAI), 137
Rehabilitative Indicators scale (RI), 139
Reinforcement, see also Motivation;
    Reinforcers
  differential, 83–84, 167
  learned helplessness and, 24–25
  negative, 167

positive, 167
Reinforcement contingencies, *see also*
     Contingency management,
     using reinforcement
  inappropriate, 62–63
Reinforcement survey, individualized,
     82–84
Reinforcers
  assessment of, 129–130
  specificity of, 218–219
Reiss Screen for Maladaptive
     Behavior, 87
Relationship Beliefs Inventory, 104
Representativeness heuristic, 31
Research design, prevalence rates and, 16
  subject selection and, 16
Research methodology, prevalence
     rates and, 17, 26–27
Residence
  model, 218–220
  prevalence studies and, 16
Residential placement, caregivers and,
     need for assessment of, 99
Residential treatment, key components
     of, 226–227
Resident Management Practices Scale
     (RMPS), 129, 139
Resource(s)
  affecting family coping, 208
  assessment of, 60, 140
  community, social support and,
     210–211
  crisis-meeting, coping and, 194–195
Resource management, assessment
     of, 140
Respite care, 210–211
Respondent, defined, 162
Respondent learning approaches,
     162–166
  clinical applications of, 163–164
  clinical examples of, 164–165
  clinical strategies using, 163
  defined, 162–163
  mental retardation and, special
     considerations with, 165–166
Response, in behavior chain, 61, 62
Response enumeration, BRAT and, 112
Response evaluation, BRAT and, 112–113
Restraint, 175
RI (Rehabilitative Indicators scale),
     137, 139
RIAI (Rehabilitative Indicators–
     Activities Indicators) scale, 137

RMPS (Resident Management Practices
     Scale), 129, 139
Role assignment, flexibility in, family
     system and, 205
Role-play situations, in BRAT, *see*
     Behavioral Role-Play
     Activities Test (BRAT)

Schizophrenia
  assessment of, 91
  prevalence of, 21–22
Screening, 48–53, *see also* Assessment
  initiation difficulties in
     related to client, 48–49
     related to significant others, 49
     related to therapist, 49–50
  problem-solving model applied to,
     50–53
  psychiatric symptom, 88
Scripts, role-play, in BRAT, 113–114
Self-control strategies, 179, 225, *see also*
     Social learning models of
     treatment
Self-generated stimulus, inappropriate
     control of, 62
Self-injurious behavior, assessment of, 94
Self-instruction, 179, *see also* Social
     learning models of treatment
  stress inoculation training and, 226
Self-referrals, goals and, 39
Self-regulatory interventions, in group
     therapy, 223–226
Service delivery systems, and gap
     between mental illness and
     mental retardation, 6–7
Setting, *see* Environment
Sexual behavior, 94
Siblings, 105, *see also* Family
Significant others, *see also* Caregivers
  initiation difficulties related to, 49
Situational analysis, BRAT and, 111–112
Situational factors, in prevalence
     studies, 16
Skills training, *see also specific type*
  functionality of, generalization and,
     135–136
  proactive, 233
  in treatment plan, 147
Slosson Intelligence Test, 77
Social consequences, 41
Social environment, 119, *see also*
     Environment
  in assessment, 126–129

Social environment (cont'd)
  in treatment, 216–217
Social learning models of treatment,
    178–183
  clinical applications of, 179–180
  clinical example of, 181–182
  clinical strategies for, 179
  defined, 178–179
  mental retardation and, special
    considerations with, 180–181
Social Problem-Solving Inventory, 104
Social problem-solving therapy, groups
    in, 224
Social skills
  depression and, 24
  training in, 179, see also Social
    learning models of
    treatment
    assessment of, 137, 139
    for employment, 232–233
    in group therapy, 221–222
    proactive interventions
      and, 233
Social support
  assessment of, 127–128
  availability of, 217
  for caregivers, 209–213
  depression and, 24
  provision of, 210–213
Social validation, 137, 139
Solutions
  alternative, see also Treatment
    alternatives
    evaluation of, 40–41
    generation of, 39–40, 64, 66–68,
      147–148
    implementation of, verification and,
      41–42, 68–69, 154–156
S-O-R-K-C acronym, in functional
    analysis, 62
Speech, assessment of, 85
Staff members, see Professionals
Standardized Assessment of Personality,
    22–23
Stimulation, environmental
  excessive, 124
  physical setting and, 216
Stimulus
  in behavior chain, 61, 62
  inappropriate control of, 62
  in respondent learning approaches,
    162, see also Respondent
    learning approaches

Strategies
  functional systems assessment,
      102–103
  tactics versus, 38
Strategies-tactics approach, alternative
    solutions and, 40, 147–148
Strengths, deficits and, evaluation of,
    81–84
Stress Adaptation Model, 194
Stress inoculation training, 226
Stressors
  affecting caregiving system, 98, see also
      Caregivers, stress in; Care-
      giving system(s)
  environmental, 124–125
Subgoals, 68
Subproblems
  definition and formulation of, 38–39
  identification of, 33–34, see also
      Assessment
Substance abuse, 94
Supervision, burnout and, 213
Support, social, see Social support
Supported employment, 227–233
Supportive groups, 220–221
Support services, formal, 210–211
Symptoms
  assessment of, 71, see also Assessment
      psychiatric symptom screening
      measures in, 88
  etiology of
    caregiving system and, 101–102
    multiple factors in, 80–81
  psychiatric, 88
    understanding of, 132–134
Systematic desensitization, 163
Systems approach, 56, see also Care-
    giving system(s)
  integration of, with caregiver training
      and stress coping, 209
  key behaviors and, 57–58
  multimatrix assessment and, 72

Tactics, see also Strategies-tactics approach
  functional systems assessment,
      103–108
  strategy versus, 38
Target problems, focal, see Focal
      problem areas
Teaching, burnout and, 212
Test anxiety, 20
Test construction, behavioral-analytic
      model of, 110

Therapists, *see* Professionals
Therapy, *see* Treatment; *specific type*
Thinking, assessment of, 85
Time-in area, 217
Time-out, 175
Timetable, in treatment implementa-
    tion, 156
Training, *see also specific skill or type
    of skill*
    of caregivers, 108–109, 116, 196–204,
        see also Caregiver training;
        Professionals, training of
    functionality of, generalization and,
        135–136
    intensive, in job setting, 230–232
Transactional/problem-solving model,
    stress in, 195–196
Treatment, 145–160
    caregiving system and, 191–214,
        see also Caregivers, treatment of
    complexity of cases and, 30
    complications in, 34–35
    design of, *see* Treatment planning
    environmental focus in, 215–234
        goal of increased visibility and
            integration and, 227–233
        key components of residential
            treatment and, 226–227
        model residence and, 218–220
        physical, 215–216
        proactive intervention and,
            233–234
        programmatic interventions
            and, 217
        qualitative aspects of, 217–218
        social, 216–217
        therapeutic groups and, 220–226
    evaluation of, *see* Treatment evaluation
    implementation of, 156
    individual approaches to, 161–190,
        see also Individual, treatment of
    individual differences and, 30
    intensive, in employment settings,
        230–232
    residential, key components of,
        226–227
Treatment alternatives, *see also* Solu-
    tions, alternative

consequences of, short-term and
    long-term, 152–154
effects of, value of, 152
ineffective, troubleshooting versus
    termination of, 158–160
positive effects of, likelihood of, 148
"Treatment cookbook," lack of, 29–30
Treatment evaluation, 156–160
    monitoring of effects in, 156–157
    predicted versus actual consequences
        in, 157–158
    unsatisfactory findings in, trouble-
        shooting versus terminating
        due to, 158–160
Treatment planning, 145–156
    decision making in, 148–154
    developmental issues in, 57
    flexibility in, need for, 34–35
    generation of alternative solutions
        in, 147–148
    problem orientation and, 146–147
    solution implementation and
        verification in, 154–156
Tripartite model, focal problems and, 55
    assessment and, 58–60
Troubleshooting, intervention termina-
    tion versus, 158–160

Unconditioned responses, 162
Unconditioned stimuli, 162
Utility, in decision making, 40

Validation, social, 137, 139
Validity
    of BRAT, 114–115
    construct, 114–115
    predictive, 115
Videotapes, in behavioral assessment, 89
Vineland Adaptive Behavior Scale, 75
Visibility, increased, goal of, 227–233

Wechsler Scales, functions assessed by, 77
Work setting, 227–233
Worldview, and problem orientation,
    36–37, 55, *see also* Problem
    orientation

Zung Self-Rating Depression Scale, 92

About the Authors

Christine M. Nezu received her Ph.D. in clinical psychology from Fairleigh Dickinson University in 1987. She has held clinical and academic appointments in New York City at Beth Israel Medical Center, where she directed a clinical psychiatry outpatient service specifically for persons with developmental disabilities, and Mount Sinai School of Medicine. She is currently director of the Predoctoral Clinical Psychology Internship and an assistant professor in the Department of Mental Health Sciences at Hahnemann University in Philadelphia.

Dr. Nezu has taught and supervised many psychology graduate students, interns, and psychiatric residents in behavior therapy. She has recently been appointed Chair of the Committee on Academic Training for the Association for the Advancement of Behavior Therapy.

In addition to presenting at numerous national and international conferences, Dr. Nezu has published many scholarly journal articles and currently serves as a guest manuscript reviewer for *Psychological Assessment: A Journal of Consulting and Clinical Psychology* and *Hospital and Community Psychiatry*. She is coauthor of two additional books, including *Problem-Solving Therapy for Depression* (Wiley, 1989) and *Clinical Decision Making in Behavior Therapy* (Research Press, 1989). Additionally, she is the primary author of the Behavioral Role-Play Activities Test, a measure of caregiver competency, included in this text. Dr. Nezu is currently interested in investigating the etiological bases of aggressive behavior problems and disinhibited sexual behavior in persons with developmental disabilities, as well as conducting clinical outcome research concerning effective psychotherapy strategies.

Arthur M. Nezu received a Ph.D. in clinical psychology from the State University of New York at Stony Brook in 1979. Currently, he is professor and director of the Ph.D. program in clinical psychology at Hahnemann University in Philadelphia. He has previously held administrative and academic appointments at Beth Israel Medical Center and the Mount Sinai School of Medicine, both in New York City; Fairleigh Dickinson University in New Jersey; and St. John's University in New York.

Dr. Nezu is a Fellow of both the American Psychological Association and the American Psychological Society. He is currently consulting editor for the *Journal of Consulting and Clinical Psychology* and editorial board member of *Behavioral Psychology*. Previously, he was associate editor of the *Journal of Dental Practice Administration*. He has published numerous journal articles and book chapters on a wide variety of topics in mental health and is coauthor of three additional books, including *Problem-Solving Therapy for Depression* (Wiley, 1989), *Clinical Decision Making in Behavior Therapy* (Research Press, 1989), and *Improving Long-Term Weight Loss* (Wiley, 1992).

Dr. Nezu has consistently been involved in providing clinical services to children and adults with developmental disabilities. Currently, he serves as codirector of the Mentally Retarded Sex Offenders Project at Hahnemann and is actively involved in research regarding affective disorders of adults with developmental disabilities.

Mary Jane Gill-Weiss received her Ph.D. in clinical psychology from Rutgers University in 1990. While in graduate school, she worked at the Douglass Developmental Disabilities Center as a classroom supervisor and as Research Coordinator and conducted research in the areas of staff burnout, the effectiveness of various teaching strategies, and stress and coping in parents of children with autism and other developmental disabilities.

Dr. Gill-Weiss is currently working at Bancroft in Haddonfield, New Jersey, where she is coordinator of the Program for Children With Autism. She has coauthored several book chapters in the areas of parent training, family stress and coping, and life-cycle issues for families of individuals with developmental disabilities. Her clinical and research interests include the enhancement of the continuity between educational and residential programming for individuals with developmental disabilities, the assessment of stress and coping in families with developmentally disabled members, the facilitation of successful coping in families of individuals with developmental disabilities, and staff training.